"THIS RASH ACT"

"THIS RASH ACT"

Suicide Across the Life Cycle
in the Victorian City

Victor Bailey

Stanford University Press

STANFORD, CALIFORNIA   1998

STANFORD UNIVERSITY PRESS

Stanford, California

© 1998 by the Board of Trustees of the Leland Stanford

Junior University

Printed in the United States of America

CIP data appear at the end of the book

To my mother, Lily Bailey,
and in memory of my father,
Fred Bailey (1914–1980)

ACKNOWLEDGMENTS

This book has been too long in the making, its completion delayed by emigration, Festschriften, and a trade union history. It gives me enormous satisfaction, therefore, to have reached the stage of acknowledging the people who, and institutions that, have contributed in various ways to the book. I never imagined I would spend close to a decade ruminating on the lugubrious theme of suicide. I had little or no association with the subject before 1988. It had impinged on me personally once only, in the early 1960's, when our landlady and neighbor drowned herself in the bathtub, and my father was called in aid by her son. Though on that occasion I was struck most by the way the incident led my mother, in unwitting imitation of Mrs. Perkins in Charles Dickens's *Bleak House*, to bury the hatchet and renew "her friendly intercourse on this auspicious occasion" with our other next-door neighbor. The discovery of an unbroken run of Victorian coroners' inquisitions and case papers was the event that brought violent death, and notably suicide, to my attention. I defy any social historian to decline a body of documents that has the potential to lift the veil of darkness from a history of private life, to reveal the personal impact of illness, desertion, bereavement, unemployment, and the like. Certainly, I could not resist the opportunity to excavate these fascinating legal records, albeit for just one provincial city. Any local study runs the risk, of course, of becoming blinkered by its particular archive. Considerable pains have been taken in what follows to avoid this pitfall. The strength of an essentially local focus is, however, the "thick description" of context, behavior, and motive it makes possible. I hope I have succeeded in exploiting this signal advantage of microhistory.

I have been assisted by many institutions and people on both sides of the Atlantic. The main body of research was completed in Kingston upon Hull in East Yorkshire, where I taught for a time. I look back fondly on those days and that city, if at first (like Richard Cobb in Aberystwyth) I was tempted to check each week that the railway tracks were still in place. I was particularly fortunate to have the research expertise and warm friendship of my colleagues in the Department of Economic and Social History, notably Joyce Bellamy, Mike Brown, Doug Reid, David Richardson, John Saville, and Donald Woodward. The Nuffield Foundation supported the first stages of the project with a generous research grant. A number of archivists helped me to locate and examine the central documents. I am especially grateful to the staff of the City Records Office. Geoff Oxley, the city archivist, Pauline Ranby, and Susan Hall all uncomplainingly fetched the hundreds of volumes of Quarter Sessions papers with which the coroners' inquests were bound. I would also like to thank the staff of the Local History Library, who made the city directories and newspapers available to me, and the staff of the Office of the Registrar of Births, Deaths and Marriages, who copied a large number of death certificates from the early Victorian period. J. T. Green, Hull coroner, provided me with the Coroners' Inquisition Books for the last two decades of the nineteenth century, while Arthur Credland, keeper of maritime history, gave me invaluable help with local maps and illustrative materials. During the long hours spent poring over dusty documents, I had the enjoyable company of the early modern historian Diana O'Hara. Her paleographic skills never failed to impress me: words I simply could not read were invariably deciphered by her. Finally, Jennifer Donnelly gave me invaluable research assistance for the last decade of coroners' inquests.

On this side of the Atlantic, I have also incurred many debts. Gene Tobin, president of Hamilton College, New York, first encouraged me to secure permanent employment in the United States. The University of Kansas supported my research and writing in many different ways; I received financial support from the university's General Research Fund and a research fellowship from the Hall Center for the Humanities. The then director of the Center, Andrew Debicki, deserves great credit for encouraging all new faculty to attend to their research. I shall always be grateful to the many scholars working in this field who generously shared their work and sources with me. They include Olive Anderson, Elisabeth Cawthon, Lisa Lieberman, and Michael MacDonald. I am especially grateful to those scholars who read and criticized portions of this book. They include Silvia Canetto, Simon Cooke, David Katzman, Angel Kwolek-Folland, Howard Kushner, Roger Lane, and Peter Stearns. My statistical struggles would have been even more parlous without the help of Joshua Rosenbloom. The tables and figures would have never seen the light of day without the dexterous and dogged work of Nancy Scott, who also contributed in many other vital and unselfish ways to bringing this book to fruition. I am grateful as well to Laura Kriegstrom Poracsky for her mapping work, to Peter Cassagrande, Dan Bays, and Tom Lewin for making money available for the illustrations and index, to Lynn Porter for her word-processing wizardry, and to Catherine S. Evans for indexing the book. Kathryn Ekstrom's applause helped carry me across the finishing line. The anonymous readers for Stanford University Press valuably helped me to tighten the argument at various points in the book. Associate Editor Peter J. Kahn handled all my queries about publication with unfailing good grace and expertise. Peter Dreyer's meticulous copy editing saved me from many stylistic solecisms, and Stacey Lynn skillfully guided me through the final stages of the publication process. Stanford's director, Norris Pope, showed me the kind of support and encouragement that only authors who have labored on a book for many years can ever fully appreciate. Lastly, the book is dedicated to my mother who remains hale and hearty at four score years of age, and in memory of my father who died of natural causes, but who was exhausted by the demands of a heavy manual occupation. I could not fail to recognize him in a number of the Yorkshiremen in this book who were worn out in the later stages of the life cycle. I have lived with the 700 or more Victorians who are the subjects of this study for many years; their names, occupations, lives, and deaths will reverberate in my head for some time yet. It is time, however, to let them rest in peace.

CONTENTS

TABLES

FIGURES

"THIS RASH ACT"

Dear Husband,
I just write this note before I do this rash act to
ask forgiveness from you. I have deceived you
ever since Friday night and I cannot bare to think
of it again. I am not worthy of the love you be-
stow upon me.

Mary Elizabeth Renton, aged 25,
a fisherman's wife, March 1894
(CQB/410/49)

My Dear Wife,
I ask the Lord & you to forgive me for the rash
act that I am about to committ but I can go no
longer. I feel very sad & while you are listening
to the word of God you little think what is going
on at home. it will be a shock for you I know.

William Brighty Nixon, aged 35,
a corn carrier, January 1895
(CQB/414/24)

Introduction

In May 1893, in Kingston upon Hull, in the East Riding of Yorkshire, Thomas Chesterfield, the 48-year-old district secretary of the Dockers' Union, attempted to kill himself by cutting his throat. It was the act of a tired and sick trade union leader, possibly in despair at the defeat of 8,000 dockers who had been on strike for seven weeks, a strike marked by considerable violence, in an effort to force the Hull shipowners to recognize their union.[1] In the search for this case of attempted suicide in the criminal records of the city, on behalf of an earlier research project, I stumbled across an unworked seam of coroners' inquests on the thousands of violent deaths during the Victorian era: drownings, accidents, infanticides, the occasional murder, and, especially intriguing, fatal acts of self-destruction. I was soon enthralled by the paradox of what Richard Cobb called "the most private and impenetrable of human acts," suicide, typically done in the privacy of the home, becoming, in the drama of the coroners' inquest, the focus of a most searching public investigation.

Those who killed themselves became, in consequence, "as much mute chroniclers of their times, in the dreadfully repetitive record of their failures, as those who kept diaries, who wrote letters."[2] The coroners' inquest constructed a detailed obituary to the deceased. Each inquest file contained the date and method of suicide; the age, sex, occupation, and abode of the deceased; and the verdict of the jury.[3] Of particular fascination were the coroners' case papers, or depositions of witnesses, recorded verbatim by the coroner. The witnesses drew me into the drama of their lives and that of the deceased. Their statements breached the walls of household, workplace, and neighborhood intimacy, and uncovered the concrete, overlapping forms of social interaction in which the suicide was imbricated. Two such inquests must suffice, at this stage, to bear witness to the rich clues that these public deaths hold to the private experience of ordinary Victorians.

On April 13, 1891, at the Whittington Inn, Commercial Road, Hull, an inquest was held upon the body of Louisa Bowen, aged 45, wife of William Bowen, master of a fishing smack. The first witness to give evidence was a fish merchant and brother of the deceased. He deposed that his sister had seemed dull and low-spirited when last he saw her, although she had made no complaint of illness. Her husband was "boxing" with the fleet in the North Sea and had been gone for eight weeks. Finally, the witness said he thought his sister might be in money trouble. The next witness, wife of a bricklayer's laborer, who had done washing for the deceased, said she had been at Bowen's home on April 8 when the deceased had complained of having had influenza. This witness was followed by a milliner's forewoman, who was in charge of Bowen's eldest daughter, Annie, aged 16, and who stated that Annie had not been at work since the 8th. Lastly, an elementary teacher and neighbor, who taught the youngest daughter, Emma, aged 10, to play the piano, said that Bowen had looked low and ill, and that when he had asked her for an exercise book for Emma, she had declined, saying money was short. Additional notes by the coroner recorded the fact that both children had been admitted to the Infirmary covered in dried blood, with cuts to the head as if made by an ax. At this point the inquest was adjourned.[4]

On the day of the inquest, the *Eastern Morning News*, under the heading "Attempted Double Murder and Suicide," reported that news of the affair had spread quickly, and the street was thronged with people as the two girls were taken away. Two days later, the same paper announced that a postmortem examination had found that Bowen had attempted to mutilate her body before cutting her throat. In that day's paper, too, a letter appeared from the vicar of St. Matthew's, declaring that Bowen was a woman of deep religious conviction and had lived an exemplary Christian life. She had suffered from bad health, however, and was depressed. If she had done the deeds described, the Reverend Robinson concluded, she was quite insane at the time.[5] On May 25, the adjourned inquest was held at the Town Hall, and after a four-hour hearing, the jury returned a verdict of death from self-inflicted throat injuries while of unsound mind.

On April 17, 1891, at the same public house, an inquest was held on the body of Tom Stephenson, aged 32, a journeyman joiner. The mother of the deceased said only that her son had been apprenticed to a firm of joiners and sawmillers, and that when she last saw him he had been more cheerful than usual. She also said that her son had not lived with her (although the morning paper claimed that Stephenson had been separated from his wife for ten days and lived with his parents). John Mail, a fellow joiner and Stephenson's bench mate, then gave evidence. The deceased, said Mail, had "talked all the morning about his wife. He said her goings on were turning his brain. He spoke sensibly & not wildly. This went on until 8 A.M. when he knocked off for breakfast." Over breakfast Stephenson went out. At 8:30, he told Mail he had seen his wife, and that "she was going to the magistrates to get an order to claim the children." "He was very excited," said Mail, "& said he felt as though he could do away with himself." Suddenly, Stephenson said he could not work, but had to go home and see his children. Two minutes later the engine of the sawmill stopped. The deceased had placed his neck between a driving belt and pulley in the pit of the sawmill. On an envelope he had written the note: "Done by a deceitful wife. God help her. God help my children & parents. Lord receive my soul."[6] The jury returned a verdict of suicide while of unsound mind. On April 20, according to the *Eastern Morning News*, Stephenson's fellow workmen, who had been granted a holiday to attend the funeral, were joined by a large crowd of women who gave vent to their feelings against the widow. As Mrs. Stephenson passed to the mourning coach, the women hooted her, and they would have assaulted her but for the intervention of the police.[7]

But how could we mine this rich lode; how could we decode the clues to lived experience in the tragic documents of the coroners' court? The obvious place to look for guidance was the vast body of research work on suicide. Sociologists, psychologists, and psychiatrists have long been at work on the incidence and causes of suicide. However, the literature on suicide has, after 175 years of bibliographic accretion, "something of the monstrous about it," to adopt Jean Baechler's telling phrase.[8] Nor is it simply a problem of bulk. Disputes in the field, particularly over approaches to the subject, and particularly in the sociology of suicide, have created a methodological minefield for historians to negotiate. Two main traditions in the sociology of self-destruction are at daggers drawn: Durkheimian positivism and ethnomethodology. The first, named for its affinities with Emile Durkheim's *Suicide* (1897), typically uses the official suicide rate to lay bare the social characteristics shared by the social groups most prone to killing themselves.[9] Most studies in this tradition have concluded that social integration or cohesion is the key variable in variations in suicide rates. The second tradition, defined by Jack Douglas's *The Social Meanings of Suicide* (1967), rejects the use of suicide rates, on the grounds that the figures are inaccurate and invalid for research purposes.[10] The figures, it is said, depend more on coroners' definitions of suicide and their search procedures than on what actually happened. Hence, ethnomethodologists recommend, instead, the study of the hermeneutics of suicide, by which they mean the courts, routines, and beliefs that promoted violent death to the status of suicide. Above all, they insist on the impossibility of distinguishing between the meanings attributed to an event such as suicide and its causes. Anyone looking for confirmation of current causative theories among suicide records will discover only a self-fulfilling cycle. Significantly, these two traditions have already left their imprint on the historical study of suicide.

Until recently, the history of English suicide had attracted little attention, with the exception of the role of suicide in literature, law, and ethics.[11] In the past ten years, however, two superb contributions to historical suicide have appeared, employing two very different approaches to the subject. Olive Anderson's *Suicide in Victorian and Edwardian England* (1987) is squarely within the Durkheimian tradition. Conversant with the faults of the official statistics, she was nevertheless prepared to use them to explore the geographical, age, gender, and occupational differences in the suicide rate, and the variation in these rates across the nineteenth century. Anderson's book is a magisterial study of the entire nation over nearly a century, and it will remain the standard authority on Victorian suicide. Its use of coroners' case papers is much less secure, however, of which more in a moment. Michael MacDonald and Terence Murphy's *Sleepless Souls: Suicide in Early Modern England* (1990) is firmly within the second sociological tradition.[12] Unwilling categorically to reject the suicide statistics, the authors nevertheless made the meaning of suicide the central theme of the study. They track the rise and fall of hostility to suicide over the early modern era, and they link this declining hostility to growing secularization, by which they mean that suicide was increasingly attributed to mental imbalance rather than to the work of the Devil.[13] The authors also investigate how suicides were identified, what states of mind and social circumstances were thought to impel people to suicide, and what role newspapers played in the creation and communication of these meanings. This study is, in my view, impressionistic and speculative, insufficiently grounded in a complete and informative source. It also adopts what I shall argue in the next chapter is an untenable hermeneutic position.

Faced with two very different approaches to the study of historical suicide, grounded in two radically different traditions in the sociology of self-slaughter, the one emphasizing structural determination, the other the meanings that actors ascribed to events, it seemed wise to begin the present study by a close engagement with the sociology of suicide from Durkheim onward. Thus, chapter 1 is an extended dialogue with the main texts in the sociology (and history) of suicide.[14] From this evaluation, there emerges an outline of a methodology, what I would define as a "refurbished Durkheimianism," that seeks to draw strength from the two traditions of patterned determination and the actor's perspective. The main steps in the argument, and the manner in which they have influenced the shape of the entire book, require brief summary.

If we are to integrate the social and material pressures of life, on one hand, and the meanings ascribed to these pressures by suicides and their entourages, on the other, we must examine a complete batch of ordinary case histories in a specific historical context. Coroners' case papers — "one of the great neglected sources of English social history" — if available in a long, unbroken run, fulfill this requirement.[15] Olive Anderson used such papers to re-create the "experience" of dying by suicide in mid Victorian and Edwardian London, and in rural East Sussex. This is the most tentative section of her book, however, since it is based on only 158 inquests, drawn from two different locations and three different time periods.[16] She has perforce to take a few cases as models for each region and era. She provides no sense of the actor's interpretations; we hear no Victorian "voices," whether of the suicides or of those closest to the deceased. In contrast, I have drawn upon 604 inquests held between 1837 and 1899 in the one city of Kingston upon Hull in which the jury returned a verdict of suicide. To these 604 inquests, I have added 125 more, found among those cases (notably drownings) in which jurors decided that, since it was unclear by what means the deceased had come to his or her death, an "open verdict" was the safest decision — but cases in which there was compelling evidence of suicidal intention. In other words, I have allocated a number of cases in which the jury returned an open verdict to the category of suicide.

It is this grand total of 729 inquests that forms the bedrock of the following historical account of suicide. All current indications are that the Hull documents, in their compass and completeness, are unique. Here is no selective and possibly unrepresentative sample of cases, but a complete population of suicide inquisitions and supporting testimony. I know of no similar unbroken run of coroners' inquisitions for a provincial city in Victorian England.[17] Hitherto, Victorian suicide has been examined only on a national basis, or where local evidence has been used, chiefly only from London. The present study thus allows us to escape from the perennial tendency to focus on the metropolis. Moreover, no previous historical study of Victorian England has used this kind of documentation in the detailed and systematic manner employed below.[18] By the use of coroners' case papers, I have been able to get closer to both the experience of suicide and its social construction than any previous study. As such, while building on Anderson's study, I have managed to go beyond it in the richness of specificity, and in more solidly based arguments on causal factors.

Of course, a full estimate of the use to which these documents can be put necessitates a close evaluation of the legal institution that created them: the coroners' court. Since 1194, it has been the duty of coroners to investigate the circumstances of unnatural, sudden, violent, or suspicious deaths. In practice, this meant that they investigated all cases of accidental death (or misadventure), homicide, and suicide; and they distinguished suicide from other sorts of sudden death.[19] Chapters 2 and 3 provide the fullest account we yet have of the workings of the coroners' court and inquest in Victorian England. They examine the rituals and social dynamics of the coroners' inquest, to see the way in which deaths were certified as suicides, and what the different jury verdicts implied about popular attitudes to suicide. Above all, these chapters confront the issue of the reliability and validity of the statistics of suicide; and they assess whether the coroners' case papers can be used as a window onto the experiences of those who committed suicide, can uncover what prompted people to take their own lives. The conclusions reached are twofold. First, suicide rates can be used to provide a rough index to the varying susceptibility to suicide shown by people of different sex, age, occupation, social class, and abode. Second, coroners' case papers can be made to reveal not only the "folk explanation" of suicide — the shared social meanings of suicide — but also what "really" drove people to kill themselves. This is not to deny that the motives for suicide are complex; that every suicide is the outcome of a cumulative and many-stranded process. It is, however, to keep faith with the view that the "real world" is reflected, at least to some degree, in texts and in language. Through the distorting effects, the "muffling blanket," of legal texts and language, the realities of suicide in ordinary life can, I contend, be seen and heard.[20]

The next step of the argument is that one of the most effective frameworks within which to evaluate the individual cases of suicide is that of the "life cycle." Above all, it is hoped that by seeking the circumstances and causes of suicide in the impact of the various stages of the life cycle, it will be possible to combine the structural and subjective approaches to the study of suicide.[21] Chapter 4 draws upon the considerable literature on the nineteenth-century life cycle to construct a gender- and class-specific model of the ages at which major life transitions took place in the Victorian city. The major transitions of the life cycle were not, in the nineteenth century, as clearly structured, sequentially ordered, or rigidly timed as they have since become. The modern life cycle, with its sharply differentiated life stages, took time to emerge. Vital to the process was the introduction of age-stratified systems of public duties and rights, notably compulsory education and retirement pensions. If the timing of life transitions in the nineteenth century was less uniform and less regulated by chronological age, the life cycle as a social institution nonetheless exerted a progressively stronger influence over the domains of family and work, and over individual experience and behavior.[22]

The nineteenth-century life cycle was made up of a number of compelling influences on individual behavior. For the large majority of working- and lower-middle-class city-dwellers, the most important influences were the age at which schooling stopped and work began, the requirement for young adults to contribute to family income, and the gendered nature of the labor market. Other compulsions followed: the age of marriage and conception, the amount of the life span spent in bearing and rearing children, the imperious demands of work on male breadwinners, and the daily struggle for married women to make ends meet. The later stages of the life cycle were as unrelenting as the earlier ones: for men, the inexorable slide down the occupational chute; for women, the change of life, an emptier nest, and renewed wage-earning under the impact of widowhood. To these main structural constraints, one must add the reversibility of the life cycle, or the life crises of desertion, bereavement, illness, injury, and unemployment. Of course, the rationale of the study is to assess these objective life-cycle constraints in conjunction with the subjective response to them. What force or combination of forces, in other words, disrupted the life-organization of those men and women who killed themselves? Coroners' case papers allow us to come as close as we can get to an answer, since they make it possible to determine the age, occupation (in both the formal and informal job market), marital status (including informal separation and cohabitation), family composition, and living arrangements of each suicide; and to hear what witnesses, the press, and the coroner had to say about the subjective responses to these life-cycle pressures.

An implicit component of the argument, finally, is that a study of the structures and subjective experiences of suicide must be rooted in a specific historical context. Although Olive Anderson relied chiefly on aggregate data, about both suicides and their social context, one of the more valuable conclusions of her study is that "to generalize about the meaning of suicide even for a single generation or in a single decade with no regard to place, must be to remain at a superficial level of understanding."[23] Reconstructing this context involves not only economic and social structures, but also the "suicide culture," the local ways of thinking and feeling about suicide. The present small theater of investigation is the borough of Kingston upon Hull, in East Yorkshire, the principal port of the region, and the third port of the country (after London and Liverpool) in point of total trade. Chapter 5 describes the main economic, social, and ecological characteristics of this Victorian city, and gives specificity, where possible, to the urban life cycle. The sea shaped the character of Hull and its people; so, too, did the city's isolation, close to the eastern seaboard, 60 miles from the woolen textile capital of Leeds, 50 miles from the South Yorkshire coalfield. Its people, growing in number from 65,000 in 1841 to 240,000 in 1901, saw themselves as tough and independent, inured to the hardships and uncertainties of constant change, and bound together in mutual self-support and friendship. Yet over 700 of its number in the Victorian era decided to suffer no longer "the slings and arrows of outrageous fortune," but rather "to take arms against a sea of troubles." Their death by suicide was indubitably affected by their habitat.

The remaining chapters of the book directly confront the significance of successive life stages for the experience of dying by suicide. Chapter 6 presents Kingston upon Hull's suicide rate according to sex, age, occupation, and habitat, with the aim of providing an index to the changing propensity to suicide of different age, sex, and work groups. This "Durkheimian" chapter seeks to uncover the social and economic characteristics that were shared by groups most prone to suicide, as a suggestive guide to the more extensive interpretation of the experience of suicide. Chapters 7 through 10 examine the experience of suicide across the life cycle. They seek to retrieve the ordinary person's experience of suicide, to reveal the paths to suicide for both men and women, in close tandem with the main stages of the urban life cycle. Chapter 7 looks at the phase of the life cycle that bridged the wide gap between leaving school and marriage. In this critical transition stage, young adults, most of whom were single, found themselves having to adjust to the demands of working life, often as lowly apprentices, to the financial and emotional claims of family life, and to the trials and tribulations of courtship. The chapter focuses on parent-child relations in the home, on the ordeal of finding a lifetime partner, and on the work discipline experienced by young people. How vulnerable were those who had the temptation of handling money for employers, or those who were live-in domestic servants? How accurate was the public, more strictly literary, stereotype of the young woman, seduced and abandoned, making "a hole in the water"?

Chapter 8 moves into the prime of life, covering the years from 25 to 44. These were years when three-quarters or more of adults were married, children were at their youngest, women were least able to add to family income, and poverty in working-class families was at its greatest. The chapter assesses the extent to which female suicide was a postpartum experience, the tragic finale in a drama of depression or unremitting pain; the extent to which male suicide was linked to anxiety about joblessness; and the extent to which both sexes were affected by family bereavement. How vulnerable were the single, separated, widowed, and bereaved, those who presumably were more socially estranged? What role did the demon drink perform in the more impulsive suicides, and in suicides associated with torrid love affairs or abusive marriages? And how valid was the public ideology that explained male suicide by his more arduous role in the struggle for existence, female suicide by her passive, not to say neurotic, dependence on familial relationships? How close was the fit between the public and private, social and personal, definitions of gendered experience? Did work shape the suicidal experience of women as well as men, if only when desertion, ill-treatment, or widowhood forced women into ill-paid work in an overcrowded casual labor market? Did bereavement and the disruption of domestic relationships lead men as well as women to kill themselves?

Chapter 9, on what I have called early old age (on the assumption that old age in the Victorian era began at around 45), confronts the transition in a man's working life that came, not with the final departure from the labor force, but with the descent to a semi-skilled or unskilled, and possibly temporary, job in his middle or late forties, as his physical strength waned. For women, a critical transition in middle and later life was widowhood, a particularly common experience for those who survived beyond the age of 50. Chapter 10 brings this life-span odyssey to an end by examining the final stage of life, 65 years and above, when widowhood was a prevalent status, when making ends meet became even more difficult, and when the workhouse cast a longer and longer shadow. These chapters investigate the propensity to suicide of men reaching the end of their working lives, of women negotiating menopause and the problems of widowhood. How often did the shedding of older workers by employers, the decline of physical strength, illness, or accident lead to employment problems for older men, and thence to suicide? Was labor-market insecurity on the rise for older workers in the later Victorian years, to judge from suicidal behavior? Was there any connection between poor-law policy changes and suicide patterns? Over how many older suicides did the workhouse cast its shadow? Were women coping better with old age, to judge from their susceptibility to suicide? Were women affected less by the loss of work-derived self-esteem, and more by the emotional and financial deprivations of widowhood, and by dependence upon kin? Or did losing a spouse equally disrupt the social and emotional functioning of older men who lacked the necessary domestic and interpersonal skills for survival?

Only one issue remains: can those who killed themselves in Kingston upon Hull bear witness to the subjective impact of English industrial and urban life? Emphasis has been placed, after all, on the local diversity of suicide patterns. What gives this study wider applicability, however distinct the social and economic setting, however special the local suicide culture, is the use of life-cycle analysis to understand the circumstances and meanings of suicide. While life-cycle structures will vary, to some degree, with location, the general impact of, and subjective responses to, these structures would be borne out, I contend, in other commercial and industrial towns. Accordingly, this assessment of suicide across the life cycle is offered as a study, from an original and singular angle, of the subjective impact of English urban and industrial life in the age of Victoria.

Placing each case in its specific socioeconomic context, and examining each stage in the life course, for each sex and at different social levels, makes it possible to assess causative factors with greater confidence than ever before. For this reason, the epilogue, in addition to drawing together the threads of suicide across the life cycle, exploits the advantages of a close-grained urban study to test the causative power of the classic Durkheimian motif, the weakening of the social ties binding people together. More strictly, this final chapter uses the full database to examine the role of social isolation, or what individuals feel when they cease to be integrated in a group.

In all these ways, the study uses suicide as a window onto the lived experience of hitherto unheard-from groups. The act of self-destruction, paradoxically, surmounts the silence of a few of those whom Hamlet called "the million." Suicide, and the reactions to it, is a means of rediscovering and reconstructing the universe of people who have left no other testament; a means of exploring the material and mental world of past generations.

1

Suicide and the Social Historian

Durkheim and Beyond

> Whenever a suicide is imposed on our attention we are
> astonished anew. For in this manner of taking leave of
> one's fellow men there seems to be a disconcerting
> mixture of free choice and of inevitability, of resolve and
> of passivity, of lucidity and of bewilderment.
>
> Maurice Halbwachs,
> *The Causes of Suicide* (1930)

The two main historical studies of
suicide in England offer only lim-
ited guidance to the sociology of suicide, the body of literature that casts
its shadow across the social historian of suicide.[1] The opening chapter of
this book therefore offers an extended dialogue with the preeminent texts
in the sociology of self-destruction.[2] The aim is to evaluate the two principal traditions in the sociology of suicide, Durkheimian positivism and the
ethnomethodological critique, the one emphasizing structural determination, the other the meanings that actors ascribe to events. Durkheimians
insist that it is possible to advance explanations of suicide by reference to
social and economic factors external to the individuals committing suicide.
They link suicide, as measured by the official statistics, to the determining
forces of urban and industrial life. The ethnomethodologists view suicide,
rather, as a product of official categorizations, which are in turn thought to
be influenced by cultural understandings. They stress the interpretative process by which some acts come to be defined as suicide. I am not convinced
by the more radical claims of either main tradition in the sociology of sui-

cide. I am not willing to accept the Durkheimian tendency to ignore the "micro-social" context of suicidal death and the meaning that individuals attached to external conditions. Nor am I convinced by the ethnomethodological penchant for discarding the statistical patterns of suicide and the "objective" reality of the structures of social and economic life. I wish to offer a modified Durkheimian approach, one that, in the attempt to explain suicide, incorporates both social structural factors and the ways in which social factors manifested themselves in the realm of individual experience. I have tried to develop a methodology, resting on the coroners' case papers and on the different stages of the life cycle, that makes it possible to explore the interconnections between the social and material conditions of life, on the one hand, and the meanings ascribed to those conditions by suicidal people and their entourages, on the other. It is a methodology designed to facilitate the job of decoding the tragic documents of the coroner's court.

I

Emile Durkheim's *Suicide: A Study in Sociology*, first published in 1897, is the classic text on the sociology of self-slaughter.[3] Durkheim's starting point was the finding of the "moral statisticians" that the suicide rate in every country remained constant over time, and differed consistently from the suicide rate of other countries.[4] This remarkable regularity of suicide rates suggested that suicide was not a purely individual act. Were it so, the suicide rates would hardly remain stable, but would fluctuate markedly from year to year. The next step for Durkheim was to discover that the rate of suicide differed between social groups in the same society. What was it, he asked, that made some groups more vulnerable to suicide than others? The answer was not to be found, according to Durkheim, in individual motives for suicide, which suicidologists had traditionally examined. Motives were nothing more than pretexts; they held no explanatory power. The personal calamities that may lead to suicide afflict all social groups, said Durkheim; the point was to discover why some groups weathered the storms of life better than others. The "incidents of private life," he argued, are but "apparent causes." "They may be said to indicate the individual's weak points, where the outside current bearing the impulse to self-destruction most easily finds introduction." The individual buckles under the weight of circumstances "because the state of society has made him a ready prey to suicide."[5] What social characteristics were shared, then, by the social groups most prone to killing themselves?

Durkheim's answer emerged from statistical tables showing that the rate of suicide was higher for urban, as opposed to rural, inhabitants; for widowed and divorced, as opposed to married, people; and for Protestants, as distinct from Catholics. Each group with the lower rate of suicide, Durkheim reasoned, was a more close-knit social or religious community. In contrast, people less strongly integrated into society—those living alone in big cities, those separated from family ties, those splintered by the schismatic proclivities of the Protestant religion—were the ones most likely to supply what Durkheim termed "the contingent of voluntary deaths for a given society."[6] This type of suicide Durkheim called "egoistic suicide," since it resulted from an insufficient integration of the individual and society.[7] In addition, there was altruistic suicide, the obverse of egoistic suicide, which resulted from *excessive* integration. Such individuals as military men, and the old and sick, killed themselves in conformity, not conflict, with the demands of society.[8]

Society constrained individuals, however, not only by binding them to the norms of social groups, but also by regulating their ambitions by defining realistic goals and the ways of reaching them. Anomic suicide, Durkheim's third main type, resulted when rapid economic and social change produced a situation in which accepted standards and limits to human behavior lost their regulative power. So, for example, the unmoderated desire for ever larger rewards, particularly among those at the top of the occupational ladder, resulted only in intense dissatisfaction and the growth of the suicidal impulse. Anomic suicide, said Durkheim, was most characteristic of modern society, since it arose not only in acute form during periods of economic boom and slump, but also in chronic form through the replacement of the traditional moral order by an urban-industrial one, distinguished by a greater division of labor and diminished control of economic life.[9]

"There is, therefore, for each people," Durkheim concluded, "a collective force of a definite amount of energy, impelling men to self-destruction." This collective inclination was composed of "the currents of egoism, altruism or anomy running through the society."[10] A change in the strength of one or more of these forces was the primary cause of the variations in the rate of suicide. Explaining differential suicide rates by reference to factors external to, and determining the wills of, the individuals committing suicide was crucial, of course, to Durkheim's project of establishing a "science" of sociology. If he could show that social forces caused the "supremely individual" act of suicide, he would have proved the truth of his claim for sociology "by the very case most unfavourable to it," in Raymond Aron's words.[11]

In all, Durkheim concentrated upon the constraints of collective life that impelled people to kill themselves. It was the socially structured situation that warranted attention, he argued, not "its distant repercussions in the consciousness of individuals."[12] This conviction underlay Durkheim's decision to ignore case histories, the "micro-social" context of suicidal death, and the ways in which social factors manifested themselves in the realm of individual experience.[13] The suicidal act, according to Durkheim and his fellow positivists, was not explicable by individual motives or reasons, but by "objective" external causes. The latter derived from society; they were opaque to individual actors, yet they determined individual behavior. Durkheim's emphasis, in conclusion, was on externality and constraint, not on the consciousness and perceptions of the actor.

II

The interpretative tradition embodied in Durkheim's *Suicide* had a deep and abiding impact on sociological research. In particular, most subsequent studies took the view that social integration or cohesion was the key variable in variations in suicide rates. Maurice Halbwachs in *The Causes of Suicide* (1930), for example, used the most recent statistics to complete a thorough reappraisal of Durkheim's *Suicide*. He essentially confirmed Durkheim's generalizations, linking suicide rates to such external factors as religious affiliation and family structure.[14] However, Halbwachs modified and simplified Durkheim's analysis by arguing that many of the factors that Durkheim found to be related to a high rate of suicide were interlocked in the context of urban life. The higher rates of suicide consistently found in urban areas, Halbwachs argued, were caused by the higher degree of detachment of individuals from their social milieu; in a word, by social isolation. This approach owed not a little to Halbwachs's interest in social ecology, or the spatial distribution of human populations. It led him to discard the typology of egoistic and anomic suicide, and to suggest instead a direct relationship between suicide rates and the degree of urbanization. Halbwachs paid more attention than Durkheim, then, to the specific impact of urbanization on suicide rates, and thus to the change from traditional agrarian society to the complexity characteristic of the urban way of life.[15]

Six years earlier, Maurice de Fleury's *L'Angoisse humaine* (1924) had attacked Durkheim's position by giving absolute precedence to the bio-psychological causes of suicide.[16] Halbwachs was one of Durkheim's most ardent followers, but he was unwilling to reject the "psychiatric thesis" out of hand. He argued, indeed, that the "social" and "psychopathologi-cal" explanations of suicide were complementary rather than antithetical, concluding thus:

It is unnecessary to believe that there are two categories of suicide, each explained by a different determinism, or that, depending on the individual, the organic deter-minism is sometimes in play, and sometimes the social determinism. Actually the suicide, every suicide, can be envisioned from two points of view. Depending on whether one places himself at one or the other, he will see in the suicide the effect of a nervous trouble arising from organic causes, or of a rupture of the collective equilibrium resulting from social causes.[17]

More significant for present purposes, this approach to the social and pathological aspects of suicide led Halbwachs to reject Durkheim's differ-entiation between the social causes of suicide and suicidal motives. While Halbwachs kept faith with the Durkheimian tradition in linking the rising tide of suicide with the lifestyle of modern urban civilization, he committed apostasy when it came to the treatment of suicidal motives.

Durkheim had insisted, of course, that motives played no part in the de-cision to kill oneself. Halbwachs opposed this view on two grounds. First, he argued that collective and individual forces complemented each other. The force of individual misfortune, "which separates or excludes them [people] from the social milieu and which imposes on them an unbearable feeling of loneliness," supplemented the impact of the collective weakening of the social ties that bound people together.[18] Second, Halbwachs con-tended that individual events, which serve as occasions or motives for sui-cide, are directly related to "group structure and style of life."[19] The former occur more commonly in a more complex urban society. It was incumbent on Halbwachs, therefore, to locate a social explanation of both collective forces and particular events. He found it in what he termed "the unique cause of suicide . . . a feeling of a solitude which is definitive and without remedy."[20] The higher level of social isolation in urban areas, he concluded, was both a structural cause of suicide and an individual motive for suicide.

This marked a significant advance on Durkheim's theory, emphasizing as it did both structural causes and individual motivations. For Halb-wachs, a satisfactory explanation of suicide rates required an analysis of both "the structure of the social body" and the manifestations of this structure "in the form of individual situations or circumstances."[21] By insisting that valid explanations of suicide had to be sought in a more experiential perspective, Halbwachs made an original turn toward the study of meanings. Indeed, Halbwachs's desire to integrate social structural factors with individual motivations in the explanation of suicide has been a major influence on the present study. Unfortunately, his improvement on Durkheim's theory of suicide was not taken up by subsequent sociologists to any great degree, in large part because the Chicago School of urban sociologists so effectively underscored the ecological thesis that suicide was an expression of the social disorganization of the modern city.

The Chicago School developed a distinctive theory, based on the assumption that cities enforce a particular way of life.[22] To explain this way of life, the Chicago sociologists introduced into urban studies the biological concept of ecology. Ecology is the study of the relationship of living organisms to their physical environment. Social ecology is the study of the relationship of social structure to the city environment. All parts of this environment, according to the Chicago sociologists, are moved by natural forces, the most important being competition for scarce urban resources such as land. The competitive struggle leads, in turn, to the creation of sub-environments or "natural areas" within the city. Each area is inhabited by a particular social group; each area imposes characteristics upon the social groups within them. In short, the experience of living in certain areas determines the behavior of the residents.

Put less abstractly, the area immediately adjacent to the city center, termed "the zone of transition," is subject to particular ecological and demographic processes: the invasion of business, housing deterioration, a shifting immigrant population. These processes weakened the influence of social rules and values on individuals and disrupted the ability of families and community to control the behavior of their members, resulting in "excessive increases in disease, crime, disorder, vice, insanity, and suicide," which were, said E. W. Burgess, "rough indexes of social disorganization."[23] Harvey Zorbaugh's study of the "rooming-house" or bed-sit area and the related "urban type" (male, single, white-collar, and lonely) first emphasized the relationship between the physical and demographic features of the city, a breakdown of social cohesion, and, for some people, withdrawal in the shape of suicide.[24] The fullest "Chicago" study of suicide and social disorganization, however, was Ruth Cavan's *Suicide*, published in 1928.[25]

Cavan's main finding was that the suicide rate was highest in the central lodging-house areas of the city, where the key social institutions of family, school, and church were decidedly weak, and that it declined gradually as one moved toward the periphery. What explained this spatial pattern? In the central rooming-house districts, said Cavan, there was "a striking lack of the intimate type of group life which is considered by some sociologists the most fundamental both for the control of the individual and for the establishment of conventional norms of conduct, and for the satisfaction of interests and wishes."[26] Lodging-house life was not conducive to community consciousness; the transient and single or divorced males were "detached, uncontrolled by the opinions of their neighbors, and often very lonely."[27] Such conditions were deemed to be favorable to suicide.

Had Cavan terminated her study at this point, it would stand as the most detailed exploration of the general relationship between social disorganization and suicide, and would confirm Durkheim's position concerning the exclusively social causation of suicide. Cavan was not, however, convinced that this general relationship had much explanatory strength. Most individuals living a rooming-house life did not commit suicide (just as most children in "delinquency areas" did not commit delinquency). How then to avoid what has become known as "the ecological fallacy," or the erroneous assumption that the pattern of association between suicide and specific variables (such as unemployment) at an *aggregate* level of analysis holds true for *individuals*?[28]

In the second part of *Suicide*, Cavan probed the relationship between the socially disorganized neighborhood and the process in the individual that culminated in suicide. Her conclusion was that social disorganization affected the tendency to suicide by causing "personal disorganization," by which she meant the failure of the individual to adjust to, or cope with, the various crises of life. Death could seem the appropriate solution to the burdens facing the individual.[29] The most common type of crisis resulting in suicide, said Cavan, occurs when the relationships that constitute "the life-organization" are shattered:

A previously satisfactory life-organization has been broken through forces outside the control of the person: through the death of someone important to him, through illness, through economic failure, through quarrels. . . . Such disturbances seem more liable to affect a whole system of interests and relationships . . . and adjustment is correspondingly difficult.[30]

What requires emphasis here is Cavan's recognition of the need to investigate the suicide's experience and interpretation of the social world.

"The essence of the suicide situation lies," said Cavan, "in the meaning which it has for the person who experiences it. . . . Economic failure does not mean the same thing to everyone, and a domestic difficulty is capable of a dozen interpretations."[31] To investigate the inner world of the individual, Cavan employed the life-history method, which stresses how the world looks to the individual, what crises the individual feels she or he has to cope with, what options the individual considers open to him or her.[32] It becomes possible thereby to understand self-destruction as the end point of a sequence of life events experienced by the suicide. Cavan even pointed to the social strains that characterized different periods of life, "the critical situations in each age group which are associated with suicide," which bears a remarkable similarity to the life-course concept, of which more later.[33]

Once again, however, the attempt to integrate personal motivation with social structural factors in the explanation of suicide withered on the vine. Subsequent diggings in the seam of urban ecology concentrated on the statistical correlation of suicide rates with social isolation, social mobility, and social disorganization.[34] Such structural forces were not greatly influenced, to judge from these authors, by individual choice or personal motivation. No space was granted, at least, for the meaning that individuals attached to external conditions.[35] It is no exaggeration to say, in conclusion, that the interpretative framework launched by Emile Durkheim on a sea of prior studies, refitted by Maurice Halbwachs, and steered deep into the twentieth century by the Chicago sociologists, became seemingly unsinkable.

III

In recent years, however, this dominant tradition deriving from Durkheim has come under attack on two main flanks, the sociological and the historical. The sociological assault, by the ethnomethodologists, is associated mainly with Jack Douglas, whose study *The Social Meanings of Suicide* (1967) challenged both the evidential and theoretical foundations of Durkheim's work.[36] Like the "moral statisticians" before him and the urban ecologists who followed him, Durkheim based his study on the official statistics of suicide. He did so on the assumption that the official rate was a reliable measure of the distribution of suicide; that the official rate bore some approximation to the "true suicide rate." Durkheim also assumed that official errors in recording the fact of suicide would be of a random nature, and would introduce no systematic bias into the figures.[37]

Durkheim's mistake, according to Douglas, was to assume that suicide is "out there," needing only to be culled and tallied by responsible officials. It is now widely accepted, however, that all officially processed social data are unavoidably influenced by the ideas and beliefs of the recording agents. All official statistics are products of complex social and bureaucratic processes that tell us as much about these processes as about the social behavior they purport to reveal. A "suicide," argued Douglas, far from being a straightforward reflection of a "real world" event, is the result of a complex interpretative process by which some acts come to be defined as suicide.

The recording of suicide is said to be complicated by two major sources of systematic reporting error. One is concealment of suicides, notably by social groups such as Catholics and families of higher social standing, who, like Mr. Power in James Joyce's *Ulysses*, looked upon suicide as "the greatest disgrace to have in the family." It is often claimed, too, that families tried, in particular, to conceal female suicides. The second source of error is said to be the misclassification of deaths by coroners, who differed in their qualifications to judge the cause of death and in the resources available to conduct their investigations. Misreporting was probably most frequent in suicides by drowning, a method used disproportionately by women. Since in law, sudden death was presumed accidental until proved otherwise, a suicide verdict tended not to be returned in drowning cases, unless someone actually saw the person intentionally make "a hole in the water." Coroners may have differed, moreover, in how they advised juries to treat the circumstantial evidence in these cases.

In addition, the way deaths come to be defined as "suicides," argued Douglas, is deeply influenced by the cultural understandings of the dramatis personae. In categorizing an unnatural death as suicide, coroners employ commonsense ideas or "shared social meanings" (although not necessarily the same ones) about the circumstances and motives "typically" culminating in such an act. The criteria used by coroners to infer suicide include the manner of death and those aspects of the deceased's past life that evinced suicidal intent, such as state of mind before death, previous suicide attempts, medical and psychological history, and marital, health, and financial difficulties. In their investigations, Douglas contended, coroners employ "folk" or commonsense theories of suicide, plus general assumptions or meanings that society associates with suicide, to structure the selection and interpretation of fact. Furthermore, doctors, policemen, relatives, even suicides themselves, also contribute to this social construction of suicide.[38] It should be emphasized, finally, that the ethnomethodological critique does not alone question the reliability of the statistics, or urge the inclusion of "folk understandings" alongside the "real" causes of suicide. It claims that an event such as a suicide cannot be understood apart from the cultural representations within which, and only within which, the event has meaning.

The implications of this entire sociological outlook are essentially threefold. First, suicide, far from being a "social fact," as Durkheim imagined, is the product of official categorization. Second, the motives that can be found in the suicide's biography—data Durkheim rejected—are central to a death being defined as a suicide. Third, the explanations of suicide offered by Durkheimian positivists may be only a reprise of the "folk theories" used by officials and others in defining a death as suicide. Even the most habitual sociological finding, that suicide rates correlate positively with areas of social disorganization, is arguably a product of systematic bias in the collection of the statistics. The poor and unattached in run-down areas are less able to conceal a suicidal death. Conversely, socially integrated groups more readily succeed in avoiding the stigma of suicide. Therefore, the higher suicide rates in less integrated urban areas may reflect this lower rate of concealment of suicidal actions. Official statistics may well be biased, in brief, in ways that support a theory of social disintegration.[39]

In all, Douglas insisted that the meanings and causes of suicide are revealed at the level of the individual case, as it appears to the suicide and the suicide's entourage. The only way in which we can decode the meanings implicit in action, he concluded, is to study the concrete or "situated meanings," which is to say, the suicide's motives and intentions in the context of the social relations surrounding the act of suicide. Douglas, in effect, is calling for a "bottom-up" case-study analysis of suicide.[40] The overly deterministic approach of Durkheim, the claim that suicide is the outcome of external social forces, is replaced, then, by one in which agents create their own social world through the meanings they use in social interaction. Countering the assumption, implicit in statistical studies of suicide, that external forces have the same impact on, the same meaning for, each individual, is the proposition that the impact of social events is a function of the meaning that individuals ascribe to those events. This orientation toward particularity, the micro-social context, the actor's perspective, is an important alternative to the Durkheimian concentration on aggregate data and abstract meanings.[41]

In the mid 1970's, the French sociologist Jean Baechler endorsed Douglas's anti-Durkheimian position. Baechler argued that suicide results neither from an external suicidogenic wave nor from an internal mental disorder; "suicide is neither a force nor a sickness; it is quite simply a logical solution to a real or imaginary problem."[42] For this reason, Baechler submitted what he termed a "strategic theory" of suicide. Like Douglas, Baechler saw suicide as a motivated act arising out of a particular situation; likewise, he insisted upon investigating the situated, or concrete, meanings of suicide, in order to uncover the general patterns or "typical meanings." And, like other interpretative sociologists, Baechler talked, not of constraint, of individuals trapped like rabbits in the snares of abstract currents or compulsions, but of action and meaning, of people making their own destinies, even on their way to death.[43]

The Durkheimian tradition has also experienced the skepticism of historians. The historical assault on the Durkheimian tradition has taken three main forms. First, historians of crime, the city, and the family have challenged the causal link between urban-industrial society and social disorganization, the link that bulked large in Halbwachs's and Cavan's studies of suicide.[44] Historians of crime have revealed how, in the unfavorable context of intensified urban change, the indices of Victorian criminality— homicide, assault, and theft—actually declined.[45] Urban historians have contested the ecological view that social disorganization is an invariable characteristic of neighborhoods in which there is ethnic diversity, poverty, and lodging-house living. Migration to the city is not accurately portrayed in terms of a transition from cohesive, close-knit communities to disorganized, impersonal slums. Although it might not appear so to outsiders, the urban poor had close kinship ties and their own social hierarchy.[46] In similar vein, historians of the family have discovered that the bonds that held families together did not dissolve; kin networks continued to play a central role in the new urban environment. Family assistance was clearly the most important source of security, especially in coping with "critical life situations": sickness, unemployment, desertion, widowhood, and death.[47]

Second, and more important, the early historians of suicide have thrown into question the positive correlation between urban disorganization and self-slaughter. Roger Lane presented a modified urban thesis, replacing the connection between suicide and disintegration with that between suicide and integration. Nineteenth-century Philadelphia, he showed, grew less not more violent, to judge from the rates of violent death. If suicide rates rose, as they did from the 1870's on, this reflected, not urban disorganization, but an industrial discipline (learned in schools, factories, and offices) that effectively curbed external aggression (homicide) and redirected it inward (suicide). Lane "read" the increased incidence of suicide as "an ironic index of civilization," a measure of social integration.[48] Two other historians of suicide have posed a more direct challenge to the view that high suicide rates are an index of "the suffering and rootlessness bred by urban industrialism."[49] Barrie Ratcliffe tested Louis Chevalier's thesis that suicide was a symptom of social breakdown in the rapidly urbanizing Paris of the second quarter of the nineteenth century. His conclusion was that the various statistical tests "lend scant support to the thesis that urbanization exacerbated social disorganization at this time, at least as far as suicide may be taken as an indicator of social pathology."[50] Olive Anderson found that those most prone to doing away with themselves in Victorian and Edwardian England were not the victims of the new industrial economy. The highest suicide rates were in rural villages and nonindustrial towns and resorts, not in industrial cities.[51]

In terms of methodology, however, all three suicide studies are still examples of what might be called "historical Durkheimianism." Olive Anderson, for example, is cognizant of the main pitfalls in the official statistics, yet she proceeds to use them extensively, with little or no discussion of the social construction of suicide and the challenge it poses to a positivist approach. Ratcliffe is more willing to discuss critically his sources, statistical and otherwise, and to assess the possible sources of distortion. He reaches the conclusion, nonetheless, that the suicide statistics for nineteenth-century Paris are reliable, and that they can be massaged to reveal something of value about the trends and patterns of suicide. In fact, there is only one historical study of suicide that has rigorously adopted an anti-Durkheimian position. It represents the third and final form of historical assault upon the Durkheimian tradition.

Michael MacDonald and Terence R. Murphy have applied the insights of interpretative sociology to the historical study of suicide in an original and imaginative way. Their book *Sleepless Souls* (1990) examines "the secularization of suicide" in England between 1500 and 1800, a legal and cultural shift in attitudes that led to suicide being seen as a secular, not diabolical, event, which should be pitied, not penalized by forfeiture of property.[52] In the third and most thought-provoking section, the authors turn to what they entitle "the hermeneutics of suicide," the "institutions, procedures, and beliefs that identified suicidal deaths and assigned them meanings."[53] They dismiss the suicide rate as "the history of illusions" (although they do examine the suicide rate of different ages and sexes), and concentrate instead upon how deaths were identified as self-murder, what psychological profile (or states of mind) inquest juries and witnesses associated with suicide, what "folk sociology" they employed to make sense of why people took arms against themselves.[54] Coroners' inquisitions and newspapers are examined for what different groups thought about suicide, how they responded to self-destruction, how suicides tried in their notes to influence interpretations of their own deaths. In short, *Sleepless Souls* discards the Durkheimian obsession with the suicide rate, and seeks, rather, to decode "the meanings implicit in social actions and in texts." [55]

In the historical, no less than the sociological, examination of suicide, the dominant conceptual framework, which linked suicide to social structure and claimed that suicide, industrialization, and urbanization were closely associated, has come under vigorous attack. The official suicide statistics are now seen at worst as elaborate fictions, at best as social constructions based upon commonsense perceptions held by the various actors in the drama of investigation and inquisition. In consequence, suicide is treated less as an empirically established "social fact" than as a cultural construction. Suicide is viewed less as the result of social causes beyond the influence of the actors involved than as the outcome of shared meanings informing the practices of everyday life. The study of "objective" structural forces has given way to a scrutiny of the way suicide data are socially constructed, and of the choices and responses made by suicidal people and their entourages.

IV

Would it be sensible, however, having dismantled the Durkheimian framework, to adopt an exclusively subjective theory of suicide? For a start, the Durkheimians could counter the indictment against the official suicide statistics. They could legitimately enquire, for example, why, if groups with greater social influence can more effectively conceal their suicides, the well-educated consistently return higher suicide rates? By the same token, they could enquire why blacks in multiracial societies have a lower recorded suicide rate than whites? And they could ask for hard evidence of social groups, as distinct from random individuals, acting to mislead the courts, and of court officials being swayed by these efforts. In a word, they could go some way toward rebutting the charge that suicide statistics are systematically distorted.[56]

The Durkheimians could also counterattack by submitting that a study of suicide that concentrates only upon the procedures by which individuals attribute meanings to the action of others, upon the way that individuals create the world around them, is as partial as one concerned only with the determining power of social structures. The claim that social life consists solely of actors' shared definitions and assumptions denies the possibility of any objective knowledge of the world. If the world is socially constructed, if society is but a "mental event," then how do we recognize it? Attending solely to actors' perceptions of society, moreover, denies the reality of structures of economic and political power within which individuals operate. Yet whether or not actors define them as real, "the hard surfaces of life," in Clifford Geertz's words, "the political, economic, stratificatory realities within which men are everywhere contained," are very real in their consequences.[57]

It seems unwise, therefore, to replace "an imperialism of the social object," in Anthony Giddens's phrase, with "an imperialism of the subject."[58] Must we rest content, however, with interpreting suicide as *either* the product of material factors *or* the result of different systems of categorization and social meanings? Is there no way of avoiding the horns of this philosophical dilemma, of escaping "the two-headed monster" of structure and agency? It is the aim in what follows, and the preeminent purpose of the entire chapter, to develop a method that unites the individual motives for suicide with a historical-material account of social structure that incorporates the chosen and the determined dimensions of suicidal behavior.

In the attempt to surmount the dualism of subjectivism and objectivism, a number of texts are suggestive, although they provide no specific blueprint as far as the study of suicide is concerned. The relationship between determinism and human agency was a central theme of E. P. Thompson's writings, both in his historical work on the "making" of class and in his vigorous rejection of structural Marxism for denying the significance of human activity and consciousness. Against the view that all human behavior is "lawed," or "structured," Thompson offered a "rule-governed structuration of historical eventuation (within which men and women remain as subjects of their own history)."[59] The process of class formation, he argued, is one of both agency (or "self-making") and conditioning. What counts, he insisted, is "the *dialogue* between social being and social consciousness."[60]

Pierre Bourdieu's work likewise concerns the ways of reconciling the notion of determining structures with the activities of people seeking to change their circumstances. Bourdieu's actors are structurally positioned, but the structures of the past are not imperious. What he terms *habitus*, or practices learned from an early age, practices influenced, to be sure, by material structures, provides the latitude for purposeful action, scope for strategic intervention. There is a constant exchange in Bourdieu's "theory of practice" between subjective experience and strategy on one hand and objective structures on the other—what Bourdieu terms "a double structuration." To adopt his simple metaphor, both the nature of the hand dealt the person or family and the skill with which the hand is played are important in the card game of life.[61]

More instructive, thanks to its direct link with the study of suicide, is Giddens's theory of structuration.[62] The theory is Giddens's way of arguing for a dialectical relationship between structure and action, for the complex interplay of constraint and agency as a matter of process in time. Basic to the notion of structuration is "the duality of structure": the notion that structure is simultaneously the unintended "outcome" of human activity and the "medium" of that activity. Our actions, the argument runs, are influenced by the structural features of the society we inhabit (actions, that is to say, are both limited and facilitated by the inequalities of power, material resources, and knowledge), but at the same time, we reproduce and transform those structural features through the continuous flow of daily practice. Giddens has always been longer on theory than empirical research, but the message for the actual investigation of suicide is the requirement to combine a view of suicide as "rationalized action, reflexively monitored by the actor" with an estimate of "the motivational components," and an examination of "the structural conditions of this behaviour, especially in the context of the nexus of social relationships in which the action occurs."[63] In short, Giddens proposes that we explore the interconnections between the social and material conditions of life, and the meanings ascribed to these conditions by suicidal people and their entourages.

V

But the question remains, what modus operandi allows us to explore these interconnections between material life and meanings? The first methodological feature is that the study of suicide must be based on individual-level data in a specific local context. The aggregate, national approach will simply not suffice. Only by "fine-comb field study in confined contexts," to adopt Geertz's description of the anthropological method, is it possible to examine the entire range of factors.[64] Suicide is decipherable only through a reconstruction of the complex setting and social meaning of the action. Regard must be had, for example, to place, to household patterns (where and with whom the suicide lived), to daily occupation, to health and wealth, to age and gender. Attention must be given also to the thoughts and feelings of the people who killed themselves, to the firsthand reactions of relatives, neighbors, and workmates to the suicidal death, and to the circumstances that ordinary people believed were conducive to self-destruction. Only thus can one begin to reveal the links between structural forces acting on individuals and the meanings given by individual actors.

A passport to this complex and bounded locality exists in coroners' inquest papers, where both a statistical profile of those susceptible to suicide and detailed case histories can be found. For each case, as stated earlier, there is the formal inquisition, giving, inter alia, details of the age, gender, occupation, and habitat of individual suicides. Also, there are the depositions of witnesses, through which the historian can vault the barrier imposed by suicide, "in an effort to fill out a life," [65] to uncover details of the marital status and living arrangements of suicides, and probe possible motivations. The statistical evidence makes it possible to provide an index to the variable propensity to suicide of different age, gender, work, and social groups, and thus to reveal what social and economic (including familial) characteristics were shared by those most prone to killing themselves. I am at my most "Durkheimian" in chapter 6, assessing the ages at which men and women were most vulnerable to suicide; the occupations that were most suicidal; the numerical reality of unemployment; and the habitats that contained the largest share of suicides. The aim is to discover pointers that can inform the interpretation of the experience of suicide to be found in the depositions of witnesses.

At this point, most likely, ethnomethodologists would interject that uncovering the experience of suicide from such qualitative sources is much easier said than done. The evidence of witnesses, they would insist, was always shaped by the coroner's questions and by the interests of witnesses themselves. Coroners did indeed have a set line of questioning, designed to elicit evidence suggestive of suicide. Such questioning might have altered over time, as lay and professional knowledge of, for example, physical and mental illness increased. When it came to witnesses, they had the difficult, if not impossible, task of serving as proxy for the suicide. Their accounts would draw, at least to some degree, upon contemporary habits of explanation, including the gender-specific motives ascribed to suicides. It was a commonplace of nineteenth-century discourse, for example, to blame male suicide upon work and financial problems, female suicide upon domestic and emotional troubles. Moreover, the fact that self-destruction is always preventable, and that family members often had a role in the causal process leading to the suicide, could well have influenced the way that witnesses reconstructed the past. It is unrealistic to expect witnesses to admit readily to deep-seated family tensions, say, when such an admission might reflect badly upon themselves or other survivors.

The hermeneutic gaze has also been turned upon suicide notes. Only a minority of suicides ever left them; those who did, it is argued, were out to control the meanings that would be assigned to their deaths. The suicide note united self-destruction with self-definition.[66] Nor, finally, the hermeneutic argument insists, can newspaper accounts of inquest proceedings be relied upon. Press reporting was selective, inclining to the unusual in methods and motives, and it embodied, not to say molded, contemporary perceptions of suicide. The interpretative sociologist would thus conclude that no historian can successfully strip away what Natalie Zemon Davis calls "the fictive elements" of these documents, and expose the "hard facts." "The glimpses of life and death," on view in the depositions, are, said Ratcliffe, "shadows that are more projections of observers' views and phantasms than the reality of self-destruction." The "assigned motive," that proffered by coroner or witness, is merely the "folk explanation" of suicide. The "true motive" (what was in the suicide's mind) is impenetrable.[67]

To the last point, one can only nod assent. The real motives that impel a person to suicide are ultimately unfathomable. "An act like this," said Albert Camus, "is prepared within the silence of the heart, as is a great work of art." Jean Baechler concurred: "Every suicide carries its secret to the grave."[68] But what of the rest of the argument? The hermeneutic critique is telling, but not ultimately convincing. Inquest depositions certainly reveal the shared social meanings of suicide: what conjunction of social and emotional circumstances were felt by contemporaries to explain suicide. But this leaves open two possible conclusions: one, that the factors cited are merely "seen to be" causes of suicide by coroner and witnesses; and two, that the factors "really are," to some degree at least, causally related to suicide. The latter represents my own conclusion. Accepting that coroners' case papers lay bare popular notions about the causes of suicide, I would argue that these notions were informed by the experience and knowledge of the pressures of daily life: the economic uncertainties, the domestic tensions, the bereavements, and the worries over ill health that, in conjunction with subjective responses to these difficulties, can and did result in the shattering of an individual's well-being. The motives or causes that survivors assigned were governed by their understanding of the victim and his or her circumstances. A deponent's consciousness of the environment was important but not all-important; a person's thoughts remained implicated in objective circumstances. The notions held by relatives, neighbors, and workmates about the paths to suicide were grounded in the interlocking reality of socioeconomic structures and subjective experiences. In fine, I have assumed that there is a reality external to the historical text, a reality that is knowable. I have supposed that clues in informants' accounts attest to something other than themselves. I subscribe to Carlo Ginzburg's view: "Reality is opaque; but there are certain points—clues, signs—which allow us to decipher it."[69]

The second methodological requirement to integrating the social pressures of life and the meanings ascribed to those pressures is a framework over which the closely woven evaluation of individual cases can be thrown. The framework chosen is that of the "life cycle," or, as historians of the family now prefer, the "life course." I see the "life cycle" as an overlapping sequence of eras or "seasons," each with its own distinctive character, with variations related to gender, class, and culture. More specifically, *life cycle* refers to the developmental stages, such as childhood, adolescence, adulthood, and old age, each with its own biological, psychological, and social characteristics, through which individuals move in the course of their lives. The concept has a long ancestry, the most recited formulation possibly being Shakespeare's seven ages of man, from "the infant, / Mewling and puking in the nurse's arms" to "second childishness and mere oblivion, / Sans teeth, sans eyes, sans taste, sans everything."[70] The term *life course* implies more variability and discretion than the deterministic language of the life cycle. It concentrates upon the major lifetime transitions: entry into the labor force, departure from the parental home, marriage, parenthood, widowhood, and exit from the labor force. The life-course perspective shifts the focus of investigation from the abstract stages of the life cycle to how (the process) and when (the timing) individuals make the transition from one stage to the next, including whether the transition occurs at all, over the entire life span, and in response to social and economic change and opportunities in the larger society. The approach also highlights the synchronization of individual life transitions with the collective experience of the family as it moves through its life course (one of the main findings of life-course research being that individual life trajectories were intertwined with family development).[71]

The causes of suicide will be sought in the impact of the various transitions of the life course.[72] What we know of the life course in nineteenth-century industrial towns, which is more fully treated in chapter 4, has led me to investigate, for example, the major transition in a man's working life that came with the descent to a semi- or unskilled, and possibly temporary, job in his middle or late forties, as his physical strength waned. This transition would inevitably have been affected by the occupational structure, stage of industrialism, and economic health of the city in question. For women, a critical transition in middle and later life was widowhood. Some widows continued to head their own households, either by finding paid work or by taking in lodgers; others moved in with kin or into lodgings. The character of the city's poor law could affect this transition, as could the demand for female labor.[73] We shall take cognizance, finally, of what Michael Anderson has termed the "reversibility of the life-cycle experience," caused by demographic and economic uncertainty.[74]

The chief merit of the life-course perspective, it should be stressed, is that it centers upon the complex relationship between individual choices and strategies, social interaction within the family and workplace, and the constraints and possibilities of the socioeconomic environment.[75] It is, therefore, an appropriate framework for a study of suicide that seeks to use prosopography, or individual case reports, to link experience, or the actors' perspective, to "objective" structures. The life-course approach makes it possible to fuse the personal and the public, to locate the individual career within a particular matrix of social relationships and life chances, to examine what Philip Abrams termed "the meshing of life-history and social history in a singular fate."[76] By placing the deceased within the life cycle or life course, we are providing the essential context for uncovering both the material pressures impinging on the deceased, and the meanings that the suicide generated. Attention to the life course, finally, compels the historian to "listen" carefully to the personal narratives of the central tragedians of the inquest, whose stories have long been disregarded by statistical analysts and social theorists. An investigation of how dying by suicide was related to the different transitions of the life course will provide only one clue to the enigma of suicide. But, as Jean Baechler remarked, "it is not necessary to be able to explain *everything* in order to try to understand something."[77]

Interpreting the Coroners' Inquest

2

"Crowner's Quest Law"

At the appointed hour arrives the Coroner, for whom the
Jurymen are waiting, and who is received with a salute
of skittles from the good dry skittle-ground attached to
the Sol's Arms. The Coroner frequents more public-
houses than any man alive. The smell of sawdust, beer,
tobacco-smoke, and spirits, is inseparable in his vocation
from death in its most awful shapes. He is conducted by
the beadle and the landlord to the Harmonic Meeting
Room, where he puts his hat on the piano, and takes a
Windsor-chair at the head of a long table. . . . As many
of the Jury as can crowd together at the table sit there.
The rest get among the spittoons and pipes, or lean
against the piano. . . .

"Well, gentlemen!" resumes the Coroner. "You are
impanelled here, to inquire into the death of a certain
man. . . . The first thing to be done, is to view
the body. . . ."

So they go out in a loose procession, something
after the manner of a straggling funeral, and make their
inspection in Mr Krook's back second floor, from which
a few of the Jurymen retire pale and precipitately. The
beadle is very careful that two gentlemen not very neat
about the cuffs and buttons . . . should see all that is to
be seen. For they are the public chroniclers of such
inquiries.

Charles Dickens,
Bleak House (1852–53)

Every borough with its own Court of Quarter Sessions had to appoint a "fit person" to be coroner. Borough coroners required no professional qualification, either legal or medical, although most were in fact solicitors. They held office for life. Local dynasties were not uncommon, the office of coroner remaining in the same family for many generations. The coroner had the duty to investigate the circumstances of unnatural, sudden, or suspicious deaths, and, from the mid nineteenth century on, of all deaths in lunatic asylums and prisons (but not workhouses), and on railways.[1] Cases were referred to him by, among others, doctors, police constables, prison governors, and asylum superintendents. The coroner had only one way of investigating these cases: by holding an inquest on the body, with the aid of a jury. Unless an inquest were held, no postmortem examination of the body could be ordered, no medical evidence could be called and remunerated.[2] The jury had the job of listening to the evidence, and certifying "who the deceased was and how, when and where the deceased came by his death."[3] Coroners had considerable latitude in the way they ran their courts. There were no strict rules of evidence; there was little or no interference from either the Home Office or the Lord Chancellor's Office. In consequence, the coroner system reflected, as Olive Anderson has remarked, "the prejudices, habits, and values of each particular locality in all the diversity of its public and private interests, conflicts, and routines."[4]

The coroners' court mandates our close attention not only because of its local diversity but also because its social and bureaucratic processes created the very documents upon which the second half of this book is based. In making sense of how, when, and where an unnatural, sudden, or suspicious death occurred, the court gathered the quantitative and qualitative data that make it possible to establish the sex, age, and occupational distribution of suicide, and the individual experience of dying by suicide. We cannot, in a word, separate the data from the legal instrument through which they were collected. As chapter 1 indicated, however, the inclination to use these data to establish the incidence, distribution, and etiology of suicide has met the not-inconsiderable resistance of sociologists and historians who question the value of court-created documents.[5] Coroners' inquests, as we shall see, brought a large body of people together to investigate the physical evidence, the events that preceded the death, and the deceased's actions, gestures, and words. The process, the critics of positivism argue, was shaped by theories of causality that determined what questions were asked of witnesses, what facts were gathered, and how they were interpreted. In a word, the cultural understandings of the actors in this public drama influenced deeply whether deaths were defined as accidents, "by the visitation of God," "open verdicts," or suicides. On the strength of such observations, the critics of a positivist approach insist that the statistics derived from inquisitions are worthless, reflecting the social construction of suicidal death, not the realities of suicide; and that coroners' case papers give us access only to the "shared social meanings," not the actual experience of suicide.

The next two chapters have the essential task, therefore, of evaluating the strengths and weaknesses of the records created by the coroners' court, by way of a "thick description" of the assumptions and methods of those responsible for establishing the cause of death. To this end, chapter 2 examines the local dynasty of coroners, their workload and remuneration; how sudden and suspicious deaths came to the coroner's attention, and the "etiquette" of discovering suicidal death. It explores where inquests were held; the social composition of juries; and the choreography of the inquest itself. Particular attention is given to the contribution of postmortem examinations and of medical witnesses, both to uncovering the cause of death and, in cases of death by suicide, to determining the deceased's state of mind. Chapter 3 looks closely at "open verdicts" and the issue of officially overlooked suicides, and at when and why juries returned the three different kinds of suicide verdict. The conclusion drawn from the evidence of these two chapters is that the inquisition and depositional data are sufficiently reliable to justify a study of both the statistical trends of suicide and the experience of dying by suicide.[6] Over and above this important conclusion, these chapters portray the rituals of the inquest, drawn not from legal treatises, but from the unique local practice of one provincial city's coroners' court.

I

The Hull coroner who bestrode the period under examination was John Joseph Thorney. His father, John Thorney, to whom John Joseph was articled, was in practice as a solicitor, and held the office of borough coroner. In 1849, John Joseph was admitted a solicitor. Partnership with his father followed, and in 1854 he succeeded him as both borough coroner and superintendent registrar of deaths. These offices he held until his death on January 10, 1897, at the age of 69. A man of "upright figure and sprightly gait," J. J. Thorney had few interests beyond the coronership. He was, however, a zealous supporter of the 1st Corps, East York Rifle Volunteers, in which he chose to remain a private, preferring the ranks to the officers' mess; he was also a confirmed mountaineer and Alpine Club member. Politically he was a Liberal-Unionist. He had six daughters and two sons, the eldest of whom, Alfred, helped to run the law firm for the final twelve years of Thorney's career, and acted as coroner during Thorney's last illness. Predictably, the Town Council appointed Alfred Thorney to succeed his father in the office of coroner.[7] Even allowing for the effusive nature of local obituaries, the town clearly felt that J. J. Thorney had discharged the duties of coroner in a painstaking and sympathetic manner. In 43 years at the helm, he held possibly 6,000 inquests.[8] It was said that, no matter how difficult the case, he mastered all the details. It was also said of him that "the law failing, the medical profession would have been enriched by the addition of his name."[9] Thorney's long tenure and his family's monopoly on the office of borough coroner would lead us to expect a reasonably high level of precision and consistency in the way that inquests were handled. The full inquest papers (containing both inquisitions and depositions) submitted by the Thorneys to the clerk of the peace also speak to a high level of efficiency.

The workload of the three coroners can be reconstructed in broad outline. John Thorney, the patriarch of the group, held approximately 90 inquests each year in the 1840's, and 100 a year in the early 1850's. J. J. Thorney's burden increased from an annual average of 110 inquests in the 1860's, to 128 in the 1880's, to 223 inquests in the five years before his death in 1897. By 1900, Alfred Thorney was holding over 300 inquests each year and investigating the deaths of another 100 persons in respect of which he did not consider it necessary to hold inquests.[10] The burgeoning workload was largely a function of both population growth and periodic extensions of the borough boundaries, which together took the population in the coroner's jurisdiction from approximately 66,000 persons in 1841 to 240,000 in 1901. As for the types of death investigated, the figures for 1864, a year chosen at random, indicate that just over 60 percent of all inquests were cases of accidental death (predominantly accidents at work and in the home), 15 percent were due to illness or natural causes (including three prisoners), another 15 percent were "found drowned" (including a destitute sloopman who had earlier threatened suicide), 4 percent were newborn children (two of whom had been killed, two found dead), and 4 percent of the inquest cases were suicides.[11] Cases of suicide were obviously a small part of the coroner's workload, although the figure for 1864 is one of the lowest. Typically, suicide cases constituted between 5 percent (in 1844, 1856, 1868, and 1896) and 11 or 12 percent (in 1846, 1869, and

1895) of all inquests.[12] The Town Council had at first no schedule of fees and allowances, but the custom was to pay the coroner and his deputies (who took possibly one-tenth or less of all inquests) a fee of £1 for every inquest (increasing to £1 6s. 8d. by 1880); one shilling to each juror; five shillings for the hire of a room at the pub or inn where the inquest was held; and £1 3s. per inquest for medical witnesses and for postmortem examination, when these were called for. Hence, the average cost of each inquest, at least until the 1880's, was between £2 7s. and £2 15s.[13]

The first stage in the process of defining a death as suicide was for the coroner's attention to be called to deaths that appeared to be self-inflicted.[14] Such bodies fetched up in various locations. A few were landed at St. Andrew's Dock, bodies of fishermen who had jumped from smacks into the Humber estuary or the North Sea. Others were fished out of the city's various docks, drains, ponds, and rivers. A few bodies were found on board emigrant ships; a few found mangled on the railway tracks. Close to 40 bodies were former inmates of the borough prison, workhouses, pauper lunatic asylums, police cells, and almshouses. The Infirmary received many who had poisoned themselves or cut their throats but did not die instantly.[15] The majority of seemingly suicidal deaths, however, were extremely private acts, prepared and executed behind closed, locked, or barricaded doors, at home or at work. Of the 52 officially defined male suicides from the 1860's, for example, no fewer than 24 were carried out in a house, hotel, or lodgings, typically in a bedroom—occasionally a water closet— with the suicide using a razor or knife to cut his throat, or a bedpost, joist, or banister from which to hang himself. A dozen more chose their place of work: a warehouse, hayloft, stable, shop, or fish house, which commonly lay in close proximity to the home, typically hanging themselves from halter, chain, or beam. Of the 21 officially defined female suicides from the same decade, 9 hanged themselves or cut their throats at home or in lodgings, not including the 7 who poisoned themselves, some of whom took the poison in a pub or in the street, but went home to die.[16]

It follows that deaths that appeared to be self-inflicted came to the coroner's notice via policemen, doctors, private individuals, and the registrars of deaths. The last, under the system of medical certification and registration of deaths, introduced in 1836, could inform the coroner of any uncertified deaths. In the discovery of suicide in public places, the town, dock, and railway company police were inevitably important.[17] For deaths in the home and at work, the key figures, as the coroners' case papers reveal, were family members, neighbors, policemen, and doctors. In April

1883, Thomas Todd, a 55-year-old joiner, hanged himself in his kitchen; his wife's screams attracted a fitter who lived nearby. A few months later, when Martin Pitman, a 59-year-old professor of music, hanged himself from the banister rail, his wife's screams roused the next-door neighbor, a clerk, who cut Pitman down. A destitute hawker of fish, hanging from the bedstead at his lodgings in June 1866, was cut down by the landlord of the Prince of Wales Tavern, who lived in the same street.[18] In January 1890, a fruiterer, aged 36, was found on the stairs by a live-in servant. His wife opened a bedroom window and hailed a policeman. When, in August 1879, the wife of a 67-year-old house proprietor discovered her husband hanging by a silk handkerchief from a closet door, she sent her daughter to fetch the constable who lived in the next terrace.[19] Often, no attempt was made to cut the hanging body down. The assistant who discovered William Goy, a 17-year-old grocer's boy, hanging from an iron bar in a warehouse window in March 1862 went immediately to find a constable. Four years later, the son of an ale and porter merchant waited for a policeman to arrive at his father's store before cutting the body down. In November 1876, Isabel Castle's son-in-law, who lived next door, found her hanging from a door by a silk handkerchief. He went immediately for a doctor, who told him to go to the police station. Several of the jury asked him why he had not first cut the body down, but the coroner observed that it was a prevailing belief, to which he did not subscribe, that when a dead body was found, it was best to leave it where it was until the police or someone had seen it. The practice certainly persisted; in July 1897, a juryman asked a young tailor who had found his employer hanging from a door in the workshop why he had run for a policeman before cutting down the deceased.[20]

On some occasions, a constable came across the body first. When, in April 1849, the shop of a widowed tailor, Thomas Webb, failed to open, a neighbor summoned a policeman, who broke into the house and found Webb hanging by a cord from an iron staple in the kitchen ceiling.[21] As for doctors, they were summoned by both family members and the police, especially if the person was still alive. Dr. Robert Nicholson was called to a 69-year-old corn meter, his patient of ten years, who was in shock from having cut his throat in the backyard in June 1875. Dr. Thomas Denison was called to Thomas Bigby, a cattle salesman, who had jumped into Prince's Dock in August 1894. As he was giving artificial respiration, the hatch boards of the lighter they were on gave way, and they all fell into the bottom of the vessel. Bigby was sent to the police station, where he later died from the shock of immersion.[22] Not all doctors responded to such appeals, however. In December 1847, George Graham, a 56-year-old shoe-maker, poisoned himself with prussic acid; a fellow shoemaker, who lived with Graham, ran for William Hendry, surgeon and apothecary. Hendry declined to attend "because he said he had been attending him before for poison & had not got paid."[23] When, in May 1897, the wife of a black-smith started shouting that she had taken laudanum, her sons gave her mustard and water, and a policeman poured hot coffee down her. A son then went to fetch Dr. George Briggs, who refused to attend, but told the son to take her to the Infirmary.[24]

An important consideration, at this stage, is the possibility of conceal-ment of suicidal death. The evidence above suggests that it would not have been easy to conceal or disguise a death by suicide, particularly among the closely packed homes of working-class districts, where little escaped neighborly attention. The subject requires further examination, however, since the critics of suicide rates set so much store by the prevalence of con-cealment. Medical certification, it is clear, did not guarantee detection of a suicidal death. There is evidence from other parts of the country that doc-tors shielded relatives by giving a certificate of "death from natural causes" in cases that warranted an inquest. As Anderson has argued, however, the amount of concealment from this source was kept in check by police sur-geons, poor-law doctors, policemen, and registrars who were familiar with the kinds of suspicious circumstances that called for investigation, and who worked hand in glove with the local coroner.[25] What of the evidence from coroners' inquests? The closest a recorded case of working-class suicide came to concealment was that of an unemployed oil miller, Thomas Atkin-son, who hanged himself from a bedpost in February 1873. His house-keeper of 25 years called a neighbor to help carry the deceased downstairs. Asked why she had not sent word to the police, the housekeeper said: "I would have kept the matter quiet if I could." But the neighbor spotted the rope round the neck.

Concealment was more possible, presumably, for those who could af-ford to summon private, especially medical, assistance. There is a hint (no more) of concealment in the case of John Oliver, a schoolmaster, who died in November 1888. His doctor certified that the cause of death was cere-bral effusion and apoplexy. The postmortem, however, revealed strychnine poisoning. Thorney let the doctor down gently, remarking that he had understandably been misled by the deceased's prolonged intemperance and recent delirium tremens, and that finding him dead, he gave a certificate to that effect.[26] The only unmistakable case of attempted concealment in the inquest files concerned the death in January 1899 of Louis Shibko, a 48-year-old Jewish jeweler. The constable deposed that, assuming that Shibko had hanged himself, he had decided to try artificial respiration. "Before I did so," said the constable, "the woman in the room tried to send me away, saying he had only fainted." Later, the family sent for the doctor who had attended the deceased for sixteen years. At the inquest, the doctor deposed revealingly: "As I went upstairs an old gentleman, whom I understand is deceased's uncle, asked me if I could certify disease of the heart. On seeing him I examined him. I saw the abrasion on the neck. I was told it was the mark of his shirt." The fact of asking this doctor to examine the body, after another doctor had already done so, "and then trying to 'wheedle' out of him a certificate of death from natural causes, was a matter," said the coroner, "which could not be passed over without comment." Shibko's life was not insured, so the attempt at concealment must be ascribed to the stigma of suicide felt by a respectable family of Jewish faith, and to the denial of burial in the city's Jewish cemetery, which a suicide verdict presumably entrained. It is noteworthy, however, that even here, a constable had been called to the house, and the family doctor could not be suborned.[27]

Of course, hanging, the method most preferred by men, was the one most difficult to conceal. It might have been easier to conceal suicide by poisoning (a common method of suicide among women) or by throat cutting (a common method among men). However, the slower-acting nature of the two latter methods could also prevent concealment by leading to medical attention or hospitalization.[28] Only drowning, a method used most commonly by women, was open to frequent misclassification, but, as I later argue, less because of purposeful concealment than of the legal injunction that a death must be considered accidental until proved otherwise.[29] It is possible that lodging-house keepers and publicans, both with custom to lose, might have tried to conceal suicides on their premises, as might a doctor who feared for the reputation of his medical practice. The city's social elite presumably had a greater desire and capacity to cover up attempted and completed suicides (although their households often contained domestic servants, whose complicity with the family could not be ensured). However, these possibilities hardly square with the context and forms of suicide discovery.

In the smaller, more personal neighborhoods of the provincial town, and particularly in districts of high-density working-class housing, people's behavior was subject to considerable public scrutiny. Nor was there much privacy inside the house, given the small size of most homes, the intrusion of business into many households, and the practice (at particular stages of the life cycle) of taking in lodgers or employing domestic servants. In addition, so shocked were families, neighbors, workmates, and landlords at discovering the dead or dying body of kin, friend, or colleague, that a constable or doctor or both were fetched immediately. Constables had no interest in concealing suicide, doctors little more; they both took a professional risk in doing so. Finally, to judge from press reports, news and rumors of a suicide were eagerly bruited abroad and quickly became public knowledge. The suicide of David Cook, a fruiterer, in June 1874, caused considerable excitement in Mytongate, in the Old Town district. His eight-year-old daughter had found him hanging on the second-floor landing, and his wife had run through the street crying, "My poor husband." When Charles Plant, a police constable, failed to appear on parade on November 17, 1880, his sergeant went to his house and found that he had killed his wife, then hanged himself from the banister by a clothesline. In view of his occupation, no doubt, the event became the subject of excited conversation throughout the town, and crowds gathered in the locality of Grosvenor Street, west of Beverley Road.[30] In all, then, it seems unlikely that many cases of suicide were subject to successful concealment.

II

The second stage on the path to registering a death as suicide was for the coroner to determine whether or not an inquest should be held. Coroners, especially urban ones, seem to have held inquests on most of the unnatural, sudden, or suspicious deaths reported to them. An inquest was the only way in which the pathological cause of death could be properly investigated, and the only means by which the coroner could receive remuneration.[31] The third stage, that of the inquest, warrants much closer attention, since it directly determined whether or not a verdict of suicide was returned.

An inquest required a room big enough to hold some 20 to 25 people: the coroner, jurymen, medical and lay witnesses, and, occasionally, representatives of relatives, the deceased, or an insurance company, and the chief constable on behalf of the police. The body upon which the inquest was held would also be present (in another room, an outhouse, or a mortuary) for the jurors to view. In Hull, the usual place of inquest was a room in a tavern, inn, hotel, or public house. A tavern or pub could always be found close to where the body lay, and to where witnesses lived, with a

A CORONERS INQUEST.

Juror— *The man's alive Sir, for he has open'd one eye.*
Coroner— *Sir the doctor declar'd him Dead two hours since & he must remain Dead. Sir so I shall proceed with the Inquest.*

London Published by The W. Leen at Haymarket 1826

ILLUSTRATION I: *A Coroner's Inquest*. Unknown artist (dated 1826). Clements C. Fry Print Collection. Cushing / Whitney Medical Library, Yale University.

room large enough for a coroner's court.[32] Inquests were also held at the police stations in Jarratt Street, Blanket Row, and Parliament Street; at the borough asylum in Anlaby Road and the borough jail in Hedon Road; at the workhouses in Whitefriargate and the Beverley Road; and at the Infirmary in Prospect Street, upon the bodies of inmates of all these places.[33] But the vast majority of inquests were held in the beery atmosphere of local pubs, particularly the imposing Whittington Inn on Commercial Road. In some cases, the deceased had been a lodger at, or the publican of, the very house in which the inquest was held.[34] The home of the deceased was sometimes the venue, but given the size of the room required, this practice was restricted to those of some social standing: a printer and newsagent, a surgeon, and a chemist and druggist, as three examples.[35] In the 1890's, in default of a purpose-built coroner's courthouse, a number of public institutions were used: the Friendly Societies Hall in Albion Street; the Fire Brigade station in Worship Street; St. George's Cocoa House in Castle Street. Inquests were also increasingly held at the Castle Street mortuary.[36] For most of the Victorian period, then, the inquest had a distinctly popular character. It was less an aloof, bureaucratic, and routinized inquisition and more an informal, accessible investigation, sited in the deceased's own neck of the woods.[37] Indeed, the essence of inquest practice was public participation and assent. This aspect of the process of establishing a death as suicide was only strengthened by the jury of local people.

The rules governing the selection of inquest juries were distinguished by their simplicity. No fewer than twelve and no more than twenty-three "good and lawful men," declared the Coroners Act, 1887, were to be summoned.[38] Hull inquest documents show between twelve and fifteen jurors' signatures in most cases, inhabitants of the deceased's neighborhood, and tradesmen, shopkeepers, and merchants all. For the 1838 inquest at King's Coffee House in High Street, on the master of a vessel plying between Hull and Antwerp, who cut his throat with a razor while at anchor in the Humber, a jury of twelve deliberated. The foreman was a jeweler and watchmaker; the other jurors included a brush manufacturer, a house and ship painter, a printer and stationer, a hairdresser, a breeches maker, an engraver, and a victualer. For the 1887 inquest at the Infirmary on a shipowner and the Danish vice-consul in Hull, who shot himself with a pistol while traveling in a cab, a jury of fifteen held court. The foreman was a fruiterer; his fellow jurors included drapers, hosiers, a carver and gilder, a dentist, and a tobacconist.[39] Men of this status were thought perhaps to have the courage of their convictions when it came to bringing in a verdict, and the responsibility to heed the summons. Jurors could be fined for failure to appear, and if an inquest were adjourned, they were bound over to attend in a recognizance of £10 each. At the time fixed for the start of the June 1898 inquest in the St. Matthias Mission Room on an unknown male who had hanged himself, two jurymen were missing. The coroner, Alfred Thorney, said that he had previously had occasion to complain of nonattendance, and that all he could do was use his powers of punishment. The last juror to turn up said that he had mistaken the notice on the summons. When a juror was late for the adjourned inquest in May 1891 on Louisa Bowen, who had cut her throat, the coroner told him that he had only just escaped a £10 fine.[40]

The inquest itself was a fact-finding investigation, not a trial. The procedure was inquisitorial, not accusatorial. No one stood accused; there was no prosecution, no defense. The rules of evidence were indulgent; hearsay, for example, was admissible. The key figure, inevitably, was the coroner, who put most of the questions to the witnesses and summarized in longhand their verbal depositions.[41] First, the coroner would charge the jury, stating that it was their duty to inquire how, when, and by what means the deceased had come to his or her death. He would also inform the jury that if they decided that the death had been self-inflicted, they would have to consider what state of mind the deceased had been in at the time.[42] The body would then be viewed by the jurors, and the examination of witnesses would begin. The first witness was usually the spouse, a relative, or a close friend, and typically the person who had last seen the deceased or who had first found the body. In only a handful of cases did a doctor certify that the widow was in no fit state to attend the court.[43] Spouses, children, siblings, and friends, under questioning by the coroner, might describe the deceased's behavior and mood prior to the act; his mental and physical history and condition; his drinking habits; his previous attempts and threats to commit suicide; the family's record of insanity; and the impact of such recent distressing events as dismissal, arrest, widowhood, or a physical injury. These witnesses might be asked by the coroner whether they had ever feared that the deceased would destroy himself; whether the deceased had lived "comfortably" with his wife; and whether their own conduct had in any way induced the suicide.[44]

Other witnesses included domestic or hotel servants, lodging-house keepers, neighbors, employers, foremen, and workmates, all of whom might describe the deceased's lowness and despondency, his drinking habits, his romantic disappointments, or his economic situation.[45] Neighbors and fellow lodgers were well placed to describe marital quarrels, conversations in which the deceased had talked of suicide, and previous suicide attempts. Then there were the police and medical witnesses. A police constable might describe how and where the body had been found; a chemist or druggist tell how the deceased had got hold of the poison; a doctor interpret his patient's symptoms, explain the postmortem findings, and speak to the deceased's actual or probable state of mind.[46] Throughout the inquest, jurymen had the right to question witnesses. In reply to a juror, the widow of a 34-year-old carpenter, who had hanged himself in April 1894, stated: "He has had no full employment & that has troubled him." Moreover, representatives on behalf of the deceased, the family, employers, and insurance companies occasionally gave evidence and interrogated witnesses.[47]

To describe the evidence of spouses, relatives, and friends is again to confront the issue of its reliability. Was the evidence really as disingenuous as some suggest?[48] The inquest was an extremely public proceeding, and one likely perhaps to induce family and friends to be economical with the truth, if the latter reflected poorly upon the deceased, the family, or themselves. This is hard, of course, to prove or disprove; only the *unsuccessful* manipulation of evidence would tend to come to light. A neighbor of Mary Wiles (who drowned herself and her child in August 1891) told the coroner that Mary's mother-in-law had instructed her, when giving evidence, "to hear all but say nowt." The mother-in-law sought to protect her son (Mary's husband) from evidence that he had quarreled with and beaten the deceased. The neighbor said, however, that she would speak the truth.[49] On the other hand, coroners typically summoned a number of witnesses, not all of whom were family or friends. It is hard to imagine that all the witnesses at an inquest lacked candor. Yet it was rare for witnesses to contradict each other, and on the few occasions when they did, they were recalled by the coroner in an attempt to resolve the contradiction.[50] The ambience of the inquest may have been colloquial, but the interrogation of witnesses was in the hands of a lawyer and experienced coroner, and witnesses were reminded that their deposition was "taken upon Oath." In the final analysis, therefore, the allegation that depositional evidence is characterized by insincerity is not particularly telling.

It is much more difficult to deny that depositions were patterned by coronorial and popular notions of what led people to take arms against themselves. Witnesses could not substitute themselves for the suicide; all they, the coroner, and juries could do was to search for "clues" to prove that the deceased had committed suicide. They expected suicide to be linked to a history of depression, intemperance, or illness; they expected people to buckle under the pressures of unemployment, bereavement, or debt. The "clues" sought, moreover, tended to differ according to gender. While economic reasons for suicide were carefully scrutinized in the case of men, domestic and biological ones were emphasized in the case of women. Was the young, single woman pregnant?[51] Was the married woman recently confined or "living uncomfortably" with her husband? And the coroner encouraged witnesses to speak to these issues at each inquest. For some historians, therefore, the glimpses of life and death the depositions provide "turn out to be shadows that are more projections of observers' views and phantasms than the reality of self-destruction."[52] While this would be a valid conclusion to reach about newspaper reports of inquests, which were selective and biased, it is less convincingly applied to coroners' case papers. The latter contain no mirror image of reality, but in addition to popular notions of what led people to kill themselves, the dossiers provide some handle upon the individual experience of suicide.

III

Coroners increasingly relied upon medical witnesses for evidence of cause of death and the deceased's state of mind.[53] From 1836 on, coroners had the power to order and pay for any medical practitioner to appear as a witness at an inquest, and, if desired, to conduct a postmortem examination. Juries could also insist that medical evidence be called, and they could oblige the coroner to call a second medical practitioner if the first disappointed. Coroners, or so the critics charged, too often entrusted autopsies to the nearest available doctor, most of whom had little experience in pathology or forensic science, and requested evidence from doctors who just happened to have attended the deceased at death or during his or her last illness.[54] The frequency with which autopsies were performed and medical evidence presented is difficult to fathom. Urban coroners seem to have ordered postmortems and called medical witnesses more routinely than their rural counterparts. In Westminster, over 16 percent of all inquests in 1835–38 included an autopsy; 50 percent in 1865–66. The figures for cases of suicide were much smaller, however; 8 and 11 percent, respectively.[55]

In Hull, to judge from coroners' case papers, close to 100 different doctors (including 44 "surgeons," 22 "general practitioners," and 14 "physicians") conducted postmortems and gave medical evidence between 1837 and 1899.[56] More to the point, postmortems were performed on 48 male and 31 female suicides, or 11.3 percent and 17 percent of all suicide inquests, respectively. The larger figure for female suicides reflects the fact that most autopsies were ordered in cases of suicide by poison, and women used this method of suicide twice as often as men.[57] Of the 48 postmortems on male suicides, poison was the method in 30 cases; of the 31 female autopsies, poison was used in 29 cases. The only other method that claimed postmortem attention in any number was suicide by gunshot; eleven male autopsies examined whether the wound was accidental or self-inflicted. Autopsies were rarely performed in cases of hanging.[58] In those done on male suicides by hanging, there were particular reasons for the examination: one body was in a state of putrefaction; one was a case of murder followed by suicide; another involved an attempt at concealment.

Postmortems were used throughout the Victorian period, but the figures—which are probably minima, since examinations were performed in more instances, one suspects, than are recorded in the documents—indicate that they were used more in the 1890's than in other decades. Of the 48 male autopsies, exactly one-half were done in this final decade (including most of the postmortems on suicide by gunshot); of the 31 female autopsies, 14 were done in the 1890's.[59] Doctors were more frequently involved in inquests as medical witnesses; they gave evidence in 27 percent (113 cases) of inquests on male suicides, 32 percent (58 cases) of inquests on female suicides. Doctors who had attended the deceased over many years or during the last illness, those who had been called in the event of suicide, and those who worked in the lunatic asylum and Infirmary, presented evidence as to cause of death, and as to the deceased's medical history and state of mind.

Individual inquests reveal other salient facts about postmortems and medical evidence. In the early years, autopsies were far from standard practice, even in poisoning cases, and the methods of examination could be relatively primitive. The only two cases in which juries were said to have requested a postmortem examination, for which the inquests were adjourned, came in 1838 and 1843, in relation to two suicides by poison. In the first of these cases, Dr. Edward Wallis said only that he thought the woman of 76 years, whom he found in her lodgings in a deep lethargy, had died from the effects of narcotic poison. The autopsy revealed opium.[60] In two other cases in the 1840's, the examination consisted solely of a chemist testing the contents of a cup in which a straw bonnet maker, who had poisoned herself, kept oxalic acid for use in her trade; and a doctor testing the deceased's vomit for arsenic.[61] The limited use and nature of postmortems was, in part, a function of the speed with which inquests were held: usually on the following day, sometimes on the same day as the death. Even when the body was examined, therefore, the surgeons who gave evidence would often state that they had not had time to make an analysis of the stomach and its contents.[62] For this, an adjournment was necessary, to give time for the doctor or (by the 1890's) the borough analyst, a chemist, to analyze the stomach.[63] Rarely did the coroner, having requested a postmortem examination, wait two or three days before holding the inquest. Speed was of the essence, however, since laudanum (opium mixed with alcohol) was rapidly absorbed; hence, some postmortems found no trace of opium in the stomach although the evidence indicated its consumption.[64]

It is difficult to know if those who did the postmortems were qualified for the task. Most were undistinguished surgeons or general practitioners, about whom little is known. Yet there were exceptions, particularly among the house surgeons at the Hull General (later Royal) Infirmary. Frederick Huntington, Edward Wallis, and Henry Pigeon were all house surgeons. Wallis was the first lecturer in anatomy at the Hull and East Riding School of Medicine, which he helped to found in 1831; Pigeon gave evidence in other inquests, including murder cases.[65] Henry Thompson was a house surgeon, and surgeon to the police; he did a number of postmortems in the 1880's and 1890's on the bodies of suicides. At the end of one inquest, he stated: "I have had a good deal of experience in medico-legal matters." Thompson it was, too, who in October 1877 used the occasion of an inquest on a licensed victualer who had hanged himself, to call the coroner's attention to the state of the dead-house where he had done the postmortem. It was badly lit, there was only one table, and there were no platters or towel and no plug in the washbasin. Thorney told him to report the matter to the proper authorities.[66] The incident stands as telling comment on the room for improvement in postmortem procedures 40 years into the Victorian era.

The most common form of medical evidence at coroners' inquests came from family doctors who had treated the deceased before death, and who described illnesses, mental and physical, that in their opinion conduced to suicide. They also might provide a professional judgment about the deceased's state of mind when he took his life, which was germane to the jury's verdict. In a few instances, it was evident that the medical testimony was influenced by what the surgeon heard lay witnesses depose about the deceased's behavior.[67] In addition, the medical superintendent of the borough asylum and the workhouse surgeon reported on the suicides in their care. Given the large proportion of lunatics manifesting a suicidal tendency (estimated at between a quarter and a third of all asylum inmates), remarkably few committed suicide, and about a third of those who did were out of the asylum "on trial" at the time.[68] With the exception of the asylum superintendent, Francis Casson, few Hull practitioners would have had substantial knowledge or clinical experience of mental illness.[69] This did not deter them from offering a diagnosis when called to give evidence. To what, then, did medical witnesses ascribe the suicidal impulse?

Not surprisingly, given the content of clinical manuals for medical practitioners, the vast majority of witnesses referred, directly or indirectly, to mental depression and melancholia.[70] Two men who killed themselves in the borough asylum were said by Casson to be lunatic from melancholia, and to have asked the surgeon to put them to death. A third inmate, who was out "on trial" at the home of the manufacturer for whom she was housekeeper, was also said to suffer from melancholia. Two years later, the asylum surgeon, John Gibson, deposed that a 47-year-old pattern maker who had hanged himself suffered from "religious melancholia."[71] Three surgeons whose patients had suffered from melancholia added explanatory riders to the effect that this form of mental disease often verged into insanity, or "suicidal mania," and almost always ended in self-slaughter.[72] Two other surgeons added that the tendency to self-destruction ran in families.[73] Melancholia was also thought to be the sequela of brain disease. In the case of a retired butcher, who had complained of head pain before cutting his throat, Dr. John Holden declared: "Long continued pain in the head is indicative of disease of the brain & may cause melancholia which frequently results in suicide." The surgeon, George Pyburn, believed that the "increasing lowness of spirits" detailed by the brother of a 19-year-old clerk who had shot himself pointed to "disorder of the brain which might turn to dementia. Melancholy frequently leads to suicide." Dr. Arthur Jessop deposed that the postmortem on an iron-yard laborer, who in November 1892 poisoned himself with strychnine, revealed "meningitis of some little standing. . . . The meningitis might be a predisposing cause towards suicide."[74]

There were certain acute diseases, moreover, that were thought to lead to depression or delirium. A 62-year-old woman, wife of a net maker, who hanged herself, was suffering from a chronic inflammation of the bowels, according to Dr. David Davy. "She was very weak & in very low spirits; suffering from melancholia," said Davy, "which would arise from her feeble health & her long continued pain." According to the medical witnesses, a 34-year-old woman poisoned herself when influenza made her more despondent than ever; the wife of a stonemason, recently confined, had been ill with influenza for three months before cutting her throat.[75] William Day, surgeon to the Hull workhouse, at the inquest on an inmate of the fever hospital who, in September 1847, threw himself out of a window, said the effect of fever was "alternately exciting & depressing & which some times results in suicide."[76] Finally, medical witnesses referred to delirium tremens arising from excessive drinking; to hypochondriasis, or the unfounded belief on the part of the patient that he was suffering from some bodily disease; to "puerperal mania," or mental disorder brought on by lactation; and to forms of mania—"suicidal monomania," "religious monomania"—that could lead to certification and to suicidal death.[77]

In short, the evidence from medical witnesses assisted the processes of registering a death as suicide and ruling upon the deceased's state of mind.

Above all, medical evidence, in addition to stating the cause of death, confirmed the lay assumption that "lowness," in the form of melancholy, and suicide were practically synonymous, that many forms of disease prompted people to self-destruction, and that most people who killed themselves were insane in the wider sense of that term. This was particularly true of the 1880's and 1890's, since medical opinion was by then all but unanimous that suicide was the product of mental defect. It was no great stretch for juries, therefore, to reach the conclusion that normally suicides were not in their right mind. In every one of the above-mentioned cases, the jury returned a verdict of non compos mentis, "suicide whilst of unsound mind."

IV

It is an accepted fact that in the nineteenth century, attempted suicide was interpreted as strong evidence of a person's insanity, and that threats of and attempts at suicide triggered many asylum committals. Families, it was believed, could not provide the necessary surveillance of those with suicidal inclinations, especially among the poor; only asylums could supply the requisite vigilance.[78] Moreover, historians of Victorian insanity have stressed the supposed decline of family and community tolerance of madness, and the substitution, particularly among the working poor, of confinement in an asylum for family care. In the wake of the Lunatic Asylums Act of 1845, which made public provision for the pauper insane compulsory, madhouses became "a convenient place to get rid of inconvenient people," according to Andrew Scull.[79] What impresses one about the coroners' inquisition papers, however, is the evidence of families doggedly coping with deranged and suicidal relatives, and of the apparent reluctance of families (and doctors) to consign patients either to the "feeble ward" of the workhouse or to the madhouse. Families did not readily dump difficult members in the new asylums, as the historians of these institutions suggest, but resisted the institutionalization of such people, even up to their suicides.

In a dozen cases, while there is evidence that the deceased had been insane for weeks or months and had been closely watched by relatives, no evidence appears that any thought had been given to asylum care. For example, the widow of a mariner, in a low state of mind for two months, had been watched night and day, according to her seaman son. She had tried to cut her throat, but had been stopped. A week later, however, she succeeded in doing so. A blacksmith who was afraid of coming to poverty had not been sane for five weeks, according to a neighbor. "I have been so much afraid of his destroying himself," she said, "that when his wife went to market I have often gone to get him to our house fearing he might come to harm." [80] The mother of a young joiner's apprentice catalogued her son's violent behavior: "He hanged himself two year ago & since then he has tried to cut his throat. I think he was not right at those times. His head was affected at times & he was quite delirious." [81] The doctor had told her that the boy had an overflow of blood to the head and would go out of his mind. In none of the dozen cases was the possibility of asylum committal raised.[82] In another case, a grocer's wife had been depressed for six months and watched for three months. "Something has been said about taking her to an asylum," her son stated, but, while a surgeon had attended the deceased for six months, no doctor had examined her for committal purposes. She threw herself out of an attic window and died at the Infirmary.[83] In many of these cases, doctors had advised family members to watch those concerned and to remove everything with which they might do themselves harm, but they had apparently said nothing about asylum care. On other occasions, doctors stymied committal proceedings. The wife of a railway clerk, low in spirits for six months, had expressed a wish to go to the asylum. A doctor was called in, but he said it was not wise to send her there. She was later found drowned in Prince's Dock. Joseph Wilkinson, aged 37, had attempted to take his life two years before under the influence of delirium tremens and had been confined in a lunatic asylum for a month. He had tried to get into the asylum a year before, but the medical men thought he posed no danger and would not admit him. Nor had they suggested additional vigilance in the months before he cut his throat.[84]

Even when surgeons did advise committal, families could reject the advice. Dr. Davy thought a painter who exhibited symptoms of insanity with delusions should go to an asylum. A friend of the deceased told the coroner: "I thought we could do with him at home." He found the deceased hanging from a bedpost. A merchant seaman suffering from "internal cancer" hanged himself. His wife told the court: "He said the devil tempted him to kill himself & others & I was afraid of him. I would not have him taken to the asylum. I preferred to run the risk." [85] For one or two people, asylum admission came too late. The 45-year-old wife of a railway gatekeeper had been low-spirited for three months, ever since her second marriage. She suffered from intense melancholia, said the surgeon; "she was insane. I should judge that she had not become so very recently." She cut her throat on November 25, 1868; on December 2, she was taken by a relieving officer to the asylum under a magistrate's order as a pauper lunatic, where she died.[86] Finally, there were patients who killed themselves after being discharged from the asylum because their relatives wanted them out.[87]

Cases drawn from coroners' papers in this unsystematic manner could hardly serve as evidence to prove conclusively that families and doctors were decidedly unwilling to seek asylum care for relatives and patients who displayed suicidal tendencies. But the cases do at least confirm existing scholarship in two regards. They suggest that the family was the primary context in which madness was defined, and in which decisions were taken concerning the assignment of relatives to the asylum. For a certificate of lunacy, a deposition had to be sworn before two justices to the effect that the individual was "a Lunatic or Insane person," and a medical examination had to be conducted. But this was merely a sequel to the family's decision that they could no longer cope with their relative.[88] Second, these cases suggest that for Hull, too, there is substance to John Walton's Lancashire-based argument that family tolerance of madness did not erode as rapidly or as thoroughly as the historians of insanity contend, even in working-class circles. Families did not, *pace* Michael Anderson, invariably behave in a calculative and instrumental fashion, casting out relatives from the bosom of the family at the first sign of difficulty. Rather, families (and neighbors) were willing to cope as best they could with deviant individuals, including round-the-clock invigilation, in order to avoid what was doubtless seen as the disgrace of asylum committal.[89]

V

The jury had now heard the evidence of the relevant lay and medical witnesses. Before reaching their verdict, however, juries in a small percentage of cases heard the testimony of one more "witness": the suicide. They did so, of course, by means of the suicide notes discovered by relatives, friends, and the police and handed to the coroner. Here was the only chance the deceased had to mold the meanings that would be assigned to his or her own death. By a suicide note, the deceased had an opportunity to turn an act of self-destruction into a form of self-expression; a private act into a public statement. A total of 53 suicide notes (41 male, 12 female) were located either in the depositions or in the press reports of the inquest. It has been assumed that the notes exclusively printed by newspapers were genuine, not fictional. Fifty-three is a minimum figure, since notes were referred to by witnesses that appeared neither in the depositions nor in the press.[90] Notes were written in almost 10 percent of all male and 6.6 percent of all female suicides. Some suicide notes were a short sentence in length; others went on for pages. A contents analysis of the notes suggests the following classification. One-quarter read like last wills and testaments; the writers disposed of their property and issued instructions for their burial. When a cooper who wished neither to be a burden nor to enter the workhouse poisoned himself, his suicide note asked for his club money to go to his sister and his clothes and belongings to other named individuals. "Don't have any row if you can help it," he thoughtfully concluded. A Humber pilot, aged 36, grieving for the wife who had died a few weeks before, left a note in a Bible saying that he left everything to his son, and that he wanted to inhabit the same grave as his wife. The wife of a painter, whose health had failed ever since her daughter's death two years before, left a note that read: "Dear husband. You will find my body in one of the top rooms. Bury me near Polly & bring little Harriet with you. Good bye & God bless you."[91]

Another one-third of the notes tried to explain why the writers were about to destroy themselves. The note left in a Bible by a lighter owner who poisoned himself in March 1886 blamed his business: "Last three years' trade bad and losses heavy. It is a fearful end, after 50 years struggling to maintain a respectable position. Heaven protect my family. They are innocent. Lord have mercy on my soul." When a constable suffering from influenza decided to poison himself, he left a note that read: "I am just writing this in my last moments life is such a misery tho me my head is all on a swim and every limb I have got hakes so good by all and I hope that every body will forgive me for doing this rash act . . . but I carnt help it life is such a misery and burden to me so may god bless me and you all." Before hanging himself, a brewery company's cellarman reassured his employers that everything was taken care of, "barring ales ordering from Burton," and then explained: "[F]orgive me for this rash act. My health has given way and I would die ten times over before I would put on a firm that has done so well for me." Implying that suicide was typically a flight from debt, he stressed he had none: "I have no cause for this rash act as I do not owe to my knowledge one Farthing and which you know I command £3-0-0 per week."[92] Amy Cullen, aged 36, poisoned herself when her fiancé called off their engagement. In her letter she explained the depth of her love:

I think I can guess your motive. You could not marry one woman while loving another. But no woman will ever love you as I did. Perhaps you hardly realized how dear you were to me. You cannot gauge the depth or intensity of that love which you thus carelessly fling away, as a thing not worth keeping. Pride would forbid my saying this to you, if I had not made up my mind not to live, but what I could not have said living, I can say, dying. For oh my darling, I cannot live without you. After the one glimpse of Heaven that you have shown me, I dare not face life with the prospect of never seeing you again. By the time you receive this I shall be no more. But do not reproach yourself, dear. It was to be & you could not have acted otherwise than you did. Goodbye Jack. If there is a God may He bless & keep you, my darling & make you happy.[93]

Other notes were by no means as forgiving. One-fifth were manifestly intended as a form of revenge. An oil-mill employee, who was too ill to work and whose wife had left him six months before, poisoned himself. The letter to his mother pinned the blame on poverty and his wife:

Do not grieve for me I shall be best out of this world where there is nothing but poverty and misery for me Mary has deserted me and you are pining and pinching yourself for me and I cannot bear it longer. I have taken forty grains of opium so it will be no use trying to bring me to but I pray God to bless you and my Child as for Mary she must take her chance as had she returned to me I should not have done this.

A 29-year-old woman, given to drink, was downhearted when the stevedore she cohabited with told her she must leave. "Dear Will, you have drove me to this dreadful deed," her note bluntly stated. A domestic servant took revenge on the employer who had frequently reproved her. A note to her mother found on her drowned body stated: "Its Mrs. Wilkins is causing all this—nothing else but grumble . . . I cannot stand swear & grumble." Mary Wilkins, wife of a shipyard manager, had to explain herself at the inquest. She described the deceased as a girl of "sullen & rather obstinate temper," "a bad getter up," and "very fond of trashy novels." She denied that she or her husband ever swore, but admitted that she grumbled at the deceased for not getting up.[94]

A few notes tried to lessen the shock and pain of the act. A corn carrier who cut his throat left two notes to his wife, the first on the kitchen table, telling her to fetch the constable before entering the scullery. The second note said: "[I]t will be a shock for you I know, but you will forgive me I hope as I pray to the Lord he will forgive me also." Other notes used their death as a moral exemplum. A watchmaker instructed "Polly," possibly his sister: "Tell everybody that it is drink that has done this for me."[95] Finally, the idea of suicide as a sin is present in some of these notes, although exclusively in the form of a request for forgiveness for the imminent act of self-destruction.[96]

It is unlikely that notes written at a time of intense emotion always laid bare the real motives for the act. Many of the notes suggest that suicides were, indeed, trying to shape the framework in which their death would be interpreted and to evoke the correct response from their audience.[97] Most notes were composed to claim the attention of family, friends, and neighbors. It was probably common knowledge that suicide notes were read by, and could influence, the coroner and jury. The wife of a dock laborer left nothing to chance; she addressed her note to the coroner: "Please don't bring it in felo-de-se. My husband has driven me to it. I can't bear it."[98] It was doubtless known also that newspapers could enlarge the audience by reprinting suicide notes. Indeed, the press must have played some part in the dissemination of the rhetorical forms and language used in many suicide notes. Even a 12-year-old newsboy, said to be much given to reading, who laid himself across the railway track when his mother learned he had forged the newsagent's name to get more papers, employed these conventions. The blood-stained note found on his body was addressed to his mother: "Please forgive me for my rash act . . . and may God bless you The reason why I have committed suicide is that my life is a burden to me and to you."[99] Nonetheless, the notes ought not to be seen as examples of artifice alone. If some notes sound like contrived attempts to safeguard reputation or apportion blame, many more sound like sincere and heartfelt attempts to explain their economic distress, their sense of despair at prolonged illness, their sense of loss at the departure or death of a loved one. As such, they not only reveal the ways in which suicides represented their deaths; they also shed light upon the reasons for and circumstances of those deaths.

At this juncture, the coroner would ask the jury if they were satisfied with the evidence they had heard. If so, the coroner would help the jury weigh the evidence as to cause of death, he would remind them that suicide was the deliberate destruction of one's own life, and the jury would then return their verdict. A majority verdict, as distinct from a unanimous one, would suffice for the coroner. The jury's verdict was the crux of the coroner's inquest. It raises a number of difficult but crucial issues concerning the records of the coroners' court, and thus warrants a chapter to itself. Let us, therefore, reserve final judgment upon the reliability and validity of the statistics derived from these court documents, and upon the value of the documents for tracing the experience of suicide, until the close of the next chapter.

3

Suicide Verdicts

The Jury learn how the subject of their inquiry died, and
learn no more about him. "A very eminent solicitor is in
attendance, gentlemen," says the Coroner, "who, I am
informed, was accidentally present, when discovery of
the death was made; but he could only repeat the
evidence you have already heard from the surgeon, the
landlord, the lodger, and the law-stationer. . . . Is
anybody in attendance who knows anything more? . . .

Now. Is there any other witness? No other witness.

Very well, gentlemen! Here's a man unknown,
proved to have been in the habit of taking opium in large
quantities for a year and a half, found dead of too much
opium. If you think you have any evidence to lead you to
the conclusion that he committed suicide, you will come
to that conclusion. If you think it is a case of accidental
death, you will find a Verdict accordingly.

Verdict accordingly. Accidental death. No doubt.
Gentlemen, you are discharged. Good afternoon."

Charles Dickens,
Bleak House (1852–53)

The first and most difficult issue to
confront is the extent to which sui-
cide was wrongly classified by coroners' courts as natural, accidental, or
undetermined death. A large number of such misclassifications would, of
course, diminish the reliability of the statistics of suicide. Olive Anderson

has surmised that in the big cities, inquests were "less likely than else-where" to end in that way.[1] She may well be right, comparatively speaking, but we still need to estimate the level of error in the city under scrutiny. It is possible that some suicides, occurring under circumstances that did not arouse suspicion of suicide, could have been put down as natural deaths. In a couple of cases discovered in the coroners' papers, a verdict of natu-ral death was recorded even when it was apparent that a suicide attempt had, at the very least, hastened death. In May 1849, an old "gentleman" was found by his housekeeper in the privy. He had taken a razor to his throat. The housekeeper told the jury that she had never seen the deceased melancholy or low-spirited and had had no suspicion that he would try to injure himself. The surgeon, who had attended the gentleman for years, de-posed that the deceased had had difficulty breathing due to heart disease and bronchitis, and that he had died of natural causes. The jury returned a bizarre verdict: died by the visitation of God after cutting his throat. In June 1894, a draper's assistant found his father, of the same occupation, kneeling on the ground and hanging from a clothesline fastened to the bed-post. His father, he said, "has threatened lately to kill himself on account [of] being dismissed." The surgeon stated that the deceased had wished to go into the workhouse, "as being unable to maintain himself." "He was of sound mind," the witness continued; "he has been somewhat strange since he failed in business about two years ago." The surgeon concluded that death was due to syncope caused by the excitement of an attempt at suicide acting on a weak and diseased heart. The jury's verdict used the same phrase, but omitted mention of the suicide attempt. In the Inquisition Book, the coroner noted: "Attempting to hang himself & died from fright."

It is also possible that some suicides, particularly by poison, drowning, or falling, and where the deceased had not communicated the intention to anyone else, were masked, intentionally or otherwise, as accidents. Even when the deceased had threatened suicide, the jury could return a verdict of accidental death, to judge from the following case. In April 1858, a 49-year-old chemist, out of work for three months, who took laudanum two or three times a week for stomach pain, came home drunk, emptied a bottle of laudanum, and went to bed. By the next morning, he was dead. His two children told the jury that he had frequently threatened to destroy himself, and that several times they had taken laudanum and prussic acid bottles, in addition to knives, away from him. The surgeon, however, said that he had not found the usual symptoms of laudanum, so a postmortem was ordered. At the adjourned inquest, the surgeon stated: "I think he died from disease of the brain accelerated by the laudanum he had taken." Hence, the jury concluded that the deceased died from brain disease, accelerated by a laudanum overdose, "taken whilst drunk & by mistake, & not with an intention of destroying his life."[2]

I

The number of natural and accidental deaths that were in fact unproven suicides can only ever be a matter of conjecture. We can take comfort alone in the hope that the incidence of misclassification was constant, and therefore does not deprive the fluctuations in the suicide rates of their significance.[3] It is not possible to be so sanguine with regard to undetermined deaths, where juries, able to affirm the fact but not the cause of violent death, returned an open verdict. On too many occasions for comfort, there is compelling evidence of suicidal intention. There were cases of death by locomotive, and even a case of death by hanging, in which an open verdict was returned. An old jobbing laborer, rather deaf and very myopic, was found at the end of the departure platform at Paragon Street station in October 1869. The foreman of the jury, according to the *Hull News*, "said there were grave suspicions of suicide, but no evidence to show positively how [the deceased] came to his death." He recommended an open verdict, "Found dead, killed by a railway carriage," and his colleagues concurred. A mat maker who was "found hanged" in a privy by a night-soil collector going his rounds on the Humber bank was a comparative stranger to the city and had been missing for a month.[4]

However, the cases in which there was evidence of suicide and an open verdict was returned were typically deaths by poison and drowning. Both methods of death posed evidentiary difficulties. It was notoriously difficult to be sure that death from an overdose of opium (or laudanum) was intentional. There was a thin line between self-medication and self-destruction in a culture in which opium, the most popular poison for suicide until the 1890's, was a mainstay of the medical profession and the most common form of self-medication, a cure-all for aches and pains, insomnia, and delirium tremens. Opium was readily available in affordable doses at corner shops, pubs, market stalls, and chemists. It differed materially in quality and strength, of course, and amounts that would satisfy a confirmed "opium eater" would kill a person unaccustomed to it.[5] A number of inquests illustrate some of the evidentiary problems facing juries.

In July 1849, Sarah Crosland, wife of a ballast-lighter owner, sent for a pennyworth of opium for her ailing husband. Subsequently, she and her husband quarreled, and she told a domestic that she had taken the opium herself. When the domestic went to get a neighbor, the deceased had prevented her, torn at her dress, and spoken of coming to poverty. The jury returned the unusual verdict of "opium taken during temporary insanity, whether taken with intent to destroy life, no evidence." A retired engineer told an inquest on the body of his wife in February 1886 that she had been intemperate since marriage and would drink spirits in any form. The surgeon's assistant deposed that he had found her under the influence of methylated spirits and a narcotic and had put it to her "that the law did not allow her to take her own life." A few days later, he called in the surgeon, who thought she had taken laudanum. The postmortem revealed symptoms of intemperance, but no laudanum. The final twist to the story came at the adjourned inquest, when the coroner told the jury that he had several letters written by the deceased to friends, from which it was evident that she meant to leave her husband, but in which way the coroner could not say. The foreman suggested an open verdict: "[A]poplexy accelerated by a narcotic poison, but how administered, no evidence."[6] In addition to opium, open verdicts were recorded in cases of poisoning by prussic acid, oxalic acid, arsenic, and carbolic acid.[7] No clearer case of the gray area between self-medication and self-destruction appeared than that of William Dossor, a chemist. He was very depressed because of the suspension of a bank to which he was greatly indebted. For heart palpitations, on the advice of his uncle, Dr. James Dossor, the deceased had taken "a bitter infusion with a little prussic acid." The postmortem examination led Dr. Daly to conclude that the deceased had taken an overdose of prussic acid; with what intent, the jury could not say.[8]

Juries were faced with the same difficulty when it came to drowning cases. They would go through the motions of asking witnesses if the deceased man's trouser fly was open, to rule out the possibility, presumably, that he had accidentally fallen in while urinating. They would investigate how deep the water was; whether the deceased's clothes were torn; if the body bore any marks of violence. However, on the legal principle that a death was accidental until proved otherwise, juries had little choice but to return an open verdict unless someone had seen the deceased jump into the water.[9] Even when an oil miller walked out of a pub and into the river, and resisted rescue, an open verdict was returned.[10] Juries were certainly not influenced by circumstantial evidence, including the existence of suicide notes (of which, however, there were few). A 16-year-old domestic servant was found drowned in Albert Dock. The suicide note addressed to her mother said she was tired of the reprimands from her employer of six weeks. The *Eastern Morning News* entitled its report of the inquest "Singular Suicide," despite the jury's open verdict, and the Coroner's Inquisition Book recorded, "supposed suicide." A young paint-works laborer was found drowned in Humber Dock Basin. Both his father and sister deposed that he had complained of pain in his head and throat. A letter to his girlfriend said he could not stand the pain any longer, and concluded, "I hope I shall be able to meet you on the beautiful shore above." The coroner, according to the press report, said the jury would have had no difficulty returning a verdict of accidental death had it not been for the letter. He left it to the jury to say whether the deceased had taken his own life. The jury gave a verdict of "found drowned." [11] Nor were juries swayed by evidence of melancholy, a family history of suicide, previous suicide attempts, or even more distressing circumstances. A single, 23-year-old paper-mill hand, found drowned in Barmston Drain (one of the open land drains of this sea-level district), was in labor when she died. The wife of a carpenter and former publican was found on her face in Spring Ditch in August 1844, her 5-month-old son in her right arm. Family witnesses said the deceased had been ill and in low spirits recently. The *Hull Advertiser*, oblivious to the jury's verdict, entitled its report "Supposed Murder & Suicide." It also quoted the coroner as saying: "There was every reason to believe that the unfortunate woman had willfully drowned herself and child, but, in the absence of all evidence to that effect, they had better return an open verdict." [12]

Inquests often resulted in an open verdict, then, where the circumstantial evidence of suicide was substantial. For the entire Victorian period in this one city, 125 cases (71 males and 54 females) were discovered, from among all open verdicts, in which there was suspicion of suicide. To add these cases to the total of suicide verdicts (604), would be to add another 20 percent.[13] The figure alone should give us pause. It suggests that a sizable number of deaths by suicide were being defined by the coroners' court, and subsequently registered, as deaths in which the cause of death was unknown. Nor can the statistical problem posed by open verdicts be circumvented by claiming that they were representative, in all important respects, of actual suicide verdicts. They were not. For a start, the sex ratio was different. Among suicide verdicts, the male : female ratio was 2.3 to 1; among open verdicts, it was 1.3 to 1. The large number of female suicides among open verdicts was a reflection, in part, of the methods (drowning and poisoning) preferred by women. The methods of suicide were even more unrepresentative. Seventy percent of the male and 85 percent of the female open verdicts were deaths by drowning. Hence, while among open verdicts there were 96 cases of drowning (50 males, 46 females), among suicide verdicts there were only 27 cases (19 males, 8 females). There were age differences, too. Over a third of the female open verdicts, for example, were young women aged 15–24.

To omit open verdicts from consideration, therefore, would be to distort seriously the incidence and experience of suicide according to age, gender, and method. Accordingly, these cases were closely examined, and they figure in the following chapters on the statistics of suicide and on the experience of suicide across the life cycle.[14] Care is taken at all times, however, to indicate the presence of open verdicts. No claim is being made that one can, by the addition of open verdicts, discover the true incidence and rate of suicide. The very mode of selecting open verdicts, by a subjective assessment of the circumstantial evidence to be found in inquest depositions, would weaken any such claim. It would be unwise, however, to throw away the advantage of a detailed study of one city's experience of suicide by refusing to consider those inquests in which juries returned a verdict of "found dead," but in which lay and medical witnesses, the local press, and at times the coroner himself were manifestly of the view that they were dealing with a death by suicide. Incorporating open verdicts into the study also helps to combat the larger underregistration of female than of male suicides, caused by the greater use women made of drowning as a method of suicide.

II

If the jury concluded that the deceased *had* died willfully by his own hand, they then had to decide whether, when he killed himself, the deceased knew he was doing wrong, or whether he was in an unsound state of mind. Juries had a choice of three verdicts. The first was felo de se, or self-murder, meant for a person, in the antiquated language of the inquisition, "not having the fear of God before her eyes but being moved and seduced by the instigation of the Devil and of her malice aforethought . . . wickedly contriving and intending . . . feloniously to kill and murder herself." The second verdict was that of non compos mentis, meant for those, again in the words of the inquisition, "not being of sound mind, memory, and understanding, but lunatic and distracted" (which coroners abbreviated to "temporary insanity"). The third or "medium verdict" was returned on

TABLE 3.1
Hull Inquest Verdicts, 1837–99

	Male		Female	
Verdict	No.	Pct.	No.	Pct.
Felo de se	4	1%	7	4%
Non compos mentis	361	85	153	84
Medium	57	14	22	12
TOTAL	422	100%	182	100%

SOURCE: Inquests, 1837–99.

those who had died by their own hands but for whom there was insufficient evidence as to whether they had been "of sound mind at the time or otherwise." The first question that needs to be answered is, with what frequency were these verdicts used?

In the last three decades of the eighteenth century, according to Michael MacDonald and Terence Murphy, over 97 percent of recorded suicide verdicts in England were verdicts of "temporary insanity," the remaining 3 percent being felo de se rulings. Since the latter verdicts were not separately enumerated in the official statistics until after 1893, for the Victorian period, Olive Anderson could say only that "perhaps as few as 3 per cent of all . . . suicide verdicts were verdicts of *felo de se*," and that the figure probably varied greatly between coroners' districts. Carolyn Conley found that only 1.25 percent of suicide verdicts (or 19 out of 1,519 cases) in mid-nineteenth-century Kent were felo de se rulings. For the period 1893–98, finally, a national annual average of 1.4 percent of male and 1.1 percent of female suicide verdicts were felo de se.[15] As for "medium verdicts," Anderson found that nationally, in 1894–99, "some 7 percent of all suicide verdicts recorded that there was no evidence to determine the state of mind of the deceased."[16] The figures for Hull shed further light on these frequencies. Table 3.1 shows that for the entire Victorian period, 85 percent of all male suicide verdicts and 84 percent of all female verdicts were rulings of temporary insanity. Felo de se verdicts were returned in only eleven cases, or 0.9 percent of all male, and 3.8 percent of all female verdicts. All eleven verdicts, moreover, were returned between 1837 and 1855; for the remaining 45 years of the Victorian era, not one of the 479 cases of suicide was ruled felo de se. As table 3.1 also shows, medium verdicts bulked larger than the national figures would lead us to expect; 13.5 percent of all male and 12 percent of all female suicide verdicts were so ruled.

Medium verdicts were, however, a late-century phenomenon. Over 80 percent of both male and female medium verdicts were recorded in the last

TABLE 3.2
Medium Verdicts, 1837–99, by Period

Period	Male		Female	
	No.	Pct.	No.	Pct.
1837–80	7	12%	4	18%
1881–99	50	88	18	82
TOTAL	57	100%	22	100%

SOURCE: Inquests, 1837–99.

two decades of the nineteenth century (see table 3.2). It is helpful, there-fore, to distinguish among early, mid, and late Victorian suicide verdicts, even though the figure for some categories is thereby rather small. Table 3.3, which displays the frequency of verdicts for these three periods, shows that felo de se rulings were still used in the early Victorian period, albeit very sparingly; that their place was taken in the mid Victorian years by a small number of medium verdicts; while in the late Victorian period, the use of the medium verdict increased considerably. One-fifth of all suicide verdicts were medium verdicts between 1875 and 1899. In the 1890's, no fewer than 28 percent of all verdicts were medium verdicts. How then do we explain these frequencies? For this, we have to look at what led inquest juries to return the different kinds of verdict, and, in particular, what circumstances led juries to grant or withhold a verdict of "temporary insanity."

By 1837, and the start of the Victorian era, juries rarely returned a felo de se verdict, and for intelligible reasons. Severe penalties, which fell on both offender and family, came in the wake of the verdict. Until 1882, the body of a felo de se had to be buried by the police in unconsecrated ground, by torchlight between the hours of nine and midnight, and without religious rites. When John Hawley, a 32-year-old extra-tidewaiter, who poisoned himself in May 1845, was given a felo de se verdict, the local newspaper recorded: "and, at midnight, his remains were consigned to the earth with all the legal horrors so truly agonizing to desolate relatives and to mourn-ing friends."[17] Until 1870, moreover, the goods and chattels of a felo de se (as of all felons) could be claimed by the Crown. In practice, the denial of Christian burial could be circumvented from mid-century on by using municipal cemeteries outside the jurisdiction of the Church of England, and forfeiture proceedings were almost a dead letter. Insurance companies, however, increasingly voided a policy in the event of a felo de se verdict (although not usually in the case of other suicide verdicts).[18] To avoid a felo de se verdict, then, was to spare a suicide's family the social disgrace of a clandestine, non-Christian burial and the financial penalties of forfeiture

TABLE 3.3
Inquest Verdicts, 1837–99, by Period

Verdict	Early Victorian Period (1837–49)				Mid Victorian Period (1850–74)				Late Victorian Period (1875–99)			
	Male		Female		Male		Female		Male		Female	
	No.	Pct.	No.	Pct.	No.	Pct.	No.	Pct.	No.	Pct.	No.	Pct.
Felo de se	3	6%	5	13%	1	0.8%	2	4%	—	—	—	—
Non compos mentis	46	94	34	87	115	95	50	89	199	79%	70	80%
Medium	—	—	—	—	5	4.2	4	7	53	21	18	20
TOTAL	49	100%	39	100%	121	100%	56	100%	252	100%	88	100%

SOURCE: Inquests, 1837–99.

and a voided insurance policy. That the social stigma of the verdict persisted is suggested by that imploratory suicide note of Elizabeth Martin, who drowned herself in December 1899, which stated: "Please don't bring it in felo-de-se. My husband has driven me to it. I can't bear it." [19]

In law, the offender had to be compos mentis, able to distinguish good from evil, and to have willed the act; and the act had to be done as part of an evil design. In practice, most historians contend, *felones de se* were marginal, minority, or propertyless members of the community (paupers, servants, foreigners, and strangers), or were prisoners awaiting judgment or execution (notably for the crime of murder). In consequence, historians argue, juries who recorded a felo de se verdict either felt no pressure to give a verdict of "temporary insanity" so as to safeguard the suicide's property for his survivors or were condemning the suicide's attempt to avoid punishment for an antecedent offense. The verdict was also at times applied, historians suggest, to adulterers, habitual drunkards, soldiers, those who took poison (a method that had always provoked alarm), and those who deliberately planned to kill themselves. In such cases, perhaps, juries were punishing those who had offended against community norms.[20]

The eleven Hull felones de se are difficult to categorize. There are overlaps with the above typology, but in fewer than half the cases was the felo de se verdict used to sanction marginality or misbehavior. A 60-year-old auction-room laborer was a somewhat marginal figure. He lodged at the White Hart tavern, where he had lain in bed for ten weeks before hanging himself from a bedpost. A tavern servant deposed: "I don't know that the deceased had any means of paying for his living," and the inquisition stated that, to the jurors' knowledge, he had no goods or chattels. A marine-stores dealer, a widower with six children, hanged himself from a beam in a police cell at Blanket Row station house, where he had been taken the previous evening and charged with receiving stolen goods. The jury may have been influenced by the apparent attempt to avoid the legal consequences of a felony, and also by a police inspector's statement that "there was nothing in his manner unusual or uncollected . . . nothing in his manner that made me think him insane." [21] In no cases of murder followed by suicide, however, was a felo de se verdict recorded.[22] The third case, a young army private barracked in the Citadel, shot himself with his musket; the depositions reveal only that he seldom spoke, that no marked change had occurred in his manner, and that no reason could be assigned for the act. The last of the four male felones de se, who poisoned himself with laudanum, had been discharged from his job as an extra-tidewaiter with the

Customs Board because of drunkenness. Perhaps the jury saw the suicide as an escape from the consequences of a moral lapse.[23]

Six of the seven female felones de se poisoned themselves, in every case with opium or laudanum. Two were single, three were married, one was a widow, and one cohabited. Intoxication was a feature of three of the cases. In two other cases, the documents suggest that the jury might have been passing moral judgment on the deceased. A widowed shoebinder, who swallowed sixpence-worth of laudanum, when told by a friend to think of her soul, replied defiantly that "hers would not be the first soul that was damned." The young wife of a fisherman took opium when a man claimed that he had told her husband about her prostitute life, and that her husband would no longer allow her to receive his half-pay while he was at sea. The surgeon who was called to attend her also stated: "The first time deceased took the opium she was quite sensible of what she was doing."[24] All but three of these eleven felo de se verdicts, finally, were returned before 1850. While mid-century commentators continued to advocate the use of the felo de se verdict, on the grounds that it defined the act as sinful and criminal, and thus deterred self-murder, the tide continued to flow in the opposite direction. As Sir John Jervis complained, the idea prevailed "that he who destroys himself *must* be *non compos mentis*, that the very act of suicide is evidence of insanity."[25]

There is less to say, ironically, about the "temporary insanity" verdict, returned in the vast majority of cases. Witnesses had only to mention some form of emotional disturbance—whether health worries, spousal quarrels, drunkenness, "lowness," or despondency—for juries to concede diminished responsibility. Evidence of "unsound mind" was, at times, wafer thin. The witnesses at the inquest of a gas worker who hanged himself in August 1889 deposed that the deceased had never seemed low, never referred to taking his life, and was never intemperate. After the inquest, the coroner inscribed in the Inquisition Book: "Nothing to shew his state of mind." Yet the jury's verdict was non compos mentis.[26] Not even a declaration of sanity could stem the tide. In a case with a Dickensian story line, a prodigal brother, back from Australia after thirty years, having received the legacy that was his, but failing to get a loan that he had demanded, put himself in the way of a railway engine. In a staccato suicide note, he wrote: "Tired of Life—the speediest and best way of getting out of it. Heaven and Hull [*sic*] a humbug. Verdict. Suicide in sober senses . . . Thursday 2pm. Adieu."[27]

Nor were medical witnesses any more influential. Dr. George Lowther thought Mary Ellerton had "flatulent dyspepsia," for which he ordered leeches to the pit of the stomach. She appeared irritable and impatient to him, but these were the only symptoms of mental malady: "The complaint was not of so violent a nature as to have a tendency to overthrow the mental equilibrium judging from the symptoms." But the jury were more impressed, it seems, by the sister's evidence that the deceased, who had hanged herself, had had pain all over and talked at random, which she was not in the habit of doing. Of a prostitute who poisoned herself, Dr. Thomas Lambert said: "[S]he appeared to me to be a person of violent passions & stubborn disposition but I saw no indication of aberration of mind about her." In both cases, however, a verdict of non compos mentis was returned, indicating that when medical definitions of "unsound mind" became too exacting, which they typically did not, inquest juries simply rejected them.[28]

In three cases of murder followed by suicide, finally, juries returned temporary insanity verdicts. Robert Hickson, a coal porter, hit his wife, who was a poorly woman, on the head with a poker four or five times, then cut his throat with a razor. The neighbor who discovered the bodies said that Hickson had never done anything to indicate insanity. Another neighbor, a mariner by trade, deposed: "I never saw any thing in his actions which would induce me to suppose him insane." However, the deceased, who was deaf and dumb and very passionate, had told his employer, a coal dealer, "that his wife had been committing adultery & that he would shoot the man, whom he described by signs which I understood." A dinnertime quarrel led to the murder and suicide. Not only was Hickson declared to be of unsound mind, but at the inquest on his wife, the jury returned a verdict of excusable homicide, killed by her husband in a fit of insanity.[29] In the other two cases, the separate verdicts on the murder and the suicide were strangely at odds with each other. Charles Plant, a police constable, and Ann, his wife, had had an unhappy marriage, according to an aunt. Ann drank to excess, and Charles was violent, as a result of which Ann had got a summons against him. Before it could be heard, however, Plant cut his wife's throat with a bread knife, and hanged himself from the banisters of the garret staircase. The police surgeon, Henry Thompson, examined both bodies, and gave the cause of death in each case. He then said of Charles Plant: "I have attended him for Rheumatism not for any head affection. I have never seen symptoms of insanity about him." The jury, however, decided that Plant was of unsound mind when he killed himself. Yet in the inquest on Ann's body, the jury rejected manslaughter, and brought in a verdict of "wilful murder" by Charles Plant, for which they had to believe there was malice aforethought.

The second case is that of 19-year-old Mary Wiles. She and her six-month-old daughter, Eliza, were found dead in the waters of the Timber Pond. Her husband, working on a keel at the time, told the coroner that his clothes had been pawned in his absence, and that he could not send his wife money, inasmuch as they were paid only when the captain drew the freight. Their routine, he said, had been for Mary and the two children to borrow from her mother, and for Wiles to repay her when he got back. A friend of Mary's then deposed that the deceased and Wiles had not always been on good terms. The policeman who helped get the bodies out found a note that said, "Good by Mother weep not for me but love my child for my sake," and a piece of paper with love poetry and the name of Wallace Webster of the keel Alphia upon it. The jury concluded that Mary Wiles had drowned herself while of unsound mind. Yet in the inquest on the child, the jury brought in a verdict of "wilful murder" against Mary Wiles, who "did feloniously, willfully and of malice aforethought murder the said Eliza Wiles." As a footnote to the entire case, the funeral at the Hedon Road cemetery was disturbed by a number of women who thought that the husband was to blame making comments against him.[30] It is difficult to know how one squares these verdicts, but it could be that a narrower definition of insanity was employed in inquests for murder, one that limited it to the intellectual incapacity to distinguish between right and wrong, along the lines of the so-called M'Naghten rules.

III

It would be wrong to conclude, however, that from the mid nineteenth century on, juries only ever condoned suicide by returning non compos mentis verdicts. The late Victorian years witnessed an important new development. In the last two decades of the century, the tide of "temporary insanity" verdicts began to ebb owing to the increasing use of the medium verdict, or "state of mind unknown." As we have seen, one-fifth of all suicide verdicts between 1875 and 1899 were medium verdicts. In what circumstances was this verdict used by juries? Olive Anderson has proposed that this verdict was returned when a jury wished neither to condemn (by returning a felo de se verdict) nor condone (by returning a non compos mentis verdict) the suicide; they chose, therefore, the "suspended moral judgment" of a medium verdict. She also suggests that it was used when there were "indications of wrong behaviour either by the deceased, or by close friends or relations" and when the deceased was "unidentified or a stranger." [31]

The Hull evidence indicates that there is much in what Anderson says, but also that the picture is a shade more complex. The medium verdict was indeed used for the handful of male strangers and unknowns who fetched up at inquests. Nothing was known of a Swedish emigrant from Gothenburg who shot himself on board a steam tug in May 1881, except that he carried birth and baptismal certificates, a ticket to New York on the Cunard line, and a continuation ticket to Chicago. An unknown man aged about 50 was found hanging to a pit prop in St. Andrew's Dock. The jury heard only that the deceased looked like a seaman, carried a National Union of Sailors and Firemen ticket, and was wearing practically his entire wardrobe: two pairs of trousers, a flannel shirt, and a woolen one. [32] The medium verdict as a "suspended moral judgment" was also evident in cases involving arrest, attempted murder, and actual murder. A number of suicides occurred in response to arrest and confinement in a police cell. Jacob Benjamin, a secondhand clothes dealer who was Russian by birth, strangled himself in a police cell after he and his wife were charged with stealing clothing. Anna Isaksen, a Norwegian, and former domestic servant, died from phosphorous poisoning while on remand in prison, charged with stealing a dress skirt from the house where she had lodged. [33] A small group of suicides involved attempted murder. When a prostitute declined to marry a passionate Italian seaman, he attempted to kill her and a lodging-house keeper and then shot himself. When a fisherman's wife declined to go away with another fisherman, the latter pulled out a revolver and said, "if we can't live together we'll die together." The woman ran toward the police station crying, "Help police"; a constable on his beat saw her but "thought it was a family quarrel & slackened to a walk." The constable eventually confronted the deceased, but he ran back into the woman's house and shot himself. [34] One suicide, finally, followed an act of murder. A former soldier, then working as a checker, became so angry at his wife's peregrinations with a female music-hall singer, a wife whom he had ill-treated for years, and from whom he had been separated for three months, that he killed her, then himself. The wife's father deposed that the deceased's mental condition was sound except when in drink. [35]

In each of these cases, perhaps, the jury were unwilling to declare the deceased a felo de se, since there was evidence of some emotional distress, but it was not sufficient to make them concede a non compos mentis verdict. In one early case, the medium verdict was a straightforward compromise between a felo de se and a non compos mentis verdict. The wife of a merchant seaman poisoned herself with laudanum in October 1860. Her young son said, "I have often heard my mother say she would poison herself," although he did not know the reason. A mariner who lodged with the deceased said that "she had got into money difficulties"; indeed, she had borrowed three sovereigns (£3) from the mariner's cashbox without his knowledge. The jury deliberated for an hour, according to the *Hull News*, but could not agree; nine jurymen were for a non compos mentis verdict, three for a felo de se verdict. The via media of a medium verdict was the outcome of the dispute.[36] The medium verdict was also given, finally, to suicides who seemed to have acted in a deliberate and rational manner, to judge from the suicide notes they left.[37] There were no cases, however, of the verdict being given as a judgment upon relatives or friends who the jury felt had acted improperly, except perhaps the suicide of the Jewish jeweler, whose family, as we have seen, tried urgently to conceal it.[38] Moreover, some juries reached a medium verdict for reasons that Anderson downplays or never came across.

For a start, the simple absence of evidence concerning the deceased's state of mind was seemingly influential in about one-third of the male medium verdicts. The widow of a yeast merchant who hanged himself in November 1889 told the jury that her husband of only six weeks had been a sober man; there had been no change in his manner, and no one in his family had been insane. The Coroners' Inquisition Book stated that it was thought that the deceased had lost money by gambling, but there was no evidence regarding his state of mind. The sister of a young grocer's assistant who was found hanging in the coalhouse deposed that her brother had been in no trouble, had had no love affair, and did not gamble. "An unaccountable act" was the entry in the Inquisition Book.[39] By late century, coroners and juries were perhaps less willing to grant a "temporary insanity" verdict when the evidence indicated no dispositional change in the deceased, no prior attempts at suicide, no marked emotional distress. Maybe those commentators who had long criticized the abuse, as they saw it, of the insanity verdict were making headway.

Second, evidence of pronounced drunkenness was present in a third of all male and a half of all female medium verdicts. Many of the female suicides given to drink, moreover, had the morally questionable status of married cohabitee. A coal dealer whose stable was next door to that of one suicide, a dock laborer who had also hawked sawdust and cinders, described the deceased as "a great drunkard." Another, a former soldier and French-polisher who died from the effects of laudanum, was given to drink and would when drunk put his wife out of the house and threaten to kill her. Harriet Grice, supposedly married but cohabiting with a stevedore, was given to drink and had been imprisoned for fourteen days for being drunk, driving her common-law spouse to ask her to leave. She hanged herself over the top of a closet door. Likewise, a dock laborer told his common-law wife, who had been drinking heavily for three weeks, courtesy of the pawnshop, to stop drinking or find another home. She hanged herself over the attic stairs.[40] In short, suicides who, in earlier years, would have been declared non compos mentis by virtue of their intemperance, were in the 1880's and 1890's accorded a medium verdict. Whereas drunkenness had once been proof of diminished responsibility, now it was seen as an impediment to judging the deceased's true state of mind. It is possible that this change in attitude on the part of juries reflected a wider unwillingness to excuse drunkenness, or a shift in the law's approach to drink as a mitigating circumstance.

The final factor worth examining is that of age. Among men of 60 years and over, only 18.7 percent of certified suicides between 1881 and 1899 were medium verdicts. The same figure was returned for men aged 45–60; while for those in the prime of life, 26 percent of suicides were medium verdicts. By contrast, among those aged 15–24, 50 percent of suicides (or 9 of 18) were medium verdicts. If anything, then, it was young males who disproportionately received this verdict in Hull. And the same was true of female suicides over the same years. No woman of 60 years and over received a medium verdict; a quarter of women in the prime of life got such a verdict; but 55 percent of young adults aged 15–24 were given medium verdicts between 1881 and 1899.[41]

There are many reasons, then, why the medium verdict was used much more frequently by juries in the last two decades of the century. It was the obvious verdict where little was known of the past life and recent behavior of the deceased, and where witnesses provided little or no enlightenment concerning the deceased's state of mind. In addition, juries were partial to medium verdicts when they heard that the deceased had been a cheerful individual, had never threatened or attempted suicide (but, rather, had condemned self-slaughter), and had penned a suicide note that read more like a premeditated last will and testament. Third, the verdict served the purpose the felo de se verdict had once served, to reprimand posthumously those who had thus escaped punishment for an earlier or concurrent crime. And, finally, when the deceased had led a dissipated life, juries, reluctant to grant diminished responsibility, reached for the medium verdict. And yet, in the tradition of jury solicitude and pragmatism, when the verdict looked likely to penalize survivors unjustly and make them a charge on the public, the verdict could be reconsidered. A police constable, whose beat was the south side of Hessle Road, told the jury that his wife, whom he had found hanging by a piece of trawl line fastened to the window sash, had been drinking lately and had "not been in the best of spirits for two or three weeks." The jury were all set to return a medium verdict, according to the *Eastern Morning News*, when the constable appealed to the jury to consider that his wife was insured, that he had a family of six children, and that he might lose what little money there would be with the verdict in that form. The deputy coroner urged the jury to banish from their minds the insurance question and to consider only whether there was evidence to show that the deceased had been of unsound mind. The jury called the eldest daughter, who worked as a domestic servant, to give evidence. She said she had noticed nothing peculiar about her mother, but that she had been excitable and had said that she would destroy herself. The jury then retired, and the foreman eventually returned to say that, while two jurors had not voted, twelve jurors had agreed on a verdict of "temporary insanity."[42]

In deciding that a death was caused by suicide, and in judging the state of mind of the deceased at the time of death, juries drew upon popular notions of what typically caused suicide and upon a popular jurisprudence of suicide. A death was categorized as suicide only when the evidence from witnesses, medical and lay, corresponded with what juries believed were the typical circumstances of suicidal death. The specific verdict reached by juries depended upon similar "clues" to the deceased's state of mind. Evidence of "melancholy" or "brain fever," or a family history of suicide, was interpreted as evidence of a predisposition to insanity and the associated suicidal tendency. A verdict of non compos mentis almost invariably followed. Not every suicide was considered to be of diminished responsibility, however. In a tiny number of early Victorian cases, juries handed out the harshest verdict, felo de se, with all its legal consequences. The popular jurisprudence of these decisions is difficult to fathom, although it could be that juries used the verdict mostly as a posthumous penalty for crime or immorality. More important, numerically speaking, juries used the medium verdict, particularly in the last decades of the century, as a middle ground between the excessive stigma of felo de se and the exoneration implied by non compos mentis. Again, the jurisprudence is complex, but the absence of evidence concerning the deceased's state of mind and evidence of dissipation seem to have influenced juries. When the usual pointers to suicidal death were absent, or when it was impossible to be sure that the death had been anything but accidental, an open verdict was returned. In reaching these decisions as to cause of death and state of mind, the coroner played an important role. He cajoled witnesses to tell the court of the deceased's last hours, his frame of mind, his trials and tribulations. He reviewed the evidence for the jury, and reminded them of their legal duties. But then it was up to the jury. They were expected to make up their own minds, and this by and large they seem to have done. They asked to see again the scene of death, they called fresh witnesses, they reconsidered their verdict in light of new evidence, they disagreed among themselves, and they pointed the moral of the inquest in the form of advisory addenda.

IV

After reaching a verdict, the jury could, and occasionally did, add a prescriptive or critical rider. When the wife of a coal heaver poisoned herself with carbolic acid in March 1894, the jury recommended that the sale of this substance be placed under the same restrictions as that of other scheduled poisons. The jury in the case of Sarah Ann Bennett, the wife of an iron molder, who drowned herself in September 1869, asked the coroner to censure the husband for his neglect. He had heard his wife threaten to drown herself and had seen her go on the Albert Dock side, but he was slow to go look for her or to report her absence to the police. Jurymen likewise suggested formal censure of a druggist who allowed his housekeeper to attend to the shop when he knew of her intemperate habits. She had poisoned herself with laudanum.[43]

Occasionally, third parties were severely admonished. Robert Hickson, the coal porter who killed his wife and then himself in November 1841, accused Charles Richardson, a fellow coal porter, of committing adultery with his wife. Richardson denied the charge, but "several jurymen," reported the *Hull Advertiser*, "expressed themselves as perfectly satisfied that this witness was morally guilty of the deaths of the deceased." The coroner was also reported as having said:

You, Richardson, are guilty in the minds of the jury, and have had recourse to perjury to cover your crime. I have no power over you, and you may retire. If you have caused the deaths of these two persons, I hope you will repent, for the offence is of a most horrible description. The matter rests within your own conscience.[44]

On other occasions, however, the coroner strove to calm neighborhood passions. In response to the rumor that Mary Tomlinson, found drowned with her five-month-old son, had destroyed herself because of her husband's ill-treatment, the coroner stated that the evidence contradicted the reported ill-treatment, and he criticized those who put around such stories. At the end of the inquest on Mary Wiles, who drowned herself and her child, the coroner stressed that no blame should be attached to the husband, although, as we have seen, this did not stop a cemetery protest against the husband. Nor could public indignation be denied in the case of a 28-year-old dressmaker who poisoned herself when she discovered that the man she was engaged to had been cohabiting with a Mrs. Kirk for five years. During the inquest, a large crowd of women assembled outside the County Hotel, ready to place the blame for Mary Richardson's death on Mrs. Kirk. Four policemen had to escort Kirk home, the crowd following, hooting and hissing all the way.[45] Such incidents belong in the catalogue of "rough music," examples of crowds directing hostility against individuals who were thought to have offended community norms.[46] Jurors, finally, might append a charitable note to the proceedings, subscribing their fees to the destitute widow and family of the deceased, to the Lying-in-Charity, or to the Infirmary.[47]

The coroner now moved to the fourth and final stage of the process of defining a death as suicide, about which little need be said. He would send a "Certificate after Inquest" to the registrar, with the information needed to register the death.[48] The resulting death certificate recorded the bare bones of the case: the name of the deceased; his or her sex, age, and occupation; when and where he or she had died; the cause of death; and the description of the informant, in this case, the coroner. In the 70 cases in which coroners' inquisition papers failed to provide such information, I was therefore able to draw upon death certificates to fill the gap.

V

The public inquest over, it was the turn of the press to define and interpret the tragic event. Typically, a brief summary of the inquest would appear in the morning newspapers; in cases that were exceptional in either motive or method, notably murder followed by suicide, the inquest would be reported verbatim. In most cases, press reports held closely to the facts assembled by the inquest, although in the briefer reports, they had a tendency to amalgamate evidence from a number of different witnesses. More important, reports included information about the deceased that did not always get entered into depositions, such as suicide notes; and recorded details of the cross-examination of witnesses by jurymen or legal representatives, of the speed and unanimity with which verdicts were reached, of the obiter dicta of coroner and jurymen, and of the reactions of relatives, neighbors, and bystanders. This chapter has benefited from such information. Press reports, finally, included other miscellaneous yet helpful details.

Depending upon when the death occurred, newspapers might report details of the event before the inquest was held and even anticipate the jury's verdict by stating that the deceased had committed suicide.[49] Headlines sometimes sought to encapsulate the case, as in "Suicide from Want"; sometimes they would contradict the jury's verdict. The headline would be "Melancholy Suicide" or "Supposed Suicide," when, in fact, the jury had returned an open verdict. Newspapers were obviously unwilling to stick to the letter of the verdict when the evidence indicated suicide. It was rare for the press openly to criticize the jury's verdict, although in May 1838, the *Hull Advertiser*'s report of the inquest on Mary Dailey, who was found to have killed herself while of unsound mind, concluded with the observation: "There was not a particle of evidence to prove that deceased had ever exhibited any symptom whatever of insanity."[50] More commonly, newspaper reports would add a judgment on the case: "A most unaccountable and deplorable case of suicide"; "The old, old story of debt, despondency and death"; or on the deceased: "Mrs. Smith was in the prime of life, and was greatly respected in the neighbourhood." Newspapers, finally, would keep track of the frequency of suicide, and when necessary refer to "The Suicidal Mania in Hull" or "The Suicide Epidemic in Hull," as the *Eastern Morning News* did in September 1883, November 1888, and again in September 1891.[51] In short, while newspapers could never be the exclusive source for a study of suicide, being selective in what was reported and stereotypical in the motives stressed, they do often help to construct the social context of the individual act of self-destruction.

VI

This concludes our examination of the processes of certifying a death as suicide and of the social dynamics of the coroner's court. It remains only to reach a conclusion concerning the degree of confidence with which we can use the documents created by these inquest procedures to plot the overall rate of suicide, to identify the sex, age, and occupational distributions of suicides, and to disclose the experience of suicide across the life cycle. One thing is certain: the documents contain no mention of those who preferred to kill themselves outside of Hull, whether in another coroner's jurisdiction, or, like Charles Lewis, a Hull merchant, in Amsterdam.[52] The two main sources of systematic reporting error, however, according to critics of the official statistics, were concealment and misclassification. Concealment led, it is claimed, to the underregistration of suicide among the middle and upper classes, whose families recoiled from a system that would wash their dirty linen in public. The preceding examination of the etiquette of suicide discovery indicates, however, that families, even those of respectability, were too shocked by the death of a relative to think immediately of concealment. Once the death was public knowledge, the chance of subterfuge was gone. Among working people, there was little chance of concealment; their houses were too close, their walls too thin, their lives too communal, and their relationship with doctors too undeveloped to make concealment feasible. And in all social classes, the presence of "extra" household members beyond the family group, notably domestic servants and lodgers, made concealment of suicide more difficult.

The misclassification of deaths poses a larger problem for would-be statisticians. Suicides by poisoning and drowning, it is claimed, were often misclassified as accidental deaths or as undetermined deaths (the latter being returned as open verdicts). Since these were methods of self-destruction used disproportionately by women, moreover, such misclassification would result in the underregistration of female suicide. The standard riposte to the charge of misclassification is to argue that the addition of the missing cases to the suicide category would not affect the relative, as distinct from the absolute, suicide rate.[53] In Hull, however, a sizable number of suicides by poisoning and drowning were misclassified, from the look of the depositional evidence, as undetermined deaths, sufficient, in fact, to add another 20 percent to the suicide total. More critically, the misclassified suicides were more youthful and female than officially defined suicides. To surmount the problem of misclassification, therefore, the present study has reserved the ability to incorporate those open verdicts in which the circumstantial evidence of suicide is compelling. A final defense of the use of these documents for statistical purposes is to underline the fact that we are investigating only one jurisdiction, and one in which the coroner's office remained in the same family for three generations. As such, the likelihood of consistency over time in the certification process is greater.

A second area of difficulty in the use of the court-created documents lies in the way that suicides were socially constructed by the coroners' court. Coroners, witnesses, and juries, it is claimed, looking for "clues" to suicide, dealt in "folk beliefs" about the state of mind that drove people to destroy themselves. The act of self-destruction was associated with a distinctive "psychological profile," one that medical opinion encouraged. Thus, the coroner prompted witnesses to tell the jury whether the suicide was "low-spirited" or "melancholic"; was given to drink; had quarreled with spouse, lover, or parent; was in debt, in straitened circumstances, or in poor health; was affected (for a woman) by the menarche, pregnancy, or the menopause; had threatened or attempted suicide; had insane or suicidal relatives; or had been in an asylum. A combination of such factors would induce juries to return a verdict of suicide. In consequence, the critics charge, coroners' case papers tell us only about the well of technical and commonsense knowledge from which coroners, witnesses, and jurymen drew; they offer nothing reliable about the actual causes and experience of suicide.[54]

There is no gainsaying the fact that the statements of inquest witnesses were frequently simply an echo of the coroner's questions. He it was who asked about the mood, health, financial condition, and family history of the deceased. He it was, too, who acted as the filter between the linguistic manner in which witnesses expressed themselves and the words that got recorded in the signed statement. To recognize that case papers disclose the causative theories that shaped the questions asked by coroners, the answers given by witnesses, and the verdicts reached by jurymen does not, however, negate their use to shed some light upon the actual circumstances of suicidal death. The coroner acted as prompter, not ventriloquist; witnesses were guided, not led by the nose. The depositions of spouses and children, friends, and neighbors, emerged from a dialogue between coroner and witness. If the voice of the coroner is audible, so too is that of the witness. Moreover, the depositions were generally based upon an intimate knowledge of the deceased, often over a long span of time. Witnesses would refer to illnesses, previous suicide attempts, and bereavements that went back ten, even twenty years. In an attempt to explain the "rash act" of a relative, friend, or neighbor, witnesses may have drawn upon popular notions of what led people to kill themselves, but they also recorded what the deceased had been doing, saying, and threatening for weeks and months; what impact being laid off or separated from a spouse had had upon the deceased; and what physical or mental illness the deceased had actually suffered from. If the text of the coroner's inquest is no mirror image of the "real world," it is no fictional invention either. The records can and will be used, in short, to reveal something about the individual experience of suicide, as well as the trends and patterns of suicide.

The Urban Life Cycle

The Urban Life Cycle in
Victorian England

All the world's a stage,
And all the men and women merely players;
They have their exits and their entrances,
And one man in his time plays many parts,
His acts being seven ages.

Shakespeare,
As You Like It 2.7.139–43

In the twentieth century, life-course transitions have become officially recognized and regulated. A series of age-related requirements, from compulsory school attendance to mandatory retirement, now imposes considerable uniformity in the timing of such transitions.[1] In the Victorian era, the timing of life-course transitions was not so uniform and was less a product of law, or institutionalized age norms, than of family economic needs. The latter might differ according to occupation, social class, generation, and region, and might be different for migrants than for nonmigrants. Moreover, high death rates meant that many Victorians did not experience the normal life-course pattern. Some died young, some were orphaned, some never married, some were childless, and some had their marriages prematurely terminated by death (and very occasionally by divorce).[2] The diversity of resources, options, and role sequences in the Victorian life course should not deter us, however, from assessing the major points of transition: entering the labor force, leaving the parental home, marriage, parenthood, widowhood, and retirement. This is the theme of the present chapter and an important preliminary to the analysis of suicide in terms of the life cycle. Deviations from the normative life cycle, the reversibility of the life cycle, and the conflict between "family strategies" and individual preferences, which all influenced people's emotional and financial stability in significant ways, are likewise examined to help us understand Victorian suicide.

The chapter is based entirely upon the abundant secondary literature on the urban life cycle in Victorian England. This literature tends to examine the urban population *tout ensemble*, and it thus fails to reveal the details of class-specific life cycles. This would be a decided limitation were it not for the fact that the bulk of the middle class were petit bourgeois shopkeepers and small producers, whose life-cycle transitions bore a close resemblance to those of the majority working-class population. Only the wealthy middle class had life cycles that differed appreciably from those of the mass of the urban population, and specific attention is paid at one point to these differences.

I

Let us start with entrance into the labor force. Working life began early in Victorian England. In 1851, 28 percent of children between the ages of 10 and 15 were at work, and this is probably an underestimate, given the likely failure to declare casual or part-time child labor to census enumerators. Boys under 15 at work outnumbered girls of the same age by two to one. The proportion of working children between the ages of 10 and 15 fell slightly to 26 percent in 1871, but then declined sharply to 14 percent in 1911.[3] At the later date, the figure is doubtless also an underestimate, since boys from as young as 9 worked before and after school as newspaper sellers, delivery boys, lather boys in barbershops, and shop assistants. The hours worked could be excessive and, on top of a school day, could result in physical and mental exhaustion.[4] The decline in the proportion at work over the second half of the century was due to child labor laws, the decline of domestic production, and compulsory school attendance (which applied to children under 10 from 1876 on). The school-leaving age was raised to 11 in 1893, and 12 in 1899.[5] Above the age of 13, full-time waged work was the norm, and these older children made important contributions to family incomes.

Between the ages of 15 (the average age at menarche for late Victorian girls) and 24, bridging childhood and independent adulthood, practically all males, and a larger proportion of females than at any other time of their lives, worked for wages. Exactly how many young women worked depended upon the local employment structure, and probably upon local custom, but parental expectation was evidently strong that daughters should enter the labor market and contribute to the family coffers. Women's labor was restricted to a handful of low-paid, low-skilled occupations: domestic service, dress (or clothing), textiles, and food processing. Only in the last quarter of the century did employment opportunities widen (without increasing overall), notably in clerical work and retailing.[6] For young men, employment opportunities were stable during the second half of the century, judging from the low and declining percentage of males aged 15–19 returned as unoccupied. By contrast, as Ellen Jordan has argued, the unoccupied figures for women aged 15–19, which varied between 31 and 41 percent in the period 1851–1911, "suggest that there was endemic female unemployment throughout these sixty years, unemployment which was a direct result of the prevailing sexual division of labour."[7] Significantly, the towns with the highest proportions of young women returned as having no particular occupation included the seaports of Cardiff, Birkenhead, and Grimsby, the last only twenty miles south of Hull as the crow flies.

But what of the young, unmarried girls who had jobs? Domestic service was their prime resort. The most recent enumeration of occupied women has reduced the number of domestic servants by half (omitting those who were performing domestic tasks at home for their kin), but domestic service for wages was an important female job, and especially for single girls.[8] In 1851, according to Michael Anderson's national sample, one-fifth of unmarried women in the age group 18–27 were employed as domestics. In 1871, nearly three-fifths of all female indoor servants were between 15 and 24 years of age. As Edward Higgs has observed, domestic service was "predominantly a life-cycle occupation," a job for women between leaving home and getting married.[9] If the stereotype of Victorian domestic service is of a young servant girl performing cleaning and cooking functions for a well-to-do family as part of a retinue of servants, the reality could be very different. Over 50 percent of all domestics in 1851 were the sole resident female servant of households that were not particularly wealthy. Domestic servants were found not only in middle-class homes. Small retailers (butchers, grocers, innkeepers) also employed domestics, as did those in clerical, artisan, and manual occupations. Many domestics migrated from the rural regions, the source of most town servants, but some were recruited from the workhouse or charitable institutions by working-class families.[10] In all social classes, need as much as status prompted the employment of servants. Indeed, according to Higgs, servant employment was related to the life-cycle needs of the families concerned. In the skilled manual class and the social classes above, servant-employing families were concentrated in the life-cycle stage of the married couple where there were children at home, but none were in employment. Servant employment was a function, too, of the domestic crisis posed by the death of the wife and mother.[11] The working life of the young, single "slavey," finally, could be harsh. Often separated from home and family, deprived of freedom and companionship, domestic servants had few kin or friends to turn to when faced with employer mistreatment, or with illness, pregnancy, or unemployment.[12]

If membership of the labor force and submission to the financial requirements of the family was one main feature of the period between leaving school and getting married, a second feature was the long-drawn-out transition to adulthood. In this regard, the relatively late age of marriage was a decisive influence. Leaving aside the regional and occupational differences in the age at marriage, the national figures for the 1850's put the median age at 24.4 for men and 22.9 for women. During the second half of the century, the median age rose, reaching 26.7 for men and 24.4 for women in the years around World War I.[13] Between leaving school and marriage, therefore, some twelve to fifteen years might elapse. Until the age of 20, four-fifths or more of children lived with parents or kin in family households. Thereafter, the proportion who left the family of origin increased, but even in their early twenties, one-half of all children still lived with parents. The other young unmarrieds (a proportion of whom would be orphaned) were in service or in lodgings.[14] Like domestic service in the lives of young working-class women, the practice of lodging commonly marked the transitional stage between leaving the parental home and establishing an independent household. In Preston, for example, around a quarter of the 20–24 age group lived in lodgings in 1851, two-thirds of whom were young men.[15] Both migrants (especially the Irish-born) and nonmigrants used lodgings. And, typically, young lodgers lived with a skilled or semi-skilled working-class family (as distinct from specialized lodging houses that accommodated itinerant and seagoing workingmen). A large proportion of young people, then, occupied what Michael Anderson calls "life-cycle-stage-specific residential statuses." In 1851, almost one-half of both men and women at age 20 were of "intermediate" residential status: neither living in the parental home nor heading (or a spouse in) their own households.[16]

The economic and psychological burdens of this prolonged transition to marriage and household headship are predictable. Many young apprentices were worked hard and paid poorly, only to be dismissed at the end of their time. While young people lived at home, they were expected to "tip-up" their wages (at least until their late teens, when parents might allow them to pay board) and accept a large measure of parental authority. In some families, moreover, the male parent doubled as employer. It would be surprising if this financial dependency and subjection to parental control (and punishment) had failed to arouse adolescent anger and family tensions. If domestic service or lodgings allowed young people to escape parental control, however, they also exposed at least some of them to loneliness, exploitation, and brutality.[17]

II

The next significant life-course transition was marriage and parenthood. Of course, by no means all women got married. The unfavorable sex ratio alone meant that a high proportion of women between 20 and 40 (almost one-third in 1851, for example) were single. In the largest Yorkshire towns in 1861, however, the proportion of women aged 35–44 who had ever married varied between 80 and 90 percent (as did the proportion of "ever-married" men in the same age group).[18] Marriage was an extremely common status, therefore, for people in the prime of life. Conception tended to follow quickly upon marriage. Parenthood, moreover, was a lifelong role. As Michael Anderson has illustrated, the "typical" woman (experiencing her life-course events at the median age for her cohort) gave birth to her last child at 39 years of age in 1831; at 33 or 34 in 1891. The combination of late marriage, high fertility, and short life expectancy ensured that bearing and rearing children filled practically the entire adult life span. Rarely was the nest empty. Yet the number in the nest varied a good bit. And since the range of family sizes was so wide, Anderson says, "the family experience both of parents and of children was very diverse" with regard both to the number of children claiming parental attention and to living standards.[19] Historians impose order on this diversity, however, by dividing the life cycles of married couples into six distinct stages, in accordance with the absence or presence of children and the proportion of children in employment. This entire construct, which is most applicable to working-class families, presumes, of course, that families passed through a series of recognizable stages.[20]

In the first two life-cycle stages, when the married couple were either alone or with only one young child, when the wife might be earning a wage, and thus when there was a high ratio of wage earners to family members, close to 90 percent of working-class families lived above the minimum poverty line. At this phase in the life cycle, fewer married couples headed their own households than would eventually be the case. In mid-century Preston, for example, during the first few years of married life, no fewer than one-half of all working-class couples lived in the homes of parents or kin or lodged with another family.[21] The third and most punishing life-cycle stage came when the married couple were in their thirties, the wife had dropped out of the formal labor market, and their children were too young to work, so that the ratio of family dependents to wage earners was at its peak. Even though the husband's wage also reached its peak in this life-cycle stage (especially that of manual workers), over two-thirds of working-class families (including even one-third of families headed by skilled workers) sank below the poverty line in Bradford in 1851.[22] Prospects could only improve in the next two life-cycle stages, when the children entered the workforce, and, at their best (when fathers were in their late forties and fifties), earned a third or more of total family income. The protracted residence of working adolescents before marriage made it possible for 90 percent of Bradford's working-class families to rise above the poverty line. In the sixth stage, indeed, nearly half of all working-class families were "in comfort," making it possible for at least some families to extend support to aged parents, to coresident married children, and to kin who were newcomers to the town.[23] In short, these studies all indicate, first, that living standards were determined less by the husband's occupational class, and more by the family's position in the life cycle. Second, that all but the most fortunate were vulnerable to economic strain, particularly in the middle stage of the life cycle, even in the most benign of times. And, third, that the collective strategies of the family were crucial to the negotiation of regular life-course transitions, and, as we shall see shortly, of what have been called "critical life situations"—deaths, accidents, sickness, and unemployment—which could take a heavy toll on a family's domestic economy.[24]

Before extending the discussion of the life-cycle stages of married couples, I should emphasize that the above is applicable largely to working-class families (although many lower-middle-class families, including the majority of clerical workers, would have experienced a similar life-course pattern).[25] For the urban middle-class family, however, the life course could take on different characteristics. For a start, the transition to marriage and household headship was even more prolonged than in a working-class family, given the high cost of establishing a middle-class household. The average age of middle-class men who married between 1840 and 1870 was 29.93 years. It is unlikely that the age of middle-class marriage fell, in view of the rising standards of domestic expenditure and the associated obsession with the "proper" time to marry. Moreover, probably fewer children of the middle class occupied "intermediate" residential status, between parental homes and their own households. Few were employed in service; and few would have moved into lodgings. It is more likely that boys from lower-middle- and middle-class families experienced a longer period of dependency, as parents became willing to keep sons at school and in professional apprenticeships, in the hope of white-collar careers for them.[26]

As with working-class families, parenthood was a lifelong role, but the middle-class family was subject to less economic strain, was much less dependent upon children's earnings, and was in a position to accommodate kin members at most stages of the life cycle. Indeed, one historian has posited the notion of a property cycle for the successful middle-class male, akin to the poverty cycle of the wage-earning family.[27] The first adult stage of the property cycle began with marriage or the establishment of an independent household, when the family depended on earned income, and when business debts were being paid off. The next stage, in the man's late thirties or early forties, coincided with the inheritance of parental property, which brought an end to indebtedness. In the final adult stage, the middle-class man in his early to mid fifties slowly withdrew from business, and lived on forms of unearned income (land, rents, and dividends) purposely acquired for old age. The most significant consequence of this cycle was that by mid-century, the bourgeois family rarely functioned as an economic unit; rather, it concentrated on domesticity. Virtually no wives of manufacturers, merchants, doctors, lawyers, or clergymen worked outside the home. Their role had become that of domestic manager, their task to create a retreat from the outside world. The lower middle class, moreover, was not immune from the ideology of domesticity.[28] Of course, probably no more than 12 or 13 percent of urban adult males headed this kind of household.

One of the points above requires further emphasis: the close association between life-cycle stage and married women's formal participation in the workforce. It has long been thought that, with the exception of Lancashire cotton and Yorkshire woolen towns, where a third or more of working-class married women had paid employment, the transition to adulthood via marriage brought departure from the labor market. Or, if wives did work, it was to solve a temporary crisis in the family economy.[29]

It now seems more accurate to say that wage-earning was a regular part of married working-class women's experience, and that it was shaped by life-course considerations. In particular, the domestic responsibilities of married women in different life-course positions shaped their wage-earning. Married women were most commonly employed before the age of 20 and after the age of 40. Between the ages of 25 and 39 (and particularly in the 30–34 age group), the rate of women's wage-earning fell. These were the years of greatest economic want for families, but years when women were busiest in the home with children. In short, married women entered and left paid employment in accordance less with economic emergency and more with their changing family situation.[30]

The proportion of occupied married women appears, however, to have declined in the second half of the century. In 1851, almost a quarter of wives were in waged work; by 1911, only 10 percent were at work. This was probably the result of the shift of work from home to factory, of the influence of the "domestic idyll" (or the view that women belonged in the private sphere of the home), of the ideology of the male breadwinner, especially pervasive among skilled workmen, and of the falling cost of living.[31] Yet if married women moved out of full-time waged employment, income substitutes were commonly found in home work of various kinds. For the working-class woman, there was no tight demarcation between public (work) and private (domestic) spheres.[32] The insecurity, seasonality, and casualness of most workingmen's lives generally required the wife to be productive when not being reproductive. Much of this irregular activity was part-time and casual — selling food, doing laundry, working with self-employed husbands in shops and pubs, taking in boarders — and was underenumerated in the census returns.[33]

By definition, therefore, it is impossible to give a reliable picture of the total employment activity of married women, but Michael Anderson suggests that by the 55–64 age group, "nearly half were probably engaged in a substantial income-producing activity" at mid-century.[34] The provision of lodgings was a popular, informal way of supplementing the family economy, particularly for those in late middle age who could use the beds of children who had left home. In Bradford, for example, just over one-third of all working-class families took in lodgers in 1851.[35] It is possible, finally, that married women's wage-earning assumed greater importance as compulsory education made inroads on child labor, although rising male wages probably reduced the need for a wife's earnings.[36]

The level of contribution made by working-class married women to the family economy was an important ingredient in what one historian has termed a "hidden matriarchy" of women, who turned kin and neighborhood networks to account in the struggle against "critical life situations." This is not to say, however, that men never performed similar services, for they indubitably did.[37] The most obvious ways in which the life cycle could be thrown into reverse were the death or illness of a spouse. In the nineteenth century, marriages came to an end through death much more than divorce, although informal separation (which might be followed by cohabitation) was not uncommon. Such were the high rates of marital breakup through death that for the cohort marrying in the 1850's, 19 percent of marriages would not have lasted 10 years; nearly half would not have lasted 25. "By fifty," Paul Thompson observes, "a married man or woman was as likely as not to have suffered widowhood." The difficulties that came in death's wake were funeral expenses (and at best only half the population were insured in burial clubs), the grief of bereavement, and one-parent child rearing.[38] Sickness was less devastating, but (like an accident or unemployment) aroused almost as much fear. Were a husband to be ill for an extended period (and the average duration of sickness in six districts of York in 1843 varied from 6 to 15 weeks), and particularly if the family were utterly dependent on the breadwinner (as most were in life-cycle stages 3 and 4), the family would soon find itself in Queer Street. Membership of a sick club or friendly society could help, but benefits were never more than one-half the average wage, and they went down after six weeks or so.[39]

The death or illness of a spouse did not exhaust life's crises. The deaths of children were likewise frequent and distressing. Among the 1861 birth cohort, for example, 27 percent of the males and 24 percent of the females died under 5; a third or more of both sexes did not reach 25.[40] The impact of heavy child mortality is in dispute. David Vincent has argued that the depth of bereavement was calibrated by material considerations. Parental grief was less for a young and dependent child than for a strapping boy who looked set to contribute handsomely to the family exchequer.[41] Such an essentially "instrumental" view of family relationships has been challenged, however, by historians who suggest that the response to a child's death was more likely to be intense grief than resignation; that women commonly sank into illness and depression after a child's death; and that grief could strike fathers as heavily as mothers.[42] In all these situations— whether of death, sickness, accident, or unemployment—the family would typically rally round, providing help in cash, kind, or emotional comfort. As negative reinforcement of the importance of family to the negotiation of life crises, one need only refer to the large percentage of single individuals with no coresident family who were below the poverty line in mid-century Bradford, and to the plight of migrant lodgers with no kin in mid-century Preston.[43] Another "critical life situation" was old age, but this warrants extended treatment as a distinct life-cycle stage.

III

When does "old age" begin? Janet Roebuck found that there was no single, official definition of old age in the nineteenth century comparable to the "retirement age," or "pension age," of over 65 for men, and over 60 for women, established in the twentieth century. Rather, men were presumed to be old when, getting on in years, they were no longer able to support themselves by their work. For women, it was less functional incapacity than biology that was emphasized; menopause was deemed to be the climacteric of the female life cycle.[44] Thus women were thought to reach old age before men, even though female life expectancy at birth (42 years in 1841, 54 in 1891) was greater than that of men (39 and 48 years, respectively).[45] The pension schemes of most friendly societies began at age 65, although the 1875 Friendly Societies Act defined "old age" as "any age after 50."[46] Once a state pension scheme got on to the political agenda, as it did in the 1890's, an official definition could no longer be avoided.[47] In the end, a combination of the age at which pauperism was said to increase sharply and national financial considerations resulted in a pension age of 70 in the 1908 act. In the course of the national discussion, however, and particularly before the Royal Commission on the Aged Poor in 1893–94, a good deal of evidence was presented in support of what a Birkenhead iron turner (and local secretary of the Liverpool District Committee of the Amalgamated Society of Engineers) disclosed about the lot of elderly workmen:

In most trades a man is at his best from 25 to 45, then the period of decline sets in from 45 onward, growing and accelerating until, at the age of 55, the earning powers become diminished, and the difficulty of obtaining anything like regular employment becomes considerable. . . . At 60 years of age the retrograde movement is more pronounced, work being intermittent, and wages, as a rule, very much below the standard.[48]

His statement, he added, would apply to all those who were not skilled artisans. It seems justifiable, then, to define "old age" as 55 and older, and to see the years 45–54 as a time when middle age was settling into old age.[49]

As such, what proportion did the old represent in the demographic pyramid? In the national population, the proportion of males and females aged 45 and above was 19 percent and 20 percent, respectively; the figures for those aged 55 and above were 10 and 11 percent. The proportion of males aged 65 and over and females aged 60 and over (or those of current pensionable age) was 4 and 8 percent, respectively, suggesting that the ratio of females to males in the elderly population was roughly two to one.[50]

The process of defining "old age" has revealed the extremely gradual manner in which men left the labor force in the nineteenth century. Middle-class men would slowly withdraw from business, working fewer hours as they approached their late forties, a rentier income allowing. The lower middle class, a main force in working-class housing, might try to retire on the proceeds of house rents.[51] For most manual workmen, the major transition in their working life was not the complete cessation of labor but the slow and often painful downgrading of skills and earnings, with more frequent periods of unemployment. From their mid forties on, manual workers would experience a reduction in earnings, due either to a decline in productive capacity in the job they had always done or to a gradual slide down the occupational chute, as strength and endurance failed, into the pool of unskilled and casual labor. A number of trades—barmen, shop assistants, drapers, barbers, and servants—cast off workers at the onset of middle age because they required either strength or a youthful appearance. Ex-soldiers, unfit for industrial work, cushioned by their small pensions, drifted into the ranks of casual labor.[52] What has been called "life-cycle de-skilling," or downward job mobility, led to concentrations of older workers in low-paid, low-status, and ill-organized sectors of the workforce. The social investigator Charles Booth found "a surplus of old men in decaying industries" (coopers, shipwrights, rope makers, and watchmakers) in late Victorian London. Other London occupations had an excess of men aged 40 and above: lightermen and watermen (often former sailors); dealers in wood, corn, and coal; builders and blacksmiths; boot and shoe workers; and gardeners. An excess of men aged 55 and above prevailed among tailors and hatters. A more recent investigation of British males aged 65 and over has showed that older workers were concentrated in the agricultural, clothing, laboring, and sales sectors in the later nineteenth century. Older workers also turned to small-scale retailing (market stalls, corner shops, and pubs).[53]

Illness (and accidents) often aggravated the plight of old workmen, since finding work on recovery could be difficult. This was as true of clerical workers, and even small shopkeepers, as manual workers. At about age 45, morbidity rates rose sharply and the number of weeks lost through sickness also went up. This was particularly true of the later Victorian years; the more life expectancy rose, the more the risk of being sick increased. Speaking of old townsmen, Charles Booth declared: "[I]f any mishap breaks the thread of their employment it is difficult for a man of fifty to make a fresh start, and even at forty-five it is, in some trades, not easy to do so." By the time Victorian workmen retired, Peter Laslett affirms, they were commonly in poor health, and suffering from various forms of disability.[54] In all, elderly males worked until disablement or death. In 1881, nearly three-quarters of British males aged 65 and over were returned in the census as occupied; even in the 1900's over 60 percent were employed.[55] They had little choice in a pre-pension era. Friendly and other provident societies enrolled between a quarter and a third of the occupied male population, but owing to prolonged sickness, unemployment, and reduced earnings, many men had allowed their contributions to lapse by the time they entered their fifties. Only white-collar workers and former servicemen had guaranteed pension schemes before 1908.[56]

It has long been considered that the plight of older workmen worsened during the "second industrial revolution" in the later nineteenth century. From 1875 on, and particularly in the 1890's, in the context of an increasingly competitive international economy, British employers in a number of industries (notably metals and engineering) sought higher labor productivity by introducing new machinery and increasing the pace of work (particularly by the piece-rate system of wage payment). Employers became much less willing to keep on older workers. Trade union resistance to aging members working for less than the recognized minimum rate of wages further diminished the older man's chances of remaining in work. New techniques in tailoring, boot and shoe manufacture, and printing allowed the substitution of female labor for that of adult men. Among the lower middle class, finally, the trade depression of the 1880's and 1890's made employment less secure for many clerks, and the economic viability of small independent shopkeepers came under threat from new forms of retail operation. The view that these new employment practices made it increasingly difficult for workers over 50 to find work was a leitmotif of evidence to the Royal Commission on the Aged Poor in the mid 1890's.[57]

In recent years, however, historians have been less convinced that skills were destroyed, labor reorganized, and managerial control asserted in the late Victorian years. Paul Johnson has, moreover, emphasized that the labor-force participation rates for men aged 50–54 and 55–59 were high and stable in the last decades of the century. In contrast, as early as 1881, 40 percent of urban men over 65 had permanently left employment. This suggests to Johnson that 65 was "an important employment threshold well before the introduction . . . of social security pensions"; and that the concern shown for the aged poor from the 1880's was a consequence of "the growing visibility of the urban industrial aged poor rather any real change in occupation-specific employment propensities for men aged over 65." [58] Yet even if we accept that the plight of older workmen did not greatly worsen in late century, it is impossible to gainsay the impact of being slowly ousted from the labor force. "It is, no doubt, always a bitterness to a man," Lady Florence Bell observed, "to have to content himself with a lighter, less well-paid, and less responsible job than the one he occupied when he was hale and vigorous." [59] For many, moreover, this was the start of a process that could end in destitution or dependence. "I do not wonder," said James Callear, a South Staffordshire ironworker who told the Royal Commission of his fellow workmen, "that some of them in old age have lost hope and heart and taken to drink, and that others unfortunately have preferred suicide after having sought to make both ends meet, to live respectably after having worked hard, and feeling a repugnance to the workhouse; I do not wonder that some have preferred suicide to dying a pauper and filling a pauper's grave." [60]

For women, the transition to old age was a rather different experience. Since the illness, unemployment, or death of the primary wage earner tended to occur in later life, old age pushed many wives and widows into the job market. Unskilled, low-paying jobs were the norm: charring, laundry work, dealing in food, and seamstressing. Alternatively, wives and widows took in lodgers. As this implies, moreover, widowhood often accompanied the transition into old age. At any time in the second half of the nineteenth century, according to Michael Anderson, 16 percent of women aged 45–54 (7 percent of men), and 30 percent of women aged 55–64 (14 percent of men) were widowed. The figure was higher still for women aged 65 and over. The results of such high levels of widowhood were, first, a large surplus of widowed women (aggravated by the tendency of widowers to remarry younger single women), and second, in view of the extended period of childbearing, a large number of widows with young children to support. [61] Yet if the position of women in old age could be as bad, if not worse, materially (and in terms of health, little better), historians have suggested that females did better at adapting to old age and widowhood. Less involved in the world of work, they argue, women suffered the shock of severance from it less. The daily routine of housework, or even part-time work, was not drastically altered by widowhood or old age. Old women had kin and neighborhood support systems to fall back upon. And psychologically accustomed to dependency, women found it easier both to enter the workhouse and to move in with married children (which is not to deny that such coresidence could be a source of family tension). In short, as Charles Booth concluded in 1894: "The position of women in old age has probably always been better than that of men, and the special disadvantages of men at the present time touch them less."[62]

IV

An assessment of the final life-cycle stage would not be complete without reference, first, to the poor law, the most important source of aid for the elderly, and second, to old-age living arrangements. A large proportion of elderly persons received some form of public assistance. Charles Booth estimated that in 1891, 28.5 percent of men over 65 in urban areas (exclusive of London) were in receipt of poor-law relief, over half of whom were relieved in the workhouse. The figure for *all* women over 65 was 31 percent, the large majority of whom were in receipt of outdoor relief. In a word, almost one in three old persons over 65 drew relief at some time during the year.[63] As David Thomson has argued, the poor law constituted "a formalized institution of income redistribution to which the two-thirds to three-quarters of the population who were non-propertied could look with a near-certain expectation of regular and prolonged assistance in old age."[64] Thomson also showed, however, that from the early 1870's on, this system of poor-law "pensions" broke down. Poor-law officials, urged on by charity reformers, launched what the Webbs called "a persistent crusade against Outdoor Relief as such, to any class or section of the pauper host." This campaign of the 1870's and 1880's led to an enormous reduction in the proportions of the elderly receiving a poor-law pension, and also to a reduction in the relative value of the pensions that were still paid.[65] Since older women, particularly spinsters and widows, had always received outdoor relief to a greater extent than old men, this "crusade" presumably had the fiercest impact on females. Between 1873 and 1892, the number of widows receiving outdoor relief fell from 53,502 to 36,627; at the same time, the number of old women in the workhouse increased. But older men were not unaffected by this policy change. Indeed, Thomson states that since "pensions" to men on the outdoor list "were cut more savagely than those to women," the proportion of old males in the workhouse remained a good deal larger than that of females. The workhouse, it seems, cast a larger shadow than ever over old men in the late Victorian period, particularly over widowers and single men, who were less able than old women to look after themselves, and whose relatives were less willing to house them. Even at the end of the "crusade" against outdoor relief, however, the rate of institutional residence for the elderly was very low. Only 5.8 percent of males (2.8 percent of females) aged 65–74 were in poor-law institutions.[66]

The elderly rarely lived entirely alone in Victorian England. In Preston in 1851, a third of people aged 65 and over lived with a married or widowed child, and just over a third with unmarried children. Only 6 percent (3 percent of males, 8 percent of females) lived alone.[67] In 1891, the proportion of elderly men and women reported as living alone in England was 13 percent (10 percent of males, 16 percent of females).[68] As for the elderly widowed, specifically, 41 percent of widows (50 percent of widowers) lived with a married child, 34 percent of widows (27 percent of widowers) lived with an unmarried child, and only 7 percent of widows (5 percent of widowers) lived with no other person in mid-century Preston. It should be added that 18 percent of widowers (but only 4 percent of widows) lived as lodgers.[69] In cotton towns, however, the child-minding needs of women factory workers led to a higher proportion of old widowed females living with their children. Yet in a sample of mid-century urban and rural areas, David Thomson also found that 40 percent of old widowed women were dependents in other people's households (half of these being their children's households); between 25 and 40 percent headed households consisting of their own children; while between 10 and 20 percent lived alone.[70] These figures, and some others, suggest not only that few among the old experienced residential isolation but also that widows continued to head independent households for as long as possible, taking in lodgers, and inhabiting the very worst housing, if necessary; and that many women continued to perform parental or surrogate parental roles in old age.[71]

A study of the life-course transitions of the nineteenth-century urban population thus reveals a number of pressure points, to which we shall have cause to return in later chapters. For those aged 15–24, there were the pressures both of working life, particularly in the shape of male apprenticeships and female domestic service, and of the possibility of conflict over the proper scope of parental discipline. For those in the prime of life, especially among manual workers, there were the pressures of the poverty cycle, particularly severe in the stage when the family was complete but children had not yet become net contributors to family income. In addition, there were the "critical life situations" of death (of spouse and children) and illness. For those, finally, in early old age and in late old age, there were the pressures for men of "life-cycle deskilling," illness, and accidents; and for both sexes, of widowhood, illness, the struggle to keep the wolf from the door, and an increasing resort to the poor law. So far, however, I have done little more than offer a generic or "heuristic" sketch of the main life-course transitions and the difficulties they might entail. The next step must be to situate the life cycle in the specific urban setting for which we have suicide data.

5

Kingston upon Hull: Economy, Society, Ecology

> Even more than most cities, Hull in our time was a place
> of revolving smells, according to the direction of the
> wind. Fish from the docks and the fish-meal factories,
> oil from the oil-seed crushing works, paint from the
> paint factories, wood from the timber yards, chocolate
> from Needler's and mixed smells from Reckitt and
> Colman's.
>
> Richard Hoggart,
A Measured Life

We now must have regard to place. It is one thing to provide an "ideal type" of the Victorian life cycle, but an equally important one to attach the life cycle to a specific urban setting. This chapter situates the Victorian life cycle in the economic, social, and ecological context of Kingston upon Hull. It examines the demographic characteristics of the town; its trading and industrial economy; its related occupational and social structure; its ecological patterns; and some features of the patterns of housing, health, and poor-law relief that prevailed.

I

The borough of Kingston upon Hull is situated on the north bank of the Humber estuary, twenty-two miles from the eastern seaboard, at a point where the deepwater channel comes close to the shore, and where

ILLUSTRATION 2: A bird's-eye view of Hull. Lithograph from a watercolor by Frank Noble Pettingell (1881). Hull City Museum.

the river Hull, flowing south from the Yorkshire Wolds, joins the Humber. The early Victorian boundaries ran along the Humber bank for about three and a half miles, and inland for about two miles. The entire area was bisected by the river Hull. The built-up area of roughly two square miles (by mid-century) lay largely to the west of the river. Immediately adjacent to the river was the old Walled Town, a "peninsula" of land surrounded by the three Town Docks: Queen's (1778), Humber (1809), and Prince's (1829). Building had spilled over the Walled Town, going north and west, in the late eighteenth century. To the east of the river Hull, building development hugged the bank of the river, moved into the area north of Victoria Dock (opened in 1850), and pushed up the Holderness Road. No hillock disturbed the dead-level topography of the town; no part was more than a few feet above sea level, and a few reclaimed areas to the east were actually below the high-water mark. As a result, open land drains intersected the moist soil of the town, and sewage disposal was a recurrent difficulty. An extensive dock system and good rail and water connections with the industrial regions of Yorkshire and the North Midlands made Hull the principal port of the region and the third port of the country in point of total trade (after London and Liverpool).[1]

The population of Hull rose from 65,670 people (30,279 males) in 1841 to 240,259 (117,453 males) in 1901, an increase of 266 percent. Until 1861, the decennial rate of increase was steady and moderate, well below that of the booming manufacturing towns in the West Riding of Yorkshire: Leeds, Sheffield, and Bradford. Migration in was considerable, especially in the 1840's, and by 1851, 50 percent of all townspeople had been born outside Hull.[2] In the 1860's, 1870's, and 1880's, however, Hull's population ex-

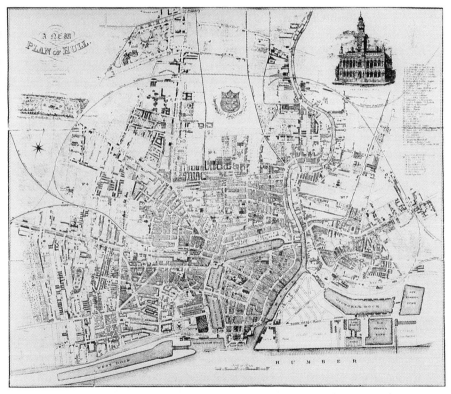

ILLUSTRATION 3: *A New Plan of Hull.* Engraved for *Stephenson's Hull Directory* (1842) by Goodwill & Lawson. Hull City Museum. By the time this plan was published, the population was over 65,000. The map shows that the line of the town walls has been entirely replaced by docks, which now mark the boundaries of the medieval town.

panded much more rapidly than the national average, and above the averages for the large industrial towns of the north of England. This growth was a function partly of a higher rate of natural increase (the excess of births over deaths) and partly of substantial net inward migration. Between 1871 and 1881, for example, net inward migration accounted for almost 9 percent of the 26 percent growth in population, or just over one-third.[3] Many migrants were displaced rural workers from the East Riding of Yorkshire and Lincolnshire, hard hit after 1874 by agricultural depression.[4]

At every census there was a surplus of females, although the ratio of women to men declined from 117 females per 100 males in 1841 to 104 females per 100 males in 1901.[5] The surplus of females was even more marked in the 15–24 and the 65-and-over age groups.[6] The surplus in the younger age group may have been due to the attraction of employment in the cotton mills from 1838; the surplus in the older age group came from the longer life expectancy of women. At every census, too, the age profile of the population remained remarkably similar, and extremely youthful. Just over one-third of all men were below 15 years of age, and over a half were under 25; just under one-third of all women were below 15 years of age, and just over a half were under 25. The peak of this youthful profile was reached in 1881 and 1891. By contrast, only 16 percent of males and 18 percent of females were aged 45 and above. The remaining 28 to 29 percent of both sexes were in the prime of life (25–44).[7] As for civil status, at each census between 1861 and 1901, approximately 37 percent of males aged 15 and above were single, 58 percent were married, and 5 percent were widowed. The figures for females aged 15 and above were 33, 55, and 12 percent, respectively. Civil status varied according to age group, of course. The largest difference was in the percentage married in the age groups, 15–24 and 25–44. In the first group, only 13 percent of males and 23 percent of females were married; the other 87 and 77 percent, respectively, were single. By contrast, in the prime of life, 75 percent of men and 76 percent of women were married, the highest rate of any age group. In the final two age groups, widowhood entered the picture, notably for the longer-lived sex. In the 45–64 age group, 25 percent of women, but only 10 percent of men, were widowed. Among those aged 65 and above, 62 percent of women and 34 percent of men were widowed.[8]

II

Hull was an important mercantile city throughout the nineteenth century. In broad outline, it imported raw materials (timber, grains, oilseed, bar iron, and raw wool) from northern Europe, via the Baltic, and exported manufactured goods (woolen and cotton yarns and manufactures, iron and steel goods, and machinery) from the West Riding, Lancashire, and the industrial Midlands. The heavy concentration of Hull's shipping trade on the Baltic led to a highly seasonal trade pattern, since the Baltic froze in winter, and to some trade disruption during European wars. In the economic history of the town, the 1860's marked a pronounced dividing line. The 1860–80 period was, it is generally thought, the most expansive economic phase of the century for Hull. An early and wholehearted conversion from sail to steam by Hull shipowners, plus reductions in railway rates and dock dues, allowed the mercantile community to share in the expansion of British overseas trade in these years.[9] The most significant developments in the second half of the century were a widening of Hull's trading connections, a marked increase in the volume of emigrant traffic, the growth of a coal export trade, an overall growth of port traffic, an expansion of dock facilities, and an enlargement of the mercantile community. Each of these changes warrants further consideration.

Successful efforts were made from the 1870's on to foster trade with the Americas, southern Europe, the Far East, and Australia. In particular, large amounts of wheat began to arrive from North America to supply the expanding flour-milling industry.[10] The volume of emigrant traffic from Scandinavia and eastern Europe also grew in the 1880's and 1890's. Most emigrants landed in Hull on the first stage of the journey to America; they were taken by emigration agents to special lodging houses in the streets near the docks before boarding the train for Liverpool and embarking on the next stage of their journey. The number passing through the port averaged between 50,000 and 60,000 per annum in the final two decades of the century. In keeping with the rest of the Baltic trade, emigrant traffic was seasonal.[11] Following the opening of the Hull & Barnsley Railway in 1885, the port also began to serve the South Yorkshire coalfield. Coal increasingly provided the export cargoes of bulk that Hull's trade had hitherto lacked.[12] Overall, shipping tonnages at the docks more than doubled between the 1870's and 1900.[13] To keep pace with these trade developments, new docks were built. Victoria Dock (1850), with its three timber ponds, was the principal landing place for Scandinavian timber. Albert Dock (1869), to the west of the Old Town, was built for larger vessels and for fishing smacks. But this was only the beginning. The center of gravity of the merchant shipping interest moved to the east of the town with the opening of the Alexandra Dock (1885), which was deep enough to accommodate the largest steam-powered cargo vessels, while the fishing smacks moved farther west with the opening of William Wright Dock (1880) and, in particular, St. Andrew's Dock (1883).[14] Finally, the size and specialization of the mercantile sector advanced in the second half of the century. Between the 1830's and 1890's, the number of merchants, commission agents, and brokers increased from approximately 380 (firms or individuals) to 1,200. By the last date, few were general merchants, but rather specialists in coal, timber, oil, fish and fruit, wine and spirits, corn or seed. In timber, corn, and fruit, the mortality of firms was high. Few mercantile firms, moreover, were equal in size and wealth to the merchants of Liverpool and London, with the exception of Thomas Wilson, Sons & Co., which had 42 ships in 1876, the largest privately owned shipping fleet in the world.[15]

The industrial development of the city was closely linked to this trading activity. A number of industries had their origins in the availability of imported raw materials, notably the oil, paint, flour, and sawmilling industries. Demand from these industries contributed, in turn, to increases in the oilseed, grain, and timber trades. The export of cotton yarn, moreover, was a causal factor in the decision to establish cotton manufacturing in Hull in the 1830's and 1840's. In addition, metal, engineering, and shipbuilding firms were established to serve the port, as well as to supply machines for the seed-crushing and flour-milling industries. From the 1840's on, finally, Hull was a major fishing port. Trawl-fishing expanded considerably in the following decades, as did the ancillary trades of shipbuilding, sail and rope making, carting, and coopering.[16] Industry in Hull was concentrated along two main axes, the Humber shore and the banks of the river Hull, forming the shape of an inverted T. Along the banks of the Hull River were ranged the seed-crushing and oil mills, the cement works, and the cotton mills. On the Humber shore, next to the docks, were the shipbuilding, ship-repairing, sawmilling, engineering, and fish-curing works. Outside of this pattern were the brewery just north of Queen's Dock, the paint and color works on Spring Bank, and the flour mills on Holderness Road.[17]

Hull's industrial economy was varied but far from expansive before 1870. The city's main manufacturing industry, in which Hull led the country, was seed crushing for the extraction of vegetable oils. It emerged around 1840, following the demise of the whale fishery; by 1858, there were 28 seed-crushing firms. Associated with this industry was paint and color manufacturing. In addition, before 1870, there were approximately 30 corn-milling and 11 shipbuilding firms. As yet these industries had no large labor force, each employing but a few hundred workers.[18] More important in this regard was the arrival in the late 1830's of cotton manufacture. At the 1851 census, cotton manufacture employed 2,235 people (1,253 women, or 12 percent of all occupied females), over half of whom hailed from the cotton towns of Lancashire and Cheshire or from Ireland.[19] The cotton mills were equipped with the latest machinery, but poorly managed. They were in financial difficulties by the mid 1850's, and the prospects for cotton workers only worsened between 1861 and 1865, when the American Civil War led to a shortage of raw cotton, short-time working, the ultimate closure of all the mills, and the resort to charity and the poor law. Production restarted, however, and cotton manufacture maintained a presence in Hull until 1894.[20] North Sea trawling was also established in the 1840's, assisted by the experience gained during whaling days of fishing in northern waters. From 1845 to 1865, trawl-fishing experienced considerable growth, to judge from the rapid rise in the annual number of fishing voyages.[21] By 1863, 270 fishing smacks were sailing from Hull, the bulk of which were in the hands of men who owned one or at most two boats, and who fished for themselves. Trawl-fishing, finally, spawned the ancillary trades of shipbuilding, sail and rope making, and fish curing.[22] Among the largest employers of male and female labor, however, were the trades supplying the clothing, food, drink, and housing requirements of the population. Millinery and dressmaking employed a large number of women; shoemaking and tailoring, "domestic" shopkeeping (butchers, bakers, and grocers), and building were numerically important for male employment.[23]

During the last three decades of the century, Hull's industrial economy grew more rapidly. It became centered around the oilseed, paint, flour-milling, cement, and fishing industries. A number of these industries were aided by the mechanization of the 1870's and 1880's. The seed-crushing industry saw the introduction of the Anglo-American hydraulic press; the flour-milling industry moved toward large steam-driven roller mills.[24] And the fishing industry took on its modern form with the transition from sail to steam trawling, which took place from 1885 on, and "the concentration of the fishing fleet into fewer and larger companies." The 1880's brought other far-reaching changes to the fishing industry: the end of the workhouse apprenticeship system (forcing owners to make do with casual labor) and the introduction of the fleeting system. No longer would individual smacks fill up with fish and return to port; in future they would "box" with a fleet of smacks and transfer their catch to a steam cutter, which would then return to port. Fleeting worsened the fisherman's lot. Ferrying the boxes of fish by rowing boat to the cutter was terribly dangerous, and voyages lasted for months on end. The adoption of winter fleeting was the final straw. Fishermen went on strike in 1880, and again in 1883, in the wake of a storm in which 23 smacks and 150 fishermen were lost— 6 percent of the entire workforce. In neither strike were the fishermen victorious. By 1900, the fishing industry was an important component of the port's economy. Upward of 450 deep-sea fishing boats belonged to the port; about 3,500 were employed as trawlermen, another 6,000 were in the 55 fish-curing smokehouses, at the fish market, and in the shipbuilding and engineering yards that supplied the fishing industry.[25] And, finally, the building industry was buoyant between 1866 and 1875, and again in the 1890's.[26] It remains only to emphasize that Hull's industry was sufficiently diverse to avoid the severe economic downturns characteristic of one-industry towns, and was composed, at least until the 1870's, of small-scale units, few of which employed more than 50 persons.[27]

III

Hull's employment structure was of a piece with the patterns of trade and industry. By the mid nineteenth century, workers in the transport trades (dock laborers, seamen, railwaymen, carmen, and carters) were the largest male occupational group, averaging 23 percent of all occupied men between 1851 and 1901. The next most important industrial groups were those working in metals and engineering (shipwrights, ship fitters, coachmakers, machinists) and in the building trades. Together, transport (essentially waterside) workers, engineers, and building workers made up approximately 50 percent of the male workforce in the second half of the nineteenth century.[28] Another important constant in Hull's employment structure was the ratio of females in the total occupied population. The average proportion of occupied females (as a percentage of total occupied population) between 1851 and 1901 was 26 percent (the proportion declining from 29 percent in 1851 to 24 percent in 1901). This figure of female employment was well below the national average of 31 percent (and in 1891 of 34.4 percent). The proportion of all women aged 15 and above who were occupied in Hull was 27 percent in 1901. This compares with the national figures of 39 percent in 1851 and 35 percent in 1911. In addition, most women workers were employed in domestic service, in the making of articles of dress, in the food and drink trades, and in textiles, in that order.[29] To these constants, however, we should add the changes that took place in Hull's employment structure in the Victorian period.

The evidence for the late 1830's is not entirely satisfactory. A survey carried out by the Manchester Statistical Society was restricted to the town part of Hull (the parishes of St. Mary's and Holy Trinity), and the occupation statistics in the 1841 census related to the town part and Sculcoates parish, not to the entire borough.[30] Even so, the broad outlines are clear. In 1839, when the Society did its survey, sailors, rivermen and boatmen, and dock laborers made up 28 percent of employed males (or 2,517 out of 9,123 occupied males); another quarter were engaged in supplying the basic needs of the population (shopkeepers, licensed victuallers, and clothing workers); and one-fifth were working in "handicrafts."[31] As for females, only 23 percent of those aged 21 and above had a definable occupation (or 2,606 out of 11,400). Of these women workers, 63 percent were domestic servants or employed at home as washerwomen, manglers, and charwomen;[32] and 18 percent were occupied in the clothing trades (milliners, seamstresses). On the basis of these figures, the Statistical Society concluded that "in comparison with manufacturing towns, a sea port affords little employment for women and children, and not very regular or constant occupation even for adult males."[33] The 1841 census confirmed these occupational patterns. Noticeable by their virtual absence were the fishing industry (though the Fishing, as it was known, arrived in the 1840's), and the oil-milling and paint trades.[34]

We are on firmer ground from 1851, thanks to improved census returns and the statistical work of Dr. Joyce Bellamy. Classification changes in the 1881 census led Dr. Bellamy to evaluate Hull's occupational structure in two stages, 1851–71 and 1881–1911, a practice I shall follow here.[35] In 1851, the manufacturing sector (notably metals and engineering, textiles, dress, food and drink, and building) accounted for half of all male workers, and transport workers made up almost a further quarter of the male labor force. The industrial groups expanding most rapidly between 1851 and 1871 were, first, metals and engineering (including shipbuilding), which went from employing just over 8 percent of all occupied males in 1851 to nigh on 15 percent in 1871, and, second, the building group, with 8 percent of the labor force in 1851 and over 10 percent in 1871. Gains were also posted by fishing (where many of the hands were apprentices below the age of 21), and by chemicals, oils, and paints. By contrast, dress and textiles lost ground, the latter badly affected by the cotton famine of the early 1860's. In the 1860's (and 1870's), the growth industries required mainly male labor; hence, employment opportunities for women were restricted principally to domestic service (50 percent of all occupied females) and dress (24 percent). The proportion of women employed in textiles (particularly cotton, where the ratio of women employed to men was 5 to 4 in 1847) fell sharply.[36]

Between 1881 and 1901, the pattern of male employment changed little.

The growth in port traffic, however, was reflected in an increasing volume and proportion of labor in transport occupations (particularly dock work and railway service). The number of transport workers rose from 10,490 in 1881 to 21,560 in 1901. Almost 30 percent of all occupied males (and over 20 percent of the total workforce) in Hull were employed in these trades in 1901. Little wonder that the town proved to be good soil for the "new unionism" in 1889, and that it should play host to a bitter, seven-week-long dock strike in 1893 during the employers' counteroffensive, which embroiled 7,500 dockers and 2,500 workers in associated trades.[37] As befitting a commercial city, there was a sizable white-collar workforce, a combination of employees in the civil service, local government, and teaching, plus clerks and commercial travelers. In 1891, 7.3 percent of all occupied males were white-collar workers. Employment in engineering and building fluctuated, the latter rising during the building boom of the 1890's from 4,727 to 7,119 workers. The proportion of fishermen also fluctuated, but this was owing mainly to changing methods of census enumeration. Moreover, the proportion of workers listed under "fishing" took no account of the numbers in other occupational orders who were dependent on the fishing industry.[38] The structure of employment was influenced in these years by the development of mechanization. Economies in the use of manpower were created in shipping and fishing (with the adoption of steam), and in flour milling, seed crushing, and cement manufacture, such that the labor force in these industries did not increase proportionately with output. In dock work and railway work, by contrast, there were few comparable economies, and the number employed in these occupations continued to rise.[39]

The pattern of female employment proved more changeful. If the ratio of females in the total occupied population stayed the same, the distribution within the occupational orders changed a good deal. The proportion of women workers in the food trades doubled between 1881 and 1901 owing to growth in the wholesale and retail distribution of food and in fish curing; the proportion in chemicals and oils quadrupled owing to the manufacture of "black-lead" and metal polishes. At the same time, the proportions to be found in domestic service, dress, and textiles declined.[40] By the end of the century, then, a more varied employment pattern existed for women. Yet, even in 1901, 45 percent of all occupied females still worked in domestic service. They included the 1,000 charwomen, many of whom were doubtless widows or the wives of unemployed husbands; and the 1,000 laundresses, half of whom were married or widowed, who supplied the heavy laundry needs of the shipping industry.[41]

This brings us to the relationship of occupation and age, for which we have a limited amount of evidence. It is possible to examine the proportions working in each of five groups of ages, and the types of work at which they were employed, at the end of the Victorian era. In 1901, among those aged 10–14, 15.6 percent of boys and 7.2 percent of girls were employed, the former mainly as messengers, porters, and watchmen, the latter in domestic service, chemicals, and dress. These figures doubtless underestimate the proportions of children in regular employment. Among those aged 15–24, 95 percent of males and 50 percent of females were occupied, the former in "the conveyance of men, goods and messages," in metals and building, in clerical jobs, and in the food, drink, and lodging trades; the latter in domestic service, dress, chemicals, teaching, and textiles. Significantly, young women workers constituted 37 percent of the labor force (male and female) in this age group. Practically all men in the prime of life (25–44 years) and in early old age (45–64) were employed; whereas only just over 17 percent of women in these age groups were listed in the census as occupied. In both age categories, men were employed, in rough order of priority, in transport, in metals and engineering, in building, in the food, drink, and lodging trades, in commercial and clerical work, in chemicals and oils, and as general laborers. Women in both age groups were employed as domestic servants, chars and laundresses, dressmakers, food dealers, lodging- or eating-house keepers, teachers, and nurses. Finally, only 59 percent of old men (aged 65 and over) were occupied, confirming that 65 was an employment threshold even in the pre-pension era. Old men worked in transport, building, and metals, and as tailors, boot- and shoemakers, food dealers, and general laborers. Only 11 percent of old women were occupied, in exactly the same jobs as women in early old age.[42]

The same evidence allows an assessment of the age profile of different occupations at the end of the century. Occupations that had a larger-than-expected proportion of young male workers aged 15–24 were the building trades of carpentry, joinery, and plumbing; clerical work; and cellarman and barman jobs in the drink trade. Most male clerks were under 35 years of age, and many were under 25. Fishing was also a young man's trade, few fishermen lasting into middle age. Large proportions of those in the prime of life, aged 25–44, worked as fishermen, railwaymen, and carmen and carters. Workers in early old age (45–64) were overrepresented in agriculture, dock work, boot- and shoemaking, and among shipbuilders and publicans. Indeed, the job of bobbing (or unloading fish) was kept for old fishermen. Workers in late old age (65 and above) were overrepresented

TABLE 5.1
Social Class Distribution in Hull in 1851
(20% sample of household heads)

Social Class	Pct.
I. Professional, managerial	5%
II. Lower professional, small employers	12
III. Skilled nonmanual workers	14
IV. Skilled manual workers	34
V. Semi-skilled manual workers	18
VI. Unskilled manual workers	18
TOTAL	100%

SOURCE: Tansey, "Residential Patterns," p. 45.
NOTE: Total has been rounded.

in agriculture, tailoring, and hawking.[43] Young female workers were to be found especially in domestic indoor service, teaching, and oils, chemicals, and paints. Those in early old age were overrepresented in charring, laundry work, and nursing, and among food dealers, and lodging- and eating-house keepers; those in late old age in charring and laundering. The civil status of occupied females was also recorded: 78 percent were unmarried, and 22 percent were married or widowed. Unmarried women were especially prominent in domestic indoor service and in dress, and important in teaching, food and lodging, and oils, chemicals, and paints. Married and widowed workers were also important in domestic service (especially charring), dress, and food and lodging.

The occupational data were reconfigured in 1973 to present a snapshot of the social stratification of the town at one point in time. Table 5.1 displays the findings of a 20 percent sample taken from the census enumerators' books for 1851 by P. A. Tansey. By combining classes III and IV, and thus adapting the Hull data to W. A. Armstrong's social stratification scheme, it is possible to compare Hull's social structure with those of other selected towns at mid-century.[44] The results are in table 5.2. The comparative figures suggest that Hull, like the other seaport listed, Liverpool, had large numbers in social classes IV and V, which is to be expected given how Hull's economy was heavily weighted with transport workers (dockers, seamen, keelmen, and watermen), and with oil millers and cement workers.[45] It is difficult to make much of the figures for class III, since they combine several distinct types of occupation: skilled manual workers, small shopkeepers, and nonmanual (especially clerical) workers. There was little class identification between these groups. Table 5.1 is more useful in this regard, suggesting that skilled manual occupations (in the building,

TABLE 5.2
Social Class Distribution in Selected Towns, 1851–71
(%)

Social Class	Hull, 1851	York, 1851	Liverpool, 1871	Camberwell, 1871
I. Professional, managerial	5%	8%	1%	2%
II. Intermediate	12	14	15	14
III. Skilled	48	51	44	65
IV. Semi-skilled	18	14	18	12
V. Unskilled	18	13	21	7
TOTALS	100%	100%	100%	100%

SOURCE: Dennis, *English Industrial Cities*, p. 189.
NOTE: Totals have been rounded.

clothing, provisioning, textile, and metals and engineering trades) were not unimportant to this industrial town. A full-fledged "aristocracy of labor" is not evident, however. The figures for classes I and II indicate, finally, that Hull's middle class was small in size, and its lower middle class less so, although both groups were roughly on a par with those of other seaports and industrial towns.[46]

This class catalogue neglects, however, the role of the lower middle class. Hull had a large petite bourgeoisie, made up of small businessmen, shopkeepers, builders, and publicans, plus white-collar salaried clerks, commercial travelers, and schoolteachers. As table 5.1 reveals, 26 percent of household heads in 1851 were small employers, lower professionals, or skilled nonmanual workers. The number of clerical workers in commerce and insurance expanded, moreover, with the structural shift in the late Victorian economy from manufacturing to services. Small producers persisted in the consumer trades, in particular: in clothing, boots and shoes, food and drink, hardware, and building (especially of working-class housing). In fact, it is no exaggeration to say that via retailing, services, and secondary manufacturing, small enterprise provided the infrastructure of Hull's economy and gradually took local government out of the hands of the substantial bourgeoisie. In a study of suicide, it is appropriate to emphasize, too, that this was an extremely fragile and unstable area of the local economy. Low capitalization and tight credit made the small producer especially vulnerable to economic fluctuation. Hence, small enterprises continually experienced a high turnover. The threat of failure cast its shadow over every small businessman and shopkeeper, exacerbating their anxieties about family status.[47]

IV

We should pursue the theme of employment security over a wider terrain. For this, we must turn to evidence of trade depression, strikes and unemployment; of underemployment, associated with the casual and seasonal nature of work; and of the hazardous nature of some occupations. I shall deal with each point in turn. Hull's economy was, as noted already, a diversified one, making the city less vulnerable to the rhythms of the trade cycle. Nonetheless, local evidence, supplemented by what we know of the state of the national economy, points to a number of difficult periods for sections of the Hull workforce. Trade depression affected the entire country in 1837, 1842, and 1848, and it would be surprising if Hull had escaped the impact. The late 1840's were indeed difficult years for the town. In 1847, many of the cotton workers in the Groves district of Hull were destitute owing to a strike to resist a wage reduction introduced by the manager in consequence of the Ten Hours Act. The Danes blockaded the Baltic in 1848–49. And in the summer of 1849, unemployment reached 2,000, or about 9 percent of the male labor force, just prior to the disruptive cholera outbreak of that year.[48] Two years later, the *Hull Advertiser* reported that the shipbuilding trade was in the doldrums, that shipwrights could find little or no work, and that the knock-on effect was hurting the town's tradesmen and shopkeepers. During the Crimean War, another Baltic blockade reduced the importation of Russian linseed and closed over 20 of the 27 oil mills for a time in 1855.[49] The early 1860's, as we have seen, were disturbed by the cotton famine. By 1862, cotton operatives were experiencing distress, as also were some 300 of the town's sailors, for whom Trinity House (which relieved "decayed master mariners" and their widows) came to the rescue, setting them to picking oakum, or old rope, a task typically given to prisoners and paupers.[50]

The national rate of unemployment went up at the end of the 1860's, but Hull seems to have weathered the storm. The building industry certainly remained buoyant in these years. The 1870's were relatively good years, although there was a downturn in building activity in 1877–78, and the national trade cycle dipped in 1879.[51] The next two decades were more troubled. In 1881, Hull dockers, seamen, and marine firemen struck for higher wages; they were defeated after four weeks.[52] In line with the national picture, 1884–86 were years of distress, particularly in wintertime. East Hull was worst hit, in part because the Alexandra Dock was opened in 1885 and those employed on its construction, navvies and skilled craftsmen both, were let go. A lot of rice and oatmeal was eaten, soup kitchens were resorted to, and weddings were postponed. The employment position was aggravated by migrants from the rural districts of the East Riding.[53] Likewise, the early and mid 1890s were difficult years. In 1891, severe weather caused distress among Hull laborers. Trade turned down in 1892, by the end of which 6,000 men were unemployed (or 10 percent of the male labor force), and a further 9,000 had only part-time work and reduced wages. In early 1893, the *Eastern Morning News* discovered from the local clergy that distress pervaded the town, with the exception of the fish dock and the seed-crushing mills. Within a few weeks, the continuous upward trend in the value of imports came to a grinding halt as the dock strike began. This was followed by the notoriously cold winter of 1894–95. To make matters worse, the Kingston Cotton Mill closed its doors in 1894, putting 1,000 operatives out of work. Distress was still evident in 1895, and in 1896 the engineers at Earle's shipyard, east of Victoria Dock, were on strike for four months.[54]

More consequential, because more pervasive, than unemployment, however, was gross underemployment, characteristic of towns with a high proportion of jobs that were casual or seasonal, or both. Trawlermen were essentially casual laborers; they never knew when they would be "on the fish" again.[55] Dock work was notoriously casual. Only the preferred dockers, known as "ticket-men," were assured of full employment; the casual docker had to join the pool of labor outside the dock gates each morning. Dock work was also seasonal, since the Baltic ports were icebound from December through May. For the same reason, most seamen were unemployed for two to three months each year. Seasonal fluctuations in the supply of raw materials, moreover, affected timber working and oil milling. The former was dormant during the winter (when the Baltic froze), and the latter was slack in the summer. Building workers earned less in the winter and were usually laid off in bad winter weather.[56] Seasonality was surmounted, wherever possible, by "dovetailing," or the planned integration of different jobs. In the summer, for example, oil millers would join the dockside competition for work. Married women could also dovetail, working as chars or laundresses during seasonal troughs in the male work cycle. And, lastly, short-time working was a standard feature of flour milling and rope making.[57]

The security of employment was also modified by accident and injury. Fatal and nonfatal accidents and injuries were a common event for fishermen, lightermen, watermen, seamen, dock and railway laborers, and building workers, occupations in which Hull was overendowed.[58] The fishing industry was more hazardous than coal mining; the losses of the great storms of, say, 1883 and 1894 punctuated an annual death rate of about 1 percent of the workforce. Injuries were more common still, and they tended to cause permanent incapacity, given the time taken to get medical treatment. Dockyard work was also accident-prone; possibly as many as one-third of all days lost in a dockyard were due to injuries. Those who managed to escape injury through accident still suffered a heavy physical toll from their labor.[59] The role of injury and physical exhaustion in the experience of suicide is emphasized in the second half of this book.

V

In view of the insecurity of employment, it seems likely that Hull was a town of considerable poverty. Further assessment of this fact requires an examination of the numbers in receipt of poor relief. The numbers relieved in Hull Union in the half-year ending March 25, 1851, were 839 indoor (i.e., in the workhouse) and 4,697 outdoor, a total of 5,536, or 10 percent of the total borough population aged 15 years and above. Since the borough population included a large part of the Sculcoates Union, the percentage relieved for Hull Union alone would have been higher still.[60] As the percentage of out-relief to in- and out-relief (85 percent) indicates, outdoor relief was used considerably at mid-century, the workhouse far less. The latter offered no solution, of course, to the problem of casual or seasonal employment, since it prevented the unemployed docker or sailor from searching for work. Significantly, petitions to the Poor Law Board in London reveal that the Hull poor-law guardians were well aware of the inadequacies of indoor relief.[61] Official poor-law policy, however, was to abolish outdoor relief, and this was vigorously pursued between 1871 and 1876. Nationally, the total number of outdoor paupers fell by a third. Nor were all those struck off the out-relief rolls relieved in the workhouse; the Poor Law Board hoped to shift more of the burden, especially of the aged, back onto families.[62] This policy seems to have affected Hull. In the week ending January 1, 1876, the numbers relieved were 841 indoor and 2,841 outdoor, a total of 3,682, or 4.2 percent of the borough population aged 15 and above. The percentage is less than half that of 1851, although it should be said that 1876 was a relatively good year for employment. It must be noted, too, that the percentage of out-relief to all relief was still at 77 percent.[63] The restriction of out-relief continued until the early 1890's. The upshot presumably was that fewer people received out-relief as a form of old-age pension between 1876 and 1893.[64]

What was the condition of the Hull poor, then, by the 1890's? First, we know that there was considerable local distress between 1892 and 1895. The boards of poor-law guardians refused, however, to organize relief through public works. By 1895, in Sculcoates Union, the numbers relieved were 584 indoor and 3,448 outdoor, a total of 4,032, or 3 percent of the total population in the Union. Again, the percentage of out-relief to all relief was 85 percent.[65] Second, and more important, the group most dependent on poor relief (and this was doubtless true of earlier periods) were the aged poor, those over 65. While only 3 to 4 percent of those aged 16–65 were relieved in Hull and Sculcoates in the twelve months, 1891–92, 29 percent of the over-65s in Sculcoates and 33 percent of the over-65s in Hull were granted relief.[66] In Hull, old women tended to be given out-relief, old men indoor relief; in Sculcoates, both old men and women were given out-relief most commonly. In Hull Union, according to Charles Booth, the parish gave the aged poor 1s. 6d. and bread, to which children added 1s. and charity 9d., making a total of 3s. 3d. Many spent a half of this on rent for a room in some large, insanitary house. Some of the aged, among whom women preponderated, earned a few shillings a week by charring, sewing, rag sorting, envelope folding, or nursing. The mariners' almshouses held about 600 aged poor. In Sculcoates, old women did laundry work and nursing, while old men could find little but odd jobs. "Younger men," said Booth, "are pressing old out of employment."[67] And, finally, figures provided by Seebohm Rowntree indicate that at the end of the century, the number of persons in Hull in receipt of poor relief was 2,907, or 3.5 percent of the population. This was a higher percentage than in York (2.1 percent), in the industrial towns of Bradford (1.3 percent), Leeds (2.0 percent) and Sheffield (1.8 percent), or in England and Wales (2.5 percent).[68] Hull's reputation as a town of poverty remained intact.

VI

It remains only to establish the ecological development of Hull, and the related housing and health characteristics of the population. Nineteenth-century Hull had four distinct residential regions (see fig. 6.13). First came the medieval nucleus, or Old Town district, 90 acres of low, damp land enclosed by the Hull River to the east and the town docks to the north and west. In 1801, 17,500 people, 58 percent of the borough population, lived within this ancient core in conditions of ever-increasing overcrowding. Most homes, let off in tenements of single or double rooms, were in confined courts or "entries," between four and nine feet wide, reached by narrow archways, "like entries to a beehive," which perforated the front line of shops, licensed houses, warehouses, banks, and offices of merchants and shipowners.[69] Poor artisans were at least close to their workplaces on the docks and Hull River. The immigrants from Brixham and Ramsgate, for example, who founded the trawling industry in the 1840's, were concentrated in Humber Street. Indeed, many immigrants were attracted to the rented accommodation and lodging houses (in Blanket Row and Salthouse Lane), not to mention the brothels, of the Old Town. Moreover, the town center had a high proportion of small households, with few families in the child-rearing stage of development.[70] Additionally, many skilled nonmanual workers lived in this area, where much of the retail trade and office employment was concentrated. Through 1861, the population was stable, but it declined thereafter (to 11,000 in 1881) as more dwellings were converted into shops and warehouses or demolished to make way for the new town hall.[71] If there is one area, then, that can serve as a test of the hypothesis that the rate of suicide was high in central, business-district, lodging-house, and migrant districts, it is the Old Town.

The second of Hull's four main regions was the "inner" town beyond the docks, essentially to the north and west of the Old Town. This region had been developed from the 1780's by the Hull Dock Company. The streets due north of Queen's Dock—Savile and George streets—were full of shops and business premises; beyond this—in Bond, Jarratt, and Albion streets—were fashionable houses owned by the professional and middle classes, plus the Royal Infirmary. Still farther north were streets of terraced houses occupied by the respectable working class.[72] Going west from the town docks, however, between Savile Street and the Paragon train station, and north of the station, a maze of narrow, crooked streets contained some of the worst jerry-built and insanitary housing in Hull. To the west of Prince's Dock were the brothels of Waterhouse Lane, Junction Dock Place, and Carr Lane; clustered around the railway terminus were many eating and lodging houses; and north of Paragon Station were the streets (West, Mill, Collier, and Brook) that formed the heart of Hull's Irish quarter, "Little Ireland." The last had an age structure typical of an immigrant district: a disproportionate number of young adults, many of whom used the lodging houses in Mill and West streets.[73]

The third main region was the secondary belt of working-class housing in the subdistricts of Drypool (or East Hull), Sculcoates, and Myton. This large area was the location of the best part of the town's working-class population in the second half of the century and was dominated by "terrace" or "bye-law" housing. This meant either conventional terraces along thoroughfare streets or cul-de-sac courts, 18 to 20 feet in width, running out from the main street, in which two rows of houses (between 12 and 22 in number) faced each other, with a pathway between them. The cul-de-sac terrace allowed higher building densities than the orthodox terraced street, and led to lower rents.[74] For the sake of clarity, each subdistrict will be treated in turn. First, in Drypool, residential development was confined to the southern end of Holderness Road, and to the streets between this road and the Victoria Dock to the south. The population reached 6,617 in 1861, then doubled to 12,425 in 1871. Further housing expansion in East Hull had to wait upon dock development, notably the Alexandra Dock (1885), and the associated growth of employment.[75] Second, to the north of the "inner" town lay the housing on both sides of the river Hull. To the west, in the eastern meander of the river, were the streets laid out by the Kingston Cotton Mill Company on land south of its huge factory in Cumberland Street. Hard by were the oil mills, flour mills, color works, and seed-crushing and cement works that made it Hull's most industrial area. On the east side of the river, to the south of the meander loop, near the mills of the Hull Flax and Cotton Mills Company, was a block of seven streets known as the Groves. The housing was insanitary and extremely overcrowded; the inhabitants were largely Irish-born cotton operatives.[76] The Irish-born were the most segregated population in the city, the spatial separation reinforced by occupational and religious difference.[77] In a city known as "the metropolis of Methodism," particularly Primitive and Wesleyan Methodism, St. Mark's Catholic Church was an anomaly.[78] Other features of this district were the large number of women cotton workers and the presence of Irish lodgers in Irish households.[79]

The final subdistrict was Myton, or the area at each side of the Hessle Road. The population of Myton rose substantially between 1831 (15,000) and 1851 (32,500), and by the latter date the area contained 38 percent of all townspeople and the most extensive block of high-density, working-class housing. In the next 40 years, with the arrival of trawlers, railways, and docks, Hessle Road expanded dramatically, shifting the town's center of gravity west. For many health and housing campaigners, Hessle Road was a region of overcrowded housing, high mortality, and unrelieved poverty, the depths of which were to be found in three notorious streets—Strickland, Wassand, and Walcott—at the rear of the William Wright Dock, jokingly known as "Faith, Hope & Charity."[80] But the spatial isolation of the district at the western end of the town and common dependence upon one industry created a tight-knit community, the likes of which were not normally met with outside coal-mining villages. Although fishermen were only a small proportion of the Hessle Road population, the industry dominated the area. The occupational bond was reinforced by internal recruitment: fishermen begat fishermen. Ancillary trades, even pubs and shops, moved to the beat of fishing. And when the elements in the North Sea took their toll, the community mourned. What impact the special conditions of the industry had upon family patterns, it would be intriguing to know. It is likely, however, that the long absences of deep-sea fishermen, and thus the need for women to assume most of the responsibility for the children, the home, and its finances, created a matriarchal support community in which women had some freedom of speech and action. It was the women who seem to have held the community together, including the elderly, who almost invariably lived in the same street or terrace as their married daughters and grandchildren. The strongest bond of all was between mother and daughter.[81] Thus, the Hessle Road district can serve as an area in which to test the hypothesis that the rate of suicide was low in tight-knit communities.

The middle-class suburbs constituted the last of Hull's four main regions. In this category were included the Beverley Road, and points west (particularly around Pearson Park, and along Spring Bank and Princess Avenue), the Anlaby and Holderness roads, and the Boulevard, the broad avenue between the Hessle and Anlaby roads, which became the desirable address for clergymen, doctors, merchants, and smack owners.[82] The most significant feature of these areas was their relative exclusiveness. In Hull, as in other industrial cities, the scale of residential segregation was less marked than once thought. Levels of segregation were particularly low within the working classes. Most residents of mid-century Hull, it seems, lived in districts with a range of occupational and class strata, from skilled to unskilled.[83] In these districts, too, there were high rates of residential mobility. The insecurities of employment and the narrow margin between income and subsistence needs meant that housing quality was determined less by occupational status than by income and the related stage of the life cycle (although proximity of workplace and the pull of community could also be influential).[84] Only among the most affluent stratum of the middle class was residential segregation at all marked before the end of the nineteenth century. The only significant social and spatial divide, then, was between class I, the upper business and professional class, and the rest, among whom there was much less residential differentiation.[85]

Rapid population expansion, a general worsening of overcrowding, and occasional severe epidemics caused Hull to have one of the highest mortality rates in the country throughout the century. Cholera struck in 1832, and typhus fever in 1847.[86] Cholera returned in 1849, and struck with an intensity that gave Hull the distinction of having the highest cholera death rate in the land: 287 deaths per 10,000 inhabitants. The distribution of cholera deaths shows that over 40 percent of victims lived in South Myton, or the Hessle Road district, and 26 percent in the Old Town. Sculcoates, to the northwest of the Old Town, was less affected, with 20 percent of the deaths, despite having been built up earlier than Myton and being as densely populated. The response of the poor-law guardians was to order the recipients of outdoor relief (at the risk of losing their relief if they failed to comply) and the Irish poor to "cleanse" their houses, and to produce certificates signed by landlords to show this had been done. A more meaningful response was the creation of a local board of health, which created housing bylaws to improve the standards of new cul-de-sac courts.[87] The next epidemic crisis came in 1881, when an outbreak of scarlet fever carried away over 600 people, most of whom were children. Between 1889 and 1894, finally, Hull was affected by the influenza outbreaks that racked the country.[88] A much more serious problem than periodic epidemic crises, however, was the heavy and prolonged mortality from infantile diarrhea. The maps of deaths from infectious disease, in the annual reports of the medical officer of health, plot the close relationship between disease and death on the one hand and housing conditions on the other. Most of the deaths from diarrhea occurred in overcrowded parts of the city: in "Little Ireland," Witham, and Wincolmlee, and on the south side of the Hessle Road, east of the Beverley Road, and north of the Queen's Dock. As late as 1908, Hull had the second highest death rate from diarrhea in the country, two and a half times higher than the average of the 76 largest towns.[89]

VII

In conclusion, for most of the period under scrutiny, Hull was at a stage of urban development in which population, trade, and industry were growing at their fastest; the occupational structure, at least for males, was at its most open; and housing supply just about kept pace with demand, albeit a high-density, poor-quality accommodation. In consequence, Hull attracted large numbers of young immigrants from the surrounding rural regions in East Yorkshire and Lincolnshire, especially from the mid 1870's on, when British agriculture faced hard times. They found jobs in the expanding transport sector, or in the cotton, cement, and oil-milling concerns that faced each other across the river Hull. Only a small proportion of the workforce had been born farther afield, notably the Irish who peopled the cotton mills. Hull was a heavily proletarian town, 70 percent of its household heads at mid-century being manual workers (36 percent being semi-skilled and unskilled workers). But a mercantile city also requires large numbers of skilled nonmanual employees: clerks, bookkeepers, customs collectors, dealers, agents, merchants, and salesmen, and Hull was no exception. It also had a middle-class elite of merchants, tradesmen, and professional men, although a parsimonious and slow-moving lot, if the doings of the Council and Board of Health are anything to go by.

A reasonably diverse economic base kept the more catastrophic depressions, characteristic of single-industry towns, at bay, but what Hull gained in this regard, it lost in the economic insecurities caused by the casual and seasonal nature of some of the main occupations. Many inhabitants must have faced a catch-as-catch-can existence, particularly in the winter months. In addition, the mortality of firms in the mercantile sector was high and the turnover of small domestic shopkeepers even higher; late-century mechanization ousted labor in the seed-crushing, flour-milling, and trawl-fishing industries; and dock work and fishing were notoriously dangerous occupations. Nor could women take up much of the economic slack, since Hull was a poor town for female waged labor, domestic service and clothing aside. For the sizable body of widows, there were only the worst-paid forms of domestic service, charring and laundry work. The elderly were particularly vulnerable in a job market where physical strength mattered, and in an era, notably the 1870's and 1880's, when the poor-law guardians pulled in their horns.

This, then, is the specific urban theater in which we shall examine the impact of life-cycle stages on the patterns and experience of suicide. The first step is to present the statistical patterns of suicide according to age, gender, occupation, social class, and habitat. These patterns offer important clues to the interpretation of the experience of suicide, which occupies the last section of this book.

Statistics

6

The Incidence of Suicide

Despite the observed inadequacies of the official statistics of suicide, they constitute a rough index of the numerical trend and distribution of suicide. While the figures undoubtedly understate the actual rates of suicide, I have accepted them, with certain qualifications, as representing the proportional rates in the respective sexes, age periods, and occupations. In this chapter, I make extensive use of the statistics collected from the cases of the coroners' inquests. The aim is to present in tabular and graphic form the main contours of suicide in Kingston upon Hull: the secular trends in the rate of suicide; the age, occupational, and social-class incidence of suicide; and the ecological distribution of suicide. While we need these measures in and of themselves, they will also be scrutinized for valuable clues to the subsequent exploration of the experience of suicide across the life cycle.

I

The database consisted of 493 male suicides (422 suicide verdicts; 71 open verdicts, in which there was strong affirmative evidence of suicide) and 236 female suicides (182 suicide and 54 open verdicts), making a grand total of 729 cases of suicide, extracted from inquests held between 1837 and 1899. I began by tracking the annual rate of suicide per 100,000 living in Hull across the Victorian era.[1] As figure 6.1 shows, however, the year-on-year fluctuations of the city's suicide rate between 1840 and 1899 were so volatile that they defy interpretation. In a few years, the rate leaped upward (in 1843, 1851, 1874, and 1895 for males; in 1846–47, 1869, and 1897

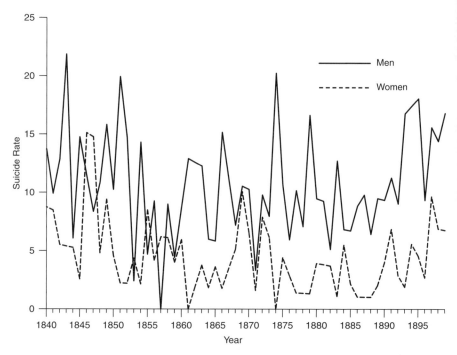

FIGURE 6.1. Annual Rates of Suicide, Measured by Suicide Verdicts Only, per 100,000 Living in Hull, 1840–99. Sources: Inquests, 1840–99; population censuses, 1841–1901.

for females); in other years, there were no recorded suicides at all (in 1857 for males; in 1861 and 1874 for females). For this reason, the seven-year moving average was employed. From figure 6.2 it is evident that through the 1840's, the male and female suicide rates remained fairly constant and were at a high level relative to subsequent years. From 1850 on, the rates sank sharply, until 1856 for males and until 1864 for females. The male suicide rate rose quickly between 1856 and 1864, then more steadily to 1877. The fall in the male rate in the late 1870's and early 1880's was followed by a steep rise from 1887 until the end of the century, for the first time exceeding the rates of the 1840's. The female suicide rate also rose quickly from 1864 on, but from 1870 on, it fell back to a low in 1877, where it hovered until 1886, after which it too went on a late-century ascent, but one that failed to reach the level of the 1840's. The inclusion of open verdicts has little or no impact upon the abovementioned trends in the seven-year moving average (see fig. 6.3). It seems, then, that the highest suicide rates for

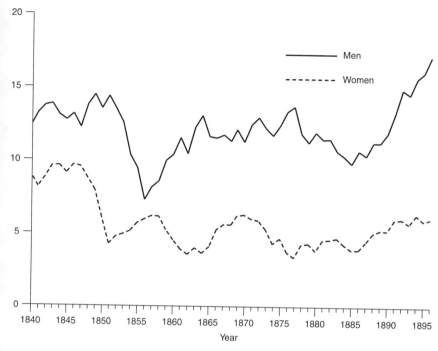

FIGURE 6.2. Seven-Year Moving Average of Rates of Suicide Only per 100,000 Living in Hull, 1840-96. Sources: Inquests, 1840-99; population censuses, 1841-1901.

both men and women were reached in the decades that act as bookends to the Victorian era, the 1840's and the 1890's.

It is difficult to know what to make of these rhythms of change in the scale of suicide. To assist an interpretation, I have calculated the average annual suicide rates for each decade separately (see table 6.1). The 1840's, a bleak decade economically speaking, looks to have been a particularly suicidal decade for both sexes, although whether this was a new phenomenon or the continuation of a longer trend, it is impossible to say. From the 1850's on, the male rate seems to approximate the national pattern—that is, a steady rise throughout the Victorian era, with an acceleration in the final decade.[2] Moreover, in the decade 1861-70, to judge from Olive Anderson's taxonomy of urban suicide in provincial England, the average annual rate of male suicide was higher—although not by a lot—in seaport towns of over 100,000 population (in which category Hull was included) than in similar-sized textile towns (including Bradford, Leeds, and Manchester)

FIGURE 6.3. Seven-Year Moving Average of Rates of Suicide and Open Verdicts per 100,000 Living in Hull, 1840–96. Sources: Inquests, 1840–99; population censuses, 1841–1901.

or iron and engineering towns (including Sheffield and Birmingham).[3] The rates for each decade (table 6.1) suggest, however, that the rise was not steady and continuous in Hull, and both in Hull and in the East Riding of Yorkshire, the 1880's saw a fall in the rate of male suicide.[4] It is possible that this fall is related to the fact that Hull's economy and population expanded rapidly in the 1870's and 1880's, resulting in a more youthful and employed (and thus less suicidal) population. The female rate, with the exception of the rise in the late 1860's, fell continuously from mid-century on, until a decided upward move in the 1890's. The rates for each decade (table 6.1) confirm this pattern, except that when open verdicts are added, the female rate rises slightly in the decade 1881–90. The national female rate, by contrast, rose slowly from mid-century until the upward leap of the 1890's.[5] We are still in need of a convincing explanation for the late-nineteenth-century increase in suicide. It is evident, however, that no explanation based on local conditions could comprehensively explain the

TABLE 6.1

Average Annual Suicide Rates per 100,000 Living in Hull, by Decade, 1841–99

Decade	Suicide verdicts			Suicide and open verdicts		
	Males	Females	Ratio	Males	Females	Ratio
1841–50	12.2	7.6	1.6 : 1	13.4	8.6	1.5 : 1
1851–60	8.7	4.6	1.9 : 1	10.1	5.2	1.9 : 1
1861–70	10.4	3.8	2.7 : 1	12.6	4.9	2.6 : 1
1871–80	10.1	3.1	3.3 : 1	12.3	4.1	3.0 : 1
1881–90	8.4	2.5	3.3 : 1	10.5	4.6	2.3 : 1
1891–99	13.8	5.2	2.7 : 1	14.4	5.9	2.4 : 1

SOURCES: Inquests, 1841–99; population censuses, 1841–1901.

NOTE: The population for each decade was calculated by taking the arithmetic mean of the population recorded in the two adjacent censuses.

phenomenon of a rising suicide rate that seems to have been a feature of the entire Western world.[6] It is also clear, from national figures, that the suicide rate continued to rise in the first decade of the twentieth century.[7]

What of the differences between the sexes? The difference in male and female suicide rates was by no means constant over the Victorian era. Using the seven-year moving average, we see that the male rate in 1840 was 1.6 times that for females, compared to a multiple of 2.9 in 1896. The most divergent point came, however, in 1876, when the male rate was 4.5 times that for females. Using the average annual suicide rates for each decade, we see that the ratio increased from 1.6 males to 1 female in the first decade, to a high of 3.3 males to 1 female in the decades 1871–80 and 1881–90, before dropping to 2.7 to 1 in the final decade (see table 6.1). The inclusion of open verdicts has the tendency to lower the male : female ratio in the last two decades of the century. In short, in the 1840's and 1850's, the suicide rates of the two sexes were closer than they were to be again in the nineteenth century, and after 1861, there were on average three male suicides to every female one.

At this point, however, it is necessary to say something about the ratio of attempted suicides to completed suicides. For every completed suicide, according to contemporary analysts, there are anywhere between six and twenty-five attempts. It is also estimated that women attempt suicide 2.3 times more frequently than men. I have made no systematic examination of attempted suicide in Hull. I did, however, search the local press for the first year of each decade between 1851 and 1891, or five years in all. Sixty-six cases of attempted suicide were reported, two-thirds of them in the years 1881 and 1891. Forty-four women attempted suicide, or a ratio of two female attempts to every one male attempt. Three-quarters of the females tried either to poison or to drown themselves. The age of the attempters was rarely given, but where it was, youth is evident: three were teenagers, four were in their twenties, three in their thirties. The occupations of the women included two domestic servants, two prostitutes, a waitress, and a brothel keeper; six others were the wives of laborers, a lumper, a lighterman, a plumber, and a blacksmith. The male attempters included a beerhouse keeper, a jeweler, a painter, a plasterer, a shoemaker, a brushmaker, a fisherman, a seaman, a boilermaker, and an army pensioner. From the brief press reports of these cases, it is evident that many attempts took place in police cells following arrest for some offense; a number were non-residents, visiting or passing through the city; many were rescued by, or handed over to, a police constable; many were intoxicated at the time; many had quarreled with a spouse or lover before the attempt; and a few had previously attempted suicide.

Attempted suicide was an indictable offense, triable in a higher court and liable to a maximum sentence of two years' imprisonment. In fact, however, all but one of the 66 cases were heard by the police magistrate, and practically all were dealt with leniently. They were remanded to prison or the workhouse for a week, then either ordered to find sureties for good behavior or admonished and discharged into the safekeeping of a husband, family member, or friend. In only one case did the magistrate commit to the Assizes, on the grounds that attempted suicide in Hull prison was becoming a common occurrence. The judge at the York Assizes was not convinced that the woman should have been committed, and he discharged her. When she attempted suicide again, however, she was sent to the Leeds Assizes, where she got nine months' imprisonment. In short, the Hull evidence bears out Norwood East's examination of 1,000 cases remanded to Brixton prison between 1907 and 1910, which found that male attempters were young (half were under 35 years of age); and confirms East's and Anderson's remarks on the lenient attitude of magistrates from large urban areas, who sent for trial only the most hardened offenders.[8]

II

Victorian suicidologists were aware, as S. A. K. Strahan puts it, "that self-destruction increases proportionately as age advances."[9] More specifically, as the government statistician Dr. William Ogle showed, the suicide rate between 1858 and 1883 in England and Wales rose "steadily in each successive age period, reaching its maximum in the 55–65 years period of life, when, after remaining almost stationary for another decennial period, it again falls." This statement was said to be true of both men and women, although with certain differences. The male and female rates, Ogle demonstrated, "diverge more and more widely with the advance of age, but . . . the regularity of the scale is broken at two periods, namely in the 15–20 and in the 45–55 years periods." The latter break was put down to the menopause; the former (in which the male and female rates were inverted for the only time) was ascribed to the effects of puberty.[10] More recently, Douglas Swinscow, showing the suicide rates by decades from 1861 to 1921, and by four age groups, has revealed that among males the rates increased with age, the age group 65 and over having the highest rate among men; whereas among females the rates increased with age up to the 45–64 group, but fell in the age group 65 and over.[11] Anderson's contribution to this discussion was to reveal the changes that occurred between the mid and late Victorian years, notably, the sharp increase in suicide among males in their late teens, and especially in old age. Between 1860 and 1914, she claimed, the difference between the sexes became greatest among people over the age of 65, as old men became considerably more suicide-prone. In addition, the difference in suicide rates of males at different stages of life became more pronounced. Already in the 1860's, in industrial towns, suicide was 21 times more common among men aged 55–64 than among youths aged 15–19 (while in all other provincial towns, the suicide rate was 12 times more frequent). Anderson also notes, however, that between 1860 and 1900, suicide grew at a similar speed for both men and women in the prime of life (25–44 years), and that "it was women of this age who were chiefly responsible for the massive increase in the female suicide rate which occurred in the 1890s."[12]

Let us turn, then, to the age- and sex-specific figures for Kingston upon Hull. First, the absolute incidence of suicide at each age. Figures 6.4 and 6.5 indicate that there was a peak of male suicide at 45 years of age, with secondary peaks at 46, 50, 55, and, if open verdicts are included (not shown in the figure), 57 years of age.[13] The peak of female suicide came earlier, at 40 years of age, with secondary peaks at ages 45, 48, and 56. When open verdicts are included (not shown in the figure), secondary peaks of female suicide appear at the younger ages of 18, 25, 27, 30, and 34. The mean age of male suicide was 45 (46 with open verdicts added); the mean age of female suicide was 44 (42 with open verdicts). The median age of male suicide was identical with the mean; the median age of female suicide was 43 (41 with open verdicts). These figures alert us to the possibility of life-

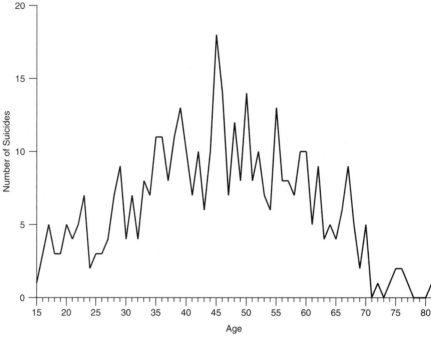

FIGURE 6.4. Incidence of Male Suicide, Measured by Suicide Verdicts Only, at Each Year of Age from Fifteen Years in Hull, 1837–99. Source: Inquests, 1837–99.

cycle pressures: for men as they began to enter old age and experienced the transition from regular work to less work or unemployment; for women as they began to negotiate the "change of life," widowhood, and poverty.

Table 6.2 presents the suicide rates for each sex at eight different groups of ages in each of the Victorian decades. The rates are rather volatile, as a result of the small number of cases in, for example, the over-75 age group. Taking the rather safer average figure for all the decades, we can see that the male suicide rate rose in each successive age period to a maximum at 55–64, after which it fell; whereas the female suicide rate rose until 45–54, fell in the next age period (55–64), and reached its maximum at 65–74 (at least for the first three decades and the last decade of the Victorian period). In short, the female rate for Hull differs from the national rate, which reached its maximum at 55–64. The range of female rates was smaller than that of male rates. This is evident from the differences in suicide rates at different stages of life. In the 1890's, suicide was nine times more common among men aged 55–64 than among men aged 15–19, and over fourteen times more common than among men aged 20–24. By contrast, suicide

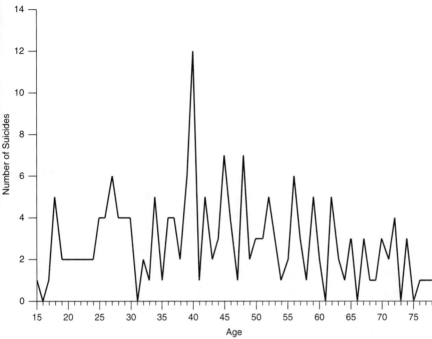

FIGURE 6.5. Incidence of Female Suicide, Measured by Suicide Verdicts Only, at Each Year of Age from Fifteen Years in Hull, 1837–99. Source: Inquests, 1837–99.

TABLE 6.2
Average Annual Mortality from Suicide by Eight Age Groups per 10,000 Living in Hull, 1841–99
(suicide verdicts only)

	Age group							
	15–19	20–24	25–34	35–44	45–54	55–64	65–74	Over 75
Male								
1841–50	6.1	8.9	10.1	16.8	50.1	35.8	21.2	0.0
1851–60	4.8	9.7	2.8	7.4	38.4	42.0	19.3	0.0
1861–70	7.8	3.9	7.0	24.9	19.5	47.5	15.5	48.5
1871–80	0.0	6.5	5.4	20.9	26.7	40.3	65.9	0.0
1881–90	2.5	9.2	7.3	15.8	22.0	23.1	51.6	32.9
1891–99	4.8	3.0	14.8	23.8	41.0	43.2	18.3	36.4
AVE.	4.3	6.9	7.9	18.3	32.9	38.6	32.0	19.6
Female								
1841–50	0.0	6.9	8.7	8.3	23.7	13.9	31.6	19.9
1851–60	4.4	2.0	5.1	6.8	7.1	14.7	26.7	0.0
1861–70	1.9	1.8	4.4	7.4	7.9	3.0	27.8	14.3
1871–80	0.0	1.5	4.5	4.9	10.1	10.0	4.5	0.0
1881–90	0.0	1.2	4.3	9.5	6.7	2.1	0.0	0.0
1891–99	5.4	1.8	4.5	9.2	10.5	14.9	17.5	0.0
AVE.	1.9	2.5	5.2	7.7	11.0	9.7	18.4	5.7

SOURCES: Inquests, 1841–99; population censuses, 1841–1901.

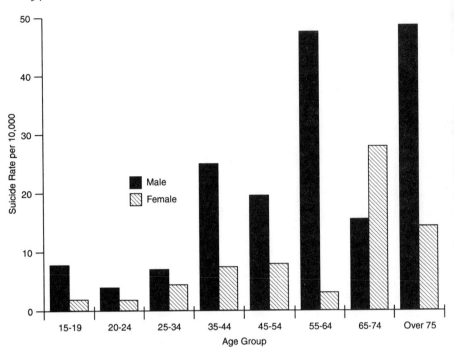

FIGURE 6.6. Average Annual Rates of Suicide, Measured by Suicide Verdicts Only, by Eight Age Groups per 10,000 Living in Hull, 1861-70. Sources: Inquests, 1861-70; population censuses, 1861 and 1871.

was only three times commoner among women aged 65-74 than among women aged 15-19, and only four times commoner than among women aged 25-34. Figures 6.6 and 6.7 show the information for the one decade of 1861-70.[14] Comparing these figures with comparable ones in Anderson's national study, the Hull profile approximates most closely the profile of what Anderson called "industrial towns," as distinct from "non-industrial towns" (in which seaports like Hull were included).[15] The Hull profile (see fig. 6.7) also follows, at least to some degree, the typical female pattern of a rise in suicide at puberty (15-19 years) and menopause (45-54).

Tables 6.3 and 6.4 and figures 6.8 through 6.11 present the suicide rates for each sex at only four different groups of ages. Again, the Hull figures diverge from the national picture. The age group 45-64 turned in the highest rate among men (with an average of 35 suicides per 10,000), not the age group 65 and over. Among women, the highest suicide rate belonged to the age group 65 and over, not the age group 45-64. As the figures also indicate, the female suicide rate in all four age groups was highest in the decade

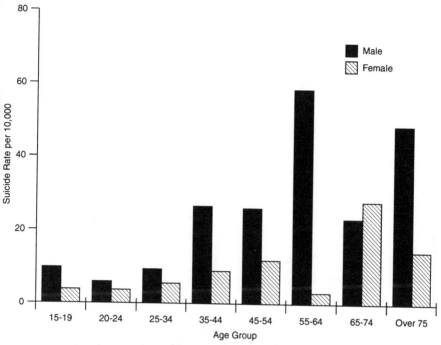

FIGURE 6.7. Average Annual Rates of Suicide and Open Verdicts by Eight Age Groups per 10,000 Living in Hull, 1861-70. Sources: Inquests, 1861-70; population censuses, 1861 and 1871.

1841-50. The rate for males aged 45-64 fell from the 1840's until the sharp rise of the 1890's. And the rate for males aged 65 and over rose considerably in the 1870's and 1880's, at the same time as the rate for females aged 65 and over (in marked contrast to the first three decades) declined rapidly (even with open verdicts added, for which see fig. 6.11). Indeed, there was no recorded verdict of suicide by a woman over 64 between 1874 and 1894 inclusive.[16] Thus the figures bear out Olive Anderson's argument that the statistics of suicide "point to an experience of old age which became more harsh for men but not for women from the 1870s."[17]

Additional figures allow us to underscore the contribution of the aged to the suicide toll. Men aged 45 and above constituted, on average, 26 percent of the Hull male population aged 15 and above in the Victorian era, yet 54 percent of all male suicides (67 percent in the 1851-60 decade). As much as 45 of the 54 percent was contributed by men aged 45-64. The equivalent figures for women aged 45 and above were 28 percent of the total female population aged 15 and above, yet 47 percent of all female suicides

TABLE 6.3
*Average Annual Mortality from Suicide by Four Age Groups
per 10,000 Living in Hull, 1841–99*

(suicide verdicts only)

	Age group			
	15–24	25–44	45–64	65 and over
Male				
1841–50	7.5	12.8	44.7	15.6
1851–60	7.2	4.8	39.8	14.0
1861–70	5.9	14.6	29.9	23.5
1871–80	3.2	11.9	31.9	51.1
1881–90	5.7	11.1	22.4	47.4
1891–99	3.9	18.7	41.8	22.5
AVE.	5.6	12.3	35.1	29.0
Female				
1841–50	3.7	8.5	19.9	28.3
1851–60	3.2	5.8	10.0	19.2
1861–70	1.8	5.7	6.0	24.0
1871–80	0.8	4.6	10.0	3.3
1881–90	0.6	6.5	4.9	0.0
1891–99	3.6	6.4	12.2	12.5
AVE.	2.3	6.3	10.5	14.5

SOURCES: Inquests, 1841–99; population censuses, 1841–1901.

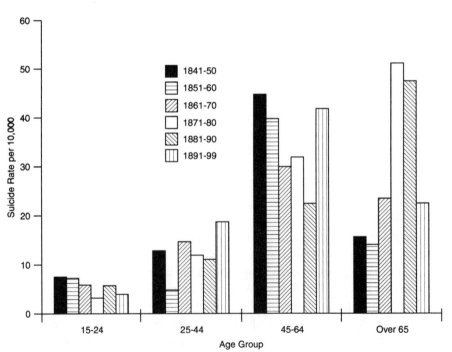

FIGURE 6.8. Average Annual Rates of Male Suicide, Measured by Suicide Verdicts Only, by Four Age Groups per 10,000 Males Living in Hull, and by Decade, 1841–99. Sources: Inquests, 1841–99; population censuses, 1841–1901.

TABLE 6.4
Average Annual Mortality from Suicide by Four Age Groups
per 10,000 Living in Hull, 1841–99
(suicide and open verdicts)

	Age group			
	15–24	25–44	45–64	65 and over
Male				
1841–50	9.0	12.8	49.2	23.4
1851–60	7.2	5.6	43.2	35.1
1861–70	7.8	16.6	38.1	29.3
1871–80	4.8	14.0	40.6	55.8
1881–90	7.0	13.1	30.2	54.7
1891–99	5.9	19.0	47.1	28.1
AVE.	6.9	13.5	41.4	37.7
Female				
1841–50	6.1	9.4	21.7	28.3
1851–60	3.2	5.8	12.9	24.0
1861–70	3.7	6.9	8.3	24.0
1871–80	2.3	6.2	11.0	6.6
1881–90	5.2	9.4	7.3	2.6
1891–99	5.4	8.4	12.9	14.5
AVE.	4.3	7.7	12.3	16.7

SOURCES: Inquests, 1841–99; population censuses, 1841–1901.

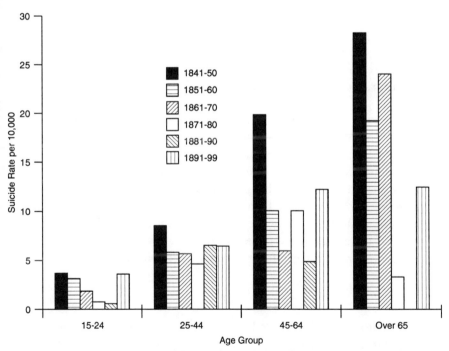

FIGURE 6.9. Average Annual Rates of Female Suicide, Measured by Suicide
Verdicts Only, by Four Age Groups per 10,000 Females Living in Hull, and by
Decade, 1841–99. Sources: Inquests, 1841–99; population censuses, 1841–1901.

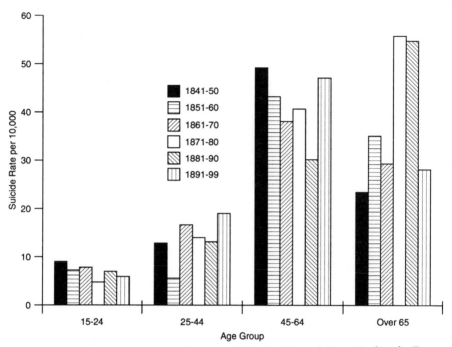

FIGURE 6.10. Average Annual Rates of Male Suicide and Open Verdicts by Four Age Groups per 10,000 Males Living in Hull, and by Decade, 1841–99. Sources: Inquests, 1841–99; population censuses, 1841–1901.

(although the figure fell to only 26 percent of suicides in the 1881–90 decade).[18] The ratio of male to female suicides among the elderly was also greater than in the general population. For the age group 45 and above, the male suicide rate was greater than the female by a ratio of 3.7 to 1 for the Victorian period, although this was a combination of a low ratio for the years 1841–70 and a high ratio for the years 1871–99. The average ratio also masks the fact that the male : female ratio was highest in the age group 55–64 (averaging 6.6 males to 1 female), lowest in the age group 65 and over (the ratio being in favor of females between 1841 and 1870).

III

In what seasons did people kill themselves? It was a commonplace of nineteenth-century suicidology that self-destruction increased from January to June, along with the increase of daylight hours. Suicide was commonest, then, in spring and summer. William Ogle explained this cyclical

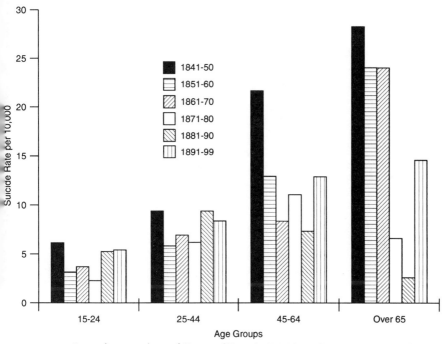

FIGURE 6.11. Average Annual Rates of Female Suicide and Open Verdicts by Four Age Groups per 10,000 Females Living in Hull, and by Decade, 1841–99. Sources: Inquests, 1841–99; population censuses, 1841–1901.

regularity in the following manner: "[A]s the days grow longer, the movement of life . . . becomes more and more active; and . . . the changes in the amount of suicide correspond to the consequent changes in the amount of mental excitement." [19] At the century's end, Emile Durkheim likewise linked the rhythm of suicide to the "seasonal fluctuations" of "social activity." [20] Historians have confirmed these cyclical findings, at least for the early modern period. From the sixteenth century on, according to Michael MacDonald and Terence Murphy, the peak months for suicide were the spring and early summer. One third of suicides in eighteenth-century Paris killed themselves in March, April, and May.[21] And the data from twentieth-century Britain, with one twist, also establish that "the favourite season for committing suicide is clearly from spring to about midsummer." [22] The twist is that some contemporary studies point to a second peak (especially for female suicides) in October–November. It would be surprising if Victorian Hull failed to correspond with this barrage of findings.

In the five months of March to July, 45 percent of all male suicides and

FIGURE 6.12. Average Number of Suicides by Month and Sex in Hull, 1837–99.
Source: Inquests, 1837–99.

46 percent of all female suicides occurred. April was not, however, "the
cruelest month." As figure 6.12 shows, the cyclical peak differed between
the sexes: male suicides peaked in June; female suicides in March, with a
secondary peak in July. The figure also illustrates that for both male and
female suicides in Hull, there were two cycles. If the first was spring and
early summer, the second was late autumn; more specifically, an October peak for women, a November peak for men. The explanation of this
seasonal distribution is not immediately apparent. If the spring and summer peak had indeed to do with increased social activity (business and
pleasure), then how to explain the October–November peak? If men were
affected by the annual employment cycle, say, why were there not more
suicides in the winter months (December to February)? One hypothesis is
that the high number of suicides in March to June is "a delayed effect of
conditions in the winter months, when the weather is bad, sickness . . .
is rife, and many industries suffer seasonal unemployment." By the same
token, the lower number at the end of the year "could be due to a persis-

TABLE 6.5
Methods of Suicide According to Sex, 1837-99

Method	Male				Female			
	Suicide verdicts		Suicide and open		Suicide verdicts		Suicide and open	
	No.	Pct.	No.	Pct.	No.	Pct.	No.	Pct.
Hanging or strangling	206	48.8%	208	42.2%	67	36.8%	67	28.4%
Drowning	19	4.5	69	14.0	8	4.4	54	22.9
Cutting, stabbing	62	14.7	62	12.6	30	16.5	30	12.7
Poison	71	16.8	83	16.8	71	39.0	78	33.1
Firearms	47	11.1	47	9.5	0	0.0	0	0.0
Jumping from height	4	0.9	8	1.6	5	2.7	6	2.5
Railway	9	2.1	12	2.4	1	0.5	1	0.4
Other	4	0.9	4	0.8	0	0.0	0	0.0
TOTAL	422	100.0%	493	100.0%	182	100.0%	236	100.0%

SOURCE: Inquests, 1837-99.
NOTE: Totals have been rounded.

tence into the early winter of the effects of the contrasting benefits of the summer months." [23]

How did Victorians kill themselves? Statistics for the entire country suggest that in the third quarter of the nineteenth century, 40 percent of male suicides used the method of hanging or strangulation, 20 percent cut their throats with knives and open razors (appropriately known as "cut-throats"), 15 percent drowned themselves, 7 percent used poison, and another 7 percent used firearms. By contrast, only one-quarter of females hanged themselves and 13 percent cut their throats, while one-third drowned themselves and 17 percent used poison. Hardly any women used firearms. In short, women resorted to drowning and poison twice as often as male suicides.[24] The same statistics also suggest that during the last quarter of the century, a smaller proportion of men hanged themselves and a larger proportion used poison and firearms, while more women used poison. Indeed, the proportion of suicides ascribed to poison almost doubled between the mid Victorian and Edwardian years.[25] In the case of Hull, the figures for suicide methods bear some approximation to the above, but also display some marked differences. As table 6.5 shows, nearly one-half of all male suicides in Hull hanged themselves, 16 percent used poison (over twice the national proportion), nearly 15 percent cut their throats, and 11 percent used firearms. Less than 5 percent of male suicides drowned themselves, a sizable reduction on the national figure of 15 percent. Among female suicides, almost two-fifths used poison (much greater than the national figure of 17 percent), 37 percent hanged themselves (again greater than the national proportion of a quarter), and 16 percent cut their throats. Only 4.4 percent drowned themselves, which is considerably lower than the national figure of one-third. Only when open verdicts are added do the proportions of those who drowned themselves increase: 14 percent of male "suicides" and 23 percent of female "suicides." Obviously, without open verdicts, drowning would be remarkably under-represented in this port city.[26]

If the Hull figures confirm that a smaller proportion of male suicides hanged themselves and cut their throats at the end of the century, they do not signal any proportionate increase, let alone a doubling, in the use of poison. The percentage of males using poison fell from 22 percent in 1837–59 to 14 percent in 1860–79, and it rose only slightly, to 16 percent, in 1880–99. The figures for females were 41, 35, and 39 percent, respectively. The addition of open verdicts does little to alter this pattern. The main change over time is to be found in the use of firearms, which increased from 8.4 percent of male suicides in 1860–79 to 14.2 percent in 1880–99. During the Hull dock strike, the sale of revolvers was said to have risen sharply, and in the two subsequent years, 6 of the 37 male suicides (or 16 percent) shot themselves.[27] Railway suicide was always a minority method. Even in the period 1880–99, only 2.3 percent of male suicides used trains to destroy themselves.[28] The methods of suicide varied according to age. Hanging was the main method of choice for male suicides aged 45 and above, 60 percent of whom hanged themselves, while only 17 percent used poison or firearms. By contrast, 50 percent of those aged under 35 years used poison or firearms, and only one-quarter hanged themselves. It is hard to explain why younger men should have preferred poison and guns, to which presumably they had no greater access than older men.[29] For one suicide method, finally, that of poisoning, we can provide an additional breakdown, the type of poison used.

The most frequently used poisons were laudanum and other opiates, accounting for 34 of the 71 male suicides (43 of the 83 suicide and open verdicts) for the period 1837 to 1899, and 34 of the 71 female suicides (37 of the 78 suicide and open verdicts), or almost one-half of both male and female suicidal poisonings.[30] As Anderson notes, moreover, the choice of poisons was influenced by simple accessibility. Poisonous cleaning materials and household remedies for common ailments were frequently turned to, especially by women.[31] Between 1870 and 1899, 68 percent of female self-poisonings involved vermin killer, carbolic acid (a popular disinfectant), oxalic acid (used in the home to clean brass and straw bonnets), and laudanum (used as a medication). Close to one-half of *all* female suicidal poisonings were with products found around the house (oxalic acid, arsenic, vermin killer, carbolic acid, strychnine, corrosive sublimate, and phosphorous), all of which would have caused painful deaths.[32] Employed also were poisons used as tools of certain trades.[33] Cyanide of potassium (used in electroplating and in photographic development) was used by a 20-year-old photographer to kill himself in May 1886, by a banker's clerk who had taken up photography as a hobby two months before his suicide in October 1879, and by an ironmonger who used the substance in his business and in his suicide in August 1894. A taxidermist used corrosive sublimate in his job and to kill himself in July 1896; two surgeons swallowed prussic acid (hydrogen cyanide).[34]

IV

Next we turn to the occupational and social class (see table 5.2) distribution of suicides. As before, we begin with the evidence that has come down to us. William Ogle's 1886 article dealt particularly with the impact of occupation upon suicide rates. He calculated the suicide rate among males for various occupations in England and Wales for the years 1878–83, adjusted for age. The least suicidal occupations, to judge from Ogle's findings, were those that involved heavy manual labor, "carried on in the open air, and by men who are comparatively uneducated" (miners, quarrymen, general laborers, shipwrights, bricklayers, gardeners, and fishermen). The most suicidal were "sedentary occupations" (particularly the professions of law and medicine, including chemists), and "callings that notoriously lead to an intemperate mode of life" (soldiers, publicans and innkeepers and their servants, butchers and greengrocers, domestic servants, and commercial travelers, brokers, and agents). In addition, commercial and law clerks were highly suicidal. Ogle attributed the high rate among professional men to access to the means of destruction ("the medical man and the chemist in his poison chest") and to the strain of "prolonged mental work." Soldiers— who headed the entire list, with a suicide rate close to twice that of the next most suicidal occupation—also had access to a means (their rifles), and they were notoriously intemperate, as were publicans, and also butchers and grocers, who often fortified themselves with spirits at early morning markets.[35] To Ogle's explanation for soldiers' proneness to suicide, a discussant added the point that the army was the refuge of "people of bad character and habits."[36] Retired, as distinct from active, soldiers were also probably highly suicidal, given the difficulties—both occupational and financial—faced by discharged soldiers in adjusting to civilian life.[37] The middle ranks of Ogle's table of suicide were occupied by skilled artisans (tailors, shoemakers, painters, blacksmiths), factory hands, farmers, and general shopkeepers. In short, while industrial occupations and those characteristic of seaports had average-to-low suicide rates, professional, artisanal, and service jobs had high suicide rates.[38] A common denominator of the high-rate group, moreover, was that many were in some form of independent business for themselves, and not employees, with all the financial strains this might entail.[39] Finally, Ogle pointed to the correspondence between high suicide rates and higher levels of education; and to the parallelism of high suicide rates, high insanity rates, and high general mortality rates among lawyers, medical practitioners, soldiers, commercial travelers, publicans, and hotel servants, the last two groups being vulnerable to tuberculosis, caught from their transient customers, and prone to alcoholism. As he concluded, "the same occupations and habits of life as conduce to general unhealthiness conduce also, in general, to self-destruction."[40]

We are less well served when it comes to social class variations in suicide rates. What evidence we have from the period, and that from the first third of the twentieth century, suggests that suicide among both males and married women was most frequent in table 5.2's social class I (professions; highest ranks of business) and especially in class II (entrepreneurs, managers, clerks, and retail traders); was least frequent in social classes III (skilled workers) and IV (semi-skilled workers); and went up again in social class V (unskilled workers). In short, as Anthony Giddens has concluded, "rates of suicide tend to be highest at both ends of the class hierarchy, with rates among those in the very lowest strata matching or even [exceeding] those of men in the highest class groups."[41] The highest rates among the laboring classes are said to have been among migratory and casual workers, whose employment security was most precarious and who were most subject to spells of unemployment. Thus suicide was most frequent among those of changeable economic status.[42] This was particularly the case in later life. At age 65 and over, the male suicide rate was highest in social class V, followed closely by class III (skilled workers).[43]

The occupational data for Hull do not allow a direct comparison with William Ogle's findings. Suicide rates can be calculated for broad occupational groups and a few individual occupations for the 1890's only. Nor is it possible to adjust for the fact that the age distribution of employed males differed considerably in the various industries and professions. Table 6.6 presents the suicide rate of 23 occupational groups for the final Victo-

TABLE 6.6
Suicide Rates per 10,000 Males Living in Hull by 23 Occupational Groups, 1890-99

Occupation	Suicide rate	Occupation	Suicide rate
Agriculture	51.3	Paper and books	32.6
Fishing	41.6	Building	22.5
Mines and quarries	—	Gas, water, and electricity	17.5
Bricks and glass	20.3	Transport	14.5
Chemicals and oils	23.8	Commerce	28.4
Metals and engineering	21.8	Government*	25.0
Precious metals	29.6	Defense	—
Textiles	35.4	Professions	26.3
Skins and leather	31.2	Domestic/other service	58.0
Dress	47.0	Other occupations	4.5
Food and drink	25.2	Without specified occupation	4.8
Woodworking	11.7		

SOURCES: Inquests, 1890-99; census for 1901, PP, 1902, 121: 228-29.
   NOTE: Since the 1901 population of each occupation was used to create the suicide rates, it is possible that the rates are lower than they should be.
   * National and local.

rian decade. The highest suicide rates fall into the occupational categories "agriculture," "fishing," "dress," "defence," and "domestic offices or services." The small number of suicides listed under "agriculture" (a market gardener, a jobbing gardener, and a cattle salesman) and "domestic services" (two grooms and a coachman) make each of these rates unreliable. The high suicide rate among soldiers, found by Ogle, was not repeated in Hull, although three men were army pensioners (then working as a dock laborer, a butcher, and a fisherman). The suicide rate for "fishing" (based on five fishermen) would be relatively low (14.3 per 10,000) if the total number of males employed in the industry is taken to have been 3,500 (according to reliable contemporary estimates) and not 1,202 (the 1901 census figure, which omitted those at sea on enumeration day). This leaves only the category of "dress." The high rate for "dress" was a function mainly of the suicides of hairdressers, tailors, and shoemakers. While hairdressers were high on Ogle's list, too, tailors and shoemakers had suicide rates only slightly higher than average. To go further, we must examine the other occupational groups for specific occupations.

The occupational group with the largest absolute number of suicides in the 1890's was "transport" (31 suicides, including two open verdicts). Only one of these was a railway worker, out of 5,000 men working on the railways in Hull in 1901, confirming Ogle's finding of a low suicide rate for this occupation; and only eight were dock laborers, out of a total workforce of 5,573 dock and wharf laborers (a low suicide rate of 14.3 per 10,000). A slightly larger number of suicides (11) were seamen, mariners, or marine firemen, out of 3,647 so employed (or a higher suicide rate of 30 per 10,000).

The next largest category numerically is "metals and engineering." Nineteen workers under this heading killed themselves, including six open verdicts. Four were fitters, three blacksmiths, and three boilermakers. The individual rates for each of these occupations were low to average.

In the "building" category, the suicide rates for bricklayers and joiners were average, in line with Ogle's findings, but the rate for painters and paperhangers was higher than average. In the "food and drink" category, three butchers and three grocers killed themselves, but it is not possible to compare individual rates for these occupations. We can do so, however, for licensed victuallers and cellermen, whose suicide rate was high, in line with Ogle's findings.

In "commercial occupations," eight commercial and business clerks killed themselves out of 3,250 males so employed (or an average suicide rate of 24.6 per 10,000). Ogle found both clerks and commercial travelers and agents to have much higher-than-average suicide rates. Professional men in Hull were not particularly suicidal in the 1890's, a finding that stands in stark contrast to that of Ogle.

In all, the occupational distribution of Hull suicides in this one decade confirms some of Ogle's findings (such as the high suicide rate among publicans and the low rate among building, railway, and metal workers) but fails to confirm others (such as the high rate for professional men and for commercial travelers and clerks). In addition, the Hull figures suggest that tailors, shoemakers, and painters and paperhangers there were more suicidal than in the country as a whole. The first two occupations had higher-than-average proportions of men aged 45 and above, and especially aged 65 and above.

Another available occupational distribution is that between the percentage of Hull males occupied in broad occupational categories and the percentage of Hull male suicides in the same categories. The comparison is made possible by Joyce Bellamy's work on Hull's occupational structure. Tables 6.7 and 6.8 make it possible to compare the 1837–80 and 1881–99 time periods.[44] For the earlier decades, it is evident that while the three main occupational groups in Hull—transport, building, and metals and engineering—were less suicidal than might be expected from the proportions they constituted in the occupational structure, three categories—food and drink, commerce, and domestic service—were more suicidal than might be expected. This overrepresentation was a function of the following spe-

TABLE 6.7
Occupational Distribution of Suicide According to Sex, 1837-80

| | Male | | | Female | | |
| | Ave. % of total males in occupation, | Suicides 1837-80 | | Ave. % of total females in occupation, | Suicides 1837-80 | |
Occupation	1851-71	No.	Pct.	1851-71	No.	Pct.
Agriculture	1.8%	6	2.9%	0.5%	—	—
Fishing	1.7	1	0.5	—	—	—
Mines and quarries	0.8	2	1.0	0.1	—	—
Bricks and glass	0.6	1	0.5	0.1	—	—
Chemicals and oils	3.3	6	2.9	0.4	—	—
Metals and engineering	11.6	21	10.2	0.6	1	5.0%
Precious metals	0.7	1	0.5	0.2	—	—
Textiles	4.8	12	5.9	9.1	—	—
Skins and leather	1.2	4	2.0	0.3	—	—
Dress	6.8	13	6.3	24.2	4	20.0
Food and drink	8.2	27	13.2	3.2	1	5.0
Woodworking	5.1	10	4.9	0.6	—	—
Paper and books	1.2	2	1.0	0.4	—	—
Building	8.7	10	4.9	0.1	—	—
Gas, water, and electricity	0.2	—	—	—	—	—
Transport	23.0	32	15.6	1.0	—	—
Commerce	3.9	18	8.8	0.1	—	—
Government *	1.8	6	2.9	0.2	—	—
Defense	1.0	4	2.0	—	—	—
Professions	2.6	6	2.9	5.7	—	—
Domestic/other service	2.1	10	4.9	50.7	14	70.0
Other occupations	9.0	13	6.3	2.5	—	—
TOTAL	100.0%	205	100.0%	100.0%	20	100.0%

SOURCES: Inquests, 1837-80; Bellamy, "Occupations in Kingston upon Hull, 1841-1948," pp. 39-40 (tables 3 and 5).

NOTE: Totals have been rounded. Enumeration changes in the 1881 population census made it necessary to examine the occupational distribution of suicide in two separate time periods, 1851-71 and 1881-99. Moreover, in the first period, to enlarge the number of cases of suicide, I used all the suicides returned between 1837 and 1880. This step rests on the assumption that Hull's occupational structure did not change markedly between 1837 and 1880.

* National and local.

cific occupations. In "food and drink," two main occupations dominated — butchers and grocers — followed by "cowkeepers" (one of whom owned a dairy). All three occupations are high in Ogle's table. In "commerce," railway, merchants', and bankers' clerks were the most frequent occupation, followed by commercial travelers and brokers.[45] In "domestic service," the predominant occupation was that of licensed victualler or publican. In all, the occupations that were especially prone to suicide in Hull between 1837 and 1880 are those high in Ogle's table. Four other categories warrant attention. "Agriculture," "government," "professions," and "defence" were also

TABLE 6.8

Occupational Distribution of Suicide According to Sex, 1881–99

	Male			Female		
Occupation	Ave. % of total males in occupation, 1881–1901	Suicides 1881–99		Ave. % of total females in occupation, 1881–1901	Suicides 1881–99	
		No.	Pct.		No.	Pct.
Agriculture	1.0%	4	2.0%	0.1%	—	—
Fishing	2.4	8	4.0	—	—	—
Mines and quarries	0.6	1	0.5	0.1	—	—
Bricks and glass	0.5	1	0.5	0.1	—	—
Chemicals and oils	3.9	8	4.0	2.6	—	—
Metals and engineering	12.5	17	8.5	0.7	—	—
Precious metals	0.6	3	1.5	0.2	—	—
Textiles	2.0	4	2.0	5.7	—	—
Skins and leather	0.9	4	2.0	0.3	—	—
Dress	3.3	8	4.0	19.7	—	—
Food and drink	7.2	20	10.0	5.4	1	11.1%
Woodworking	4.2	7	3.5	0.7	—	—
Paper and books	1.5	4	2.0	2.1	—	—
Building	8.9	22	11.0	—	—	—
Gas, water, and electricity	0.6	2	1.0	—	—	—
Transport	26.3	44	22.0	0.5	—	—
Commerce	6.2	15	7.5	0.8	—	—
Government *	1.5	3	1.5	0.2	—	—
Defense	0.2	—	—	—	—	—
Professions	2.7	8	4.0	7.8	—	—
Domestic/other service	2.1	12	6.0	50.6	8	88.9
Other occupations	11.1	5	2.5	2.3	—	—
TOTAL	100.0%	200	100.0%	100.0%	9	100.0%

SOURCES: Inquests, 1881–99; Bellamy, "Occupations in Kingston upon Hull, 1841–1948," pp. 39–40 (tables 3 and 5).

NOTE: Totals have been rounded. The average percentage of males and females in each occupation was calculated from Bellamy's occupational figures for 1881, 1891, and 1901. The last year for which the number of suicides was available was 1899.

* National and local.

more suicidal than expected. The first category was composed essentially of retired farmers and former agricultural laborers; the second of customs officers and policemen; the third of surgeons and teachers. The final category, "defence," consisted of three serving soldiers, two of whom shot themselves with their rifles in the Citadel garrison, and one old army pensioner, who was in Sculcoates workhouse at time of death. No serving soldier killed himself after 1858 in Hull, a result possibly of the 1869 order that removed service ammunition from pouches and placed it in regimental magazines.[46]

In the second time period, 1881–99, five categories were more suicidal than might be expected from the proportions they constituted in the occupational structure (see table 6.8). As might be anticipated, the data concerning specific occupations are not dissimilar to the findings from the above section on the 1890's. In "dress," tailors and shoemakers were the most prominent occupations; in "food and drink," fruiterers, butchers, and grocers were most numerous, again followed by cowkeepers. In "commerce," clerks were predominant, followed by commercial travelers and agents; in "professions," schoolteachers stood out; while in "domestic services," licensed victuallers were most numerous. No serving officer killed himself in these years, but three suicides were army pensioners, then working as a butcher, a dock laborer, and a fisherman.

It is possible, also, to compare the proportions of occupations and suicides for the opposite sex (see tables 6.7 and 6.8). In both time periods, approximately 20 percent of Hull female suicides were waged workers. In 1901, 24 percent of all Hull women were in waged employment. Between 1837 and 1880, two-thirds of all female suicides were in "domestic service," mainly young domestics, plus a number of housekeepers and chars. This was a larger proportion than in the occupied female population as a whole, since only one-half of all occupied women were in domestic service. A quarter of all suicides were in "dress," almost the exact same proportion as in the occupied female population. The specific occupations were dressmakers and straw bonnet makers. No female suicides were in either "food and drink," "professions," or "textiles," in which approximately 3, 6, and 9 percent, respectively, of all occupied females were employed.[47] Between 1881 and 1901, over 80 percent of all female suicides were in "domestic service," in contrast to 50 percent or less of all occupied women. Again, the suicides were predominantly domestic servants in their teens and twenties, older housekeepers, and a laundrywoman. The suicides of two paper-mill hands led to an overrepresentation of "paper and books," but obviously the numbers are too small to be reliable. In these later decades, finally, no female suicides were in either "dress," "professions," or "textiles," in which approximately 19, 8, and 6 percent, respectively, of all occupied females were employed. The overall conclusion is foregone: domestic servants and housekeepers were the most suicide-prone female occupations.[48]

Finally, a similar comparative exercise was completed for men aged 45 and over for the 1890's. Table 6.9 contains the results. In addition to the overrepresentation of "food and drink" (a product of the suicides of fruiterers, grocers, and publicans), two of Hull's main occupational categories, "building" and (when open verdicts were added) "metals and engi-

TABLE 6.9

Occupational Distribution of Male Suicides Aged 45 and Above, 1890–99

Occupation	Percentage of occupied males aged 45 and above, 1901	Suicide verdicts No.	Suicide verdicts Pct.
Agriculture	1.1%	3	4.0%
Fishing	1.0	1	1.3
Mines and quarries	0.7	—	—
Bricks and glass	0.4	—	—
Chemicals and oils	3.4	4	5.3
Metals and engineering	11.4	8	10.8
Precious metals	0.7	1	1.3
Textiles	1.1	3	4.0
Skins and leather	0.9	1	1.3
Dress	3.0	4	5.3
Food and drink	7.7	7	9.5
Woodworking	3.7	1	1.3
Paper and books	1.1	1	1.3
Building	8.8	9	12.2
Gas, water, and electricity	0.8	1	1.3
Transport	25.0	15	20.3
Commerce	4.4	5	6.8
Government *	1.4	2	2.7
Defense	0.1	—	—
Professions	2.0	2	2.7
Domestic/other service	0.9	2	2.7
Other occupations	8.5	—	—
No specified occupation	11.3	4	5.3
TOTAL	100.0%	74	100.0%

SOURCES: Inquests, 1890–99; census for 1901, PP, 1902, 121: 228–29.
NOTE: Totals have been rounded.
* National and local.

neering," were overrepresented for the first time. Painters, plumbers, and bricklayers killed themselves in the first category; shipyard fitters, boiler-makers, blacksmiths, and mast and block makers in the second category. We shall have cause in subsequent chapters to examine the suicide of the aged, but these figures alert us to the vulnerability of older workers in the building, metals and engineering, and food and drink trades.

A direct comparison with the national figures for social class variations in suicide is likewise not possible, since we do not have the figures to compute suicide rates for each class. We must fall back upon the percentages of suicides in each class, which we can put alongside Hull's social structure for 1851. Table 6.10 shows the percentages of suicides among occupied males in each social class for the years 1837–60, and table 6.11 gives the percentages for occupied males and females together. These are compared with the class distribution for economically active household heads (essentially males) and for the total economically active (male and female)

TABLE 6.10
Distribution of Occupied Male Suicides by Social Class, 1837–60

Social class	Occupied Household Heads in 1851 (20% sample)	Suicide verdicts		Suicide and open verdicts	
	Pct.	No.	Pct.	No.	Pct.
I. Professional and managerial	5.0%	3	3.6%	3	3.2%
II. Lower professional and small employers	12.0	7	8.3	7	7.5
III. Skilled nonmanual workers	14.0	21	25.0	22	23.7
IV. Skilled manual workers	34.0	30	35.7	33	35.5
V. Semi-skilled manual workers	18.0	14	16.7	19	20.4
VI. Unskilled manual workers	18.0	9	10.7	9	9.7
TOTAL	100.0%	84	100.0%	93	100.0%

SOURCES: Inquests, 1837–60; Tansey, "Residential Patterns," p. 45 (table 5).
NOTE: In the first column, the total has been rounded.

TABLE 6.11
Distribution of Occupied Male and Female Suicides by Social Class, 1837–60

Social class	Total occupied in 1851 (20% sample)	Suicide verdicts		Suicide and open verdicts	
	Pct.	No.	Pct.	No.	Pct.
I. Professional and managerial	3.0%	5	5.2%	5	4.6%
II. Lower professional and small employers	9.0	7	7.2	7	6.4
III. Skilled nonmanual workers	12.0	21	21.6	22	20.2
IV. Skilled manual workers	35.0	31	32.0	36	33.0
V. Semi-skilled manual workers	28.0	21	21.6	27	24.8
VI. Unskilled manual workers	14.0	12	12.4	12	11.0
TOTAL	100.0%	97	100.0%	109	100.0%

SOURCES: Inquests, 1837–60; Tansey, "Residential Patterns," p. 45 (table 5).
NOTE: In the first column, the total has been rounded.

population of Hull in 1851.[49] The most compelling finding is the overrepresentation of suicides in class III, skilled nonmanual workers. While only 14.3 percent of Hull's economically active household heads were in this class in 1851, 25 percent of male suicides between 1837 and 1860 were. This figure is probably exaggerated by the inclusion in class III of suicides who properly belong in class II, by virtue of having employed more than one

TABLE 6.12

Distribution of Occupied Suicides by Social Class and Sex, 1837–99

	Suicide verdicts				Suicide and open verdicts			
	Male		Female		Male		Female	
Social Class	No.	Pct.	No.	Pct.	No.	Pct.	No.	Pct.
I. Professional, managerial	10	2.5%	2	6.3%	11	2.3%	2	4.0%
II. Lower professional, small employers	48	11.9	1	3.1	54	11.4	1	2.0
III. Skilled nonmanual workers	98	24.2	1	3.1	111	23.5	1	2.0
IV. Skilled manual workers	134	33.1	3	9.4	158	33.4	5	10.0
V. Semi-skilled manual workers	80	19.8	19	59.4	96	20.3	34	68.0
VI. Unskilled manual workers	35	8.6	6	18.8	43	9.1	7	14.0
TOTAL	405	100.0%	32	100.0%	473	100.0%	50	100.0%

SOURCE: Inquests, 1837–99.
NOTE: Totals have been rounded.

assistant or servant, information that is rarely given in the inquest depositions. Were we able to make this adjustment, the percentage of suicides in
class II would doubtless increase, possibly to the point of overrepresentation, but it is likely that class III would remain particularly suicide-prone.
By examining the individual cases that make up the percentage for classes II
and III, it is clear that most of the suicides in class II were master mariners (not all of whom perhaps properly belong in this class), vessel masters,
merchants, agents, and managers; while the suicides in class III were clerks
(especially to merchants), licensed victuallers and publicans, greengrocers
and fruiterers, and dealers (in marine stores, coal, and game). In addition,
there were commercial travelers and assistants (to a chemist, a grocer, and
a draper) in class III.[50] Another significant finding is the underrepresenta-
tion of suicides in class VI, laborers and unskilled workers (including dock
laborers). While 18 percent of Hull's household heads were in this class
in 1851, only 10 percent of male suicides were. The percentage of suicides
in class VI among the total economically active was slightly higher, owing
to the inclusion in this class of female chars and laundresses. The larger
percentage of suicides in class V among the total economically active population is the result of the concentration of the female occupied in class V,
semi-skilled workers (in domestic service, textiles, and dress). This is more
evident still in table 6.12, which tabulates the percentage of Hull suicides
in each class for the entire Victorian period. Nigh on 60 percent of all

TABLE 6.13
Distribution of Married, Widowed, and Cohabiting Female Suicides by Social Class,
1837–99

Social Class	Suicide and open verdicts	
	No.	Pct.
I. Professional, managerial	10	2.5%
II. Lower professional, small employers	48	11.9
III. Skilled nonmanual workers	98	24.2
IV. Skilled manual workers	134	33.1
V. Semi-skilled manual workers	80	19.8
VI. Unskilled manual workers	35	8.6
TOTAL	405	100.0%

SOURCE: Inquests, 1837–99.

NOTE: The total has been rounded. The social class of female suicides was taken from the class of husband, deceased husband, or cohabitee.

female suicides who were in waged work were in class V; the figure rises to 68 percent if open verdicts are included. Moreover, women suicides who were married, widowed, or cohabiting (for whom I have used the occupation of husband, former husband, or cohabitee) were concentrated in class IV, skilled manual, and class V, semi-skilled, for which see table 6.13.

What, also, of the relationship between suicide and unemployment? Historians of suicide have generally failed to explore this issue, owing to a shortage of reliable information. Fortunately, the Hull coroners seem usually to have asked witnesses about the deceased's work history, making it possible to offer some quantitative estimates of the frequency with which unemployment was associated with suicide. It should be recognized, however, that reference to unemployment could have become more frequent in inquest evidence from the 1880's on, as unemployment became a topic of political conversation.[51] Eighty-nine male suicide and open verdicts were unemployed at time of death, which was 18 percent of all male suicides. Sixty percent of these unemployed suicides came from the last two decades of the nineteenth century, constituting 22 percent of all male suicide and open verdicts between 1881 and 1899. In other words, over one-fifth of all male suicides in the last twenty years of the century were unemployed. Unemployment was particularly common among the older male suicides. Of the 89 unemployed suicides, 42 (or 47 percent) were aged 45–64, and 54 (or 60 percent) were aged 45 and above. As for the usual occupation of the unemployed suicides, 24 percent were transport workers (mainly dock laborers, master mariners, merchant seamen, or sloopmen) and 8 percent were building workers (almost all joiners or carpenters). The most over-represented occupations, however, were from the chemical and oil industries (notably oil millers and color-maker's laborers) and from the metal and engineering trades (boilermakers, shipyard laborers, blacksmiths, and mast and block makers). Eleven percent and 17 percent of the unemployed were drawn respectively from these two occupational categories. The metal and engineering trades had a concentration of unemployed suicides between 1894 and 1899. This could have been related to the economic condition of the shipbuilding industry, as engineers at Earle's main shipyard were on strike for four months in 1896.[52] Every social class, except class I, had an unemployed suicide, but most came from class IV, skilled manual, and class V, semi-skilled workers. Compared with the class distribution of the Hull workforce, semi-skilled workers who killed themselves seem to have been most affected by unemployment. Few women suicides, finally, were unemployed, but then few women suicides were in waged work. Of the handful of unemployed female suicides, most were either young domestic servants or old housekeepers.[53]

V

We turn, lastly, to the ecology of suicide. Was the incidence of suicide associated with particular socioeconomic habitats, and hence ecological? Peter Sainsbury, for example, established correlations between the incidence of suicide in different districts of London in the 1930's and their socioeconomic characteristics. He hypothesized that where social mobility and social isolation were pronounced, community life would be unstable and without purpose, and that this would be reflected in the suicide rates. He concluded that suicide rates "were highest in the West End and North-West London where both class and spatial mobility are highest, small flat and boarding-house accommodation preponderates, shared mores are absent, and relationships impersonal. Suicide rates were low in the peripheral southern boroughs where family life and stability prevail, and in many of the working-class districts whose residents are locally born and where life is more neighbourly."[54]

No previous study of Victorian suicide has confronted this issue, in the main because the parish named in the formal inquisition referred to the place where the body lay, which may or may not have been the deceased's place of residence. Inevitably, then, any ecological study is affected, not to say undermined, by the sizable number of suicides that took place in drainage canals, docks, and rivers, or less commonly on railway lines. It is possible to surmount this problem, however, by digging out the deceased's

TABLE 6.14

Average Annual Suicides per 10,000 Living in Six Subdistricts of Hull, 1841–50

Subdistricts	Suicide verdicts		Suicide and open verdicts	
	Male	Female	Male	Female
Drypool	13.2	—	13.2	—
Sutton	16.6	3.6	16.6	7.1
Humber and St. Mary	11.1	7.4	13.4	8.4
Sculcoates, East	12.4	7.2	14.5	9.0
Sculcoates, West	10.2	3.9	10.2	3.9
Myton	11.0	10.9	11.7	11.6

SOURCES: Inquests, 1841–50; population censuses, 1841 and 1851.

NOTE: The population was calculated by taking the arithmetic mean of the population recorded in the two adjacent censuses. The rates for Humber and St. Mary and for Myton were affected by the location of various institutions. In Humber and St. Mary, two of the male suicides were in the workhouse. In Myton, one male suicide was in the old jail, and one was in the fever hospital; one of the female suicides was in the Master Mariners' Hospital, and one was in the Hull & East Riding Refuge.

TABLE 6.15

Average Annual Suicides per 10,000 Living in Six Subdistricts of Hull, 1890–99

Subdistricts	Suicide verdicts		Suicide and open verdicts	
	Male	Female	Male	Female
Drypool	8.1	4.6	9.8	5.7
Sutton	3.1	3.2	6.1	4.8
Humber and St. Mary	29.1	6.9	31.3	9.2
Sculcoates, East	14.0	1.4	19.6	1.4
Sculcoates, West	11.3	3.7	12.9	5.5
Myton	17.3	7.3	18.5	7.9

SOURCES: Inquests, 1890–99; population census, 1891.

NOTE: Only the 1891 population figure could be used for Humber and St. Mary and for Myton, rather than the arithmetic mean of the 1891 and 1901 populations. This would have the effect of increasing the suicide rate for Myton, but depressing the rate for Humber and St. Mary, since the population of the latter doubtless continued to fall between 1891 and 1901.

place of residence from the depositional evidence.[55] This has been done for two decades, 1841–50 and 1890–99, the two with the highest suicide rates for both sexes. Suicide rates for the city's main registration subdistricts, for which there are population figures, were then computed. The spatial incidence of suicide is presented in tables 6.14 and 6.15 (in conjunction with fig. 6.13).[56] It should be said immediately that the administrative divisions are far from adequate to our purpose. They cover large areas, and, in most cases, contain a number of more natural regions or neighborhoods. On the other hand, the number of suicides per decade is, with the exception of the 1890's, too small on which to base reliable rates for six districts.[57] These limitations aside, what do the rates suggest?

The most telling finding is the high suicide rate for the "Old Town" districts of Humber and St. Mary (which I have combined) in the 1890's. This

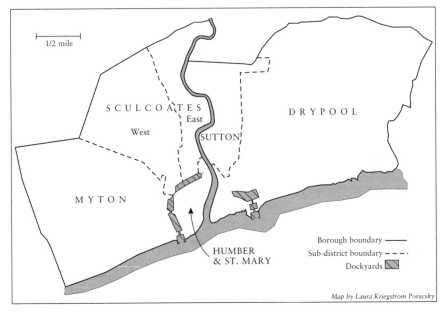

FIGURE 6.13. Registration Subdistricts of Victorian Hull. Source: Atlas of Coroners' Districts, East Riding of Yorkshire, Home Office Papers, H.O. 84/3, Public Record Office.

was particularly true for males, but when open verdicts are included, it is true also for females. In the 1840's, by contrast, the Old Town did not post an unusually high suicide rate. Other districts had higher rates, although the returns for Sutton and Drypool are based on only a handful of suicides. The difference between the two decades, I would suggest, is a reflection, at least in part, of the demographic and socioeconomic character of Hull's inner core. In the 1840's, on average, 25 percent of the borough population lived in the Humber and St. Mary divisions (although falling from 29 percent in 1841 to 21 percent in 1851). Already an area of shops, pubs, warehouses, and offices, and affected by overcrowding, the Old Town housed many of the regular laborers and artisans of the city. By the 1890's, however, less than 5 percent of the borough population lived on the central "island," in what had become the main business and retail quarter, full of licensed premises and lodging houses, a district of high migrant status, and one in which there seems to have been a high proportion of small households (with less emphasis on family life), and of skilled nonmanual workers (attracted by jobs in retail and commerce).[58] The occupational, residential, and civic status characteristics of individual suicides, on which the rates are based, bear out these different descriptions.[59]

In the 1840's, the male suicides who resided in the Old Town were predominantly married men of 45 years and up (some with children), working in the food and drink trades (butcher, greengrocer, publican, and victualler), in metals (whitesmith, blacksmith), or in commerce (warehouseman for a wine merchant, customhouse boatman). In addition, there were an old waterman, who had lodged with a widow for over five years; a widowed marine-stores dealer with six children; and a young laborer and an old bacon factor who were paupers in the workhouse. The female suicides, in a decade in which women were particularly suicidal, were either married (to a carpenter, and a ballast-lighter owner) or widows (of a sailmaker, a confectioner, and a mariner), one of whom had two children and worked as a shoebinder. One of the widows lived with her daughter's family, one with her grown sons, and one lodged with a publican. Only two women were young singles, both of whom lived in lodgings. In the 1890's, by contrast, there were as many single and widowed as married men. All but one of the single men were in lodging houses or hotels; the exception was a live-in draper's assistant who was on remand for attempted murder. Likewise, a chemist's assistant from Southampton, found in a Queen Street hotel, was wanted by the police for stealing watches. Most of the singles were in their forties or fifties; one was an unemployed driller, one a destitute seaman, one an indebted commission agent. Of the married men, one was an army pensioner and dock laborer; one an unemployed ship's steward, who was working as a newsagent in the meantime; and one a brewery company's clerk, whose drinking had led to a threat of dismissal. There were only four female suicides from the Old Town in this decade, two of whom were poverty-stricken widows in their thirties. In short, the high suicide rate of the Old Town district in the 1890's can be linked, at least to some degree, to the ecology of an inner-city business, migrant, and lodging-house district.

The next two highest suicide rates in the 1890's, after the Old Town, were returned by the Myton and East Sculcoates districts. Of East Sculcoates, the main finding must be the absence in the suicide roster of workmen from the main industries in the eastern meander of the river Hull: oil and flour milling; cotton, cement, and paint manufacture. Only one male suicide in the 1890's came from the streets around the Kingston cotton mill, and he was a retired confectioner.[60] In addition, two suicides in their fifties were oil millers, one 17-year-old was a paint-works laborer. The rest, however, were drawn from a variety of trades: cooper, tailor, butcher, blacksmith, and compositor. As for females, the suicide rate was the lowest of any city district; only one woman, the wife of an oil-mill foreman, killed herself. The second of these districts, Myton, contained both the Hessle Road fishing community and the group of streets that constituted "Little Ireland." Both these subdistricts warrant examination to assess the ecology of two heavily, although different, working-class communities.

The fishing community was essentially bounded by the administrative division of South Myton, south of Anlaby Road, with the western addition of parts of the Hessle district. It had a couple of streets of desirable middle-class residences, and two female suicides (one a spinster, aged 27, who lived with her solicitor brother; the other a 72-year-old widow who lived with her cattle-salesman son) lived along the Boulevard. It also had streets of the very poorest inhabitants, namely, Strickland, Wassand, and Walcot streets. Seven suicides (3 male, 4 female) came from these three streets in the one decade, although one of the males, a painter and paper-hanger from Halifax, was only visiting his sister, the wife of the skipper of a fishing smack, in Strickland Street. The other two male suicides were an intemperate bricklayer's laborer and an unemployed fish-dock laborer. Of the four women suicides, one was a young domestic servant, one was the wife of a fisherman, and two were widows (of an iron-yard laborer, and an iron molder), of whom one lived with her brother and the other had a lodger. A striking thing about the Hessle Road district, an area dominated by the fishing industry, is the relatively small number of suicides of men working in fishing and ancillary trades. In 1900, around 3,500 men were employed as trawlermen; another 6,000 in fish curing, in the fish market, and in the shipbuilding and engineering yards. Many, if not all, would have lived in South Myton. Of the 32 male suicides from South Myton in the 1890's, only one was a fisherman, aged 20, who lodged with a fisherman's family and wanted the wife of another trawlerman to leave her husband for him. Three more Hull fishermen killed themselves at sea, and their bodies were landed at St. Andrew's Dock. The depositions do not reveal their place of residence, but they probably lived in South Myton. It is probable, too, that all three were single, and certainly no spouse appeared at any of the inquests. A final fisherman lived in North Myton, but he had not been to sea for a year, having been injured in rough weather on his last voyage, and did odd jobs on shore instead. In addition to this handful of fishermen, one male suicide was an out-of-work fish-dock laborer.[61] It is possible that suicide among fishermen was underregistered, in view of the fine line between fatal risktaking at work, on the one hand, and suicide on the other.[62] But the numbers, taken at face value, suggest that the rate of suicide was low among fishermen and those dependent upon the fishing industry. Should we conclude that this was a function of the group solidarity of the fishing occupation, and of the tight-knit society of the Hessle Road district? Possibly, but the wives and widows of the fishing trade, those who were renowned for holding the community together, were not immune to the suicidal impulse. Five such women, most of whom were in their forties, killed themselves. Two wives did it while their fishermen husbands were at sea; one widow was in a state of bereavement and another in great poverty.

Nine suicides (six male) were living in the fewer than one dozen streets that made up "Little Ireland" in North Myton. The most striking characteristic of these few cases is a solitary or troubled living arrangement. A 55-year-old dock laborer, who had lived alone for ten years, hanged himself in a depressed state on account of illness. A 48-year-old dustcart man, who had lodged with a widow for two years, was said never to have got over his wife's death and drowned himself. An old laborer, a sailmaker by trade, with four children, was separated from his wife, who had left because of his violence. A 42-year-old tailor who took poison had also ill-used his wife; they both drank heavily and quarreled over money. And a young spinster who cohabited with a rullyman had been drinking every day for a month before hanging herself. Similar cases could be found for other districts, but the uniformity of isolation or family breakdown in the "Little Ireland" suicides reflects a district to which the single, the widowed, and the immigrant gravitated; a district of poor housing and lodging houses; one with no strong occupational bond like the Hessle Road.

One of the lowest suicide rates was posted in the 1890's by the fast-growing Drypool division, which consisted of the streets north of Victoria Dock, Earle's shipyard, and the timber yards, and of the Hedon and Holderness roads. The latter roads contained a number of desirable residences, including those of two men who poisoned themselves, one a 28-year-old surgeon to the prison, the other a game dealer. The suicides of this division appear, however, to have been more occupationally representative than those in other working-class communities. Over half the male suicides worked either in metals and shipbuilding or in marine transportation, and almost all the female suicides were wives or daughters of men in the same trades. The final district worth exploring is that of West Sculcoates, the populous area to the north and west of Queen's Dock, including one of the largest middle-class areas, the Pearson's Park region, between Spring Bank, Beverley Road, and Princess Avenue. Accordingly, a good half of the male suicides held professional and skilled nonmanual positions. Four suicides were clerks: one to a solicitor, one to a Guardian Society, and two to a provision dealer and a newspaper proprietor, respectively. A fifth suicide was an unemployed wine-merchant's clerk. In addition, the manager of a navigation company and a lithographics artist, both of whom had business troubles, killed themselves, as did a single schoolmaster, two greengrocers (one a former musician), a licensed victualler, and the master of the SS *Yorkshireman*. Bourgeois quarters in Victorian cities invariably sheltered other social groups, particularly domestics, and West Sculcoates was no exception. A tobacco manufacturer's groom and a shipbuilder's coachman, both suicides, lived in this district. Among the female suicides, by contrast, only one was the wife of a professional or clerical worker.

What are we to make of this ecological survey? With one exception, the suicide rates of the different divisions were not markedly different. The exception is the Old Town division, the only area sufficiently small and bounded to have a discrete demographic and socioeconomic character. For the rest, we have to conclude perhaps that the arbitrarily defined census enumeration districts did not sufficiently correspond to the main urban "communities." Hull's districts, in consequence, were possibly too similar in demographic composition, housing type, morbidity history, and occupational character to generate a noticeable association between suicide and ecology. Alternatively, it could be that the similarity of suicide rates was a function of working-class communities—whether dockside, shipbuilding, or fishing districts—in which the main labor process delivered considerable occupational and social integration, and a common identity.[63]

VI

With this, our statistical work is at an end.[64] It remains only to gather together the most suggestive findings to take with us into the final section of the book on the experience of urban suicide. The best clues are to be found among the age, occupational, and social class indices of suicide. The male suicide rate rose in each of eight successive age periods, reaching its maximum among those aged 55–64; the female suicide rate rose in each age period up to and including the 45–54 age group, but fell among those aged 55–64, before reaching its high point in the 65–74 age group. The figures suggest that whereas men were most vulnerable in the decade before the present-day age of retirement, women were more vulnerable during the next ten years, when many were widowed and living in penury. When the age periods were reduced to four, a similar profile emerged. Men were most suicide-prone in the 45–64 age group; women in the 65-and-over age group (with the exception of the 1870's and 1880's). Moreover, the old of both sexes, defined as those who were 45 years and above, were considerably overrepresented in the suicide toll. Just over a quarter of Hull's population were aged 45 and above, yet a half or more of all suicides were in this age group.

The occupational findings are not perhaps as clear-cut, but they nonetheless offer a number of clues to the interpretation of the inquest depositions. The highest occupational rates of suicide among men belonged to licensed victuallers or publicans in the "domestic" sector; to butchers, grocers, and fruiterers in the "food and drink" sector; to tailors and shoemakers in the "dress" sector; to clerical workers and commercial travelers in "commerce"; and to painters, plumbers, and bricklayers in the building trades. Among waged women, domestic servants in their teens and twenties and older housekeepers were the most suicidal female occupations. These findings suggest the possible influence upon male suicide of work in the drink trade (publicans); of the financial risks associated with small businesses (grocers, butchers); of trades in which older workers were tending to congregate (tailors, shoemakers); of service or commercial occupations (clerks and travelers); and of the seasonal pressures associated with the building trades. Female suicide was evidently linked to the trials and tribulations of domestic service, at least among waged workers. When the occupational data were converted into social class categories, skilled male nonmanual workers in class III were found to be particularly suicidal, which is hardly surprising, since class III includes publicans, clerks and commercial travelers, greengrocers and fruiterers. Semi-skilled women workers in social class V were especially suicidal, reflecting the inclusion in this class of domestic servants, and women workers in textiles and the clothing trade.

One significant clue remains, the bane of unemployment. Close to one-fifth of all male suicides between 1837 and 1899 and over one-fifth of all male suicides in the last two decades of the Victorian era were out of work at the time of self-destruction, owing to shortage of jobs, prolonged illness, old age, or an accident (often incurred at the workplace). More specifically, well over half of all out-of-work suicides were aged 45 and above, and close to a half were aged 45–64. And workers from the chemical and oil industries (oil millers, color-makers' laborers), and the metal trades (blacksmiths, shipyard laborers) were particularly affected by unemployment. These figures, moreover, make no mention of the suicides in the workhouse or those who suffered from irregular work or underemployment, a common characteristic of port labor markets. It all suggests that work problems, especially, although not exclusively, among men, and particularly among men in their later working years, deserve close attention in the following examination of suicide across the life cycle.

Suicide Across the Life Cycle

7

Early-Life Transitions

I would there were no age between sixteen and three and
twenty, or that youth would sleep out the rest; for there
is nothing in the between but getting wenches with
child, wronging the ancientry, stealing, fighting.

Shakespeare,
The Winter's Tale 3.3.59–63

It is time to examine the experience
of suicide across the life cycle. In
this chapter, I deal with the phase of the life cycle that spanned the gap between leaving school and marriage. As we have seen, life-cycle transitions
in the Victorian era were less uniform than they were to become. Not until
the 1890's, perhaps, were young people living through a well-defined life-
cycle stage. Even so, there were common patterns of experience. For most
of the century, young adults adjusted over a long period of twelve years or
more to work, to the financial demands of the family, and to courtship.[1] If
young adults by their late teens were economically ready for independence,
their parents typically wanted a share of their increasing earning power. The
needs of the family economy could thus limit their freedom to leave home or
to marry; girls were perhaps less independent of parental control, required
both to help within and work without the home. For those in apprenticeships, family control was compounded by that of the employer. The lot of
the apprentice was not a happy one: he was hard worked for little pay and
could be dismissed at the end of the apprenticeship. Many young clerks,
especially in trades such as ship chandlery, suffered this fate. The passage
from adolescence to marriage was also an emotionally charged one, as the

search for a spouse began. In all, this transitional phase in the life cycle had considerable potential for conflict with parents, employers, and lovers.[2]

I

"Up to 16 years," Durkheim says, "the tendency to suicide is very slight, due to age, without considering other factors."[3] Victorian Hull bears out this statement. Among official verdicts of suicide, only two males were under 16 (one was 15, one 12); among open verdicts in which there was affirmative evidence of suicide, two more males were under 16 (one 15, one 13). No female suicides were under 16. These youthful cases were a late-century phenomenon, three of them occurring in the years 1895-96. As we have seen, the 15-24 age group of both sexes had the lowest average rate of suicide in Victorian Hull. Furthermore, the suicide rate for both sexes in this age group declined over the Victorian era, with the exception that the rate for females aged 15-24 rose appreciably in the 1890's. In addition, the suicide rate among males of this age group exceeded that of females in every decade. In the 1890's, however, the rate for females aged 15-19 was larger than that for males of the same age group.[4] In absolute numbers, there were 39 male suicides and 19 female suicides aged 15-24 in this one Victorian city. To these I have added 12 male and 19 female open verdicts, making a total of 51 male and 38 female suicides in the life-cycle stage between childhood and independent adulthood. I shall evaluate the suicide and open verdicts en bloc. As the numbers indicate, however, the inclusion of open verdicts makes a considerable difference to the profile of young adult suicide. One-quarter (12 of 51) of young male verdicts, and one-half (19 of 38) of young female verdicts were open ones in which the evidence of suicide was thought to be compelling.

The aim of this chapter is to uncover the civil status of the suicides, their residential and occupational details, and, most important, their motives: the pressures that conduced, or were thought to have conduced, to the suicidal act. With regard to motives for suicide, we have explored them under five main headings: economic and work-related difficulties (unemployment, business worries, destitution); bodily and mental illness; disturbances in personal relationships (family quarrels, bereavement, emotional disappointment); drink and drugs; and disturbances in social relationships (public disgrace, loneliness, impending legal action, and life seen as "meaningless").[5] It is not possible to find a motive in every single case; some simply defy categorization. Nor is it entirely valid to allocate every case to only one of the above categories. There are obvious overlaps, for example, between heavy drinking and mental illness, particularly depression. Such overlaps will be pointed to in relevant cases.

II

We begin with civil status. Of the 51 male suicides in the 15-24 age group, 4 were married, 1 was cohabiting, and 46 were either definitely or probably single.[6] The five males who were married or cohabiting were all in the 20-24 age group. Of the 38 female suicides aged 15-24, 5 were married, 1 was a widow, and 32 were seemingly single. Two of the married suicides were from the 15-19 age group; the other marrieds and the widowed suicide were from the 20-24 age group. In short, 90 percent of the male and 84 percent of the female suicides were single, which was marginally higher than the figures for the entire age group in nineteenth-century Hull (87 percent of males and 77 percent of females were single).[7]

As for residential status, 25 (or approximately one-half) of the male suicides aged 15-24 were living with parents or kin in family households. Six were living in lodgings (five of whom were in the 20-24 age group); seven were "institutionalised" (three in prison, one in the workhouse, one in the asylum, and two in the military garrison); four lived with spouses and one cohabited with a prostitute; one lived with his employer, a matmaker; one was a cabin boy from Hamburg; and one a cook on a fishing smack at the time of death. Seventeen (or 45 percent) of the female suicides aged 15-24 were living with parents or kin; twelve (or almost one-third) were in service; five lived with spouses; one was in lodgings, one was in prison, and one was in a brothel. The first conclusion of note is the proportion of young suicides living with parents or kin in family households, which is lower than the figure for all young people. We noted previously that until the age of 20, 80 percent or more of all children lived with parents or kin; and that even in their early twenties, 50 percent of all children still lived with parents.[8] By contrast, only 60 percent of suicides under 20 years of age and only 36 percent of suicides aged 20-24 lived with parents or kin. Yet if suicides were less frequently to be found with kin, the practice of lodging—an important stepping-stone, especially for men, between leaving the parental home and establishing an independent household—did not take up the slack. In mid-century Preston, one-quarter of the 20-24 age group were in lodgings; in Victorian Hull, less than 13 percent of suicides in this age group were in lodgings, and even the figure for males alone was below

18 percent.[9] As important, especially for men, was residence in one of the Victorian city's institutions: prison, asylum, workhouse, and garrison; while for women, especially those aged 15–19, the next most important residential status to living with kin was being in service. In all, these young suicides were far from being socially isolated individuals. Most lived with family, few were in lodgings. Only the young women who were in service were truly vulnerable to loneliness.

In what ways did young adults destroy themselves? Poison was the preferred method of suicide for young women, if suicide verdicts alone are examined. Of the 19 women concerned, three-quarters poisoned themselves. When open verdicts are included, however, drowning and poison share the honors, since practically all the 19 open verdicts were cases of drowning. Young men preferred hanging, poison, and the gun. Of the 39 suicide verdicts, almost one-third hanged themselves, one-quarter used poison, and one-fifth the gun. When open verdicts are included, hanging remains the most favored method, with one-quarter of the 51 male suicides hanging themselves, but drowning moves into second place as the method chosen by close to a quarter of all young men.

Practically all urban males between 15 and 24 years of age worked for wages. The Hull suicides were no exception. Among male suicides aged 15–19, only one had no stated occupation; he was in prison at the time of death. Of the occupied suicides, most were either apprenticed (as bookbinder, cabinetmaker, wood turner, joiner, merchant's clerk, or whitesmith) or employed as a "boy" or assistant (whether a grocer's boy, bricklayer's boy, cabin boy, newsboy, lather boy, or stationer's errand boy). One suicide was also a pupil teacher. In addition, two were clerks, two were hawkers (of fruit and firewood), one was a cook on a fishing smack, and one a soldier. Among male suicides aged 20–24, occupations were given for 26 of the 28, although 3 of those with occupations were either in prison or the asylum at the time of death. The variety of occupations was wide. Three were in food and drink (victualler, pork butcher, baker); four were in the wood trade (two cabinetmakers, a joiner, a saw-mill laborer); four were in transport (marine fireman, marine steward, boatman, cartman); two were tailors and one a draper's assistant. When occupation is translated into social class, and when the proportion of male suicides aged 15–24 is compared with the social class distribution of household heads in mid-century Hull (in table 5.1), we see that skilled nonmanual workers (notably clerks, and assistants to grocers, chemists, and drapers) and skilled manual workers (apprentices in the wood and tailoring trades) were overrepresented among suicides. So, too, were semi-skilled workers (notably soldiers and young adults in the fishing and transport industries). The pattern for young women suicides, by contrast, was much more uniform.

The number of young women between 15 and 24 years of age who had waged work always depended upon the local employment structure. Seaports like Hull were typically poor towns for female employment. Yet even in these towns, the largest proportion of women wage earners were young adults. In Hull, just over a half of all occupied women were aged 15–24. Young Hull girls were prominent in domestic indoor service and in dress, and important in food and lodging, in oils, chemicals and paints, and in teaching.[10] Domestic service was essentially "a life-cycle occupation," a job for females between leaving school and getting married.[11] Among female suicides aged 15–24, two-thirds (or 25 of 38) were in waged work, or had recently been in work, which is probably the same proportion as for all Hull females in waged work in this age group. Of the 38 female suicides aged 15–24, 18, or almost one-half, were in some form of domestic service. Twelve were domestics, three had recently left a situation and returned home, one former domestic was in prison, one was a housekeeper, and one helped her mother to clean offices. This means, furthermore, that of those suicides who were in waged work, 72 percent (or 18 of 25) were in domestic service. Among all occupied women in Hull in the last half of the century, no more than 50 percent worked in domestic or other service.[12] It all suggests that domestic servants were considerably overrepresented among young female suicides. In addition to domestics, finally, two female suicides were straw bonnet makers, two were paper-mill hands, one worked in the Hull cotton mills, and one in Reckitt's starch works. Three suicides were deemed to be prostitutes, but these have not been included in the figures above. It goes without saying, therefore, that in terms of social class, most young female suicides were either semi-skilled or unskilled workers. The handful who were married, finally, were wives of semi-skilled workers.

III

With these details in mind, we shall concentrate for the rest of the chapter on the young adult experience of suicide. I shall deal with each sex separately, starting with males. First, the main categories of motive. For the entire group of male suicides aged 15–24, physical and mental illness was the main factor leading to suicide in 31 percent of cases (16 of 51). Economic or work difficulties were responsible for 14 percent of cases. Public disgrace (mainly embezzlement), which I have previously categorized as a disturbance in social relationships, was responsible for 10 percent of cases. In another 10 percent of cases, heavy drinking, and the impassioned behavior it could generate, seemed to precipitate the act. Finally, disturbances in personal relationships (particularly family quarrels) were responsible for 20 percent of cases. We need to examine these categories more fully, taking into account the differences between male suicides aged 15–19 and those aged 20–24, and recognizing the extent to which categories could overlap in specific cases.

First, bodily and mental illness. As noted, close to a third of all male cases could be laid at this door. Illness was a commonplace experience for both suicides aged 15–19 and those aged 20–24. In October 1874, Josiah Curry, a 16-year-old joiner's apprentice (son of a deceased scripture reader), was killed by a railway train. His widowed mother said of her son: "He was very queer in his head. He hanged himself two year ago & since then he has tried to cut his throat. . . . His head was affected at times & he was quite delirious." The doctor had told her that her son had an overflow of blood to the head. The press report of the case queried whether the act was linked to a scolding the mother had given the deceased.[13] Henry Penny, a 19-year-old corn-merchant's clerk, six months shy of finishing his apprenticeship, shot himself with a revolver in August 1883. He and his brother (a timber merchant's clerk) lived with their father, a solicitor. The brother stated at the inquest: "For some time the deceased has appeared very silent and reserved, and in low spirits. We have noticed it for the last two years. It has increased of late." He also said that Penny had not been physically ill but had had a very violent temper. The surgeon who treated Penny deposed that the symptoms detailed by the brother "point to disorder of the brain which might turn to dementia. Melancholy frequently leads to suicide."[14]

Illness played a slightly larger role among males in their early twenties. John Hawdon, a 20-year-old workhouse inmate, cut his throat in the privy with a sailor's knife in June 1849. He was said to be laboring under nervous depression occasioned by lung disease.[15] In August 1854, James Rayner, a 21-year-old tailor, escaped from the Anlaby Road lunatic asylum, having been admitted four days earlier as a person unfit to be at large, and laid his head upon a railway line. Edward Casson, asylum surgeon, told the coroner that Rayner was in a low, melancholy, and suicidal state of insanity. "He made use of expressions to the effect that it was no use his living & that he had better die."[16] A 23-year-old hairdresser was found drowned in the Humber in September 1891. According to his widow, he had been ill and depressed with stomach pain for two weeks or more, for which he took no medicine. "He attended to his business but it seemed a great trouble to him to do so." A few days earlier, he had complained of his sight failing him.[17] Two more cases point to the overlap between bodily illness and depression on the one hand and work-related difficulties or accidents on the other. A 21-year-old oil miller, Thomas Holdstock, was found drowned in the Old Harbour in March 1876. An oil miller with whom Holdstock had lodged stated that "he seemed to be low since Hull fair ever since he cut his thumb & it kept him five weeks from working." He had been paying off debts ever since. Holdstock had been ill for over two weeks before he went missing: "It seemed to pull him down & make him very low. . . . The last week he would not speak to any one. He would throw food off his plate to the table if it did not suit him. Before he was a lively pleasant man. He was not quarrelsome but low."[18] In May 1885, a cartman hanged himself in the stable where he worked. His employer deposed that a horse had broken the deceased's leg three months before, since when he had been an Infirmary outpatient. During the previous week, he had complained of pains in his head, back, and chest, and was dull and depressed.[19]

Work- or economically motivated suicides were approximately half as common among young male adults as those inspired by illness. For those aged 15–19, the status of apprentice or "boy" was a vulnerable one, leading at times to reprimands, fear of failure, and dismissal. In November 1866, Thomas Firth, an apprentice bookbinder, aged 17, drowned himself in Barmston Drain. His boilermaker brother thought Firth "was rather affected in his head. He had a fall about 18 months ago out of a window & was laid up some time." Firth's sweetheart, a book sewer, attributed the act, however, to troubles at work. When she had last seen the deceased, he had said that he was not going back to work; another man had cut some books wrongly, but the foreman had reprimanded him. She went on: "He said he & the foreman had had some words about the work. He seemed much troubled. . . . He said he had been blamed for everything others had done for the last fortnight." She tried to persuade him to return to work, but he said he would drown himself. The witness concluded: "He said he had no complaint to make of home but of the shop."[20] A Nottingham pupil teacher, Thomas Tylee, aged 18, was found drowned in the Humber in April 1885. He had left home ten days before. His father, an insurance agent, found a letter in which Tylee said he was going " 'to carve out a way for himself.' He has frequently expressed a wish to go to the colonies. His letter said he could not face failure. He had to undergo an examination shortly."[21] George Ellis, a 13-year-old lather boy for a barber-hairdresser, was found drowned in Queen's Dock in November 1896. His mother said that her son liked his master, that he had never complained of ill-treatment, and that "his master was satisfied with the boy." In fact, the employer had given Ellis notice to leave because he had grown careless at his work: "I told him I should let his mother know about him by letter on Monday. He was I think a nervous lad."[22]

Male suicides in their early twenties were also affected by business worries and by dismissal. William Miller, a 23-year-old married pork butcher, of German nationality, cut his throat in February 1851. There was some suggestion, according to the coroner, that Miller was troubled by the fact that his wife "had been previously married to a man who was reported to have died during the cholera, but who was seen so late as the last Hull fair." But the other witnesses referred to the state of business. His wife deposed: "He [the deceased] said that trade was very bad, and he would go to Hamburg." Likewise, his father-in-law, who lived with them (and whom Miller had struck with a shovel while he sawed in the back shop), stated: "His business did not answer very well. He did not succeed well in his shop."[23]

Another 10 percent of young adult suicides were related to the social disgrace of embezzlement or gambling-related money troubles. As historians have noted, responsibility was often given to young employees to handle money, and employers were ever ready to suspect embezzlement.[24] To judge from the present cases, clerical workers were particularly vulnerable. A 16-year-old apprentice merchant's clerk, Alfred Pearson, poisoned himself with opium in his lodgings in July 1851, after it was discovered that he had misappropriated £23 12s. of his employer's money. His employer, a shipping agent, had told Pearson to come to the office as usual and had reassured him that he would not be discharged.[25] Thomas Lovitt, a 15-year-old timber merchant's clerk, shot himself with a pistol in May 1855. His mother deposed: "[H]e has been in a very desponding way during the last ten months. When he first manifested this despondency I enquired of him the cause and he said that his master was constantly finding fault with him and that he could do nothing to please him." His father, a cabinetmaker, stated, however, that his son's employer had told him that his son was suspected of stealing various sums of money. The father also noted that large sums passed through Lovitt's hands in his capacity of customhouse clerk.[26] In the most poignant and youthful suicide of all my cases, Charles Glew, a 12-year-old newsboy, son of a locomotive engine driver, placed himself on the North Eastern Railway line before an approaching train in October 1895. His mother told the inquest that her son had sold newspapers in the street for two months. The newsagent from whom her son got the news-papers had called on the witness and told her that Glew had got papers to the amount of £7 10s. by forging the newsagent's name. The mother agreed to pay the sum "to get it taken out of the police's hands," but she never saw her son again after talking with the newsagent.[27]

In April 1878, George Butler, a 21-year-old solicitor's clerk, poisoned himself with strychnine. A fellow clerk recorded that Butler had been low-spirited the previous week; he had been betting nearly every day and drink-ing too much. The solicitor's managing clerk stated that when it was dis-covered that Butler had used money entrusted to him to pay an account of his own, the deceased had said his father would repay it. Hence, the witness told him to get his father to come to the office immediately. Instead, Butler wrote his father a suicide note: "I have taken some of the office money & spent it. the amount is £12. 12s. 3d. which I ought to have paid but did not do so. please pay it for me. I owe different people little amounts also paid them. Give my love to all. Your affectionate But misguided Son."[28] And, finally, a 22-year-old baker, Albert Hill, put himself in the way of a goods train in June 1899. He had been out of work for three weeks owing to what his shoemaker father called "tender feet." The father also stated: "I did not know he had been betting or had owed any one money." The coro-ner, however, produced a book in the deceased's handwriting containing entries of betting transactions, and a suicide note to his brother:

Dear George, There is 15s. in that box mother has. That and what I have will get my watch and chain out of pawn. Get it and keep it in memory of me, as I don't think you will see me again alive. I have so much on my mind I can't stand it. what with going to the pawn shop and still owing £8 I can't get over it. I am sorry to say I have been living on mother this last three weeks.[29]

Heavy drinking took the same toll on young male adults as public dis-grace. Those in their early twenties were most affected, particularly in the mid Victorian years. Alcoholism typically caused depression, but it also worked its effect by stimulating behavior that damaged personal relation-ships. A 24-year-old bombardier in the Royal Artillery threw himself into the Humber in July 1858. A fellow soldier stated that the deceased, who had enlisted the previous October, had been in Hull since May. He had never been sober; he had suffered from delirium tremens; and he had been cen-sured for neglect of duty. A cooper, playing quoits on the Humber bank, saw the deceased walk into the river, and, ignoring the witness's shouts, keep on going. His uniform was discovered fifty yards from the waterside.[30]

Edwin Whitaker, a 22-year-old tailor, who lived with and was employed by his widowed father, poisoned himself with laudanum in March 1863. Whitaker's father told the inquest: "He was addicted to drinking when he could obtain the means & has been so for some time." The father stated that he had never known his son either to take laudanum or opium or to threaten to destroy himself, but he also told how he had called a policeman into his house to turn out his son, whom he had discharged the previous day for his violent conduct to the family.[31]

In March 1866, John Cartwright, a journeyman basket maker, aged 23, shot himself while intoxicated. He had lived with a prostitute as her husband since the Hull Fair in October. For two months he had been unemployed, but then worked as a basket maker. A week before he had come home drunk. Cartwright gave his common-law wife 3s. 4d. out of his wages, which were usually between 10s. 6d. and 13s. a week. It was his custom to buy the meat for the following week on Saturday night, but he had failed to do so. When asked why, he said "he would be dead in a fortnight. He said he was trouble." While his wife was with a neighbor, who had mangled some clothes for her, Cartwright came in and asked her if she loved him: "I smiled & said 'No' because I thought it silly of him to talk so before people. . . . He said 'you don't' & I said 'no.' He said 'all right' & went behind the bed curtain & I could not see him. Directly he fired a pistol. . . . I ran out screaming."[32]

This leads us into the final category of motive, that of disturbance in personal relationships. One-fifth of young male suicides seem to have been provoked by bereavement, romantic disappointment, and family tension or quarrels. Bereavement was a factor in only one case. Henry Tindall, a 16-year-old bricklayer's boy, hung himself in June 1862. His father, a man of drunken habits, said he had noticed nothing peculiar in the boy's conduct. Tindall's sister, however, declared that he had "often talked about his mother who was burnt to death about 13 months ago. He has not seemed comfortable since."[33]

A more common impetus to suicide was romantic disappointment, notably for males in their early twenties. Alfred Hawksley, a 22-year-old marine fireman, hanged himself from a window-shutter fastener in Pease Place in January 1873. When ashore, he had lived with his father, a fishmonger and auctioneer. For days at a time, however, he had also lived with Ann Duffill, "a gay woman," or prostitute, although he did not keep her or allow her a weekly sum. She lived in Pease Place, a dark narrow square of six houses. Late one night, a neighbor, making bread at the time, was forced to deal with Hawksley in passionate temper. He said he would get into Ann's house or she would find him dead on the step. Ann had refused to admit him on other occasions, the witness said.[34]

In April 1890, George Broadley, a 20-year-old fisherman, shot himself with a pistol. He had wanted to stay the night with Eliza Reynolds, the wife of another fisherman. When she objected, Broadley pulled out a revolver. Reynolds fled the house, but Broadley caught her and started to drag her back, saying, "If we can't live together we'll die together." A policeman took up the story at this point. Hearing Reynolds call, "Help police," he had run toward her. But when Broadley caught hold of Reynolds, said the constable, "I thought it was a family quarrel & slackened to a walk." He caught up with the couple as they reached the house. A struggle with Broadley ensued, during which he fired twice at the constable. He then ran into the house and shot himself. Reynolds concluded her evidence by stating: "On Saturday, he asked me to leave my husband & go away with him."[35]

Family tension or quarrels, in contrast, affected teenagers more, especially in the 1890's. A 16-year-old wood-turner's apprentice was found drowned in Prince's Dock in June 1891. His father, a dock laborer, said that he had argued with the deceased and threatened to stop his pocket money. That evening, the father found that a box had been forced open and ten or twelve shillings taken out. Hearing that his son had enlisted, the witness went to Beverley barracks and to the Hull recruiting stations, but could not find him. Ten days later, a fisherman found the body.[36]

John Ramsay, a 15-year-old errand boy, was found drowned in Prince's Dock in January 1895. His mother had died when he was a baby; he had been adopted seven years before, his adoptive parents promising that the boy would not go into the workhouse. A month before his death, his adoptive mother had used a penny cane, kept to correct the dog, across his shoulders for mixing with a bad character. She herself deposed: "I gave him a good flogging. . . . He cried when I caned him. He never said anything about drowning himself." A surgeon told the inquest that the cane must have been used severely, given the bruises on Ramsay.[37]

It may be significant that many of these cases of dispute between teenagers and their parents took place in the final decade of the century. It is conceivable that they reflect a sharpening generational conflict, as adolescents bridled at the prolonged semi-dependent status of youth and became less willing to submit to parental discipline. In this scenario, suicide was a family strategy of resistance with tragic consequences.

IV

So much for young adult males. I shall delay drawing the threads together until after the evaluation of young adult female suicides. For the entire group of female suicides aged 15–24, physical and mental illness was the second most important factor leading to suicide. Just over one-fifth of female suicides were so touched, as compared to one-third of male suicides. Economic difficulties were responsible for only 5 percent of cases; drink for another 5 percent. Far and away the most important determinant of young female suicides was disturbance in personal relationships (bereavement, romantic disappointment, and family quarrels); 42 percent of female suicides were so affected, over twice the proportion for male suicides. The figure would rise to 53 percent if we were to add the four suicides in which illegitimate pregnancy was involved. These cases have been treated separately, however, since it was impossible to determine which category they belonged to: economic difficulty, disturbance in social relationships (in the sense of public disgrace), or disturbance in personal relationships. If, however, these cases are deemed to be examples of public disgrace, and two similar cases are added, then disturbance in social relationships was responsible for 16 percent of cases. As before, these different categories warrant detailed examination.

First, bodily and mental illness, which affected teenagers less than those in their early twenties. Ada Lunn, a domestic servant, aged 16, was found drowned in a brick pond in December 1887. Her employer, a widow, said that Lunn, her only servant, had been there a fortnight. She had complained of her head and appeared depressed. "It was her first place & I thought that was the reason. . . . I do not think she made friends with the neighbouring servants." Lunn, gloomy and depressed, went out to do errands and never came back. Her mother, wife of a cooper, testified that her daughter had a history of depression, beginning at age 14, after an attack of Saint Vitus's dance (chorea). For almost two years prior to taking the situation, the deceased had suffered no symptoms.[38]

In May 1894, Annie Marsden, an 18-year-old housemaid, poisoned herself. Marsden was an orphan; she lived with an aunt and uncle when not in service. She had been with her present employer, a corn merchant, for over eight months. Her uncle said he had noticed no change in the deceased; but he added that her father had had brain fever and had gone out of his mind. A letter found on Marsden, addressed to her aunt, declared: "[F]orgive me for what I am going to do. I am so miserable. I feel so queer. I can't be of any good to myself or anybody. I am just in despair. I can't tell you how I feel. I do want to live and be good but I can't it's no use trying." A fellow domestic, finally, referred to Marsden's religious turn of mind: "She read religious books, chiefly the Bible. . . . She talked about religion a great deal. She never seemed despondent about herself in a religious point of view."[39]

In January 1856, Mary Ellerton, a 24-year-old woman, who helped her mother clean offices and char, hanged herself from her bedpost. She had lived with her parents and brother in two lodging rooms. A neighbor and mariner's wife stated that Ellerton had complained of pain all over and had asked the witness "to put some leaches on to her stomach which I did." The surgeon who attended the deceased had thought she had flatulent dyspepsia. When the pain persisted, he "ordered leeches to the pit of the stomach." Ellerton's brother said his sister had been ill: "She talked at random at times, which she was not in the habit of doing before. One night she was singing in bed, which I never heard her do before. I heard her say she would take poison if she did not get better. Her mother told her to hold her noise & not talk so silly."[40]

In June 1873, Louisa Hodsman, the 21-year-old daughter of a stonemason, poisoned herself. Her mother said Hodsman had occasionally been in a low state of mind, brought on by ill health, which had affected her for eight years: "She seemed depressed that she had grown up & did not get better & sometimes wished herself dead." The doctor who had attended her stated that the deceased was an invalid in body and mind, and her mind had been weakened by disease. Latterly, she had not been able to wait on herself.[41]

Another suicide involved postpartum illness. Martha Thompson, the 23-year-old wife of an iron-ship plater, cut her throat in March 1890. Her widowed mother, who had lived with Thompson and her husband in order to look after her daughter, said that she had suffered from heart disease and dropsy. She had been ill since giving birth a year before and had expressed doubt about recovering from the illness. The surgeon said that Thompson had showed a melancholic turn of mind. When her husband was out collecting his club money, she had used his carving knife.[42]

Economic motives seem to have been much less common. Indeed, in only two cases was working life, or the lack of it, the clear source of the problem, both of them in the 1880's. In September 1883, Annie Bownes, a 16-year-old domestic servant, was found drowned in Albert Dock. Her stepfather told the coroner that Bownes had come to Hull from London about seven months earlier; she had been in service for six months, the last six weeks at the home of a shipyard manager. She seemed to be "comfortable in her situation," said the stepfather, but "she had rather a shortish temper." Mary Wilkins, the manager's wife, said Bownes had "a very sullen & rather obstinate temper," and she had been reproved for not getting up. "Reproof did not seem to have any lasting effect on her." The witness also recorded that the deceased "was very easily led" and "very fond of trashy novels." The constable who took charge of the body found a letter addressed to her mother in which Bownes blamed her mistress: "Its Mrs Wilkins is causing all this—nothing else but grumble—I cannot stand which has been all to day ... my little sister keep her till she is able to work for herself—Remember the others at school. Never to see you again but do not forget me. I cannot stand swear & grumble. goodbye for ever."[43]

In the other case, Kate Hird, the 15-year-old daughter of a merchant seaman, who had been depressed because she could not get a situation, was found drowned in Prince's Dock in June 1885. Hird had been at home for three months, living with her sister and father. The latter, who had gone to sea a fortnight before, had told the deceased to get a place, and she had tried, but without success. Hird's brother-in-law, assistant to a surgeon, stated: "For a long time she has been downcast. . . . She got some laudanum three months ago, but we got it. Father has not threatened to turn her out. He has asked her if she could not find a place."[44]

Nor were the effects of heavy drinking particularly evident. The suicides in which drink figured occurred in the early and mid Victorian years, the victims again typically being in their early twenties. In December 1862, an 18-year-old "singlewoman," who had come from Newcastle a fortnight before, leaped into Prince's Dock. Her widowed sister, with whom the deceased was living, said "her habits were very dissipated, she was frequently in the habit of getting drunk." A joiner, who waited in the Grapes pub of an evening, saw her standing against a wall opposite the pub: "She had the bottom of her frock turned up over her shoulders and her arms crossed."[45]

As with young male suicides, however, drink also went along with other precipitants. A 22-year-old "singlewoman," Eliza Farrow, who was said not to have been very sober, poisoned herself with opium in June 1848. She had taken ill in a public house, and was carried home by a fisherman. The landlady of the house where Farrow lived would not have her in, and she died in the fisherman's room. It would not be stretching the evidence too much to define this suicide as a case of disturbance in social relationships, notably social isolation.[46]

The next case, in contrast, hints at an overlap between drink and disturbance in personal, or marital, relationships. In October 1843, Lavinia Smith, the 23-year-old wife of a stonemason, poisoned herself with laudanum. She was said to be in the habit of drinking; she had tried to drown herself three months earlier; and she and her husband did not live happily together.[47]

By far the most common experience of suicide for young females was a disturbance in personal relationships, specifically bereavement, romantic disappointment, and family disagreement. In May 1840, Eliza Brown, a 22-year-old domestic servant for a tailor in the Land of Green Ginger (a street in the Old Town), died from arsenic poisoning. The tailor's housekeeper told the inquest: "She has been dull lately which I attributed to the death of her sister about 14 days ago."[48] And in July 1846, an apprentice straw bonnet maker, aged 18, was found next to the Floating Chapel in Junction Dock. She had been depressed in consequence of her sister's death of "brain fever." Another sister was dangerously ill of the same malady. The deceased, who had said she had not had one night's rest for the past month, had declared that if the second sister should also die, she would not be able to get over it.[49]

Strangely, bereavement as a precipitant of young female suicide then disappears until the 1890's. In September 1890, Lydia Stather, aged 21, was found drowned in the river Hull. Her dry shawl was on the riverbank. Her brother recounted how their mother had died suddenly a week before. "My sister was delicate. She never got her mother out of her mind; she was very much attached to her mother." An aunt who had come to stay with Stather said that her niece had cried every night over her mother.[50]

In July 1898, the 23-year-old widow of a steam-trawler engineer poisoned herself. Her husband had been drowned five months before, and the deceased had been terribly affected, according to her widowed mother, with whom she had lived. "I was sadly afraid that her mind was sadly affected." The deceased had found a situation as a domestic servant, but she could not settle, and came home after six days.[51]

In addition to bereavements, there were a few cases revealing romantic tensions. In November 1839, a 20-year-old domestic servant poisoned herself. Her mother explained that her daughter had been low ever since a young man "who paid his addresses to her" had left town. The deceased had borrowed threepence to buy arsenic, telling the chemist it was to wash a bedstead with.[52] The most convincing instance of this type concerned a 21-year-old domestic servant, Elizabeth Anderson, who threw herself into a timber pond in August 1869. She was in love with James Long, a driller at an iron shipyard, who had lodged with Anderson and her widowed mother. Long paid attention to the deceased, but also to Kitty Lowther who lived opposite. Anderson returned from a five-week stint in service, complaining that Long had gone with Kitty. Long received a letter from the deceased in which she said she intended to put an end to it all. In the style that characterized the entire letter, she wrote: "[M]y dear James, you and your Dear Kitty will have a little more peace once more as I think I ham a grate truble to you both." [53]

Third, family tensions, whether between children and parents, or between marriage partners, were evident in a larger number of cases. Cases of generational conflict were restricted, as with young males, to the last dozen years of the century. In January 1888, Rebecca Ashton, a 15-year-old worker at Reckitt's starch works, was found drowned in a timber pond. Ashton and her mother had quarreled about the former's club money. The deceased had been ill for three weeks and had not been working. When Ashton gave her mother eightpence of her club money, the mother asked what she had done with the other eightpence, and reproached her for keeping it back, seeing that her father was out of work. The mother then deposed: "She did not say but jumped & put on her shawl & said 'I'll go & drown myself' & went out." The witness also said that Ashton was "generally kind & affectionate—but very hasty in temper." Her shawl, hat, and apron were found on the railway line. She was discovered lying on her back in two feet of water, head toward the shore, petticoats intact, in a pose (although not a setting) reminiscent of Millais's painting *Ophelia*.[54]

Ellen Hamilton, the 15-year-old daughter of a shipyard foreman, poisoned herself in May 1898. According to her mother, she had told Hamilton to get on with her housework, to which the deceased had replied, "I shall do as I like." She then swallowed carbolic acid. Her mother further complained: "She gave way to reading novelettes and I have had to chastise her about it. . . . She had on one occasion when I reprimanded her said 'I wish I were dead.'" The inquest also revealed that Hamilton had been in a situation, but could not settle, and came home. The mother, moreover, had been in the habit of leaving the house, and most of the housework had devolved upon the deceased. A want of parental care on the part of the mother was suggested, too, by the fact, emphasized by the coroner, that three of her children had died in infancy, two the result of burning, on which inquests had been held.[55]

The cases of marital tension or disturbance were a good deal more convoluted, not to say bizarre. In all these cases, however, the husband of the deceased was at sea or away on business when the suicide occurred, suggesting that physical absence was part of the disturbance in personal relationship. Sarah Folly, the 18-year-old wife of a fisherman, poisoned herself in September 1855. The surgeon who attended her in the night found her in a brothel. She told him that she had taken opium to destroy herself, because "some one had threatened to inform her husband of her mode of life." The woman who ran the brothel said that Folly's husband had been at sea for two weeks. She also stated that a man had told Folly that he had informed her husband of the brothel, and that she need not go to the owners as her husband had stopped his half-pay going to her. According to the deceased's mother, however, the husband had done no such thing, since he had been told nothing; the man had been joking.[56]

The 22-year-old wife of a chief gunner was found drowned in June 1878. The deceased had told a friend, whose husband was on board the same ship as her own, that she had quarreled with her husband, had received no letter from him, and had been drinking heavily all week. Another friend deposed: "She told me 2 months ago that she would commit suicide because her husband ill used her."[57]

That leaves only the cases of illegitimate pregnancy. At inquests on young women, coroners and juries invariably wanted to know whether the deceased had been pregnant.[58] In four of our young female suicides, this was the case. Three of the suicides in which pregnancy was confirmed were teenagers; all four suicides took place in the final two decades of the century. In April 1881, an 18-year-old domestic servant, Harriet Crawford, was found drowned in Sutton Drain. Her widowed mother told the coroner that Crawford had come home from her situation six weeks before, saying that she "was not regular." Suspecting that her daughter was in the family way, the witness had told her to take gin and pennyroyal. A friend of Crawford's brother, a painter by trade, then deposed that Crawford had told him that she was pregnant, "and said there were two of us for it meaning me and Frederick Field. . . . She thought about drowning herself. She was rather down when she said it—She said also several times that she should not live long. . . . I offered deceased a sovereign on Sunday if she wanted help. She said she didn't need it." A surgeon testified that Crawford was not more than two months pregnant. And Field, a spirit merchant's pot washer, contested the allegation that the deceased was pregnant by him.[59]

In July 1889, Grace Postill, a 17-year-old paper-mill worker, was found drowned in the river Hull. Her aunt, with whom Postill had lived, had sent her dinner to the mill by a boy. He returned to say that she had been let go at breakfast. The paper-mill manager deposed that Postill "had not attended to her work" and so was discharged. A fellow worker stated that the deceased had made no mention of a disappointed love affair, but had often said that she wished she was dead. A surgeon declared that Postill was about six months pregnant.[60]

Another paper-mill hand, Mary Kemp, aged 23, was found drowned in Barmston Drain in March 1891. Her mother said that when last she saw Kemp, she had come in from work about 1 P.M. and lain down on the bed. "She was with child and expected her confinement at once." She had been in an excited and distracted state since Christmas on account of her condition. The surgeon then deposed that Kemp had not only been pregnant; "she was in labour when she died, the child was a full term child. The probabilities are that she would have been delivered in two or three hours."[61]

And, finally, the 18-year-old daughter of a timber-yard laborer poisoned herself in October 1896. Her father said that the deceased was the eldest of eight children; she had prepared breakfast for the family and later made the beds. Her mother was ill and near her confinement. The father said the deceased had been dull for the last week or two, but he had had no idea she was pregnant. A surgeon said she was over six months pregnant.[62]

In two of these cases, the women in question shared the fact of pregnancy with friends and family, and little in the way of remorse or self-recrimination appears in the evidence. In the other cases, however, the pregnancy seems to have been known only to the deceased, suggesting reluctance, not to say shame, about making the condition known. To some degree, therefore, these suicides could have been prompted by a disturbance in social relationships, more specifically, by a feeling of social disgrace.

Two more suicides possibly belong to this category of disrupted social relationships. A 17-year-old cotton-mill worker, Sarah Raby, was found drowned in Sutton Drain in February 1866. Her mother said that on the day Raby went missing, she had been stopped working for a day. The witness had heard that her daughter had quarreled with some other girls and had been threatened with a summons. A workmate deposed that Raby had told her she had got "the bad disorder," or venereal disease, and was ill through it. "On the Sunday she said she would think nothing of destroying herself—she often said so." Another witness stated: "She said she would try to go into the Union & that if she did not she would make away with herself." Seemingly, Raby had been given an order for her to go into the Union. In fact, the deceased's family had occasionally asked for poor-law assistance, and the deceased's mother applied to the Board of Guardians for a coffin for her daughter.[63]

In the second case, Sarah Hope, a 23-year-old domestic servant, was found drowned in Albert Dock in May 1892. A nursemaid who had worked in the same house deposed that one day Hope had entered the kitchen crying. She said she was being accused of taking money. She then asked the witness to give her watch and chain to her young man. The employer, a hatter and hosier, stated that Hope had been his general servant for eighteen months. He had suspected her honesty and called in two policemen. "Her boxes were searched but not with her consent." A purse containing £11 was found under a wringing machine in the kitchen; the deceased admitted that £7 belonged to her employer, from whom she had stolen it. She was told she would not be prosecuted, but as the employer stated: "Nothing was said about her leaving us, but it was understood that she would do so." [64]

V

It remains only to underline the essential patterns in the experience of suicide that emerge from these 89 cases. Young adult men were particularly affected by bodily and mental illness and by economic or work difficulties. Almost one-third of the young males were said to have been ill and depressed prior to the act of suicide. This was especially true of those in their early twenties, and true for the entire Victorian period. Work pressures affected young men by way of employer reproaches, dismissal, and business failure. Once again, this influence was as true of the late as of the early Victorian years. Thus the Hull evidence does not bear out Olive Anderson's view, based on London inquests, that the work situations and punishments experienced by young suicides improved during the second half of the century.[65] Young men, and notably young clerks, were also tempted by the handling of cash to embezzle from their employers. To these work-related or social precipitants, we must add that of drink, which in particular influenced those in their early twenties. The link between drink and self-destruction was strongest in the mid Victorian years, weakening thereafter, perhaps in line with the general reduction in the scale of drunkenness.[66] However, impulsive, drink-induced suicides often involved a disturbance in personal relationships. A fifth or more of the young male suicides examined fall into this last category. Romantic disappointment took its toll, as did conflict between parents and adolescent children, notably in the 1890's.

Conflict between the generations, it should be noted, was caused by money or business differences, not by questions of courtship and marriage. In all, the experience of suicide for young men was a diverse one, and external, work-related factors were not alone responsible. Illness and the emotional complications to do with family and marriage were also important.

The female experience of suicide was more homogeneous and patterned more by internal or inward-looking factors than that of young men. Illness, especially depression, affected one-fifth of young female suicides, although it was not always clear what exactly triggered the depression. Few female suicides were directly linked to the workplace, although the two that were concerned domestic service. (I shall have more to say in a moment about the indirect effects of work in the form of domestic service.) Nor was drink-induced suicide at all common. The most important precipitants of young female suicides were disturbances in personal relationships provoked by bereavement, romantic disappointment, and family dissension. The generational conflict between parents and children came to a head in the 1890's, again over money not marriage; marital conflict was associated with, perhaps aggravated by, male occupations that led to separation for weeks at a time. The evidence does not, however, endorse the stereotype, impressed upon the Victorian imagination through literary and artistic forms, of lovelorn, seduced, and abandoned girls choosing suicide over the shame of "falling."[67] The Hull depositions turned up more examples of illegitimate pregnancy than did those examined by Anderson, owing largely to the inclusion of open verdicts.[68] And there were a couple of cases of jealousy-induced suicide. But against the romantic stereotype of the lovelorn, seduced, and betrayed female suicide, we can set many more cases of bereavement, generational conflict, and physical and mental illness (although some instances of the last may have been in response to romantic disappointment).

The most significant common denominator in young female suicides, however, was domestic service. As we have seen, two-thirds (25 of 38) of female suicides aged 15–24 were in waged work. Of those in waged work, nearly three-quarters (18 of 25) were in some form of domestic service or between situations. Hence, of all the female suicides, whether in waged work or not, almost one-half (18 of 38) were in domestic service or between situations. Here, too, the Victorian stereotype of the live-in domestic, prone to drunkenness, theft, and pregnancy, cast into the street by her mistress on discovery, fell short of the mark.[69] Only one domestic servant suicide was pregnant; only one was let go because of theft. The main precipitants for domestic servants were illness (especially depression), romantic disappointment, bereavement, and work-related problems. (Being in domestic service at least relieved them, it seems, of conflict with parents and spouses.) The most satisfactory conclusion about suicides in this occupation, therefore, is that offered by a number of suicidologists: the domestic servant was young, transplanted (into an unfamiliar environment, and one often including class difference), isolated (especially in single-servant households, which was the typical situation), and tightly disciplined. Domestic service was a lonely, demanding, and never-ending occupation.[70] Such conditions were unfavorable to a stable psychic balance. In such surroundings, depression, romantic disappointment (and marriage was the main escape route for domestics), and employer admonishment could take on exaggerated dimensions. In all, domestic service provided one of the most crucial settings for the suicide of young adult women.

8

The Prime of Life

Then he remembered Nora. Although she was always
brave, and never complained, he knew that her life was
one of almost incessant physical suffering; and as for
himself he was tired and sick of it all. He had been
working like a slave all his life and there was nothing to
show for it—there never would be anything to show for
it. He thought of the man who had killed his wife and
children. The jury had returned the usual verdict,
"Temporary Insanity." It never seemed to occur to these
people that the truth was that to continue to suffer
hopelessly like this was evidence of permanent insanity.

Robert Tressell,
The Ragged Trousered Philanthropists (1914)

The next phase of the Victorian life
cycle was that of the prime of life,
covering the years from 25 to 44. One of the most dramatic changes between the young adult stage of the life cycle and the prime of life was in
the realm of civil status. In the 15–24 age group, only 13 percent of men
and 23 percent of women were married. In the prime of life, however, 75
percent of men and 76 percent of women were married, the highest rate
of any age group.[1] In addition, the most economically demanding life-cycle
stage for married couples, especially among the working class, came when
they were in their thirties and early forties. In these years, the entire family
was usually dependent upon the male breadwinner's earnings. Children
were still too young for full-time work, and wives were at their busiest in

the home. In consequence, women's wage-earning fell to its lowest level between 25 and 39 years of age, and particularly between 30 and 34. This stage of the life cycle was difficult not only for married couples. Single individuals with no coresident family, and particularly migrant lodgers, were economically vulnerable, as were those who were separated or widowed, particularly women.[2] Over and above the strictly economic pressures of the prime of life, there were the strains of childbearing (postpartum depression posing a risk for women); the grief associated with the death of spouse, children, and parents; and the tensions surrounding the establishment and maintenance of personal intimacy.[3]

I

In the Victorian era in Hull, there were 153 male and 75 female suicides in the prime of life. To these I have added 14 male and 19 female open verdicts, making a grand total of 167 male and 94 female suicides in this middle stage of the life cycle. The average annual mortality from suicide per 10,000 living in the prime of life was 12.3 and 6.3, respectively, which was more than twice the rate for young adults.[4] For both sexes, the average suicide rate was higher for those aged 35–44 than for 25–34-year-olds. The rate for men aged 35–44 was highest in the 1860's, 1870's, and 1890's; for women of the same age group, in the 1840's, 1880's, and 1890's. The rate for men aged 25–34 was highest in the 1840's and 1890's; for women of the same age group, in the 1840's.[5] As for the civil status of suicides in the prime of life, of the 167 male suicides, 34 percent were single, 52 percent were married, and 3 percent were widowed;[6] of the 94 female suicides, 27 percent were single, 63 percent were married, and 8.5 percent were widowed. For both sexes, then, but especially for men, a larger proportion of suicides than expected were single. Two other measures add to this finding. First, 43 percent of all suicides in the prime of life among both sexes were single, separated, or widowed, and thus without the financial and emotional support of a spouse.[7] Second, in the 1890's (the only decade for which we can compute a suicide rate according to civil status), the rate for single male suicides was 37.3 per 10,000 living; for married males, 14.3; and for widowed males, 31.9.[8] The rates for females were 14.4 (single), 7.1 (married), and 28.1 (widowed).[9] For both sexes, in short, the suicide rate was much higher for the single and widowed than for the married. All these measures suggest, therefore, that the single and widowed were particularly vulnerable to suicide.

Suicides of single males in the prime of life were distributed fairly evenly across the entire age range, although with a slight preponderance in the 35–44 age group, whereas almost three-quarters of single female suicides were between 25 and 34 years of age (and 42.3 percent were aged 25–29). Thus single female suicides were younger than their male counterparts. Married male suicides clustered in the 35–44 age group; over 70 percent were in this economically punishing phase of the life cycle. And 58 percent of all married female suicides were in the same life stage. Finally, and unsurprisingly, nearly all of the widowed suicides were in the 35–44 age group.

Turning to living arrangements, 87 percent of married male suicides and 98 percent of married female suicides in the prime of life lived with their spouses, and in some cases, also with their children. Three married men were alone in lodgings, and three were in a police or prison cell; one married woman was in the asylum.[10] Of the fifteen male suicides who were separated, four lived with kin, four were in lodgings, two were on the tramp, and one had just emerged from the workhouse. Of the six separated female suicides, three lived with kin and three were cohabiting. The handful of widowers were either in lodgings or with kin; widows were either household heads, cohabiting, or in lodgings. Before dealing with the living arrangements of single suicides, we have the tricky task of counting children. It is commonly suggested, of course, that the absence of children increases the likelihood of suicide. In 57 percent of male married, separated, and widowed suicides, and in 41 percent of female married, separated, and widowed suicides, no children are mentioned in the inquest depositions. These are doubtless inflated figures, since the children of some suicides might simply have escaped mention. As they stand, however, the figures suggest that a high percentage of male and female suicides were without what is considered the restraining influence of children.[11] Of the 54 single male suicides, 25, or nearly one-half, were in lodgings of some kind; 16, or 30 percent, were with kin; 2 were on board ship; and 1 was in an army barracks. Of the 26 single female suicides, only 2 were in lodgings; 11, or over 40 percent, were with kin; 5 were cohabiting; 4 were live-in domestics; and 1 was in the workhouse. So while single men were in lodgings when not with kin, single women were cohabiting or in service when not with kin.

In what ways did those in the prime of life destroy themselves? As we know already, Hull men under 35 years of age preferred poison and the gun.[12] It is no surprise to find, therefore, that of those aged 25–34, 29 percent used poison, 19 percent the gun, and another 19 percent hanged themselves. By contrast, of those aged 35–44, over 40 percent hanged themselves, 20 percent used poison, 14 percent cut their throats, and 11.5

percent shot themselves. Poison was the preferred method of suicide for women in the prime of life: over one-third of both those aged 25–34 and those aged 35–44 used this method. Among those aged 25–34, drowning was the second most favored method, followed by hanging and throat cutting; among those aged 35–44, hanging was the second most favored method, followed by drowning and throat cutting.

What, finally, of the occupational and class background of suicides in the prime of life? The largest number of male suicides in this age group worked in transport (master mariners, cartmen, seamen, dock laborers), followed in rank order by metals and engineering (boilermakers, iron-yard workers), food and drink (butchers, greengrocers), commerce (clerks, merchants, shipping agents), building (joiners, painters), domestic and other servants (licensed victuallers), and chemicals and oils (chemists and druggists, oil-press men). The number of male suicides in the prime of life, in short, corresponds closely to the occupational profile of the city.[13] However, comparing the proportions of male suicides with the proportions of all occupied males (in tables 6.7 and 6.8), we see that the proportion of suicides was larger than expected in only chemicals and oils, commerce, national and local government (mainly policemen), the professions (surgeons, teachers), and domestic and other service.[14] As such, the figures bear out, to a degree, the national finding that the most suicidal occupations in the prime of life included chemists, surgeons, and licensed victuallers and their servants.[15] When occupation is translated into social class, and when the proportion of male suicides is compared with the social class distribution of household heads in Hull in 1851 (in table 5.1), we see that while skilled manual and unskilled workers were underrepresented among male suicides, the skilled nonmanual class was considerably overrepresented.[16] In a word, the lower-middle-class group of clerks, shopkeepers, chemists, innkeepers, commercial travelers, dealers, and policemen were particularly suicidal. If to class III one adds class II (lower professionals, larger shopkeepers, smaller industrialists, agents, and brokers), then 37 percent of all male suicides in the prime of life were in these two classes, but only 26 percent of household heads.

The occupational data for women in the prime of life are less detailed, in part because few were in formal employment. Only 17 percent of Hull women in this age group were listed in the 1901 census as occupied.[17] Of the female suicides, fourteen, or 15 percent, had full-time jobs, nine in domestic service, two in dressmaking, and one in shoebinding; one ran a lodging house, and one had a market stall. Ten of the fourteen were single, three were widowed, and one was separated.[18] In addition, however, two of the married suicides took in lodgers, another kept a small laundry, a fourth went out charring, and a fifth worked at fish curing. Including the married cases takes the figure for occupied female suicides to 20 percent. This is probably a minimum figure, since casual or part-time labor might have escaped mention in the inquest depositions. One other measure can be made: the social class of the husband or cohabitee of the female suicides. As we found for all female suicides (in table 6.13), the social class of the husband or cohabitee was commonly skilled or semi-skilled manual. Indeed, 85 percent of female suicides in the prime of life were living with skilled, semi-skilled, or unskilled workingmen.

II

We now turn at length to the experience of suicide in the prime of life, treating each sex separately, and exploring the motives for suicide under the five main headings of economic difficulties, illness, disturbances in personal relationships, disturbances in social relationships, and drink. Taking male suicides first, we can dispense quickly with the handful of emigrants and prisoners who killed themselves, since little emerged from the inquests on these cases, other than the fact that the emigrants were generally Swedish and bound for North America, and the prisoners had proved refractory in prison and been punished accordingly, illustrating Durkheim's judgment perhaps that prisoner suicides were "fatalistic," the result of excessive or oppressive discipline.[19] In August 1868, Carl Hallonquest, a 40-year-old painter, arrived in Hull from Gothenburg along with 300 other emigrants bound for Liverpool and the United States. As the ship waited to get up to the pier, Hallonquest, who had seemed dull and unwell on the three-day journey, cut his throat with a razor.[20] Clearly, for a few emigrants, the emotional cost of transplantation was too heavy. All the prisoner suicides occurred, for whatever reason, between 1870 and 1875. In January 1872, for example, Timothy Cain, a 39-year-old laborer, committed the previous October to six months' hard labor for assaulting a constable, hanged himself with a towel in his cell. Cain had been unwilling to work, said the prison governor, continually getting off the treadmill, and had threatened to commit suicide. No significance was attached to these threats, since prisoners frequently made them to escape work. When he killed himself, he was in the dark cell as punishment for smashing up his usual cell. The warder who had accidentally left the towel in the dark cell stated that the prisoner used to rave about religious subjects.[21]

Two of the main categories of motive were numerically unimportant for male suicides in the prime of life: disturbances in social and in personal relationships. First, less than 4 percent of male suicides were motivated by a disturbance in social relationships; or, more specifically, by the public disgrace associated with embezzlement, fraud, or theft. In June 1861, a 37-year-old collector or clerk in the goods department of the North Eastern Railway Company, married with four children, shot himself in his back-yard after his wife told him that the railway auditor had been to see him. The deceased, who had been with the railway company for twelve years, had overcharged merchants and kept the difference between the proper sum and what he received. He had recently asked a fellow clerk, "if he were 'a stiff one' did I think the Company would seize his house." [22] In September 1876, John Brooke, a 42-year-old accountant in the town treasurer's office, shot himself with the rifle he owned as a captain of the volunteers. A committee had been charged with investigating Brooke's accounts. As an alderman and committee member told the inquest: "During the last week he has been under very considerable mental pressure. I believe he knew himself to be under the surveillance of the police." Brooke left a note that stated: "The horrors of the last ten days have unmanned me, destroyed my belief in all humanity & life is a mistake; the net which enmity, malice & injustice is weaving around me is too much for me to bear." For the coroner, the note showed that he was laboring under a delusion.[23] And, lastly, Jacob Benjamin, a Russian secondhand clothes dealer, aged about 40, was arrested in December 1893, together with his wife, for stealing clothing from a house. He strangled himself with a scarf attached to the door of the police cell.[24]

Second, only 9 percent of male suicides in the prime of life were directly associated with family quarrels, bereavement, or romantic disappointment. The vast majority of those who were so affected were single, widowed, or separated. First, cases of bereavement. Charles Jennison, a 36-year-old Humber pilot (collecting pilotage from merchants and shipbrokers), poisoned himself with laudanum in June 1867. The woman with whom he had lodged for six weeks stated that he had "often talked about his wife & said he could not live without her." She had died a few weeks before. In a note placed in a Bible, Jennison left all his belongings to his son and asked to go into the same grave as his wife.[25] A 34-year-old boatman shot himself in

May 1897. He had been low and queer since his little girl had been burned to death five months earlier, said his brother, a police constable.[26]

Another handful of cases involved the emotional and financial impact of separation. Henry John Hindson poisoned himself with opium in February 1861, six months after his wife had left him, taking their teenage daughter with her. Hindson's widowed mother, who had lived with them, stated that her son had been out of work for four months. Oil milling, at which he had labored for seventeen years, caused him indigestion and bronchitis, and he had been discharged in consequence. Mother and son had lived on what she could earn by washing and on parish relief. The note Hindson left his mother read: "Do not grieve for me I shall be best out of this world where there is nothing but poverty and misery for me. Mary has deserted me and you are pining and pinching yourself for me and I cannot bear it longer. . . . I pray God to bless you and my Child, as for Mary she must take her chance as had she returned to me I should not have done this."[27]

Passions surfaced even more in the next two suicides. Robert Hickson, a 39-year-old, deaf and dumb coal porter, was so affected by his wife's adultery that a quarrel over a wet waistcoat in November 1841 provoked him to kill her with a poker in front of the children and then cut his own throat. A fellow porter denied that he had been involved with Hickson's wife, but the coroner stated that the jury believed he was responsible. "If you have caused the deaths of these two persons," the coroner declared, "I hope you will repent, for the offence is of a most horrible description." A neighbor testified that the deceased was a passionate man and had been known to hit his wife, who had not been in good health. Even so, the inquest jury's verdict on the wife's murder was excusable homicide.[28] In September 1899, José Perez, a Spanish marine fireman, tried to kill the brush-factory hand he was in love with, before shooting himself. His suicide note accused the woman of abusing his financial generosity, and concluded: "She has always deceived me. . . . I can neither work nor anything. . . . I am going to God for ever."[29]

III

The three remaining motives were a good deal more important. Approximately 28 percent of all male suicides in the prime of life were ascribed by inquest witnesses to physical and mental illness. Both single and married males were affected by illness, but single males were overrepresented. Almost 45 percent of those driven to suicide by illness were single. If the widowed and separated are added, the figure reaches 51 percent.

Illness affected the entire age range, however, and was not restricted to those in their later prime. Illness prompted suicide throughout the Victorian period, but 25 of the 46 suicides in this category were from the last two decades of the period. Finally, physical illness was numerically more important than mental illness, although the distinction is not always so clear-cut in individual cases, to which we now turn.

George Heath, a 38-year-old mariner in the last stage of consumption, hanged himself from his bedpost in March 1838. He had been at home ill for four months and was an Infirmary outpatient. His sister and widowed mother had supported him during this time.[30] A 28-year-old merchant's clerk suffering from "hypochondriasis bordering on insanity," according to the medical witness, had brooded over his ailments for the past year. In his lodgings, in September 1885, he shot himself in the head.[31] George Kirkwood, a former private in the Royal Marines, invalided out on a small pension by reason of pleurisy, had been unfit for work since he got home and poisoned himself with carbolic acid in May 1893, aged 28.[32] A year later, a merchant seaman, aged 41, threw himself from an attic window. His mother, with whom the deceased had lived, deposed that her son had worked little since an accident four years before. He had been in and out of hospital since then and strange in his head. The doctors had wanted to operate, but the deceased had refused.[33] And, lastly, Frank Potts, a 27-year-old policeman, killed himself with opium in the final year of the century. The surgeon had thought Potts was suffering from incipient influenza. His landlady said he had had a bad cold and pain for two weeks. In a sad note, Potts had written: "I am just writing this in my last moments. life is such a misery tho me. my head is all on a swim and every limb I have got hakes. so good by all and I hope that everybody will forgive me for doing this rash act . . . forgive me but I carnt help it. life is such a misery and burden to me so may god bless me and you all." [34]

Mental illness also took a toll. Edward O'Brien, a 29-year-old soldier stationed in the Citadel, who was about to be discharged from the regiment because of mental illness and inefficiency, shot himself with a musket in March 1852.[35] Ten years later, a commission agent, aged 32, leaped from a window of the asylum where he had been committed two weeks earlier. His insanity was described as a tendency to commit suicide.[36] In November 1866, Thomas Colgan, a 44-year-old wharfinger and shipowner suffering from depression, aggravated by a stomach disorder, hanged himself from his bedstead. The doctor who had attended him for a year added: "I fancy from what deceased said that his affairs troubled him." [37] And, lastly, Henry Larkum, a schoolmaster, aged 29, who had suffered a mental breakdown and been in an asylum before coming to Hull, jumped from his bedroom window in December 1890. His landlady said Larkum often studied until the early hours, and on the night in question she had heard him running up and down the stairs, talking to himself.[38]

Another 26 percent of male suicides in the prime of life were put down to heavy drinking. In a good three-quarters of these cases, drinking was the main reason offered for self-destruction. In a handful of the same cases, drinking was associated with family violence and marital strife. In the other 20 percent of cases, drinking was closely linked with unemployment or dismissal from work. It is impossible to know, of course, whether unemployment caused the intemperance or resulted from it. I shall subsequently suggest, however, that these cases were as much economically motivated suicides as drink-related ones. Drink's weighty contribution to suicide should come as no surprise. Alcohol was used by many workingmen as a daily pick-me-up, or as Dutch courage on dangerous jobs. The public house was still the main focus of social intercourse for workingmen. Possibly as much as one-sixth of working-class family income went on drink.[39] Excessive indulgence could enhance depression; exacerbate the effects of illness, marital disharmony, or unemployment; and end in delirium tremens and mental disorder. Drink could also, it seems, release some men from the inhibition against self-destruction. Three other preliminary points require emphasis. First, as with illness, single men and those who were separated from their wives were overrepresented among drink-induced suicides. Second, while 60 percent of the heavy-drinking suicides were manual workers—mainly skilled and semi-skilled operatives—40 percent were nonmanual workers and above. Many occupations were represented in the drink-affected suicides, but the largest categories numerically were transport (seamen and dock laborers), food and drink (especially butchers), commerce (clerks), and domestic service (licensed victuallers). And, third, the influence of drink did not diminish with time. Indeed, almost one-half of all the suicides in which drink bulked large took place in the 1890's.

In what kind of case was drink deemed to be the main precipitant of suicide? Robert Kilgour, a banker's clerk, aged 31, who lived with his parents, used the chemicals needed for his hobby, photography, to poison himself in October 1879. Kilgour's brother, an accountant, spoke of his irregular, hard-drinking life, the periodic bouts of delirium tremens, and the delusions of being followed or watched.[40] Samuel Caley, a butcher with a shop in Prince's Road, where he lived with wife and three young children, cut his throat in October 1891. He had been given to drink, said his brother, a licensed victualler. The deputy chief constable then described how Caley had been charged recently with wandering in an unsound state of mind. He had been taken to court, but was discharged, the doctor being unable to certify that he was of unsound mind. The police witness thought the deceased was simply recovering from a drinking bout.[41] The final case is a classic example of the ex-soldier without trade or work who drank away his army pension. In July 1894, Joseph Lucas, a dockside laborer, aged 31, who had been drinking hard for two weeks, courtesy of his army pension, hanged himself. The deceased had told his mother-in-law: "Don't be surprised if you find me a corpse in the morning." Since he was drunk and had threatened suicide before, she thought nothing of it.[42]

A variant upon cases in which drink was the primary influence were those in which marital violence also figured. George Barnby, a 31-year-old French-polisher, formerly a soldier in India, who was given to drink, put his wife out of the house at midnight in June 1890, and not for the first time. She returned for a few things but did not stop, "as he had threatened to take my life. He tried to strangle me 3 weeks ago." She also said her husband had not worked for a week ("he was only a week on strike"), but drank every day. A policeman broke into the house and found him dead from the effects of laudanum.[43] Three years later, a 42-year-old tailor, Anton Henricks, off work for two weeks and drinking for one of them, poisoned himself with carbolic acid. He was evidently quarrelsome in his cups. He had threatened to cut his wife's throat when he began drinking and often ill-used her when quarreling over money. Five years before, he had taken rat poison and had gone before the magistrates for it; he was let off on his promise not to do it again. A neighbor finally deposed that Henricks "would be steady & work for twelve weeks or so & then break off for a fortnight's drinking."[44] Robert Pattison, a coppersmith's laborer, aged 36, employed by the Hull & Barnsley Railway Company, had been off work ill for nine weeks with erysipelas (a streptococcal infection). After a week's heavy drinking, using the £1 he got each week from various clubs, he turned his wife and three children out of the house, threatening to kill them. His wife, therefore, applied for a summons for desertion, so as to secure an order for maintenance. Six years earlier, the magistrates had ordered Pattison to allow his wife ten shillings a week. The deceased's mother, who found him hanging in the back yard, submitted that her son had injured his head on a number of occasions, that he had lost his carrier business because of drink before coming to Hull six years before, and that he seemed troubled at his wife's departure and at the summons for wife desertion.[45]

A number of these cases point to the symbiosis between drink and working life. They certainly suggest that irregular employment could provide an opportunity for sustained drinking. A number of additional cases illustrate both that drink could result in neglect of work and the threat of dismissal, and that drink could be the surface expression of what were essentially work- or business-related problems. John Oliver, a schoolmaster in Hull, aged 42, had been intemperate for eight years or more. A notice requiring his attendance at the school board office, as preface to his discharge, provoked him to take vermin killer in November 1888.[46] A brewery company's clerk, aged 33, had been drinking for ten weeks. The district manager was dissatisfied with his neglect of work and had threatened him with dismissal. In June 1894, he hanged himself from a hook on the kitchen door.[47]

Business troubles underlay heavy drinking in some instances. A charwoman, with two children, who had cohabited until recently with William Barratt, a 35-year-old fish curer, told the inquest on his body in September 1864 that he had "done very little work during the summer. He lost a good deal of money in the winter and it seemed to trouble him much. He used to fret very much about it as we were in such great distress." She also observed that Barratt was given to drink, and that it used to make him mad—"I had to fly for my life when he was so." He was found hanging in his smokehouse.[48] A 36-year-old widowed hairdresser poisoned himself with laudanum in August 1890. He told his former landlady, after drinking heavily, that he had business debts, and that "he could not meet his payments, it will come to a sudden crash."[49]

Lack of work troubled other suicides. John Steels, a 34-year-old carpenter, who had been drinking more than usual for two weeks, pushed his wife and children out into the street before hanging himself from the attic banisters. His widow, who kept a confectionery shop, said he had been under the doctor for nervous debility and depression. She also stated, in reply to a juror: "[H]e has had no full employment & that has troubled him."[50]

IV

These cases lead logically to the final motive for suicide by men in the prime of life: economic or work-related troubles. Of all male suicides in this age group, 32, or 19 percent, were out of work at the time of death. Unemployment was not the main precipitant in all these cases, but neither do they exhaust the instances in which economic difficulty was the foremost influence. In fact, I have identified 49 cases, or nigh on 30 percent of all male suicides in the prime of life, in which work or business troubles were emphasized by inquest witnesses. This figure includes those cases mentioned above in which drink led to the threat of dismissal from work, or in which drink masked business or work concerns. What can we say in general of all 49 male suicides? Seventy percent of them were married. Of the married, moreover, almost two-thirds were between 35 and 44 years of age, and thus living through the most economically difficult life-cycle stages. As for occupation, most were in the food and drink trades, domestic service, transport, metals and engineering, and chemicals and oils. Slightly over 60 percent were manual workers (mainly skilled and semi-skilled operatives); 22 percent were skilled nonmanual workers. In the latter group were clerical workers, a number of shopkeepers and dealers, a licensed victualler, and a chemist. Finally, over a third of these cases came from the 1890's; 60 percent from the last two decades of the century.

The suicides in which economic difficulty was uppermost are examined in detail under six main headings.[51] First, there were males in the prime of life whose unemployment had brought them low. Oil-mill workers were particularly affected. A 25-year-old oil presser, with a wife and child, out of work for fifteen weeks, walked into the river Hull in July 1867, telling those who shouted for him to stop that "he would make an end of himself at once."[52] Amos Paulson, an oil-mill laborer, aged 39, also with wife and child, had been discharged for lack of work six months before he drowned himself in December 1881. "He has not had regular work since," said his brother-in-law, also an oil miller, "he has been low spirited for some time."[53] And John Soutter, a single oil presser in his mid thirties, out of work for six weeks and downhearted at not getting work, shot himself in April 1899. When the man he lodged with asked him why he had done it, he said, "'cause I was out of work."[54] Seamen and dockers were also affected by unemployment. John Spink, a widowed master mariner, aged 38, had been out of work for a year, since the death of the owner of the steamer he commanded. His sister-in-law said that Spink had been low for two months owing to not getting a situation. Three years before, when his wife died, he had tried to shoot himself; this time, in August 1880, he succeeded.[55] And Robert Caley, a fish-dock laborer, aged 36, unemployed for thirteen months, poisoned himself in April 1898. His wife deposed: "He has been very bad & wild looking for a fortnight. . . . He used to earn a shilling or two at times which kept the children in bread. Work has been very bad lately." She had given birth three weeks before, and this too preyed on Caley's mind.[56]

It is not at all surprising, of course, that such occupations were prone to unemployment. Both oil-milling and water-transport jobs were casual and seasonal, the former being especially slack in the summer.[57] But they were not the only occupations in which unemployment brought men down. Herbert Belton, a timber merchant's clerk, aged 36, had been doing little for three or four years and had been particularly depressed during the last eight months. His wife said he had been annoyed recently by someone saying nasty things about his workless condition. He poisoned himself in June 1895.[58] And, lastly, in May 1874, George Stones, a street sweeper, separated from his wife, died from an overdose of opium. He and his four children had not been many days out of the Beverley Road workhouse. Unable to find a job at sweeping, Stones told a former employer: "If I cannot find my support the sooner I am out of existence the better." [59]

The second category of suicides are those in which the deceased had been discharged. In May 1839, William Garton, a 36-year-old clerk to a boatbuilder, from whose service he had recently been discharged, came home drunk and regretful that he had no money for his wife. He had already taken the laudanum that killed him.[60] The same poison was used by John Hawley, a tidewaiter in the customs service, aged 32, married with children, in May 1845. He had been discharged when a superior officer had discovered him uncharacteristically drunk on duty. He had been trying hard to get reinstated, but was despondent in consequence. The jury returned a felo de se verdict, and his body was thus interred without religious service at midnight.[61] And a 42-year-old licensed victualler hanged himself in October 1877. He had lost his job as a stevedore and, said his son, this had depressed him.[62]

The third category of economic trouble concerns male suicides whose small businesses got into difficulty. In December 1863, Thomas Iveson, a 42-year-old boot closer, cut his throat. He had married nine months before, and with money from an aunt had opened a pork shop. The business had not flourished, however, and he had gone back to boot closing in November. His wife went out to cook at different houses. She told the coroner that her husband had been low since she had persuaded him to give up drinking, and that the money he owed preyed on his mind. On the day he killed himself, Iveson complained of being poor, fretted that he should have nothing to do, and worried that his wife would have to work. The note to his wife read: "I will be a burden on you and my friends no longer. farewell. bury me in Hedon and forgive me."[63] And Thomas Clark, a 36-year-old fried-fish dealer, who had taken a shop five weeks earlier, got depressed when the business was not successful and hanged himself in October 1895.[64]

The final three categories are work troubles due to injury or illness, work strain, and workplace irritants. In December 1845, John Gray, a 37-year-old married blacksmith, hanged himself after he lost the use of an arm. A boy who had "bled" him had cut an artery instead of a vein. A lodger declared that Gray had "often stated he was afraid of coming to poverty from his not being able to work." A neighbor also said the deceased fancied he was in the way and would never work again. She was so afraid of him committing suicide that she had taken him to her house whenever his wife went marketing.[65] In September 1879, William Pool, a 41-year-old butcher, hanged himself. The deceased's widow told the court that he had had a stroke two years ago, "and we have been going wrong ever since. He could not attend to business so much and we have been very badly off and had to dispose of our furniture and things." He had often talked about destroying himself and remarked to his father-in-law "that it was a shame that people could not die when they liked."[66] A brewery company's cellarman, William Walker, whose wife sold alcohol at the pier, hanged himself in September 1894 after two weeks of back pain. As he explained in a letter to his boss:

My health has given way and I would die ten times over before I would put on a firm that has done so well for me. . . . I have been low spirited some time. I find that I am not the man I was, for to speak the truth I cared for no man in Hull as a Cellarman. I leave one of the best wives that could be also two promising daughters. I have no cause for this rash act as I do not owe to my knowledge one farthing and which you know I command £3. os. od per week.[67]

And Henry Grint, a 39-year-old fisherman, injured in rough weather during his last voyage, who had not been at sea for a year, cut his throat in February 1899. A half cousin stated that Grint's wife was unwell and had been bedfast for three weeks. He continued: "They have been in want the last few weeks, they were not on the Parish. . . . I have heard his wife say that he said he was very tired of life."[68]

Work strain was a factor in a couple of suicides, both surgeons. John Wilkinson, a 40-year-old married surgeon, poisoned himself with prussic acid (cyanide) in April 1875. His brother, a vicar, said the deceased had been overworked and in need of a complete rest. A fellow doctor confirmed that he had been depressed owing to "an excessive amount of midwifery which is a great strain on a man's powers."[69] Thomas Redhead, a 28-year-old surgeon, used the same poison in November 1894 when similarly depressed through overwork and anxiety. A few days before, his wife had given birth.[70] And, lastly, a workplace irritant underlay a few other suicides. In November 1882, for example, Francis Johnson, a 36-year-old fisherman, who sailed his vessel on temperance principles, hanged himself aboard the fishing smack he operated for his brother-in-law. The latter had put a steam capstan into the vessel, and trouble with this winch had depressed the deceased.[71]

V

Before offering my final thoughts on male suicide in the prime of life, I shall document the experience of women in this age group. In 32 percent of all female suicides, physical or mental illness was the factor emphasized by inquest witnesses. Two-thirds of illness cases were aged either 25–29 or 40–44 and were particularly afflicted by mental illness. Almost three-quarters of illness cases were married; a quarter were single. Illness was an influence over the entire Victorian period, but as with male suicides, one-half of the female cases came from the 1880's and 1890's. For just over a quarter of the illness cases, a recent confinement triggered the illness. Selina Wardle, the 27-year-old wife of a master mariner, had been ill and depressed since her confinement three months before. She tied lead to her ankles and hanged herself in July 1872, leaving four children.[72] Three years later, Elizabeth Julian, the 40-year-old wife of a French-polisher, gave birth to her sixth child four months before she cut her throat. A week earlier, she had come home with her clothes wet, telling her husband that "Satan persuaded her to go in & Jesus brought her back." After that, a woman was hired to watch her. Julian's doctor said she had "suffered under great depression of spirits & great physical debility."[73] And, finally, Eliza Panton, a stonemason's wife, aged 39, ill with influenza and low since giving birth three months earlier, cut her throat in December 1895.[74]

Beyond the impact of childbirth, women were affected by long-term illness, and by the illness of family members. Emily Heron, a shipsmith's wife, aged 42, married for seventeen years, had been ill for four years, principally in the summertime. When unwell, she was depressed. She had had no medical advice, however. In September 1880, she cut her throat with her husband's razor.[75] In August 1870, Eliza Smith, the 42-year-old wife of a brewer, with a large and young family, had also cut her throat, worn out by the combination of suckling her sixteen-month-old baby and taking care of her husband, who suffered from heart disease. Her doctor ascribed the suicide to depression owing to the husband's illness.[76]

A number of women suicides had spent time in an asylum. The wife of an engineer's pattern maker, Matilda Anderson, aged 26, had been in Hull borough lunatic asylum for a month for "simple melancholy." The superintendent had said he wanted to keep her for a few more weeks to ensure that she was completely recovered, but her husband "was urgent to have her out." He got his landlady to watch her, but in July 1883, she cut her throat.[77] In one case, the act was done in the asylum. An excise officer's wife, aged 42, hanged herself in the Hull and East Riding Refuge in October 1847. She had been a patient for five weeks, suffering from melancholy.[78] And, lastly, a number of female suicides were put down to religious mania. Elizabeth Hudson, the 28-year-old wife of a timber merchant, hanged herself from a bedpole in March 1846. For four months, said the family's governess, Hudson had been depressed, "arising from religious feelings," and often declared that she could not be saved.[79]

Slightly more than one-fifth of female suicides in the prime of life were under the influence of drink. They were evenly split between married women, on the one hand, and single, widowed, and cohabiting women, on the other. The large majority, moreover, occurred in the 1880's and 1890's. In over half the cases, the suicides had been drinking heavily for some time. Jane Gordon, a 30-year-old married woman, cohabiting with a shipwright, poisoned herself with laudanum in June 1857. A neighbor said of Gordon: "[S]he would get drunk whenever she could . . . about 3 months since she was said to have tried to kill herself with laudanum."[80] Eliza Bell, an unmarried housekeeper, aged 40, with a four-year-old son, poisoned herself with laudanum in July 1876. She kept house for a druggist, attending to the shop when he was away. She drank too much, said the druggist, and "had frequently taken laudanum for some months . . . as a stimulant which she would get out of the shop." She was also violent, threatening the life of the druggist's daughter, whom Bell suspected of wanting to turn her out.[81]

The remaining drink-induced suicides involved marital strife, often over the debt and pawning that went along with intemperance. The 37-year-old wife of a police constable, with six children, worried that her husband should discover that she had pawned an item for drink that he had specifically forbidden, hanged herself in August 1891.[82] And a boilermaker's wife, Annie Snowden, aged 39, with three adopted children, who had been addicted to drink for thirteen years, got annoyed when her husband refused to give her money for drink. "I have since heard she was being pressed for money being in debt," said her husband. "She has left home three times when in drink & I have brought her back. . . . I used to go through the house every day for bottles when I returned home."[83]

VI

Much more than men, women in the prime of life were motivated by disturbances in personal relationships. A quarter of all female suicides were ascribed to bereavement, romantic disappointment, or family disputes. If to this number are added the above cases of drink and marital disharmony, the figure climbs to one-third of all suicide cases, on a par with illness as a motivating factor. This factor, moreover, was more evident for single, separated, and widowed women than for married women. First, the death of children, husbands, and parents led to a few female suicides. Charlotte Gower, a cartman's wife, aged 40, had taken to drinking and been in a low way ever since her eldest daughter's death three years earlier. She had attempted suicide twice before she poisoned herself with opium in October 1860.[84] A 40-year-old widow, Margaret Sirvoizza, a lodging-house keeper, hanged herself in July 1869. One of her lodgers, a hawker, said "she was only in poor circumstances, & used to pawn her things." A second lodger noted that "since the death of her husband last december the deceased has been low spirited & out of order."[85] Elizabeth Richardson, a single woman, aged 25, who kept house for her brothers, was found drowned in February 1889. She had been despondent since her mother's death ten months earlier.[86]

Romantic disappointment also contributed to the list of female suicides. A dressmaker from Horncastle, Mary Richardson, aged 28, lodged with the family of her fiancé, a shipwright. They were to have been married on the day of the inquest in September 1870, but she poisoned herself with vermin killer after she found her fiancé with a woman he had been intimate with for five years. The woman required a police escort at the close of the inquest, since a large crowd of women hooted and hissed her all the way home.[87] When a rating officer in the town hall broke off his engagement in August 1890, his 36-year-old fiancée, Amy Cullen, poisoned herself.[88] In March 1885, a 26-year-old domestic servant was found drowned. Her sister ascribed the suicide to the fact that she had been unsettled since her lover had lost his arm eighteen months earlier and the marriage was postponed.[89] Lastly, one case takes us back to the early life transition. Sarah Stamp, a domestic servant from Lincolnshire, aged 25, was found drowned in St. Andrew's Dock in March 1891. Her employer, a butcher, said she had been sick occasionally. In fact, she was three months pregnant.[90]

Third, a number of suicides were embroiled in a dysfunctional marital or intimate relationship. A 27-year-old married woman, Hannah Pattinson, caught the man she had cohabited with for five years with another woman. When she challenged him, he hit her in the mouth. A friend of the deceased observed: "[S]he was right enough in her head except from her feeling of revenge & from Dick abusing her." She poisoned herself with opium in March 1853.[91] A coal trimmer's wife, aged 40, with a twelve-year-old child by another husband, was found drowned in Albert Dock in January 1870. Her husband, whom she dearly wanted to leave, was often the worse for drink. On the day the deceased went missing, the husband was drunk and had smashed the furniture.[92]

In addition, infidelity, real or rumored, could prompt to suicide. The young wife of a fisherman, Mary Renton, was found drowned in March 1894 in St. Andrew's Dock. She had been married for six years; she had had one child by another man, born before the marriage. While her husband was at sea, Renton had been unfaithful to him with her mother's lodger.[93] Ann Baker, the 34-year-old wife of a merchant seaman, with two children, who worked at a fish curers, poisoned herself in July 1860. She had come to Hull from Liverpool five months earlier, having spent nearly two years in Liverpool workhouse. Her husband had been serving a four-year sentence of penal servitude and was expected back within days. Baker's mother said only: "I fancy she feared her husband's return, but cannot say." According to the report of the inquest in the *Hull News*, however, a rumor was afloat in the neighborhood to the effect that Baker had lived with another man during her husband's imprisonment. While no inquest witness gave any credence to this story, the deceased had presumably feared that her husband would believe it.[94]

Only one other category remains, that of economic difficulty. Considerably fewer female than male suicides were put down to this cause. As we have seen, married women in the prime of life were typically too busy with domestic duties to work full time. In only 5 of the 53 married suicides was a regular occupation mentioned. The other 14 suicides in which an occupation was listed were single, separated, or widowed. Of these 19 occupied females, moreover, 7 were motivated by strained personal relationships, 3 by drink, and 2 by illness. Only the remaining handful of working suicides was affected by economic pressures. To these, however, we need to add those married women who were troubled by their family's economic condition. In 16 percent of all female suicides, then, economic difficulty was stressed by inquest witnesses. Most were married, most were in their thirties, and a small but significant number occurred in the 1840's.

In only one case was there a direct reference to a suicide's unemployment. A woman whose name was unknown, aged between 30 and 40, came to lodge at a cabinetmaker's house in October 1844, in which she poisoned herself with laudanum. According to the landlady, the deceased had been in a situation (probably domestic service) in Bridlington, and she worried a good deal on account of losing her job.[95] A husband's unemployment was a slightly more common precipitant. Sarah Rose, the 41-year-old wife of a laborer, married for eighteen months, who went out charring, had been depressed before she poisoned herself in April 1863. Her husband had had little or no work since Christmas.[96]

Poverty was posited as the motive in a number of suicides. A laborer's wife, aged 38, hanged herself from the bedstead in May 1841. A neighbor stated that she had "frequently talked about coming to poverty" and saw nothing but that before her eyes.[97] Mary Tomlinson, the 38-year-old wife of a licensed victualler turned carpenter, was found drowned, along with her five-month-old son, in August 1844. A neighbor maintained that Tomlinson's depression was caused by poverty, the public house business having failed.[98] In November 1892, Mary Barnes, a widow, aged 39, fell from a third-floor window of the house of a woman, also a widow, who had taken her in when she had nowhere to go. The good Samaritan said of Barnes: "She was very poor. She has had no work except two days a fortnight ago. She had no parish relief."[99]

A drop in economic well-being could have a similar effect. The mother of Mary Wray, a 33-year-old married woman, who died from an irritant poison in April 1897, ascribed the death to their altered circumstances. Wray's husband had kept a beer house, but was now a mast and block maker, and an out-of-work one at that.[100] Finally, mounting debt could prompt to suicide, debt accrued, in the following cases, while the husband was at sea. A seaman's wife, aged 42, poisoned herself with laudanum after raiding the cashbox of a mariner who had lodged with her for eighteen years. As the lodger said: "I think she had got into money difficulties . . . she said she had been to my cashbox and could not make it up." Her husband was expected home in three weeks.[101] And, lastly, Patrina Watthem, the wife of a ship's carpenter, Danish by birth, aged 37, poisoned herself in September 1897, on the very day her husband got home. Watthem kept a small laundry, with the help of two assistants, and took in lodgers. "I find," the husband deposed, "that my wife had lately borrowed money from anyone she could and sold and pawned all she could." He had no idea why she had done so.[102]

VII

Having examined the experience of suicide among both men and women in the prime of life, what patterns should we stress, and what do they suggest about the association between suicide and the life cycle? For men in this stage of life, what I have defined as disturbances in social and personal relationships were relatively unimportant. Only a small number of men were primarily prompted to kill themselves because of the social or legal consequences of criminal activity or the grief aroused by the death or desertion of loved ones. A handful of male suicides were accused of, or arrested for, embezzlement or theft—men in positions that allowed such activity, whether clerk, accountant, or dealer. Fewer than one-tenth of all male suicides were directly disturbed by the rupture of personal relationships through death, desertion, unrequited love, or family quarrels. The most vulnerable in this regard were men who were depressed by a wife's departure, by a wife's attempt to claim the children, or by demands from the Poor Law Union that they maintain their wives. By contrast, large numbers of male suicides were prompted by illness, heavy drinking, and economic troubles. Over one-quarter of all male suicides suffered from physical or mental illness, often of a long-standing nature. Single and widowed males were particularly prone to illness-induced suicide, possibly because they had no one to nurse them through physical illness or to help them overcome melancholia. Significantly, perhaps, a third of these singles were in lodgings at the time. Illness prefaced the deaths of the few suicides of middle-class standing (mainly shipowners). The figures also suggest that sickness and dread of disease became a numerically stronger influence on male suicide (as also on female suicide) as the century wore on. It should be added that in a fifth of these illness cases, witnesses made some reference to the fact that the deceased had not been working or attending to business before his death, that he was unfit for work, that he was bothered by business affairs, or that he was about to be discharged. It is possible, then, that in some of these suicides, the isolating effect of illness, caused by loss of work, made illness intolerable.[103] Another quarter of male suicides in the prime of life were deeply touched by heavy drinking. Once more, single and separated men were especially vulnerable; nearly two-thirds of all drink-induced suicides were of these civic statuses. A large majority of the single men were in lodgings, sometimes in inns or hotels. A number of them were seamen and clerks, the latter often having experienced, or facing, discharge in consequence. As for the married suicides who drank heavily, half of them were notorious for violence to their wives.

The final category of motive was foremost among men in the prime of life, however, at least if those cases are included in which heavy drinking was intertwined with dismissal or unemployment. Almost one-third of economic suicides were provoked by unemployment, often of a long-term character. The number affected by joblessness was extremely small in the early and mid Victorian years: a cabinetmaker in 1849, an oil presser in 1867. There were a few more cases in the early to mid 1880's, especially master mariners and an oil-mill laborer, rising to a high point in the 1890's. In that decade, those most affected by unemployment were workers in the metal trades, oil milling, and the fishing industry. In a number of these cases, moreover, the pressure of unemployment was aggravated by the illness, confinement, desertion, or death of the deceased's wife; by the deceased's inability to support his family; or by a recent egress from the workhouse. About half as many economic suicides were prompted by the failure, or feared failure, of small businesses, especially in the food trade. Indeed, of all the shopkeepers who committed suicide in the prime of life, most were linked either with business failure or with the economic effects of illness and drink. These small producers were awfully vulnerable, of course, to economic fluctuation. It is no coincidence, perhaps, that a number of small shopkeepers hit hard times in the mid 1890's, when the Hull economy was badly disturbed by poor weather, a dock strike, and a cotton-mill closure.[104] Another 15 percent were a function of drink's impact on work performance, or drink's aggravation of work and business troubles. One-fifth of economic suicides consisted of men whose injury or illness and related unemployment led them to fret about coming to poverty. And, finally, a handful of suicides were depressed either as a result of being discharged or by work exhaustion.

Why joblessness, business failure, and discharge should have led these men to kill themselves can best be explained, short of knowing more about their psychological predispositions, by reference to the life-cycle stage they were negotiating. Over two-thirds of these men had wives; over one-third had a wife and family to support, with no financial help, in most cases, from spouse or children. Most working and lower-middle-class families in the first dozen years of married life struggled to make ends meet on a regular weekly wage; how they survived periods of unemployment that could last for anywhere between three and twelve months beggars description. Nor were single or widowed men necessarily any better placed to ride out extended joblessness. Some had clearly come to Hull to find work and lived the lodger's life while they searched. Others sheltered from the storm with widowed mothers or other kin, imposing a heavy burden upon them; a few drew upon their trade clubs. Small shopkeepers, their businesses failing, or illness making it hard for them to attend to business, could be left heavily in debt, and full of fears about their future standing and well-being.

Among female suicides in the prime of life, direct economic pressures were less influential. About 16 percent of all suicides were ascribed by inquest witnesses and press reports to the fear or reality of poverty, to the plight of widowhood, or to the anxiety caused by indebtedness. In only one case was the woman's own unemployment a cause for despondency. For the most part, economically motivated suicides were married women in their later thirties, with a child or children, who were in fear of poverty owing to their husband's illness, unemployment, or business failure. Such cases grouped, to some degree, in the 1840's. In addition, one suicide was a widow, always an economically vulnerable status, and a few more were borne down by debts. In some cases, the debts grew out of independent economic activity—in laundry work or in caring for lodgers—and were racked up during the absence of spouses at sea. Female dependents of men serving in the merchant marine were not helped presumably by shipping companies paying out allowances irregularly.[105] Almost one-third of all female suicides were affected by physical or mental illness, especially the latter. Unlike men in this category, who were largely single or widowed, and commonly living in lodgings, female suicides were predominantly married, and the single females either were living with kin or were live-in domestics. This was, in part, a reflection of the significant role of postpartum illness in female suicide. Over a quarter of the illness cases were linked with this stage in the biological life cycle, although the age at which women were affected ranged from 25 to 40 years, and from the first to the sixth child.

Another one-fifth of all female suicides were seemingly induced by heavy drinking. While male suicides in this category were predominantly single or separated, women suicides were fairly evenly divided between widows and cohabiting singles (plus a single prostitute), on the one hand, and married women with children who did not, in the euphemistic phrase of the time, "live comfortably" with their husbands, on the other. Indeed, some drove their husbands to distraction by pawning household items for drink money.[106] The demon drink had, of course, male as well as female victims.

If the last-mentioned cases are joined to those in which there was a disturbance in personal relationship, then another one-third of female suicides can be put down to bereavement, romantic disappointment, and family disputes, a considerably larger proportion than in the case of male suicides. In most of these cases (at least where drink played no part), the women were single, separated, or widowed. Single women (including the two who were cohabiting) were disturbed by the postponement or cancellation of marriage plans, by jealousy, bereavement, and the reality or illusion of pregnancy. Separated women, including those who were cohabiting, were all disturbed by violent domestic partners. And widows, including one who was cohabiting, were disturbed by violence or bereavement, the latter event resulting in economic as well as emotional deprivation. The married suicides (including those in which drink did play a central role) were disturbed by bereavement and infidelity (on the part of the suicide), but mainly by the dysfunctional relationship between the suicide (sometimes in a drunken condition) and her husband. In a few cases, finally, the relationship between suicide and husband was disturbed by the latter's absence at sea. In all, then, a decisive influence upon women in the prime of life was either the continued search for intimacy or the disruption of intimacy by death, drink, or spousal violence.

These gendered patterns seem, therefore, to confirm the traditional dichotomy between male and female suicide, encapsulated in Rowlandson's 1810 drawing *She Died for Love and He for Glory* (see illustration). While male suicides were said to be victims of powerful social or physical calamities, their self-esteem and independence threatened by unemployment, business failure, or severe illness, women were thought to be beset by loss or conflict in personal relationships.[107] My categorization of motives does indeed suggest that the suicide of urban men in the prime of life was commonly an act of opposition to forces, whether material or physical, that menaced male pride, performance, and independence. The suicide of urban women, by contrast, was frequently a response to the disruption of personal attachments, whether to lover, husband, or child, upon which they were emotionally dependent. While men in this life stage were particularly troubled by the economic and hubristic impact of joblessness, business failure, accident, and illness, women were tormented by the affective adversities of securing and sustaining personal intimacy and by the physical and emotional demands of childbirth, child care, and child mortality.

Yet we should resist the temptation simply to endorse this conventional dichotomy. For a start, the documents are somewhat biased in this direc-

ILLUSTRATION 4: Thomas Rowlandson, *She Died for Love and He for Glory*. Drawing (1810). Henry E. Huntington Library and Art Gallery, San Marino, California.

tion, since conventional attitudes to suicide in men and women could well have influenced the way witnesses deposed and juries disposed. Second, the higher risk of suicide in men who were single, separated, or widowed, which our figures reveal, is open to more than one interpretation. It could mean, as it is typically taken to mean, that personal relationships play a minor role in male suicide. Just as plausibly, it could mean that men killed themselves because of the absence of a personal relationship. Marriage, in other words, could have protected men as well as women against suicide. Third, by concentrating on primary motives, we have inevitably diminished the number of male suicides that were associated with the rupture of personal relationships. If the suicides of men primarily affected by disturbed personal relations are added to the suicides, categorized differently, in which men were troubled by the death or illness of their wives, or by separation from their wives, then almost one-fifth of all male suicides in the prime of life were troubled, to a greater or lesser extent, by the disruption of personal attachments. And, fourth, suicidal women were not always victims of what tends to be depicted as a neurotic dependence upon personal relationships, but also victims of dysfunctional relationships, involving spousal neglect and abuse, and victims of the unsatisfactory alternatives for women. A number of disturbed personal relationships were examples less of women clinging to a love-object than of women fleeing for their lives; for some, the choice came down to daily torture at the hands of their legal or common-law husbands or suicide. And the usual lot of "deserting" and deserted wives, as well as widows, was irregular work, dependency upon kin, and dire poverty.[108]

It remains valid, of course, to underline the poverty cycle in single-breadwinner families, to accentuate the daily struggle for a living, the imperious demands of work, when evaluating suicide in the prime of life, and especially for men. Yet in view of the size of the workforce in the prime of life, and the number of dependents reliant upon that workforce, the number of men and women who killed themselves for essentially economic reasons was exceedingly small. Even in the economically hardest stages of the life cycle for married people, few chose the path of self-destruction. This is perhaps a testimony, in part, to Hull's diverse and expanding economy, particularly in the second half of the century, and to the employment prospects of men in the prime of life.[109] A much firmer line needs to be scored, then, for both male and female suicide, under what has been termed "the reversibility of the life cycle," and notably under illness, death, and desertion. One-quarter of male suicides and one-third of female suicides in the prime of life were the product of illness, whether persistent, long-standing ill-health or postpartum complications. One-quarter of male and one-fifth of female suicides were linked to heavy drinking, and in a sizable number of cases to the related breakdown of formal or informal marital relations. Between a quarter and a third of male suicides were put down to economic causes, but, as we have also noted, the ills of male unemployment were at times intensified by the confinement, desertion, or death of suicides' wives. Lastly, one-third of female suicides were linked to the disruption of personal relationships, whether by bereavement, romantic disappointment, or family disputes. In the last camp were those separated and married women who suffered the wrath of abusive partners. And when primary and secondary influences are added up, male suicides, too, were clearly affected by the death or desertion of loved ones, by the dissolution of the family unit. Suicide in the prime of life emerged from the things that really mattered to most people: marriage, family, home, and drink.

9

Early Old Age

When I thought it likely that I should be thrown out of
employment, it seemed to paralyze me completely. . . .
I used to sit at home brooding over it until the blow
fell . . . the fear of being turned off is the worst thing in a
working-man's life, and more or less acutely it is always,
in the case of the vast majority, present in his mind.

> Statement of an operative brushmaker,
> in Charles Booth, *Life and Labour*
> *of the People in London* (1903)

The penultimate phase of the Victorian life cycle was that of early old age, covering the years from 45 to 64. Between 45 and 54, middle age was settling into old age, and between 55 and 64, old age was decidedly under way.[1] From their mid forties on, manual workmen were vulnerable to "life-cycle deskilling" or downward job mobility, with the associated drop in earning power and problem of obtaining regular employment. By their late fifties, work could be even more intermittent, and earnings well below the standard. Illness and accidents, by further disrupting the continuity of employment, could further aggravate the plight of older workmen. Physical and mental deterioration, combined with chronic illness and chronic pain, could lead to depression and feelings of hopelessness.[2] And then there were the emotional and financial losses associated with this life stage: the loss of life partners and close friends; and the loss of the parental role (not to mention earnings), as the eldest children left to form their own households.[3]

Men and women in this life stage might face other difficulties as well. On average, one-quarter of the women (and one-tenth of the men) in this age group were widowed, many still with dependent children, and to make ends meet, widows often had to take in lodgers or rejoin the labor force. For men, the loss of a life partner could be a severe emotional blow, disrupting their entire domestic life. In women, the biological event of menopause had the potential to influence mood and behavior.[4] Finally, in this life-cycle stage, there was perhaps greater likelihood of myriad losses—physical, emotional, and economic—reacting synergistically to reduce the quality of the individual's life to a point where death seemed preferable.[5]

I

In the Victorian period in Hull, there were 186 male and 64 female suicides in early old age. To these, I have added 35 male and 12 female open verdicts, making a grand total of 221 male and 76 female suicides in this penultimate stage of the life cycle. Let us look, first, at the age-related suicide rates. In England and Wales in the nineteenth century, the suicide rate rose in each successive age period, reaching its maximum between 55 and 64 years of age, "the refuge mainly," said J. N. Radcliffe, "of those who are worn out in a bitter and hopeless struggle against accumulated ills."[6]

In Victorian Hull, this progressive rise was true of men, but not of women. The average annual mortality from suicide per 10,000 living was 32.9 for men aged 45–54; 38.6 for men aged 55–64. The latter rate was the highest for any decennial age period. The rates for women were 11.0 and 9.7, respectively, but these rates were exceeded by women aged 65–74.[7] For the entire age group 45–64, the average annual mortality from suicide was 35.1 for males and 10.5 for females, higher in both cases than the rate for people in the prime of life.[8]

One final measure underlines just how suicidal this age group was. Those aged 45–64 made up, on average, 22 percent of the city's male population aged 15 and above, and 21 percent of the female population. Yet this same age group was responsible for no less than 44 percent of all male suicides and 32 percent of all female suicides in the Victorian era.[9] In short, suicides by those in early old age far exceeded their proportions in the population at large.

We turn, next, to the civil status of these suicides. Of the 221 male suicides, 14.5 percent were single, 61.5 percent were married, and 14 percent were widowed; of the 76 female suicides, 6.6 percent were single, 60.5

percent were married, and 30.3 percent were widowed.[10] Both unmarried men and widowers were responsible for larger proportions of suicides than would be expected from their proportions in the total population. The single and widowed committed 28.5 percent of all the male suicides in this age group, yet constituted, on average, only 18 percent of the male population. In contrast, the marital status of elderly female suicides compared closely with the marital status of the total female population in this age group. The single and widowed committed 37 percent of all the female suicides (30 percent by widows alone), and made up, on average, 33 percent of the female population. Nonetheless, over a third of female suicides were committed by single or widowed women. If we add the married but separated to this figure, then the single, separated, and widowed (or those deprived or bereft of the support of marriage) committed 35 percent of all male suicides and 41 percent of all female suicides aged between 45 and 64, slightly fewer than those in the prime of life, but still a sizable proportion.[11] In the 1890's, finally, the only decade for which we can provide a suicide rate according to civil status, the rate for single males was 83.7 suicides per 10,000 living; for married males, 35.7; and for widowers, 76.2.[12] The rates for females were 17.6 (single), 13.1 (married), and 10.7 (widowed). The suicide rate for single and widowed men was, therefore, over double the rate for married men. And widowers had a markedly higher suicide rate than widows, lending support to Durkheim's remark: "Man thus loses more than woman in passing from marriage to widowhood, since he does not preserve certain of the advantages which he owed to the conjugal state."[13]

As for the living arrangements of suicides in early old age, one-third of the single men (or 11 of 32) were in lodgings, three lived alone, one lived on board ship, one was of no fixed abode, and in nine cases the living arrangements are not given (although in three of these cases a housekeeper is mentioned). Only six single men lived with kin, mainly brothers and sisters. The handful of single women in this age group either were housekeepers (one of whom was home on trial from the asylum) or were living with mother and sister. Eighty-five percent of married male suicides (or 116 of 136) lived with their wives. In addition, one married man was in prison at the time of death, one was an emigrant, one was from out of town and staying with a brother-in-law, and two were in lodgings (their wives being in prison or the workhouse). Of the fifteen married men who were separated, five were with their children, six were in lodgings, one was cohabiting, one was in the process of selling up his home, and two were of no fixed abode. Ninety-three percent of married female suicides (or 43 of 46) were living with their husbands (one of them in an institution for old fishermen, and another in the home of the couple's daughter and son-in-law). Of the three separated women, one was cohabiting, and two lived alone. Of the 31 widowed men, 19 (or 60 percent) were with unmarried children, two lived with married children, four lived in lodgings, three lived alone, one was on board ship, one in prison, and one was of no fixed abode.[14] The proportion of widowers with dependent children is perhaps noteworthy. Durkheim suggested that while children "attach the widower to life," equally "they make the crisis through which he is passing more intense":

For not only is the conjugal relation destroyed; but precisely because a domestic society here exists, there is an impairment of its functioning too. An essential element is lacking and the whole machine is thrown out of gear. To reestablish the lost equilibrium the husband has to shoulder a double burden and perform functions for which he is unprepared. . . . It is not because his marriage is ended but because the family which he heads is disorganized. The departure, not of the wife but of the mother, causes the disaster.[15]

Of the twenty-three widowed women, nine were with unmarried children, one was a housekeeper, one was in Trinity House Hospital (an almshouse), four were in lodgings (most of whom had recently been in service), two lived alone, one lived with her brother, one with a married daughter, and three took in lodgers. Two final measures deserve mention. First, no children were mentioned in the inquests of 53 percent of both male and female suicides who were married, separated, or widowed. Thus, over half of the male and female suicides of these civic statuses were without the restraining influence of children. Second, 15 percent of all male suicides (and 36 percent of single and widowed male suicides) were living alone or in lodgings, or were of no fixed abode.

In what ways did those in early old age destroy themselves? Almost three-quarters of the men on whom suicide verdicts were returned hanged themselves, 15 percent cut their throats, 10 percent used poison, 7.5 percent used a gun, and 4.3 percent drowned themselves. When open verdicts are added, however, the figures for hanging, throat cutting, and firearms fall to 50, 12.7, and 6.3 percent, respectively, while poison increases slightly to 11.8 percent, and drowning increases by 10 percent to 14.5. Of the women on whom suicide verdicts were returned, 47 percent hanged themselves, 22 percent cut their throats, 28 percent used poison, and 1.6 percent drowned themselves. When open verdicts are added, the figures for hanging, throat cutting, and poison fall to 39, 18.4, and 25 percent, respectively, while drowning leaps to 15.8 percent.

Finally, we need to observe the occupational and class backgrounds of suicides in early old age. The largest number of male suicides worked in transport (as mariners, seamen, sloopmen, dock laborers, and cartmen), metals and engineering (as fitters, boilermakers, blacksmiths, and mast and block makers), food and drink (as fruiterers, butchers, cowkeepers, and especially grocers), building (as painters, joiners, bricklayers), commerce (as travelers, brokers, and clerks), dress (as tailors and shoemakers), and domestic service (as lodging- and eating-house keepers and licensed victuallers). This list is very similar to that for males in the prime of life and corresponds closely with the occupational profile of the city. However, comparing the proportions of male suicides with the proportions of all occupied males aged 45 and above in the 1890's (in table 6.9), we see that the proportion of suicides was larger than expected in agriculture (cattle dealers and gardeners), textiles (sailmakers and drapers), dress, food and drink, commerce, and domestic service. The proportion of suicides was also slightly larger than expected in metals and engineering.[16] What stand out in these listings are the occupations that older workmen tended to move into: small-scale retailing (corner shops and pubs), shoemaking, tailoring, cowkeeping, gardening, building, dealing, and blacksmithing.[17] What also stand out are trades in which higher labor productivity was sought in the 1880's and 1890's by the introduction of new machinery, or new forms of retail operation, and a faster pace of work: metals and engineering, tailoring, boot and shoe manufacture, independent shopkeeping, and clerical work.[18] When occupation is translated into social class, and when the proportion of male suicides is compared with the class distribution of household heads in mid-century Hull (in table 5.1), we see that, as in the prime of life, skilled nonmanual workers were considerably overrepresented among male suicides.[19] In early old age, however, the skilled manual class was also slightly overrepresented. Again, then, the lower-middle-class group of clerks, shopkeepers, innkeepers, dealers, and commercial travelers was particularly suicidal. But so, too, were skilled workmen in the building and the metal and engineering trades and in tailoring, sailmaking, and shoemaking.

The occupational data for women in early old age are more fragmentary. Only 17 percent of Hull women in this age group were listed in the 1901 census as occupied. Of the female suicides, eleven (or 14.5 percent) were in formal employment, eight in domestic and other service (one of whom looked after her husband's pub), one in a lead mill, one in a grocery shop, and one relied upon the rents from house property. Additionally, however, one woman took in washing, two did dressmaking at home, and three took in lodgers. Altogether, then, seventeen (or 22 percent) earned a living of some sort. Predictably, twelve of the seventeen earners were widows, two were single, and three were married. Two of the married ones looked after the husband's business; the other (the wife of a laborer) worked in a lead mill. Finally, the social class of the husband (living or deceased) of female suicides was mainly skilled or semi-skilled manual, as with women in the prime of life. In fact, three-quarters of female suicides in early old age were with skilled, semi-skilled, or unskilled workingmen.

II

Let us proceed then to look at the experience of suicide in early old age, again exploring the motives for suicide under the five main headings of economic troubles, illness, disturbances in social and personal relationships, and drink. Two of the main categories of motive were numerically of less importance for male suicides in this age group (as they were for men in the prime of life): disturbances in social and in personal relationships. Less than 5 percent of male suicides were motivated by the public disgrace associated with theft, embezzlement, or impending legal action. In May 1842, John Jackson, a 45-year-old widower and marine-stores dealer residing on the North Walls with his six children, hanged himself in a police cell. The previous evening, he had been brought to the station house on a charge of receiving stolen brass.[20] Robert Collison, a 47-year-old coal merchant, was found drowned in the Humber in October 1887. He had defrauded a building society, of which he was secretary, out of a sizable sum. In a letter to his wife, Collison blamed the attempt to maintain respectability:

I had hoped to keep on until some of the Boys were earning sufficient to keep you in comfort as I have tried to keep you & the family but alas at other peoples expense. . . . Oh for the days when we lived & paid our way in Sykes St. Would that I could go back to that. trying to keep up appearances & too proud to appear poor has been my ruin. . . . I hope that amongst our numerous friends some will come forward to give a helping hand to you & the girls but am afraid that my conduct will be a blot upon you.[21]

Impending legal action triggered a number of other suicides. A 45-year-old lodging-house keeper (and rag-and-bone man) had gone away to evade a police court summons brought by a man with whom he had quarreled. He was found lying in the Corporation Field, dead of laudanum poisoning. His widow deposed, however, that a head injury years ago had affected his mind, and that if he got drink, "he was like a cracked man and shouted and screamed." She also said, "[W]e were very badly off. he left me without a halfpenny or a bit of bread in the house."[22] Likewise, a police sergeant, aged 50, had to appear before the justices on an assault summons in September 1894. On the day before the hearing, he hanged himself from the balustrade of his house. His children (one a railway fireman) stated that their father had been ill, insomniac, and depressed for three months.[23]

Ten percent of male suicides were motivated by a disturbance in personal relations. In two-thirds of these cases, bereavement was the issue, whether of wife, child, parent, or friend. The commonest of these subcategories was the death of a wife. In November 1864, Anthony Wood, aged 51, hanged himself in a brew house attached to his home. He was landlord of the Whittington Inn, which his family had kept for 70 years. According to a nephew, Wood had had an attack of insanity twelve years earlier and still suffered from a persecution complex. In his will, he erroneously reiterated that he had been reported to the magistrates and his license withdrawn. At times, also, he had drunk heavily. A domestic servant at the inn emphasized his wife's death six weeks before, however. A week before his death, his late wife's children had fetched her clothes away. "It seemed to hurt him very much," said the servant, and it had made him more despondent than ever.[24]

All the other cases of suicide involving grief at a wife's death occurred in the 1890's. George Adamson, the 46-year-old captain of a steamer lying in Victoria Dock, had been depressed since his wife's death a year before. He had broken up his house and since then had lived on board ship. Adamson's son had not heard from him in a year. His chief mate deposed: "He had told me that his wife was buried at Hull, & that she died while he was on a voyage. He seemed more despondent on approaching Hull." The superintendent of Hull cemetery said he had taken Adamson to his wife's grave on September 9, 1892. As the superintendent walked away, he heard a shot from the graveside.[25]

In November 1862, Philip Whitworth, a 57-year-old grocer, was found drowned in the river Hull. He had left home in the morning saying that he was going to receive money. By nightfall, worried that he would get to drinking, his wife and children went looking for him. "Ever since we lost a son two years ago," said Whitworth's widow, "he has been very low & depressed in his spirits. He always was rather so but has been worse since my son's death & still more so lately." She added: "He was formerly manager of the weaving department at the Cotton Mill. He did not like shop keeping." By late 1862, the Hull cotton mills were closed owing to the American Civil War and the resulting cotton famine.[26]

A river sailor (or waterman), aged 47, cut his throat with a penknife in April 1870. He was a single man who had lived on board a keel (a flat-bottomed vessel) in the Old Harbour. His brother, a ship painter, said: "A great change took place in him since his mother's death 7 weeks ago. He was very much quieter & altered in his manner."[27]

Finally, there were a few cases in which the sudden death of an employee or colleague seems to have deepened the morbid introspection of the suicide. In September 1874, William Mudd, the master of a floating lightship, aged 58, hanged himself from a willow tree in a plantation in front of the borough coroner's residence. He was a month afloat and a month ashore, and he was to have gone to the ship on the morning of his death. Mudd's wife said he had been silent and low for a year and much affected by the death of the captain of another lightship. A surgeon who had known the deceased for 30 years agreed that the other captain's death had affected him, and said also: "He spoke sometimes as if he had a presentiment that something was going to happen."[28]

The next most important subcategory of disturbance in personal relations was that of family violence. All the cases come from the final two decades of the century, two being rare Victorian instances of murder followed by suicide. In November 1880, Charles Plant, a police constable in his late forties (and entitled to a pension in a few weeks' time), murdered his wife of only nine months and then hanged himself from the banisters. In a short space of time, excited crowds gathered in the locality of Grosvenor Street. Both Plant and his wife, Ann, had been widowed before they married each other. Their marriage was extremely "uncomfortable." Plant had a quick temper and often beat his wife; Ann drank to excess and refused to let Plant have access to money invested in a savings bank. The denouement to this tragedy came when Ann got a summons against Plant to be heard in two weeks' time. According to Ann's aunt, Plant beat his wife the day the summons arrived and "told her that she had Done him." Neighbors heard Ann singing as if to provoke Plant before all went silent. When Plant failed to appear on parade to get his week's wages, his sergeant went to enquire after him. He found Ann with her throat cut and Plant hanging in the garret staircase.[29]

John Henry van Kooten Duinkerk, aged 47, a cabinetmaker by trade, but lately at work as a checker, killed his wife, then shot himself in September 1896. He had served fourteen years in India, but had been invalided out of the service. Duinkerk and his wife had lived "uncomfortably" for fourteen years; he was a drinking man and had ill-treated his wife. The murder followed by suicide had been provoked, according to the deceased's own statement, by his wife's trips to Chatham and Leeds with Nellie Melrose, a music-hall singer, which had led to his selling up the house; and by the attempts of his wife's parents to separate them. Finally, Duinkerk's sister said that she had heard her brother threaten to kill his wife and himself if she did not come back to live with him.[30]

III

As with men in the prime of life, the three remaining motives were numerically more important. Seventeen percent of male suicides in early old age were ascribed to heavy drinking. In a handful of these drinking cases, intemperance was linked to family strife and violence; in almost 30 percent, there was a link between intemperance and work dismissal or poverty. Just over one-third of these suicides were single, separated, or widowed, the rest being married (although in two of the latter cases the wife was either in jail or in the poorhouse). While 55 percent of the drinking suicides were manual workers—especially semi-skilled—almost 30 percent were skilled nonmanual workers (notably clerks, shopkeepers, and licensed victuallers). And, lastly, the influence of drink was consistent over time. Although one-half of the drinking suicides came from the last two decades of the century, almost one-third took place in the 1850's and 1860's.

First, the cases in which drink was the main precipitant of suicide. In December 1842, a blacksmith with a shop in his house, aged about 60, hanged himself after having auctioned off his effects. A shoemaker friend stated: "[H]e was very crazy when he was drunk. his wife is a very respectable woman. he often sent her out at midnight for drink."[31] In October 1854, Edward Skerrow, a cowkeeper, aged 64, poisoned himself with opium. A paperhanger who had known Skerrow for twenty years deposed: "He has always broken off drinking for a fortnight or three weeks now & then." He also said that the deceased would not go home, because his wife was threatening to put him in "Charity Hall." A stonemason friend confirmed the fact by stating: "He said I've been so browbeaten at home by my wife that I shall have done with it altogether now."[32] In August 1872, William Clark, a dock pilot and widower, aged 55, hanged himself from his prison cell window. He had been committed to prison for fourteen days' hard labor for nonpayment of a fine for being drunk. Clark's son, a timber merchant's clerk, said his father had never been the same since breaking two limbs some years earlier. He had tried to kill himself before.

For some time the deceased had been drinking to excess, which had affected his mind.[33]

In a few cases, finally, drinking was associated with marital violence. In September 1895, Philip Gilsenan, a gasworks stoker in his mid forties, hanged himself. His 15-year-old son, a saw-mill laborer, told the inquest: "Mother left him. . . . I have a brother & a baby sister, we all came with mother. My mother left him because he threatened to kill her and she was afraid of him. He used to often ill use her. He was about the worst drinker there was round Courtney Street." Gilsenan was alone after his family left. The boy had heard that his father was trying to hang himself, so he and his brother went to the house, got a man to help cut him down, and called the police.[34]

A number of additional suicides show how work dismissal (threatened and actual), unemployment, and poverty could flow from, and aggravate, the effects of intemperance. Samuel Hodgson, aged 46, was found drowned in the New Timber Pond in June 1873, his pockets full of chalk stone and gravel. A widower, he had lived with his mother and aunt, but the aunt's illness had led him to move in with a man whom he had known for many years. The latter told the inquest that Hodgson had been a hard drinker and had lost his situation as a timber merchant's clerk a few days earlier through drink.[35] In February 1890, Joseph Morris, aged 46, George Cooper's groom, poisoned himself with laudanum. Cooper said that Morris had been drinking all the previous week, as was his wont, and that he had forgiven Morris hundreds of times for getting drunk. Morris's body was found where he was lodging, a book opened at a page on which was written: "Dear George, I thought you would not forgive me so took this in preference to walking about. But loved you to the last."[36] And in April 1897, an unmarried stockbroker's bookkeeper, aged 49, shot himself. His employer stated that the deceased had been with the firm for 37 years. For the last year or two, he had drunk to excess, and his work had deteriorated. "During the last 12 months I have had no confidence in his accuracy." He had been told that the firm could not overlook one more irregularity and had then been suspended for ten days. "I think he was aware that he was no longer fit for business."[37] Henry Woodhead, a 60-year-old shipbuilder's laborer, lately a fish hawker, hanged himself in June 1866 in the lodging house where he had lived since his wife's imprisonment. Said his landlady: "When he first came he was full of trouble & out of work. He then got better. He got drunk at Beverley fair about a month ago & has been drinking ever since." All his belongings had been pledged for drink.

A few days before, she continued, Woodhead had been very low "and said he had ruined himself & did not know what to do, & thought he should have to go into the Union."[38]

Another prominent category of motive among men in early old age was illness. Thirty-five percent of all male suicides in this age group were motivated by physical and mental illness. The most marked difference from males in the prime of life was that only 13 percent of suicides caused by illness in early old age were single (as compared with 45 percent in the prime of life), and only 7.7 percent were widowed. Over two-thirds of illness-induced suicides were married. Thus no civil status was over- or underrepresented among suicides caused by illness. Illness affected those aged 45–54 (58 percent) slightly more than those aged 55–64 (42 percent). And illness prompted suicide throughout the Victorian period. The first three decades contributed 43 percent of cases (the 1840's alone occasioning 18 percent); the final three decades contributed 57 percent of cases (the last two decades producing 48 percent). In terms of occupation and social class, illness particularly affected men in metals and engineering, food and drink, building, and the professions (solicitor, teachers, surgeon). Hence, one-third of suicides were from the three highest social classes (and particularly from the skilled nonmanual class), while over one-half were from the skilled working class. Close to a quarter of illness cases (or 18 of 78), finally, were ones in which illness and work-cum-business troubles were interlocked. Indeed, 9 of the 18 were unemployed at the time of death. We shall deal with these cases separately. But, first, let us look at suicides in which illness was the preeminent motive, only a small sample of which can be presented.

In August 1839, George John, a surgeon aged about 50, shot himself. Dr. Casson, who had attended John for the past few weeks, stated that his illness, which was not specified, had led to such depression that the deceased had feared he should go insane.[39] John Walker, aged 48, a patient in the Fever Hospital of the workhouse, threw himself out of a third-story window in September 1847. The surgeon to the workhouse said Walker had been in a state of delirium arising from fever.[40] Joseph Jacobs, a 45-year-old solicitor, fell from the billiard-room window of his home in December 1883. He was president of the Hull Literary and Philosophical Society, a classical scholar, and a mason. According to his surgeon, Jacobs had been ill for three months and unable to sleep.[41] Henry Capes, aged 55, a dock laborer, hanged himself in September 1895. He lived alone and had been ill for five weeks. His doctor said he had suffered from diarrhea and sickness at first, then from debility. A neighbor had occasionally helped Capes with his housework, and she had attended him when ill, looking in on him several times a day. His brother, also a docker, said he seemed low on account of his illness.[42]

A handful of suicides were in the asylum at the time. George Shaw, aged 57, strangled himself in the Hull and East Riding Refuge in October 1845. The keeper said Shaw had been an inmate for six months. "He used to say he thought he had lost all his religion . . . all hopes of heaven. he should never get there."[43] Others feared ending up in the asylum. John James, a shoemaker, aged 50, shot himself on the Humber riverbank in September 1851. He stuck a note to his wife on the grass with his penknife. "If I live, I must go to the asylum," he wrote. "It is better to fall into the hands of God than man. I pray Him to pardon His erring creature, and bless you all. . . . I have felt insanity coming on me from the first. There will never be any more chance of sleeping in comfort again in this wicked world."[44] A paperhanger in his late forties, in a low state for some time, cut his throat in October 1899. The evidence showed that the deceased had lived in daily terror of being sent to Willerby asylum.[45] Another suicide failed to get admitted in time. Elias Peachey, aged 64, a builder, was found drowned in October 1889. Said his son, "[H]is intellect has been failing for two years since my mother's death. . . . He lost 6 stones in weight during 12 months— which affected him very much." In late August, he had attempted to cut his throat, and so was removed to the Infirmary. The Infirmary surgeon stated that Peachey had been delusional and suicidal. "I insisted on his being watched by the police while in the Infirmary." He returned to his son's house, where he was watched, and while arrangements were made to take him to an asylum. He was willing and was to have gone on the day he was found drowned.[46]

Long-term illness was bound to have a detrimental effect upon a man's capacity to work. Small tradesmen felt unable to meet their orders. William Scott, aged 63, a tailor, hanged himself in September 1854. His daughter told the coroner that her father had had an apoplectic fit three years before and had since been unwell. More recently, he had been afraid that he would not be able to execute some orders for mourning clothes; the night before he killed himself, he had asked the boy who worked for him to stay late, but the latter had refused.[47]

Many more men were unable to work at all. A laborer on the Hull and Barnsley Dock, aged 54, cut his throat in December 1887. His wife said he had been ill with bronchitis and nervous depression and had not worked for seven months. They received parish relief.[48]

Lastly, illness could lead to a drop in earnings. Henry Spencer, a 45-

year-old painter and paperhanger, cut his throat in January 1898. His wife deposed that he had been under the club doctor for congestion of the lungs. He had fallen several times lately and had begun to talk to himself. While she slept in the front room with their 6-month-old baby, he had occupied the back room with their young daughter, since his cough woke the baby. Spencer was a quiet, hardworking man, said his wife, but he had given her only £1 in each of the past two weeks: "He should have averaged 30/- a week in full flush work. . . . He was depressed at not earning so much as he had earned before. . . . The last year the work has been worse than at any other time. I was never angry that he made no more money." [49]

IV

The category that warrants the closest attention among male suicides in early old age, however, is that of economic difficulties. Close to one-fifth of male suicides in this age group were unemployed at the time of death. Moreover, most of the unemployed were motivated to kill themselves, either primarily or secondarily, by economic worries. [50] Others besides the unemployed, however, were influenced by economic factors. In fact, 28 percent of all male suicides in early old age (or 61 of 221 cases) were directly motivated by economics, and the figure increases to 41 percent (or 90 of 221) if we add those cases in which drink or illness were associated with work problems. This figure is a good bit higher than the figure (30 percent) for men in the prime of life. What can we say in general of these 90 suicides? A significant proportion—40 percent—were single, separated, or widowed. They were divided fairly equally between the two age groups 45–54 and 55–64, with close to a quarter aged between 60 and 64. As for occupation, most were in metals and engineering, food and drink, building, transport, and commerce. Just over a third were skilled manual workers, just over a fifth were skilled nonmanual workers. Finally, nearly one-third of these cases came from the 1890's; just over one-half from the final two decades of the century.

The male suicides in which economic troubles were paramount are examined under five main headings. Once more, it is possible to present only a sample of cases. First, there were men in early old age whose unemployment was the problem. One-third (or 20 of 61) of the main economic suicides were troubled by unemployment. Most were formerly employed in sea transport, metals and engineering, building, or oil milling. Most were semi-skilled workers, followed by skilled and unskilled workers.

In June 1843, Thomas Hutton, aged about 50, hanged himself in prison, where he had been remanded on a charge of theft. His former employer stated that Hutton "was a labouring man and has not had any employ since he left me [seven months ago] excepting for occasional jobs. He was extremely poor and I expect he has been low spirited on account of being out of employ." A neighbor agreed. Hutton, his wife, and three children, she said, had had relief from "Charity Hall": "I believe Hunger and Starvation have brought deceased to a weak state of mind." [51] In April 1883, Thomas Todd, a joiner, aged 55, hanged himself from a hook in the kitchen ceiling. His wife deposed: "He has been very despondent since Christmas. Business was bad. He had worked at Eastons 19 years & he left at Christmas — and seemed to take it to heart very much." [52] And, lastly, in July 1891, an oil miller, aged 50, unemployed for seven weeks, cut his throat. He was separated from his second wife, and he looked after his ten-year-old daughter by his first wife. Said his former mother-in-law: "He had been out of work some time & was much in debt which affected his spirits." [53]

The second category of economic suicides were small traders whose business was failing. John Davey, a butcher, aged 50, used one of the tools of his trade to cut his throat in March 1848. For three weeks, according to the inquest report in the *Hull Advertiser*, Davey had complained to a customer that he did not know what he should do, as he did not think his shop would answer, in the phrase of the time.[54] Those working in the drink trade were particularly vulnerable. Henry Greenwood, aged 56, formerly a manager in Kingston Cotton Mill, had taken the Brewers Arms a month before he was found drowned in two feet of pond water in August 1879. His wife stated that her husband had been depressed for three weeks. The beer house had not come up to his expectations.[55] And in May 1897, George Ward, a fruiterer in his mid forties, owner of a market fruit stall, hanged himself in his warehouse. His wife said he had been troubled of late "as he had got into debt through his trade being bad & it preyed on his mind." His son-in-law agreed: "he told me he owed a number of people money & could not pay. He had not sufficient capital to carry on his business." [56]

The third category of economic suicide concerned the impact of accidents on working life. Patrick Duffy, a laborer, aged 60, separated from his wife, cut his throat in January 1852. He had broken his leg in a fall at work and had spent nearly four months in the Infirmary. On discharge, he was given a note to the workhouse for relief. However, "he seemed much depressed because they would not take him into the Charity Hall," the keeper of the lodging house where Duffy had lived said. "[T]hey gave him nothing." By this time his leg had become gangrenous. The *Hull Adver-*

tiser entitled its column on the inquest "Suicide from Alleged Neglect of Parish Authorities."[57] The chief engineer of a steamship, aged 47, hanged himself from the boiler in June 1879 as the ship lay in Prince's Dock. Two years before, the engines had broken down at sea, and the deceased had got steam in his throat, which had prevented him from eating and drinking. Said the second engineer: "He was afraid of not being able to keep his situation."[58] And John Hudson, a laborer at Earle's shipyard, aged about 60, died from an opium overdose in December 1898. He had not worked for six months owing to an accident. He had been in the Infirmary and at a convalescent home. The rent collector said Hudson lived alone, and that his claim against Earle's for compensation had not been disposed of. "I am sure it preyed somewhat on his mind."[59]

The fourth category were suicides who were troubled by debt. A dock gateman at the Old Dock, aged 48, hanged himself in July 1851. His wife said her husband was troubled by a doctor's bill, the money for which could not be found. A fellow gateman added: "[H]e has often complained to me of the trouble he had at home from debts & his wife drinking. I have seen him & her quarrel upon the Quay when she was intoxicated. he attributed his debts to the irregularities of his wife."[60] And Robert Clark, aged 62, a widowed merchant's clerk, hanged himself in December 1879. He had lost both his situation and a lawsuit, and had been forced to make over his furniture to a creditor. He had nothing to live upon, and his house was to be broken up. Clark left a note that said: "I cannot bear this any longer . . . with love to all. I hope to be forgiven for this rash act."[61]

A final category of cases involved men over whom the workhouse cast its shadow. A 58-year-old paint-works laborer, who lived alone, strangled himself in August 1893. A neighbor stated that he could not work on account of illness and had had no pay for three weeks. "I heard he was to go into the workhouse tonight. His landlord gave him notice to quit tonight. . . . He said he could not go 'up Beverley Road'—he could not bear to. I took it that he referred to the workhouse."[62]

V

The experience of suicide among women in early old age was different in many regards. Economic troubles and drink together provoked only one-quarter of all female suicides in this age group. Another one-fifth were associated with disturbances in personal relationships. The majority of female suicides (51 percent) were ascribable to physical and mental illness.

These categories will be examined before I offer conclusions about the pattern of suicide for both sexes in this life stage. Only 13 percent of women suicides (or 10 of 76 cases) were directly affected by economic troubles, slightly fewer than women suicides in the prime of life. Just about every Victorian decade had a case or two of this kind. Close to three-quarters of these women were widows, those who were most commonly involved in the world of waged work, or were dependent upon working children.

Jane Jackson, a sailmaker's widow who lodged with a publican, hanged herself in June 1842, aged 52. She had formerly been housekeeper for twelve years to a man who had married a year before, but she had lost her situation, which "preyed considerably on her mind," Jackson's landlord said. "She often expressed fears of coming to want although she has sufficient property to keep her." She also said she did not deserve to eat, as she did not work.[63]

Mary Hill, a 62-year-old widow, poisoned herself with laudanum in January 1892. Her neighbor disclosed: "Last Friday she was sold up for rent & her lodger left. . . . She was rather distressed at losing her furniture and lodger. she had no means of living that I know of." She had thereupon taken to drink.[64] And Rebecca Frazer, a mariner's widow, aged 58, cut her throat in February 1850. Until a few years before, she had been a sweeper at the Mariners' Church. At the time of her death, she lived with her two sons and two male nephews. One of her sons, a seaman, said: "We have been out of work 3 months & she thought that we should want." For six weeks, she had been depressed, insomniac, and suicidal.[65]

The next case is a classic illustration of the impact of poor-law policy on the widowed. Clarissa Kennard, aged 46, a fisherman's widow, hanged herself in December 1896. She lived with her son, a baker's laborer, who earned 10 shillings a week; another son and a daughter occasionally sent them 2s. 6d. After paying rent of 1s. 6d., Kennard and son had only 8s. 6d. a week to live on (well below the poverty line that Seebohm Rowntree would devise in 1901). Kennard's son said she was weak and ill from hunger. Having at one time received parish relief, she applied again, but it was refused because her son was in work. His testimony continued: "I have often heard my mother say she wished she were out of the road. . . . I was greatly surprised to hear that my mother had destroyed herself. . . . There was food in the house. We had no money at all. Some rent was owing but there was no threat of distress. She was at times depressed & low." The wife of a dock laborer, in whose house Kennard lived, stated that they owed six months' rent, since the son had been unemployed for a long time and owed for a week's food. "We never threatened to turn her out on account of the rent."[66]

It was not widows only, however, who were afflicted with economic troubles. Jane Holmes, aged 45, wife of a gasworks laborer, died from the effects of oxalic acid in October 1861. Her husband stated that she had been depressed for weeks. "Owing to the badness of work at the factory where several of our children were employed our expenses have been greater than our earnings." He was referring, presumably, to the New Hull Flax and Cotton Mill, which was in the street in which they lived. Some of the eldest children, he went on, had behaved badly, and there had been differences with them about their wages. He concluded: "She has several times hinted at drowning herself if it were not for the baby." A friend, finally, said that Holmes had got into debt for her children and thought she should never get it paid.[67]

The same proportion of suicides (around 13 percent) were motivated by drink, which was less than among women suicides in the prime of life. One-half of these suicides were single, separated, cohabiting, or widowed; one-half were from the 1880's and 1890's. In a few of the drink-induced suicides, intemperance had led to debt and poverty. Sarah Major, aged 48, a cabinetmaker's widow, who lived with her two sons (aged 12 and 13) and a woman lodger, was found drowned in Queen's Dock in February 1881. One of her sons, a boot-dealer's errand boy, had given the 5s. 6d. he earned to the deceased; the other boy, at the time of the inquest, was in the workhouse. Both boys testified to their mother's drinking habits. One of them added: "We hadn't over much to eat." A fish laborer who knew Major stated: "The last time I saw her she complained that she was so poor she did not know what to do."[68]

In a larger number of drink-induced suicides, intemperance had resulted in marital disharmony. Mary Parker, aged 57, a shipwright's wife, poisoned herself with opium in February 1855. Her husband, who lived with his daughter and son-in-law, stated: "She has been drinking & never sober since Christmas. She has not been living at home all the time. She has been living in a room in the neighbourhood as she thought she would do better there. . . . She got the money by disposing of her clothes. I allowed her so much a week."[69] And Mary Stokell, aged 53, a blacksmith's wife, poisoned herself with laudanum. Her son stated that Stokell's husband had not lived with her for weeks, although he came and paid the shop bills. "My father has lived away on account of her drinking habits. . . . She has lived on ale this last fortnight." The son also said: "My mother was distressed at his absence."[70]

Another one-fifth of female suicides in early old age (or 16 of 76) were motivated by disturbed personal relationships, and particularly by a husband's death. Over half of these suicides were widows. Elizabeth Apple-yard, 48 years of age, widow of a licensed victualler, hanged herself in October 1855. She had lived with her 14-year-old stepson, a railway clerk. The latter stated: "She had some means from my late father, something from dressmaking & my wages to keep us on." A surgeon who had known Appleyard for many years, and considered her to be "a most reputable woman," said she was affected by her husband's death two years before.[71] Martha Arnett, 57 years old, a cordwainer's widow, hanged herself in February 1869. She lived in lodgings and took in washing for a living. Her son deposed: "She has never been right since father died about a year ago. She has been much changed since."[72] And Mary Dent, aged 56, poisoned herself in July 1881, ten days after her husband's death. She had little or no income without her husband, who had been a pensioner of the Coast Guard Service. Dent's lodger stated: "She has on several occasions said she should commit suicide because she had lost her husband."[73]

The death or loss of other kin also caused grief. Harriet Reynolds, aged 46, a lathrender's widow, hanged herself in September 1881. Her sister stated: "She has been very low since her brother was drowned in the Columbine about a fortnight ago."[74] Ellen Smelt, aged 52, a painter's wife with three children, hanged herself in May 1895. Her husband said her daughter had died two years earlier, "and she has seemed to fail ever since." A suicide note declared: "Dear husband you will find my body in one of the top rooms. Bury me near Polly & bring little Harriet with you."[75] And Elizabeth Hanson, aged 47, a soap manufacturer's wife, cut her throat in October 1846. Her husband said she had been out of her mind "since my son was transported" some two years before.[76] Finally, the loss of a daughter through marriage could evoke despair. Ann Sweeting, aged 50, a licensed victualler's wife, cut her throat in June 1886, on the day of her daughter's wedding. A policeman took her by cart to hospital, but bronchitis set in and she died six days later. She had looked after her husband's tavern during the day, while he acted as a brewer's town traveler. They had no servant. Her husband told the coroner: "She used to say that when my daughter married she would not be able to manage the business. . . . There had been trouble between my daughter and wife about the marriage as deceased thought she would not be able to manage the house." On the day of the wedding, Sweeting said she could not live in the house by herself. "She said I can't live, I can't live. I had no idea that she meant suicide."[77]

VI

Illness was the motivating force in the vast number of female suicides in early old age. In just over 50 percent of all cases (or 39 of 76), suicide was ascribed to physical or mental illness, higher than the figure (32 percent) for women suicides in the prime of life. In some of these cases, however, the evidence was not overwhelming, and "head pain" or "lowness" was the bare explanation witnesses advanced for the self-destruction. There was nothing unusual in the civic status of illness-induced suicides. Two-thirds were married, one-third were single and widowed. Twice as many were aged 45–54 as were aged 55–64. Every decade contributed illness cases to the total, but the 1840's and 1890's were the most prolific decades. I can present only a small sample of these cases, beginning with organic illness.

In October 1858, Mary Crossland, aged 62, a brewer's widow, who lived with her daughter and son-in-law, hanged herself. Her daughter said her mother had been ill for over a year and had been laid up with a bad leg the previous winter. The witness added: "She was dependent on her children, but never complained of being so."[78] Sarah Blenkin, aged 63, a retired clerk's wife, cut her throat in May 1891. Her husband said she was usually depressed in the spring. Ten years before, she had tried three times to kill herself, once by drowning, once by cutting her throat, and once by jumping from a height. A neighbor added that inflammation of the eyes during the winter had further depressed Blenkin. The deceased had asked her neighbor, "What do you think I have done it for?" and the neighbor replied, "Because you have been ill."[79] And Martha Naylor, aged 48, a single woman who lived with her mother and sister, poisoned herself with carbolic acid. A tendency to depression had been aggravated, said her sister, by influenza two months before. A neighbor stated: "She said she had a dreadful feeling but did not complain of pain. . . . I have heard her say she wished she was in heaven."[80]

The most common form of mental illness was religious despondency. After Sarah Gilliard, aged 53, was found drowned in the Old Harbour in May 1866, her husband, a joiner, said she had been low for eight months: "She said she was a lost woman after some prayer meetings in Glasshouse Row were given up. I believe she meant lost in religion. . . . She was desponding for months about religion."[81]

Mary Simpson, aged 48, who had been separated from her husband for over two years, hanged herself in October 1868. She had been in the asylum twice before marriage and twice since, and had been discharged four months earlier. Her husband visited her two or three times a week at her lodgings. Her landlady deposed: "She used to say that she wanted to be good but could not and that God did not love her. I persuaded her to read the bible every day." [82]

Other suicides were affected by melancholia. Harriet Thompson, aged 45, a railway gatekeeper's wife, cut her throat in December 1868. Her brother-in-law, in whose house she killed herself, said she had been depressed since her marriage three months earlier. "I have no reason to think that there was discomfort between her & her husband. He was a widower with a family. She had not been married before." Following her suicide attempt, a relieving officer took her under a magistrate's order to the asylum as a pauper lunatic, where she died. The surgeon said she had suffered from intense melancholia. [83]

Finally, Sarah Loveday, aged 45, a single housekeeper, hanged herself in July 1873. She had been in the asylum for a year suffering from melancholy. For the last three weeks, she had been permitted to go out on trial to her employer's house, where she killed herself. [84]

VII

What does the inquest evidence reveal about the experience of suicide in early old age? For men, early old age was the most suicidal stage of the entire life cycle. Suicides in early old age greatly exceeded their proportions in the city population. Just over one-fifth of Hull's male population was aged 45–64, yet over two-fifths of all male suicides were drawn from this age group. The male suicide rate reached its maximum, in fact, between 55 and 64 years of age. Unmarried and widowed men had a much higher suicide rate than married men (and a much higher rate than single and widowed women). Moreover, over one-third of these single and widowed male suicides were living alone or in lodgings, or were of no fixed abode, and as such were deprived of the socially integrating force of family life. The most striking impression conveyed by the documents is the frequency of reference by witnesses to the difficulties of earning a living in later life. This economic theme must be understood, not only as a "factor" underlying suicidal death, but as a cultural pattern and a way of thinking about suicides in later life. Witnesses probably clutched at statements by suicides about their unemployment and fear of dependence to explain the deaths of these men. Nevertheless, the evidence also suggests that the end of working life was a truly vulnerable phase in the life cycle of the urban male, leading in some cases to self-destruction.

Men in their mid forties and above could find it impossible to cope with the drop in income and the blow to personal status and identity that might flow from unemployment, business failure, or industrial injury. For others, the pressure of debt or the threat of the workhouse was the final straw. The trades in which unemployed suicides worked were sea transport, oil milling, building, and metals and engineering. With the exception of the last, these were some of the most casual and seasonal jobs in the Hull economy. Occasionally, discharge ended a protracted relationship between man and firm, thus seeming to cause a deeper emotional affront. Small retailers—many of whom had only recently taken to penny capitalism, possibly because they felt no longer competent for manual labor—were often overwhelmed by business failure, especially those in the drink trade, but also cowkeepers, coal dealers, and shopkeepers. A further threat to material sufficiency—notably for railmen, seamen, dockworkers, and others in dangerous trades, and particularly prior to the 1897 Workmen's Compensation Act—was industrial injury.[85] Injured suicides in Hull had worked at the occupations of marine engineer, master mariner, railway gangsman, coal cartman, boilermaker, and dock, shipyard, timberyard, and boilermaker's laborers.

All told, some 28 percent of male suicides in early old age were primarily motivated by economic troubles. The temporal distribution of these suicides was by no means even, however. Three-quarters of the suicides in which unemployment was a motivating factor, for example, occurred in the years 1879–99. This late Victorian crescendo might be a function of the political attention that was increasingly accorded the "worn-out worker." But it might be a function, too, of labor-market insecurity, as employers increasingly shed older workers to improve industrial efficiency. Or it might be a reflection of trade depression in the local economy, which hurt older men most. There was a definite downturn in the trade cycle in the late 1870's. While the statistics of suicide are not renowned for responding sensitively to economic change, it so happens that 15 percent of all the economic suicides—including cases of unemployment, business failure, and injury—occurred in the two years 1878–79. Trade turned down again in 1886 and in the 1890's.[86]

The contribution of the economic motive rises even higher, to just over two-fifths of male suicides in early old age, when one includes suicides in which drink or illness resulted in work or financial difficulties. Excessive drinking over a prolonged period ultimately damaged a man's work performance, especially, it seems, in the clerical, bookkeeping, and domestic service occupations. In close to 30 percent of drink-induced suicides, intemperance acted via work dismissal (actual or threatened) and poverty. By definition, illness jeopardized a workman's greatest asset, especially in a low-welfare society: a fit and healthy body. In close to a quarter of illness-induced suicides, sickness had made it difficult, and in some cases impossible, to attend to work or business, or had caused a drop in earnings. If, finally, we add to these economic suicides those that were motivated by the public disgrace attendant upon theft or embezzlement, then close to 45 percent of all male suicides in early old age were achievement-related and, as such, fit squarely within the gendered image of why men kill themselves.

Women suicides, by contrast, seemed to have been weighed down by different loads. Women in early old age were much less affected by the material and psychological strains of waged working life. Only 11 suicides out of 76 were in formal employment, with another 6 taking in washing or lodgers—a reflection, in part, of the fact that Hull was a poor town for female employment, aside from domestic service. Only 10 suicides (or 13 percent of all female suicides in this age group) were directly motivated by economic troubles. Almost three-quarters of these women were widows, who typically took their largest role in the waged economic life of the community at this point in the life cycle. Individual cases illustrate the disadvantaged economic status of older women, the result of segregation in low-paying jobs and of discontinuous work histories. Women who had been homemakers for most of their adult lives often ended up supporting themselves following widowhood. However, female suicide emerged much more from the family relationships within which they largely spent their lives, and from prolonged physical and mental illness. One-fifth of suicides in early old age were induced by a disturbance in personal relationships, and notably by the death of a husband or other kin. Of course, a husband's death could involve both financial and emotional loss. In addition, in over half of the drink-induced suicides, intemperance was linked to marital discord, including impending or actual separation.

Far and away the commonest explanation offered for suicide in older women was physical and mental illness, occasionally prefaced by attempted suicide and asylum admission, and almost invariably entailing some form of melancholia. In some of these cases, the evidence was not overabundant, suggesting that illness and insanity were privileged categories in the construction of female suicide, just as economic pressure was for male suicide. The belief that pain could lead to depression and insanity legitimized the explanation of why the sick killed themselves. But if illness was a way of conceptualizing the suicide of older women, it was also a concrete force.

A large number of female suicides in early old age were afflicted with religious despondency, loss of memory, hypochondria, insomnia, influenza, and specific organic illness, leading at times to anxiety about ever recovering. It is possible, too, that the menopause, a psychological as well as physical watershed, was behind some of this illness. One-half of the suicides who were ill were in the menopausal years of 45 to 50.

It would be inaccurate, however, to leave the impression that male suicide in early old age (any more than in the prime of life) was primarily a product of working life, and that female suicide was an outcome of domestic life. As we know, Victorian commentators commonly portrayed male suicide as an effect of the stresses associated with men's roles and responsibilities, and female suicide as a result of deviation from traditional domestic roles.[87] Perhaps coroners, friends, and families likewise assumed that men killed themselves for achievement-related as distinct from domestic or relational reasons, and thus inclined toward work-related explanations for male suicides and domestic ones for female suicides. If so, it is surely significant that slightly over one-half of male suicides in early old age were *not* attributed to work-related problems. We need, therefore, to escape these gendered assumptions. To do so, we need to perform two tasks. The first is to turn the assumptions inside out: to investigate the role of interpersonal factors in men's suicide and that of extrapersonal factors in women's suicide. The second task is to assess why men in early old age, and particularly widowers, had a much higher suicide rate than women. The explanation, I shall argue, lies as much in personal and relational factors as in achievement and economic ones.

On the surface, only 10 percent of male suicides in early old age were primarily motivated by a disturbance in personal relations. In two-thirds of these cases, the suicide was mourning the death of a wife, a death that had led in some instances to the breakup of the marital home and to residence in lodgings. Most of the remaining cases involved domestic violence. But below the surface, things look a little different. Interpersonal difficulties were a contributory factor in another 13 percent of male suicides. In a handful of illness-induced suicides, the illness was aggravated by the death of kin or marital discord (owing to the wife's drunkenness).[88] In another seven cases, heavy drinking on the part of the suicide was bound up either with marital violence and separation or with retaliation by kin (including the threat of being sent to the workhouse) against a drunken husband or father.[89] More important, in just over one-fifth of the economic suicides (or 19 of 90), interpersonal difficulties were again present. This was particularly true of economic suicides who were single, separated, or widowed (and 40 percent of all economic suicides were so placed). Among the latter were men who had no friends or family, or felt deserted by them; men who were troubled by the behavior of wives or lovers (one of whom was asking for support for an illegitimate child); men whose wives had died and whose homes were to be broken up; and, lastly, men who were to enter the workhouse, who were in the workhouse, who had just emerged from the "House," or who had been refused entry to it.[90] Among the married economic suicides were men whose wives were in jail or the workhouse, and who faced resort to the "House" themselves; men whose kin had recently died; and men who quarreled with their wives over either the latter's intemperance or their own.[91] When these cases are added to those primarily influenced by interpersonal factors, close to one-quarter of all males in early old age were affected by personal and relational pressures.

When it comes to investigating extrapersonal factors in women's suicide, the evidence is less convincing. Even so, to the 13 percent of female suicides in early old age that were motivated primarily by economic difficulties, it is possible to add another 10 percent, drawn from the drink and illness categories, in which extrapersonal (largely economic) factors were also evident. Heavy drinking had financial as well as physiological consequences, leading in a number of instances to debt, poverty, and even hunger.[92] Illness could affect the work of women even if it was not waged. There were, for example, wives who could not attend to housework. Illness could result in dependence upon children. And illness could be aggravated by money troubles.[93]

The second task is to assess why older men, especially widowers, had such a high suicide rate in early old age. Was it related, as conventional theory would have it, to problems arising from occupational performance? On the basis of the inquest evidence, it would be difficult entirely to gainsay this interpretation. But it was probably only part of the story. Another part had to do with disrupted interpersonal relationships. Men were typically the more "privatized" partner in marriage. However sociable at work, men tended to occupy a more isolated position within the street community.[94] Women were the ones who kept in touch with family and friends, who bore the burden of parenting responsibilities, and who cultivated support networks in the neighborhood. Women were the ones, too, who attended to the personal care and emotional stability of their husbands. It seems likely, then, that losing a spouse, either by death or separation, disrupted the domestic life of a man more than that of a woman. In one fell swoop, he lost the person who ran the home, took care of the children, and ministered to his health and comfort. The needs of dependent children (and 60 percent of widowed male suicides had unmarried children) only added to the burden inherited by the widower, as Durkheim noted.[95]

Of course, the same interpretation helps to explain the lower suicide rate of older women, including widows. Older women were more likely to be living alone and to be poor. Losing a spouse could threaten a woman's entire financial status. But they still did better at adapting to old age and widowhood. Less involved in waged work, they suffered the shock of severance from it less. And by early old age, they had grown more accustomed to coping with a low and precarious income. The daily routine of housework, and even of part-time waged work, was not drastically altered by old age or widowhood. Widows were better prepared to manage their own households, dependent as this was upon the domestic tasks performed by women. Women experienced more continuity in their social relationships, resting as they did upon kin, neighbors, and friends. Accustomed to dependency, psychologically prepared for the normative experience of widowhood, women found it easier to move in with married children, to accept parish relief, or to make ends meet. Accustomed to the constant physical and emotional adjustments required by childbirth and parenting, to movement in and out of the labor market, women reached old age more resourceful, more flexible, more able to adopt different coping strategies, and more independent in personal and social life. In short, the gender differential in death by suicide reflected not only the stresses inherent in the economic role and responsibilities of the male breadwinner, but also the much greater disruption by losing a spouse of the domestic and emotional lives of old men than of old women.

Late Old Age

Seventy years is the span of our life,
eighty if our strength holds;
the hurrying years are labour and sorrow,
so quickly they pass and are forgotten.

The New English Bible, Psalm 90, verse 10

The final phase of the Victorian life cycle was late old age, covering the years 65 and above. We have already seen that well before the introduction of old-age pensions in 1908, the age of 65 was an important "employment threshold." By 1881, as Paul Johnson has observed, around 40 percent of urban men over 65 had permanently left employment.[1] For many, it was "infirmity" retirement, enforced by illness, failing strength, or industrial injury.[2] For others, it was "jobless" retirement, a function of the inability to find work in an economy less accommodating of the older workman, and in a society increasingly expecting retirement.[3] Still, this meant that some 60 percent of urban males aged 65 and over were returned in the census as occupied, even in 1901. In Hull itself, the figure was 59 percent. Predictably, old men congregated in trades where the work was lighter and the wage rates were lower. Old men in Hull in the later Victorian period worked in transport, building, and metals; and as tailors, shoemakers, small-scale retailers, and general laborers. They were particularly overrepresented in tailoring, hawking, and gardening. Around 11 percent of old women were in formal employment, mainly as chars and laundresses, domestic servants, dressmakers, and lodging- or eating-house keepers.[4] For many of the old, in short, the continued need to earn a living scotched any thoughts of retirement and ensured that economic insecurity would remain a fearful concern of this life-cycle stage.

Widowhood, as we have also seen, was a main characteristic of late old age. In Hull, on average, one-third of men and 62 percent of women aged 65 and above were widowed.[5] For a significant proportion of the elderly, notably widowers, moreover, public assistance was a vital source of financial aid. Charles Booth estimated that close to one in three of the over-65s drew relief at some time each year.[6] In the Hull Union in 1891–92, one-third of the over-65s were indeed granted relief; the aged poor, and especially old women, were granted 1s. 6d. and bread, which, with a spot of charring or sewing work, sufficed for the rent of a room and physical survival. In addition, the mariners' almshouses accommodated some 600 of the aged poor.[7] This patchwork of survival strategies was jeopardized, however, by the curtailment of outdoor relief in the quarter century between the early 1870's and the mid 1890's. The proportion of the elderly receiving a poor-law "pension" fell, as did the relative value of the out-relief still granted. Older women, and particularly widows, were probably the worst affected by this change in policy, but men on the outdoor list were also required to seek family assistance or enter the workhouse. The extra rigor with which the poor-law authorities dispensed outdoor "pensions" forced some men, in consequence, to brood over swapping the autonomy of working life for the dependency of the workhouse.[8] In all, the late Victorian period could be a particularly difficult one for those in late old age, and particularly for old men. Changes in the pattern and pace of work, combined with stingier poor relief, aggravated the customary tribulations—somatic illness, depression, loneliness—of old age in a pre-pension era.

I

In the Victorian era in Hull, there were 40 male and 23 female suicides in late old age. To these I have added 10 male and 4 female open verdicts, making a grand total of 50 male and 27 female suicides in this last stage of the life cycle. Over three-quarters of the male suicides (or 39 of 50) were aged 65–74; fewer than one-quarter were aged 75 and over. By contrast, almost 90 percent of the female suicides (or 24 of 27) were aged 65–74. Only three women in Hull aged 75 and over were deemed to have committed suicide in the entire Victorian period. The average annual mortality from suicide per 10,000 living was 32 for men aged 65–74, only a fraction less than the 32.9 for men aged 45–54, yet rather less than the high of 38.6 for men aged 55–64. The figure for men over 75 years of age was 19.6. For women, the rates were 18 per 10,000 living for the 65–74 age group, the highest of any decennial age period (which was true of all industrial towns and for London in the decade 1861–70) and 5.7 for the over-75 age group.[9] Lastly, for the entire age group 65 and over, the average annual mortality from suicide was 29 for males and 14.5 for females, compared with 35.1 and 10.5, respectively, for the 45–64 age group.[10] The suicide rate for males aged 65 and over rose considerably in the 1870's and 1880's, at the same time as the rate for females declined markedly. One final measure illustrates that like early old age, late old age was a decidedly suicidal phase of the life cycle. Men aged 65 and over made up 5.2 percent of the Hull population (aged 15 and above), but accounted for 10.1 percent of all male suicides. The figures for women aged 65 and over were 6.6 percent and 11.4 percent.[11] Thus suicides by those in late old age were almost double their proportions in the population at large.

We turn, next, to civil status. Of the 50 male suicides, 4 percent were single, 48 percent were married, and 36 percent were widowed; of the 27 female suicides, 3.7 percent were single, 33.3 percent were married, and 63 percent were widowed.[12] Married men were responsible for a smaller proportion of suicides than would be expected from their proportions in the total population. They committed 48 percent of all the male suicides in this age group, yet they constituted on average 60 percent of the male population. Marriage, it seems, protected old men against suicide. Married women were responsible for a slightly larger proportion of suicides than would be expected from their proportions in the total population, committing 33.3 percent of female suicides, yet constituting 29.3 percent of the female population. Marriage, it seems, was not the protective for old women that it was for old men. Widowed men were slightly overrepresented among suicides, committing 36 percent of male suicides, yet constituting 33.8 percent of the male population. The proportion of suicides committed by widows was identical to their proportion in the female population aged 65 and over, or 63 percent. The single, separated, and widowed (or those outside of marriage) together committed 56 percent of all male suicides and 70 percent of all female suicides aged 65 and over.[13] In the 1890's, finally, the suicide rate for single males was 47.4 per 10,000 living; for married males, 18.8; and for widowers, 65.7.[14] The rates for females were 20.6 (married) and 13.3 (widowed).[15] The suicide rate for widowed men was, therefore, three and a half times higher than the rate for married men. Yet the rate for married women was higher than the rate for widows.

As for the living arrangements of suicides in late old age, all of the 19 married male suicides lived with their wives. The handful of married men who were separated were either in lodgings, with a married daughter, with unmarried children, or of no fixed abode. Of the 20 widowed men, 45 percent were dependents in the home of a son or married daughter, or the home of other kin; 25 percent still headed their own households and had kin living with them; 15 percent lived alone; and 10 percent were in lodgings. One man, finally, was in an almshouse, and two were in the workhouse. The eight married female suicides lived with their husbands; the one separated suicide lived in her son's house. Of the 17 widows, 41 percent were dependents in the home of a married or widowed son or daughter; 18 percent lived alone; and 23 percent were in lodgings. Two women, finally, were in almshouses. These figures suggest that most male suicides resided with wife or kin, whether as household heads or as dependents in other people's households. Only two separated men and one-quarter of the widowed males lived alone or in lodgings. Few of the male suicides, then, had experienced residential isolation. By contrast, 40 percent of the widows lived alone or in lodgings, and thus had some acquaintance with residential isolation.[16]

In what ways did those in late old age destroy themselves? Of the men on whom suicide verdicts were returned, 55 percent hanged themselves (as compared with 75 percent by men in early old age), 22.5 percent cut their throats, 12.5 percent used poison, 5 percent strangled themselves, and another 5 percent put themselves in front of a train. When open verdicts are added, the figures for hanging and throat cutting fall to 44 and 18 percent, respectively, while 12 percent drowned themselves, and 4 percent jumped from a height. No old man used a firearm. Of the women on whom suicide verdicts were returned, 48 percent hanged themselves, 8.7 percent cut their throats, 26 percent used poison, and 4 percent each resorted to strangulation, choking, jumping, and a train. When open verdicts are added, the figure for hanging falls to 41 percent, while 11 percent drowned themselves.

Finally, there is the question of the occupational and class backgrounds of suicides in late old age. Three-quarters of male suicides were still occupied, although in some cases very fitfully; one-quarter were retired. Most male suicides worked in transport (watermen, sloopmen, dock laborer), food and drink (butcher, grocers, cowkeeper), metals (marine store dealer, mast and block maker), dress (shoemaker, tailor), and commerce (clerk).

Comparing the proportions of male suicides with the proportions of all occupied males aged 45 and above in the 1890's (in table 6.9), we see that the proportion of suicides was larger than expected in dress, food and drink, and commerce.[17] What stand out in these listings, as with suicide in early old age, are the occupations that old workmen moved into: small-scale retailing, shoemaking, tailoring, and the job of waterman.[18] What also deserves remark is that eight suicides (or 16 percent of all male suicides) had changed occupations in recent years. Three had exchanged a proper trade (sailmaker, corn meter) for laboring work; two had become small-scale retailers; and one had left boilermaking for gardening. When occupation is translated into social class, and when the proportion of male suicides is compared with the class distribution of household heads in mid-century Hull (in table 5.1), we see that skilled nonmanual workers were again overrepresented among male suicides.[19] In this age group, however, the semi-skilled class was also overrepresented. In short, the lower-middle-class group of shopkeepers and dealers was particularly suicidal, but so too were semi-skilled workmen (watermen, sloopmen, color maker's laborers, a gardener, and a cowkeeper), a reflection, presumably, of the concentration of older workers in these occupations.

The occupational data for women in late old age are again fragmentary. Only 11 percent of Hull women in this age group were listed in the 1901 census as occupied. Of the female suicides, five (or 18 percent) were involved in economic life, broadly defined, few of whom would have been listed as occupied. One went out cleaning, one was an annuitant, two lived on house rents, and one helped her butcher husband. Three of these women were widows. The social class of the husband (living or deceased) of female suicides was once again mainly skilled or semi-skilled manual. Finally, four widows (or 15 percent of all female suicides) had received parish relief before their deaths, although this is probably a minimum figure.

II

Let us now look at the experience of suicide in late old age, beginning with old men. No male suicide was motivated by public or legal disgrace, and only 6 percent of male suicides were motivated by a disturbance in personal relations, notably a wife's death. In March 1871, Christopher Fairbotham, a widowed shoemaker, aged 87, who had not worked for some time, fell from his bedroom window. His widowed granddaughter, with whom he lived, stated that he had been ill and bedridden for a few days. She had got a parish order for the doctor to attend him. Fairbotham seemed childish from old age, the witness continued, and he was difficult to manage. His wife had been buried two weeks before. "He used to fret about her death & wish he had gone first. I had removed his razors & any rope as I did not think he was to be trusted with them."[20] In May 1897, Jacob Hewitt, aged 75, a widowed beer-house keeper, poisoned himself with laudanum. His married daughter, who lived with him, said Hewitt had been low and nervous and always ailing since his wife's death five years earlier.[21]

Another suicide arose from severe marital disharmony and intemperance. John Douse, a 69-year-old general laborer, hanged himself in May 1890. According to his 15-year-old son (the eldest of four young children), Douse had been drinking for six weeks, since his wife had left him. He had been threatening to kill himself for days because his wife would not come home. The witness continued: "My father objected to my mother attending the [Wesleyan] Mission where she was employed." Douse's widow testified that she had left him, not for the first time, on account of his violence: "He used to threaten to cut his throat and also to cut my throat. He was very violent when in drink. . . . He was a sailmaker by trade but had been out of regular employment for two years. He did not earn sufficient to keep the family." For that reason, she worked as a domestic servant and also as a cleaner at night at the Wesleyan Mission. To judge from two pixilated letters addressed to the police, Douse blamed the Mission for having persuaded his wife to leave him and the children. On the day he killed himself, in fact, Douse had tried to stab Thomas Nicholson, a merchant's clerk, who was a teacher at the Mission.[22]

As with both men in the prime of life and men in early old age, the three main motives, numerically speaking, were intemperance, illness, and economic difficulties. Eighteen percent of male suicides were ascribed to heavy drinking. Most of these old men were single, separated, or widowed, especially the middle status. They were all manual workers, with the exception of an army pensioner.

Jacob Crowther, a 66-year-old sloopman, was found drowned in the shallow waters of a timber pond in March 1860. His widow said he was very much given to drinking, he had been in a low way for many years, and had attempted suicide on a number of occasions. "About 20 years ago he had a fall & ever since then when he got a little drink he has been raving." She had not lived with him since Hull Fair, "when he sold the bed from under me" and drank the proceeds.[23]

In September 1880, a shoemaker, aged 65, separated from his wife for over ten years, hanged himself in his workshop. His son, also a shoemaker, said his father had lived in a lodging house, although he had often slept in the workshop when drunk. He was, said the son, a heavy drinker.[24] In one case, finally, there was a connection between intemperance and the fear of dismissal. Richard Jackson, a timber merchant's laborer, aged 66, a widower who lived alone, hanged himself from his bedpole in August 1874. His married daughter said he had been given to drink for five years. In the past few days, he had not been at work and had been very low. "He would scarcely answer when spoken to." She added: "He said he dare not face his masters again. He was off a month or so ago. & was told that he would not be taken on again if he went off again."[25]

III

The most prominent category of motive was illness. Sixty percent of all male suicides in late old age were ascribed to physical and mental illness, or senility. One-half of illness-induced suicides were married, the other half widowed, which means that the widowed were overrepresented. Sixty percent of ill suicides were aged between 65 and 69; one-third were in their seventies, and the remaining few were in their eighties. Over three-quarters of the illness cases came from the last three decades of the century. Finally, over one-third of illness cases (or 11 of 30) were ones in which illness and economic troubles were interlocked. First, however, we shall deal with suicides in which illness was the preeminent motive.

Somatic illness prompted a number of old men to kill themselves. In January 1885, William Carlisle, a former fisherman, aged 74, a widower who lived with his married daughter, despaired of getting better and so hanged himself. His son-in-law, a mariner, said Carlisle had been ailing for a year and was unable to work. He did not undress when he went to bed, because it pained him to do so. On the night of his suicide, "he said he wished the Lord would take him." The doctor who had attended Carlisle for severe rheumatism and heart disease stated that he considered him an unlikely candidate for suicide, being a man of strong character and self-willed. He seemed to have an antipathy to anything doctors could do for him and always refused to take his medicine. The doctor added, however: "He had no possibility of getting better & he knew that he would never have any comfort or ease. His existence was getting to be intolerable to himself."[26]

George Willingham, a 68-year-old color maker's laborer, cut his throat in February 1887. He had lived with his wife and grandchild. His married daughter told the coroner that Willingham had not worked for eighteen months on account of an ulcerated leg, which pained him night and day. The pain depressed him, and he had been low for a fortnight.[27] And James Bowen, a widowed clerk, aged 76, hanged himself in March 1892. He lived with his daughter and grandson. The latter stated that his grandfather had had an illness in his bowels for years, which caused him great pain. In addition, however, Bowen had fretted about the death by suicide of another daughter a year before.[28]

Head pain was mentioned in a number of other suicides. Thomas Leonard, a retired butcher, aged 67, who lived with his wife in Harrison's Hospital, cut his throat in January 1860. His widow said that he had been in very bad health and had complained of pain in his head. The surgeon who was called to see him deposed: "Long continued pain in the head is indicative of disease of the brain & may cause melancholia which frequently results in suicide."[29] Simple old age seemed to be the affliction in other cases. The widower John Hibbs, aged 87, formerly a master mariner, hanged himself in the mariners' almshouse in December 1890. The surgeon of the Trinity House Corporation had frequently attended Hibbs for indigestion and mental depression. The wife of Hibbs's nephew, who got his tea ready and read the Bible to him, said he had been wandering in his speech for nearly a month.[30]

Other suicides were victims of insanity. Thomas Fenwick, aged 75, late Humber pilot, a widower living with his son-in-law and granddaughter, hanged himself in February 1867. He had made two attempts to drown himself in the preceding six weeks. Two years before, he had been in a lunatic asylum for six months. Dr. Usher, who was called to see Fenwick after he had been pulled out of Humber Dock, stated that he suffered from religious melancholia.[31] And Thomas Martin, aged 65, a widower living with his oil-miller son, hanged himself in April 1869. His son stated that Martin had been a farm laborer and afterward worked in the drawing room of the cotton mill. Three years ago, he had been in Lincoln County Asylum, but he was discharged on "our agreeing to look after him, & we wanted him out." He had been low recently and talked about killing himself.[32]

Illness could have a damaging impact on a man's working life, adding the insult of economic insecurity to the injury of bodily and mental pain. In the first place, a number of sick old men feared for the future. Robert Hardy, a 70-year-old twine spinner, married for nine years, and a regular Wesleyan chapelgoer, hanged himself in July 1856. His widow stated that Hardy had been weak in legs and limbs since the winter and in a low way.

He had worked a little, but not as much as formerly. She also observed: "He has latterly been worritting himself that he would not last long, & that he would not be able to work."[33] Thomas Inman, a retired butcher, aged 68, poisoned himself in April 1872. His niece, who lived with him, and who had kept house for him for 29 years, deposed that Inman had had a stroke four years earlier and fits since then, leaving him disabled, irritable, and low. "He began to think that he was not able to help himself & that he was going to be a great trouble," she said. "Sometimes he used to say that if he lived long he would not [have] sufficient to live on. The Sunday before he was taken ill he said he wished the Lord would take him." Inman also told his doctor that "he believed his property would not suffice to keep him & that he was living on his principal, & that he was no use in the world."[34]

Second, there were suicides whose illness was linked with business troubles. In May 1885, James Garrod, aged 67, a pensioned police officer and grocer, hanged himself. His widow said he had been low for weeks and not strong enough to open the shop, so they had done no business for a fortnight. The surgeon who attended him stated that he had been in a state of "great depression, anxiety & mental worry." "His ailment was altogether mental. He was feeble from age." A schoolmaster who joined the crowd around Garrod's house discovered a cryptic suicide note nailed to a wall: "Take warning dishonest customers a few shillings would have saved [?] me this fate."[35]

Third, there were suicides who were tormented by the shadow of the almshouse or workhouse. William Teal, aged 70, a married color maker's laborer, employed at the largest paint works in Hull, hanged himself in May 1891. His daughter emphasized that he had been despondent on account of his health and because he was about to stop working and go to live in the almshouses. A surgeon who had seen Teal a week earlier said that he had had a dilated heart. "He felt that his powers of working were failing him, partly thro age & partly thro his weak heart. This very much depressed him."[36]

IV

The category that also warrants attention among male suicides in late old age is, once again, that of economic difficulties. Just over one-fifth of male suicides in this age group were unemployed at the time of death, although most of these men were not motivated primarily by economic worries, but by illness. A large majority of the unemployed suicides were in their seventies or older; they had worked in transport, fishing, metals, and shoemaking, and most killed themselves between 1884 and 1894. Others besides the unemployed, of course, were influenced by economic troubles. In fact, 16 percent of all male suicides in late old age (or 8 of 50) were directly motivated by economics, and the figure increases to 40 percent (or 20 of 50) if we add those cases in which drink and especially illness were associated with work problems. This enlarged figure is almost identical to that for men in early old age. Of these 20 economic cases, almost two-thirds were married; one-third were single or widowed. Two-thirds were aged between 65 and 69; one-third were in their seventies. As for occupation, they were mainly shopkeepers and dealers, workers in water transport and metals, or laborers. Practically all these suicides occurred in the last three decades of the century.

The male suicides in which economic troubles were uppermost are examined under two main headings and one supplemental one. First, there were men in late old age whose unemployment was the trigger to self-destruction. Thomas Lacey, aged 70, a superintending stevedore for a Russian firm, cut his throat in April 1884. His widow said that he had received a letter six weeks ago from the Russian firm saying that it could not engage him that season on account of depression of trade. "It affected him very much, & he has not been the same since. . . . This was a great blow to him." She had watched him constantly for a month, since "he often wished he could make away with himself without pain." [37]

John Wray, aged 65, cut his throat in March 1885 behind a pile of boards on the dockside. His son-in-law stated that he had been dismissed as foreman to a forwarding agent fifteen months earlier and had not been employed since (except as an occasional dockside laborer). Wray's former employer allowed him four shillings a week. "He was discharged because he was past work," it was noted. In addition, however, he had been troubled by a urinary complaint and by the drowning of his grandchild nine months before. [38]

The second main category of economic suicides concerns cases in which business losses were the problem. Frederick Sutton, aged 66, an ornamental tile and pottery-ware agent, poisoned himself with sulfuric acid in October 1874. His son and clerk told the coroner that his father had been agent to an iron company and a tile works, both of which had scaled down their business. "I think the loss of employment preyed upon his mind. Both business [*sic*] have fallen off during the last summer & that affected him still more." [39]

In August 1884, James Porter, aged 70, a retired North Sea pilot, hanged himself in an outhouse. His widow said that he had been superannuated two and a half years earlier, and that they had taken a pork shop three weeks before his suicide. Porter had been very dissatisfied with the business. "He complained of being worried by the business which seemed to prey upon his mind."[40]

The supplemental category of economic suicide was fear of poverty. William Page, aged 68, a marine-stores dealer, hanged himself in his shop in the North Walls in May 1861. His son-in-law, a cabinetmaker, said Page had lived by himself since his wife's death three weeks earlier. He further deposed:

His intellect has been failing for several years. His wife used to manage the business chiefly. He had an overwhelming idea of coming to poverty. He had seemed worse since the death of his wife, & scarcely to know what he was doing. His idea of coming to poverty was unfounded. . . . He felt the loss of his wife very severely, especially in business matters. Last Sunday week he spoke of committing suicide & said that any one doing so would go to hell.[41]

V

The experience of suicide by women in late old age resembles that for old men. The most prominent category of motive was illness, which was influential in 55 percent of all female suicides. Heavy drinking led to over one-fifth of female suicides, and economic troubles to another 15 percent. Work problems were associated with a few of the drink and illness cases, however, and if these are added to the economic suicides, the number of women suicides affected by economic troubles increases to just over one-quarter. Disturbances in personal relationships were evidently unimportant as a motive. These categories will be examined before I present conclusions about the experience of suicide for both sexes in this life stage.

Only one old woman was directly affected by a disturbed personal relationship. Eliza Fowler, aged 67, a farmer's widow, poisoned herself with carbolic acid in April 1896. She lived with her married daughter and sometimes quarreled with her, said her grandson. She was bad-tempered and depressive. The day before her death, Fowler had struck her daughter in the face and gone upstairs. She was later found poisoned.[42]

Drink and drugs took a heavier toll, notably in the mid-century decades. They could be associated with disturbed personal relations, as the first case reveals, or with economic troubles, as in the second case. Hannah Simpson, aged 74, separated from her husband for seventeen months, hanged herself in August 1855. Her daughter-in-law, with whom Simpson had lived, stated that she was in the habit of taking opium. The doctor had told them that she was killing herself with it, so they had not let her have any for six months. "She used to become violent if deprived of it by us. She has often threatened to destroy herself. . . . She always said that she could not live without it."[43]

Ann Ayton, aged 74, a widow, hanged herself in a lodging house in May 1865. Her landlady said of Ayton: "She lived on the relief of the parish & sale of some of her effects. She used to keep a lodging house . . . about 4 or 5 years ago. She seemed perfectly in her mind when she was sober, but she was very often in drink."[44]

Finally, Mary Cain, a 70-year-old widow and house proprietor, hanged herself in September 1859. Her tenant, a baker, stated that she had lived on her rents, and had been drinking since the tenant of her other shop decided to leave. "She had before gone off drinking when one of her shops or cottage was unlet."[45]

Over 50 percent of female suicides in late old age (as in early old age) were ascribed to physical or mental illness, or senility. There was nothing untoward in the civic status of these suicides, two-thirds of them being widows. One-third were aged 65–69, two-thirds were in their seventies; almost two-thirds are from the early and mid Victorian decades. A number of old women were ill and desponding. Mary Chamberlain, aged 69, a widow, hanged herself in January 1846. Her daughter-in-law, with whom she lived, stated that she had had a fit on Christmas Eve and had been in a low way since. The night before her suicide, she had been arrested for having taken two potatoes. The witness and her husband, Chamberlain's son, had gone to the police station to get her bailed out, but she had been discharged. By the time they got back home, she had committed suicide.[46]

Dinah King, aged 71, a soldier's widow, poisoned herself with opium in October 1866. Her eldest son, a policeman, deposed that she had lived with her youngest son for a month, but they could not agree and he had turned her out. She had then moved into a rented room. "I do not know what she had to live on. She had 2/- a week & a small loaf from the parish. Her rent was 1/3d. a week." He added that he and his sister had contributed to her support. More to the point, she had been low for a year. "About a year ago a crate fell on her head & she has never seemed right in her mind since."[47]

Other women suffered from religious melancholia. Martha Carrick, aged 72, a lighterman's wife, hanged herself in March 1870. Her daughter-in-law said that Carrick had been despondent for six months or more. "She was a very religious woman. She said on Sunday that she thought she could not be saved & that she had been tempted to make away with herself two or three times. She said she had been a hypocrite all her life." A domestic servant added that it was Carrick's usual custom after breakfast to go into the bedroom to pray. This time she had hanged herself from a bedpost.[48]

Finally, a number of illness-induced suicides were associated with straitened economic circumstances. Pleasant Robinson, aged 74, a builder's widow and owner of six houses, hanged herself in September 1854. One of her lodgers stated that Robinson had been low through illness in recent months. "I think her circumstances were worse. She could not get her rents in & seemed to make a great trouble of it."[49]

The last case leads us logically into the suicides who were affected, at least to some degree, by economic troubles. Most of them were in their late sixties, and most were married. All the wives had husbands who were unemployed, and in two cases bereavement may well have been a factor. Phoebe Gansby, aged 70, fourteen years older than her laborer husband, cut her throat in May 1856. A cordwainer who lived in the room above the Gansbys stated that her husband was extremely deaf. "She has been in a low way some time in consequence of his not being in regular employment. She went to the asylum about 6 months ago & stayed there about 8 weeks. . . . She was under the impression that they would come to want."[50]

Elizabeth Joys, aged 66, a butcher's wife, was found drowned in the Old Harbour in February 1874, a flatiron tied to her waist. Her husband, who had been ill and confined at home since Christmas, said she had been low for some time. She had been affected by a brother's death and had fretted that she was not able to do her husband's business.[51] Lastly, Mary Squires, aged 67, a publican's widow, was found drowned in Cottingham Drain in March 1895. Her sister stated that Squires had gone out cleaning and had two shillings a week from the Union. She had complained lately of not being well and had been depressed because she had insufficient work.[52]

VI

What, then, does the inquest evidence suggest about suicide in the final season of life? The first point must be that remarkably few people killed themselves after they reached their mid seventies. The number of male suicides aged 75 and over barely reached double figures, almost one-half of which are from the final decade of the century, and only three women of this age in the entire Victorian period were adjudged by an inquest jury to have killed themselves, all three before 1870. Various explanations were offered for the decrease in the frequency of suicide after 75 years of age. William Ogle of the General Register Office argued, first, that "when the expectation of life becomes small the value attached to it becomes greater," and second, that "before this advanced age is reached, those who are unable to withstand the shock of adversity have been . . . weeded out, and that those who remain behind are on the average made of harder metal, that does not yield so rapidly to the pressure of despair." [53] Dr. S. A. K. Strahan added that "the most trying periods of life have been passed and comparative calm attained," and that many potential victims had instead developed "mental aberration," and thus were oblivious of either internal or external spurs to suicide. [54]

The second point is that while the suicide rate for women aged 65–74 was the highest of any decennial age period, this was a function of the earlier Victorian decades and the later 1890's, with a remarkable hiatus in between. [55] Indeed, from 1875 to 1894, inclusive, no woman aged 65 and over was adjudged by a jury to have killed herself. By contrast, the highest suicide rates for men aged 65–74 came in the 1870's and 1880's. Nearly 60 percent of all male suicides aged 65–74 took place in these two decades, with another 20 percent in the 1890's. The conclusion must be that for old men, much more than for old women, the later Victorian years were difficult ones to negotiate, of which more in a moment.

Third, few of the suicides in late old age were in residential confinement at the time of death. One widow was in the master mariners' almshouse, another in Trinity House almshouse, while a third was temporarily in the Infirmary for a cataract. [56] Two men were in the workhouse, one was in the master mariners' almshouse, and one was in Harrison's Hospital. [57] Not surprisingly, three of the seven were over 75 years of age, and three more were in their seventies. They were all suffering from some form of physical or mental illness.

The fourth point to be noted is that the change in poor-law policy that led to a reduction in outdoor relief from the early 1870's through the mid 1890's had no visible impact on any of the suicides in late old age. Poor relief was mentioned in only four cases, all widows, all living alone or in lodgings, and all of whom were receiving two shillings a week from the Union (and one got a small loaf in addition). [58] Three of these suicides, however, took place before the policy change, the fourth in 1895. No male suicide was said to have been receiving out-relief, which may in itself speak volumes, given the number who were too ill to support themselves. But, then, only eight male suicides in this age group were living alone or in lodgings, the ones most likely to be granted relief. Most of the rest were living with their wives and children or with other kin.

As for the experience of suicide, both sexes were heavily affected by the physical and mental changes of this life stage. Over half of all suicides, male and female, were ascribed to some form of illness or senility. Illness was no respecter of class. Almost one-third of the male illness cases were of the skilled nonmanual class and above: small retailers and dealers, clerks, master mariners, a river pilot, and a house proprietor.[59] The timing was different for the two sexes, however. Two-thirds of the female illness cases came from the early and mid Victorian decades, whereas over three-quarters of the male illness cases took place in the last three decades of the century. Illness, moreover, had a much more marked effect on the working lives of male suicides. In over one-third of the male illness cases, it was difficult to separate the impact of illness from the effect of the unemployment or business trouble that illness had prompted. And in a third of the remaining illness cases, illness had occasioned retirement, which, in a pre-pension society, could have depressing economic consequences.[60] It would be unwise, then, to draw too sharp a distinction between illness and economic difficulties in the case of male suicide, so large was the overlap between these categories.

Few old men had the kind of economic security we take for granted today. For that reason, almost two-thirds of those aged 65 and over remained part of the workforce, vulnerable to irregular employment, periodic discharge, and the final indignity of the workhouse. This was particularly true, it seems, of the later Victorian years. The vast majority of suicides in which the old man was unemployed (and frequently sick) at time of death occurred between 1884 and 1894. At least two-fifths of the male suicides in late old age were affected by economic troubles, whether directly or by reason of sickness, almost all in the later Victorian years, from 1870 on. Nor was it only manual workers who were so affected. Economic difficulty was the primary factor in the suicide of a pottery-ware agent, a water clerk (or superintending stevedore), a lighter owner, and a retired sea pilot turned pork butcher.[61] As noted previously, small businessmen, dealers, and agents were terribly vulnerable to downturns in trading activity. A sudden drop in income for those who thought they had achieved financial security could well, moreover, be more suicidogenic than chronic poverty.

Yet again, however, we must not rest content with endorsing the traditional image of male suicide as essentially a response to forces that undermined masculine pride, performance, and independence. What about personal or domestic pressures? Strictly speaking, disturbed personal relations were unimportant in the suicide of old men. Only 6 percent of suicides were directly ascribed to this influence. But is this really plausible? The life structure of old men typically relied upon a few significant relationships, the death or disruption of which could be traumatic. They were in a life stage when the frequency of death or serious illness among friends or loved ones was bound to increase. Over one-third of male suicides, moreover, were widowers, most of them living with kin. It is unsurprising to find, therefore, that a sizable number of the suicides I have categorized as motivated by drink, illness, or economics also involved domestic disruption. Another ten suicides included the recent death of a wife, daughter, brother, or grandchild; separation from a wife and the breakup of the home; or a request by kin for the suicide to quit the home.[62] If we add the men who were resident in a workhouse or almshouse,[63] who by definition were beyond the pale of domestic life, then sixteen suicides (or 32 percent of all male suicides in late old age) contained a stratum of personal disturbance in their creation.

By the same token, female suicides in late old age were not alone affected by loss or conflict in personal relationships upon which they were emotionally dependent. Indeed, a disturbed personal relationship was rarely the cause of suicide in old women. Only one woman was manifestly disturbed by family conflict, although another five suicides (making a total of six, or one-fifth of all female suicides) were influenced, if only in part, by the death of kin or by the voluntary or enforced departure from the home of a child.[64] The evidence suggests, therefore, that old women, almost two-thirds of whom were widows by this stage of the life cycle, generally established a modus vivendi of some stability and were not commonly disturbed by loss or conflict in personal relations. A more important influence, affecting over half this group of suicides, was illness or senescence. Widows were particularly vulnerable, it seems, since ten of the seventeen widows who committed suicide were motivated by illness and despondency. But aside from illness, a significant proportion—just over one-quarter—of old women, both married and widowed, were troubled by economic adversity. Married women were disturbed by the husband's unemployment or his inability to transact business; widows were disturbed by shortage of work or by the pressures of managing property.

How, finally, should we explain the fact that old men became more suicidal (while old women became less suicidal) in the later Victorian years?[65] Ill health could be a part of the explanation. Old men had a shorter life expectancy than old women, and although mortality is not the same as morbidity, or day-to-day health, this suggests that old men were the less resilient gender. In addition, ill-health or failing strength was bound to have more impact upon the working lives of men. In a workforce dominated by the transport, building, oil-milling, and fishing trades, endurance and strength were at a premium, and the older worker was at a disadvantage. Most old men experienced a drop in income; many slid down the occupational ladder to lower-paid, casual employment, or chanced the economic vagaries of small-scale retailing. Significantly, of the fifty men aged 65 and over who killed themselves, 21 were not working, 4 were in the workhouse or an almshouse, 1 was about to stop work and enter an almshouse, and 1 marine-stores dealer's wife had to run the business that he was too ill to manage. Around two-thirds of these men committed suicide in the 1880's and 1890's. If to these 27 suicides we add the handful who had worked only irregularly, then 32 of the male suicides, or 64 percent of the total, were experiencing difficult or distressing employment conditions, in a society where few qualified for a retirement pension. The experience of old age was harder for men in other ways, too. They tended to get out-door relief less readily than old women, and they thus more often suffered the prospect or reality of the workhouse. Tellingly, at least one of the male suicides thought he had to go to the Union, and another two men killed themselves in the workhouse. And, as I emphasized in the conclusion to chapter 9, men were less able to look after themselves in old age and widowhood. They typically reached the final season in life with a limited range of domestic and interpersonal skills, they were generally unused to managing their own households, and they were less useful as housekeepers or child-minders for married children. It was for these reasons, in all likelihood, that an increasing number of men of "threescore years and ten" could think of nothing better to do after giving up work than to die.

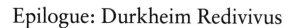

Epilogue: Durkheim Redivivus

The term "motives" must be retained for these events:
mental illness, loss of money, mourning, or love pangs,
since they are so many different particular forms hiding
the same condition. The unique cause of suicide,
however, is the condition itself, that is, a feeling of a
solitude which is definitive and without remedy.
                              Maurice Halbwachs,
                    The Causes of Suicide (1930)

The preceding chapters have suggested that urban suicide in the age
of Victoria was associated, to some degree at least, with the main characteristics of the various stages of the life cycle. In the first stage, young
adults, predominantly single and still housed by parents, were subject to
the disruptions in social (and economic) relations caused by charges of
embezzlement or by out-of-wedlock pregnancy, to disruptions in personal
relations caused by family or generational dispute, and to the work discipline imposed upon novice apprentices, assistants, and domestic servants.
Among young men, family disagreements and physical and mental illness
were more likely to lead to suicide than were economic difficulties; among
young women, likewise, the most well-trodden paths to suicide were illness
and personal troubles (bereavement, romantic disappointment, and family
quarrels). By contrast, the role of the seduced and abandoned woman,
prominent in the literary portrayal of suicide, was negligible to nonexis-
tent. Domestic service, the lonely, arduous, and ill-paid occupation of most

of the employed suicides, was a more important common denominator among young women.

In the prime of life, illness was again a prominent factor, particularly for single men in lodgings and for married women who had just given birth. Prominent, too, were economic troubles for men (notably skilled nonmanual workers such as clerks, shopkeepers, innkeepers, and dealers), particularly when cases in which drink and illness had economic consequences are added; and personal troubles for women, particularly when cases in which drink led to marital strife are included. Over two-fifths of male suicides in the prime of life were, however, single, separated, or widowed (suggesting that they were affected by lack of married life), and, in fact, almost one-fifth were troubled, either wholly or in part, by a disruption of personal attachments (especially the death of, or separation from, their wives). Those women induced to commit suicide by disturbed personal relations were, moreover, not all dependent, self-effacing, and family-centered, as the gendered theory of suicide would have it. Many were victims of violent, dysfunctional relationships; others experienced the economic adversities of "deserting" or deserted wives, and of widows.

Early old age was a truly vulnerable phase of the life cycle for men, since working life could become especially troublesome. Over two-thirds of male suicides in this life-cycle stage (if we add the drink and illness cases that had decided economic overtones) were induced by the financial and psychological difficulties of employment. The occupations that older workmen tended to shift into—shoemaking, tailoring, small-scale retailing, building, and dealing—were particularly prominent in this regard. Two-fifths of the economic suicides were, moreover, single, separated, or widowed, many of them living alone or in lodgings, bereft of spousal and sometimes even family support. Women suicides in early old age, by contrast, were affected more by physical and mental illness and by disturbed personal relations, notably the death of, or conflict with, their husbands. Once again, however, the fact that over half the male suicides were not attributable to economic difficulty gave pause for thought. Over one-third of all male suicides in early old age were without spousal support; and almost one-quarter were affected, either wholly or in part, by disrupted interpersonal relations, whether through bereavement or marital conflict. In explaining why men in early old age, and particularly widowers, had a much higher suicide rate than women, therefore, I have felt the need to underline not only economic and achievement-related factors, but also personal and relational ones. Old age for men was both economically hazardous and, if widowhood descended, socially and domestically unstable. Many of the same patterns were true of late old age, the final life-cycle stage.

Once more, two-fifths of male suicides were induced by economic difficulties, widely defined. Indeed, almost two-thirds were experiencing difficult employment conditions, in a pre-pension era, at the time of death. Once more, small-scale retailers, shoemakers, and tailors were prominent, as were those in such semi-skilled jobs as cowkeeper, waterman, and sloopman, where many old workers fetched up. Inevitably, the physical and mental degeneration of this life stage was at the back of many male suicides, although in a high proportion of illness cases, it was difficult to untangle the strands of ill-health and economic misfortune. Women suicides in old age were likewise affected by illness and senility, but were much less troubled than in the previous life stage by disturbed personal relations. Instead, for both married and widowed women, economic adversity bulked larger. And once again, finally, old men were affected by domestic or personal torments as well as by economic ones. Over half of all male suicides in late old age were single, separated, or widowed, many of whom seemed to lack the domestic and interpersonal skills for daily survival.

If to study suicide across the life cycle is to reveal the subjective impact of urban and industrial life, and I think it is, then our evidence points up the need to adjust the ideology that explained (and continues to explain) male suicide by his more arduous role in the struggle for existence and female suicide by her more passive dependence on personal relationships. The strains of working life, compounded by ill health and work accidents, were clearly evident in a large number of male suicides, especially among older workmen. This was particularly evident in the later Victorian years, when, to judge from the incidence and experience of suicide, labor-market insecurity increased. So, too, the strains of personal and domestic life were manifest in a large number of female suicides, especially among the single, separated, and widowed, and in every life-cycle stage bar the final one. It would be unwise to deny that women do participate in "collective life" in a different way than men—do inhabit different social worlds—and that this circumstance explains some of the difference in suicidal behavior between men and women. But such an accounting is far from complete. The barriers between public and private life were more permeable, the links between work and home more fluid, than the ideology presumes. Thus, the loss of loved ones by death or separation, family quarrels, and romantic disappointment (inflamed in many cases by intemperance) affected men as well as women. The hardships of working life and economic survival, especially for young domestics and older widows, affected women as well as men. And physical and mental illness took a high toll on both sexes. It would be in line with the inquest evidence to conclude, therefore, that the fit between the public (male) and private (female), or the social and personal, definitions of gendered experience was nowhere near as tight as the Victorians imagined, and as modern-day suicidologists contend.

I

The best part of this study has gone into erecting a life-cycle framework and attaching the hundreds of individual suicides to it. It is time to throw caution to the wind, to reverse the process, to take away the scaffolding, and to see what other ligaments hold the entire construction together. Forced metaphor aside, it is time to ask: how convincing is the leitmotif of the texts that launched the modern study of suicide—that each society has a collective suicide rate that varies according to the degree to which individuals are integrated into that society? To answer this fundamental question, we must return to Durkheim, or, rather (my own preference), to his pupil and authenticator Maurice Halbwachs, whose *Les Causes du suicide* (1930) is an extensive reexamination of Durkheim's *Suicide* (1897).

Halbwachs's book is a painstakingly detailed and ponderously written study, but it reaches a number of important conclusions that are germane to present purposes. First, Halbwachs believed that suicides had to be studied within comprehensive social milieux, within regions defined by their ways of life. A way of life, for Halbwachs, was the entire set of customs, beliefs, and behavior that arose from the occupations and mode of residence of the population. The advantage of "envisioning the suicides in a region defined in this way, and recalling the total milieu where they appeared," declares Halbwachs, is that it "assures us of not allowing any circumstances to escape which could explain them."[1] There is a fundamental difference, he adds, between urban and rural ways of life, particularly in the frequency and density of social interactions, and ipso facto in the occasions for, and rate of, self-destruction. There is, in short, a direct relationship between suicide rate and degree of urbanization. Urban communities have high suicide rates because they encourage the detachment of individuals from stable relationships with others.

Second, Halbwachs insists that individual motives for suicide are indispensable explanatory categories; and that valid explanations of suicide have to be sought in a more experiential perspective, have to account for the individual interpretation of the situation. He argues that the causes of suicide are to be discovered, not only in the weakening of traditional customs, beliefs, and social ties (which Durkheim emphasized), but equally in the individual and unpredictable situations of suffering, conflict, disappointment, and pain that the increasing complexity of social life creates. Durkheim was wrong to neglect these individual reasons for suicide, Halbwachs says. They are as much a result of the social structure, as much social facts, as the collective weakening of the social ties binding people together. Individual motives, he insists, are not random occurrences; they are linked to social causes. "This may not be perceived," he writes on the final page of the book, "if the major currents of collective life are arbitrarily separated from these particular accidents as if there were no connection whatever between them":

However, family sentiments, religious practices, and economic activity are not entities. They become embodied in the beliefs and customs which connect and bind individual lives to one another. Replaced in the social milieu, circumstances are no more than an aspect of general evolution. We therefore would really be going further than Durkheim along the route he committed himself to since we would be explaining by social causes not only the major forces that are deterrents to suicide but also the particular events which are not its pretexts but its motives.[2]

Third, in line with his decision to introduce consideration of individual motives, Halbwachs attributes suicide to the social isolation of the individual. Solitude, or what an individual feels when he ceases to be integrated into a group, leads to suicide. He argues, moreover, that not only "physical sufferings, pangs of love, jealousy, money worries, shame, fear of dishonor, fear of punishment, or sorrow caused by bereavement," but also "the other category of motives one distinguishes, namely, morbid mental factors" are "obstacles to the integration of the individual in society." Just as "an abandoned, unmarried mother," "the merchant who is ruined," "the family head whose means are abruptly reduced," those who "have lost a being who was dear to them," "those suicides of passion which follow the separation or threat of being separated from the loved object," and the patient who has given up hope that the pain will subside are "declassed," are "lost to society," are "expelled from social milieux" and feel themselves alone, so, too, "the frenzied and the depressed," the psychopathic, kill themselves because "they are on the periphery of society and can no longer find a point of support anywhere but within themselves."[3] It is precisely those mental disorders causing a failure of adaptation between the individual and his or her milieu that result in suicide. "If depressed," Halbwachs observes, the mentally ill person "isolates himself, burrows as if into a hiding-place, and turns in upon himself."[4] In all cases, the feeling of a relentless and irremediable solitude is the "unique cause of suicide." Halbwachs would have no truck, therefore, with the psychiatric thesis that psychopathic suicides, and suicides committed under the influence of drunkenness, constituted a separate category "different from all others in escaping social influences."[5] There is no evidence, Halbwachs contends, that even when the psychopath or the habitual drinker "is dejected and in a somber mood . . . the family and religion no longer mean anything to him or he is totally incapable of relating to life, for concern for others is not completely dead in him. . . . Why should the thought of their next of kin and of ties connecting them to one another not persist, like a flickering light, to the moment when consciousness is close to giving way?"[6]

It is these sociological insights that will now be applied to the suicide data examined in this book. To be sure, Halbwachs had a different inquiry in mind from the one I am pursuing here. He advocates comparing suicide rates with such measurable features as the density and type of social groupings, or the predominance of an urban or rural way of life. Instead, I have sought evidence in the Hull coroners' case papers of that "unique cause of suicide . . . a feeling of a solitude which is definitive and without remedy." As such, the exercise concerns the individual experience of suicide, not its statistical ramifications.

II

It has become a commonplace of historical work on suicide to discount the role of loneliness and isolation in the etiology of suicide. Olive Anderson observes that the inquest papers "so rarely show social isolation as a possible predisposing factor to suicide." Rather, "life at close quarters with a variety of relations and step-relations, landlords and lodgers, had been the usual experience of these people."[7] Barrie Ratcliffe, speaking of Paris in the first half of the nineteenth century, agrees that "suicides had not been alone and that even newcomers to the city were quickly integrated into networks formed by extended family, other immigrants from their place of origin, workplace, and neighbourhoods."[8] The Hull inquest papers confirm such statements, in the sense that most suicides were indeed living cheek by jowl with spouses, kin, lodgers, or landlords. There were cases, however, in which no relatives appeared at the inquest, or in which the relatives who did appear had had little or no contact with the deceased for many a long year.[9] And it was not uncommon for those testifying at inquests (notably landlords) to have had only a contractual relationship with the deceased. The police sergeant who testified at the inquest on William Maltby, a 53-year-old cordwainer (shoemaker), who hanged himself in July 1868 in his shop, where he had lived alone, stated: "He appears to have no friends or relatives in Hull. No one has claimed his body." The licensed victualler who ran the tavern opposite Maltby's shop deposed: "I know of no one with whom he kept company of late. He told me that he went away from his house 15 or 20 years ago without any reason, & did not return."[10] More to the point, as Peter Sainsbury has emphasized, "social isolation is a wider concept than living alone": it has to include the sense of social rejection of the unemployed and the pauper; the loss of relatedness to the community of the criminal, the bereaved, and the sick; the solitude of old age; and the cultural isolation of the immigrant.[11] It is to these categories of suicide that I now turn to illustrate that the concept of social isolation has the explanatory strength to encompass such diverse phenomena.

Unemployment was a life crisis that could weaken an individual's social ties, especially if they were already tenuous. Only a neighbor gave evidence at the inquest on George Crosskill, a 61-year-old bricklayer, in June 1879. She testified that Crosskill had been at home alone, unable to work for some time, afraid he should come to want.[12] William Lawsley, a driller, aged 55, hanged himself in March 1899 in the lodging house he occupied after giving up his home. A laborer who had gone to see Lawsley said he was living there by himself. "He was destitute, had been out of work a long time & looked as if he had been drinking hard."[13] Mary Barnes, aged 39, widow of an iron-shipyard laborer, who had to work where she could, fell from a third-floor window in November 1892. A fellow widow stated: "Deceased had nowhere to go & I took her in a month ago. She was very poor. She has had no work except two days a fortnight ago. She had no parish relief."[14] Unemployment and business failure, however, were not merely economic catastrophes. They took away a man's ability to fulfill the traditional breadwinner's role and separated him from the workplace community. Gertrude Obee, the daughter of Thomas Obee, aged 45, late a managing clerk for Wilson & Sons, a wine and spirit merchant, who shot himself in February 1891, said that her father had been unemployed for five months. She added that he had seemed to miss his occupation with Wilson's. Obee himself wrote to his wife: "I have done my best as a husband and father, and am not able to bear the strain any longer."[15] Thomas

Iveson, aged 42, had been depressed since the failure of his pork shop. He had taken to boot closing again, and his wife went out to cook at different houses. On the day he cut his throat, he had complained of being poor, that his wife should have to work, and he should have nothing to do. To his wife he wrote: "I will be a burden on you and my friends no longer."[16]

Illness could also lead to separation from the workplace community. William Pettit, an engineering draftsman, aged 46, shot himself in October 1897. His wife said that illness had kept him from work and he had got depressed in consequence. His suicide note stated that he had lost all hopes of ever being able to resume work.[17] Edward Carter, a 63-year-old sloopman of no fixed abode, separated from his wife, was found drowned in January 1864. Unable to work because of illness, he had been in the workhouse several times, and on the day he drowned, he had been trying to get into a lighter to spend the night.[18]

Economic reversals might also involve loss of social standing, or what Halbwachs defines as expulsion from a familiar social milieu. John Gibson, a lighter owner, aged 67, poisoned himself in March 1886. He and his wife had been living with their daughter for the past five months. His suicide note said it all: "Last three years' trade bad and losses heavy. It is a fearful end, after 50 years struggling to maintain a respectable position."[19] Mary Wray, aged 33, died from an irritant poison in April 1897. Her husband, a mast and block maker, said that he had not been working lately, and that his wife had been depressed. Wray's mother added that she had not seemed to want to speak to anyone she knew, and that she had very much felt the fact that her husband had come down in the world, having once kept a beer house.[20] The sharpest loss of social status was surely occasioned by resort to the workhouse. The sister-in-law of William Harford, a licensed porter, aged 67, who hanged himself in August 1891, stated that he had lived alone for eight years, had done everything for himself, and had neglected his health since his wife's death. She added: "he has been unwell, I think with old age, for some months & unable to work; this weighed on him badly: he said he had got back with his rent & must go to the Union."[21] John Sykes, a 58-year-old laborer in Blundell's Mills, a paint and color works, strangled himself in August 1893. He had lived alone, had kept neither the house nor himself clean, and had been off work ill for three weeks. His landlord had given him notice to quit. He told a neighbor that he could not bear to go into the workhouse.[22] William Teal, aged 70, who also worked at Blundell's, hanged himself in May 1891; he had been despondent because of ill health, and because he was to have given up working and gone to live in the almshouse.[23] To the reproach of having to enter "the House," one might add the isolation of living there. William Sissons, aged 81, a former keelmaster (barge captain), strangled himself in the workhouse in July 1869. He was in the bedridden ward and scarcely spoke unless spoken to. He told the pauper who cleaned his room: "I wish I was dead, that's all I want."[24]

Another category of suicide in which a diminished relatedness to the community may have prevailed involved social disgrace, whether by reason of embezzlement, arrest, infidelity, or bastardy. In all these cases, infringement of a social taboo was at stake, plus the fear or fact of social ostracism. Robert Collison, a coal merchant, aged 47, was found drowned in October 1887, having defrauded the building society of which he was secretary. The suicide letter to his wife blamed his embezzling upon "trying to keep up appearances." "I hope that amongst our numerous friends," he added, "some will come forward to give a helping hand to you & the girls, but am afraid that my conduct will be a blot upon you."[25] A number of suicides took place in the police or prison cells, or in response to a legal summons. A marine-stores dealer, aged 45, a widower with six children, hanged himself in a station-house cell in May 1842. He had been taken there charged with having received stolen goods.[26] William Grainger, a police sergeant, aged 50, hanged himself in September 1894, greatly disturbed at having to appear before the justices on an assault summons.[27]

Crimes that escaped prosecution could still have an impact. Sarah Hope, a 23-year-old domestic servant, was found drowned in May 1892. Her employer said he would not press charges even though she had stolen £7 from him and two policemen had been called to search her boxes. It was clear, if unstated, however, that she would have to find another situation.[28] Infidelity and bastardy could generate their own form of social disgrace. Mary Renton, aged 25, the wife of a fisherman who was at sea, was found drowned in March 1894. The letter to her husband declared: "I have deceived you ever since Friday night and I cannot bear to think of it again . . . tell Mother and brothers that I cannot disgrace them any longer."[29] Mary Kemp, a 23-year-old paper-mill hand, was found drowned in March 1891. Kemp's mother said she had been in a distracted state of mind for a few months owing to her pregnancy. A fellow worker who knew Kemp well nonetheless knew nothing of her condition. A postmortem revealed that the deceased had been in labor when she died.[30] And, lastly, Martha Stringer, a 30-year-old unmarried dressmaker, with a five-month-old child, poisoned herself in September 1868. The father of the child, a marine fireman, would have married Stringer, but being unemployed was unable to keep her. She had stated to more than one witness that since the child had been born, her brother had slighted her, and that she would kill herself on account of his behavior.[31]

A third category of suicide involved the weakening or severance of family, romantic, and neighborhood ties. This could occur in a number of ways. There were young adults who were unhappy with their home lives. William Sharp, a druggist's assistant, aged 21, took prussic acid (cyanide) in March 1870. He told the chemist he worked for: "I do not know what will become of us at home, my father is continually coming home drunk; my mother has not had a penny from him for some time, & I am really tired of my life."[32] There were singles who experienced the ruptured bond of a broken engagement. Amy Cullen's fiancé wrote to ask to be absolved from his promise of marriage. Before poisoning herself, Cullen replied: "I cannot live without you. After the one glimpse of Heaven that you have shown me, I dare not face life with the prospect of never seeing you again."[33] There were husbands who felt betrayed by their wives. Tom Stephenson, a joiner, aged 32, killed himself in April 1891, affected by his wife's "goings on" and by her seeking a magistrate's order to claim the children. To his mother he wrote: "Done by a deceitful wife." At his funeral, a large crowd of women mobbed his widow as she passed to the mourning coach, and the police had to intervene.[34] And there were wives who suffered from what can only be termed a sense of "moral isolation." Elizabeth Swift, aged 25, was the wife of a merchant seaman who had gone to sea two weeks before she hanged herself. She was from Cornwall, and she had no child and no relatives in town. According to a neighbor, she was reserved, did not speak much, and had been quieter than usual when her husband was away. The neighbor had helped Swift write a letter to her husband, which closed by saying: "Goodbye & God bless you & if we do not meet again on earth I hope we shall meet in heaven."[35] Separation and widowhood, by definition, could result in feelings of solitude. George Coltam, a 29-year-old wagonette driver, drowned himself in July 1891. He had been low since separating from his wife, and he told his father that he could not live without her. To compound his emotional state, his child had died three months before.[36] Charles Jennison, a 36-year-old river pilot, poisoned himself in June 1867. He told the landlady where he lodged that he could not live without his wife, who had died a few weeks before. A suicide note asked that he be put into the same grave with her.[37] Finally, a number of female suicides were associated with quarrels with neighboring women. Sarah Bennett, the 28-year-old wife of an iron molder, in poor circumstances, drowned herself after her husband had scolded her for arguing with the neighbors. The latter had accused the deceased of keeping a bad house.[38]

The next category of suicide involves the isolating effect of physical and mental illness, including old age, and of alcoholism. The physically sick, often suffering from unbearable pain, often bedridden, often despairing that they would ever recover, might gradually retreat from the world. James Leake, aged 66, a bricklayer, who had not worked regularly for five or six years on account of rheumatism and bronchitis, placed himself in front of a train in August 1896. A suicide note read: "I cannot bear my misery and pain any longer. I can't sleep night nor day my head is all on fire."[39] John Dixon, a 62-year-old grocer, suffering from cirrhosis of the liver and kidney and from influenza, shot himself in May 1898. His widow stated: "He has not been out this year."[40] And Sarah Auckland, the 27-year-old wife of a lathrender, cut her throat in September 1863. She had been ill for seven months since her confinement and could not go out. She had said she thought she would not get better, according to her husband.[41]

The unrelenting pain of mental illness could lead to a similar attitude of isolation and hopelessness, of being permanently attached to a bed of nails. Elizabeth Hudson, aged 28, the wife of a timber merchant, hanged herself in March 1846. She had been depressed for four months, said her children's governess, "arising from religious feelings." The deceased had often been heard to say she could not be saved, and she had kept to her bed when thus despondent.[42] John James, a 50-year-old shoemaker, shot himself in August 1851. His suicide note read: "If I live, I must go to the asylum. It is better to fall into the hands of God than man. . . . I have felt insanity coming on me from the first. There will never be any more chance of sleeping in comfort again in this wicked world."[43]

If there were mentally ill suicides who felt like "despairing patients cut off at the onset from the rest of the world" (in Halbwachs's words), there were numerous alcoholic suicides who for various reasons felt themselves "out of joint in relation to the groups to which they belong."[44] A high number of such suicides were linked with financial, employment, and health problems, and particularly with the disruption of interpersonal relationships. Elizabeth Smith, aged 26, the wife of a storekeeper, hanged herself in February 1882. Her husband said that she had been "at times addicted to drink," and that "we were never on friendly terms." She had regularly pawned household items for drink. "I have had shops before," he continued; "I had to leave the second shop through her drinking & leaving it without attention." On the last morning, he said he would not live with her any longer.[45] Thomas Clayton, an oil miller, aged 56, cut his throat in August 1892. He had turned his alcoholic wife out of the house two weeks before, and he was about to break up his home.[46] James Story, a 67-year-old tailor, strangled himself in October 1893. According to his son, Story lived in lodgings, took a good deal of drink, "and had become estranged from his family."[47]

And, finally, the many illnesses of old age could narrow the old person's social circle and limit conversation with others. Thomas Colbridge, aged 76, a widowed and retired master mariner, hanged himself in his lodgings in December 1886. None of his family lived in town. He was subject to fits and had almost lost his speech.[48] Samuel Thompson, aged 67, a jobbing laborer, was infirm on his feet, rather deaf, and very short-sighted. He was killed by a railway carriage in October 1869. He had been depressed for six months. He could no longer read, which made him impatient, and he used to wander about without any object.[49] And Esther Gosschalk, a 72-year-old widow who lived with her son, poisoned herself in August 1898. She had been in great pain with gout and had not been out for nearly two years. Her daughter-in-law stated: "She used often to say she was tired of her life as she could do nothing. She had been a very active woman in her time."[50]

The final category of suicide is a rather miscellaneous one, but in each case, there is evidence of a loosening of social bonds. In a small number of suicides, there was specific mention of friendlessness. A 54-year-old grocer, in poor circumstances, who complained "that his friends would not look upon him & that he was deserted," hanged himself in November 1843. A month later, a single 29-year-old chimney sweep spoke of "not having a friend . . . of being then in Hell" before poisoning himself.[51] In a few instances, the suicide was an army pensioner, struggling to fit back into civilian society. Henry Welborn, aged 31, a butcher, had been in the army for eight years. Unemployed for ten months, he was in the habit of drinking until his pension money was exhausted. He told the policeman who found him with his throat cut: "I want to die like an English soldier."[52] And a few suicides were foreign nationals, a long way from home. Anna Isaksen, a 19-year-old Norwegian of no fixed abode, poisoned herself in a police cell in April 1899. She had left her job as a domestic servant with the Norwegian government agent, only to be arrested for stealing a dress from her lodging house.[53] Finally, in a number of cases a combination of social breaches prompted suicide. Robert Clark, a 62-year-old merchant's clerk, hanged himself in December 1879. His wife had died two years before; he had lost his situation and could not find another; one of his sons had committed suicide, and another was in the lunatic asylum; and he had

had to make over his furniture to a creditor. Little wonder his suicide note declared: "I cannot bear this any longer." [54]

The well is not yet dry. The concept of social isolation also helps explain the high incidence of suicide among particular occupational groups and particular civic statuses. If occupations with a low suicide rate tended to foster group solidarity and a companionable quality, those with a high suicide rate did not. Thus, it is claimed that innkeepers and publicans suffered the impersonal, transient world of the public bar. Domestic servants were socially detached, lonely, and of lowly status. It is perhaps telling that Catherine Jones, who had just left a situation as a domestic servant, when asked why she had taken vermin killer, could only reply: "I have no home." [55] Shopkeepers were occupationally mobile, looking for an independence and status denied jobs in the workshop or factory. Failure in business, which they typically ascribed to individual incapacity, dropped them back into their former class position. As for civic status, it is notable that those who either had not adopted the family role or had been parted from it—the unmarried, separated, and widowed—had the highest suicide rates. Evidently, the bonds of family life—whether marital responsibilities, the aid of networks of in-laws, or the presence of children—were deterrents to suicide. Halbwachs even argues that the higher the number of children, the larger the deterrent to suicide, a conclusion that applied to both sexes, but more strongly to women.[56] The concept of social isolation also corresponds, finally, with my ecological findings and explanation for the higher suicide rate of old men. The ecology of suicide suggested that the highest suicide rates were generated by the inner-city business and retail area of Hull, where a more transient, unmarried, lodging- and public-house population was to be found. The lower rates were a feature of communities, like the dockside urban districts, the shipbuilding area, and the fishing region, where the major labor process gave rise to a common sense of identity and greater occupational and social integration.[57] As for those old men, their suicide rate was partly a function of the fact that with few or no gender-based networks, and with slender neighborhood ties, they had much less social support than old women to relieve the impact of bereavement, unemployment, and the rest.[58]

III

The Victorians were firmly convinced that suicide was linked to urban and industrial centers, the core sites of modern civilization. The first sociologists drew on this widespread conviction to explain suicide's historical incidence. They theorized that suicide, industrialization, and urbanization were closely associated. High suicide rates were an index, said Durkheim, of the weakness of social bonds in the urban industrial setting. Modern historians have seriously qualified this long-standing belief, citing statistics showing that suicide was commoner in nonindustrial towns than in industrial centers. Yet as Olive Anderson, one of those historians, has herself said, "[T]here may well have been some distinctive suicide pattern in the industrial areas . . . even though that distinctiveness was not one of magnitude." [59] Quite so. As I have been at pains to show, suicide can be meaningfully related to the subjective experience of urban life in the different stages of the life course. Nonetheless, the classic Durkheimian approach, as modified by Halbwachs, may yet have some merit. Social isolation remains an essential explanatory concept for the interpretation of the incidence of suicide and the meaning of those men and women who willed and accomplished "this rash act."

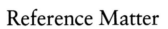

Reference Matter

NOTES

Abbreviations used in the notes include: *EMN* = *Eastern Morning News*; PP = Parliamentary Papers; CQB = Coroners' registers and case papers.

Introduction

1. In a note written before the suicide attempt, Chesterfield said: "I cannot face the misery I see before the men through the action of the Shipping Federation. They don't intend to perform their part of the agreement, but mean to crush our men to the very best" (*Hull Daily News*, May 23, 1893). The case is mentioned in Brown, *Waterfront Organisation*, p. 90. For a contemporary account, see Abraham, "Hull Strike," pp. 357–63.

2. Cobb, *Death in Paris*, pp. 101–2.

3. This information eventually became the basis of official suicide statistics in nineteenth-century England. The findings of coroners' juries were returned to the Home Office and the General Register Office, and from the later 1850's on, they appeared annually in the table of coroners' returns in the judicial statistics published in Parliamentary Papers, as well as in the mortality statistics published in the reports of the Registrar-General of Births, Deaths and Marriages. See O. Anderson, *Suicide*, pp. 427–28.

4. CQB/399/24 (Louisa Bowen).   5. *EMN*, Apr. 13 and 15, 1891.

6. CQB/399/9 (Tom Stephenson).   7. *EMN*, Apr. 21, 1891.

8. Baechler, *Suicides*, p. 3. Baechler also wrote: "It is probable that suicide is the most unremittingly studied human behavior" (ibid.).

9. Durkheim, *Suicide*.

10. Douglas, *Social Meanings of Suicide*. See also Atkinson, *Discovering Suicide*.

11. See, e.g., Gates, *Victorian Suicide*; Havard, *Detection of Secret Homicide*; Sprott, *English Debate on Suicide*.

12. MacDonald and Murphy, *Sleepless Souls*.

13. Thus, coroners' juries increasingly returned a verdict of non compos mentis (not in right mind), as distinct from one of felo de se (self-murder), which found the suicide guilty of "not having the fear of God before his eyes but being moved and seduced by the instigation of the Devil."

14. I am not competent to the task of evaluating the main texts in the psychology of suicide. Anyway, such an evaluation would not help the present study, since

the coroners' case papers, on which the study is based, do not permit a classification of suicides according to psychiatric categories.

15. Sharpe, "History from Below," p. 30. It should be emphasized that the coroners' case papers were augmented by newspaper reports of inquests (in almost every suicide case), by death certificates (for cases where basic data on age or occupation were missing), by city directories (for occupational information on jurymen and suicides), and by the Coroners' Inquisition Book, which contains a brief listing of every inquest, and a summary of cause of death.

16. Of the 158 cases, 101 came from mid Victorian London, 34 from mid Victorian East Sussex, and 23 from Edwardian London.

17. "Coroners' records in local record offices," declared F. G. Emmison, "are so rare that nothing need be said about them" (*Archives and Local History*, p. 31). This is the result of the Public Record Office Schedule, dated 1921, which allows the destruction of coroners' records that are more than fifteen years old. See O. Anderson, *Suicide*, p. 37 n. 77, and also Gibson and Rogers, *Coroners' Records*. The Hull inquests survived, it would seem, because they were delivered periodically by the coroner to the clerk of the peace, and were bound with the Quarter Sessions books.

18. Barbara Hanawalt has used coroners' inquests to reconstruct life in medieval peasant households: the material environment, household economy, patterns of child rearing, and life-cycle stages. See Hanawalt, *Ties That Bound*; id., "Seeking the Flesh and Blood," pp. 39–43.

19. Suicide was legally defined as "the intentional act of a party knowing the probable consequence of what he is about" (*Clift v. Schwabe*, Common Bench Reports, 1846).

20. The reference to "muffling blanket" appears in Cobb, *Sense of Place*, p. 135.

21. Olive Anderson has already made some suggestive points concerning suicide and the life cycle, but she has not systematically analyzed the inquest evidence in terms of the life cycle; see her "Did Suicide Increase with Industrialization," pp. 165, 172. For contemporary examples of suicide and the life cycle, see Levinson et al., *Seasons of a Man's Life*, and id., *Seasons of a Woman's Life*.

22. M. Anderson, "Emergence of the Modern Life Cycle," pp. 72–87.

23. O. Anderson, *Suicide*, p. 164.

Chapter 1

1. See O. Anderson, *Suicide*; MacDonald and Murphy, *Sleepless Souls*.

2. The history of *psychological* explanations of suicide is beyond my compass. Sociologists have, however, been involved in an ongoing dialogue with the advocates of psychological approaches to suicide.

3. Durkheim, *Suicide*. The following appraisal of Durkheim is based upon Aron, *Main Currents*, vol. 2; Giddens, *Durkheim*; Taylor, *Durkheim*; Lukes, *Emile Durkheim*; and Parkin, *Durkheim*. Most of the sociological theories discussed in this chapter were framed with particular reference to *male* suicides. For the inadequate

manner in which Durkheim, for example, treated female suicides, see Kushner, "Suicide, Gender, and the Fear of Modernity."

4. The "moral statisticians" include Guerry, Quetelet, and Morselli. For evaluations of their work on suicide, see Giddens, "The Suicide Problem," p. 4; id., *Durkheim*, p. 41; Douglas, *Social Meanings of Suicide*, p. 9 n. 10, and pp. 16–18. For another of Durkheim's progenitors, see Buckle, *History of Civilization*, 1: 28. Buckle's contribution is discussed in Porter, *Rise of Statistical Thinking*, p. 63.

5. Durkheim, *Suicide*, pp. 151, 215. Cf. the section on Durkheim in Bohannan, ed., *African Homicide and Suicide*, p. 25.

6. Ibid., p. 307.

7. In addition to *Suicide*, this account of Durkheim's classification of types of suicide (which are more strictly types of social structure producing high rates of suicide) is informed by Aron, *Main Currents*, 2: 32–34; Lukes, *Emile Durkheim*, pp. 205–9; Giddens, *Durkheim*, pp. 45–46; id., "Typology of Suicide," pp. 278–79; Taylor, *Durkheim*, pp. 13–16.

8. Durkheim, *Suicide*, bk. 2, ch. 4.

9. Ibid., bk. 2, ch. 5. See also Gay, *Bourgeois Experience*, pp. 56–57. For the nineteenth-century belief "that suicide was associated with urban life and industrial towns because both alike were centres of modern civilization, and suicide was stimulated by modern living," see O. Anderson, "Did Suicide Increase with Industrialization," p. 168. The obverse of anomic suicide was fatalistic suicide, of which Durkheim has little to say. The term referred to the self-destruction that resulted from *excessive* regulation or oppressive discipline, such as the suicide of a slave or of a prisoner.

10. Durkheim, *Suicide*, p. 299.

11. Aron, *Main Currents*, 2: 27. Cf. Lukes, *Emile Durkheim*, p. 194; Taylor, *Durkheim*, p. 10. As Dominick LaCapra states: "Suicide was of primary interest to Durkheim, not as an isolated tragedy in the lives of discrete individuals, but as an index of a more widespread state of pathology in society as a whole" (*Emile Durkheim*, p. 144). For Durkheim's hope that sociology, by establishing a "civil religion," would provide "the normative cement for modern secular society," see Tiryakian, "Emile Durkheim," p. 191.

12. Durkheim, *Suicide*, p. 149.

13. See LaCapra, *Emile Durkheim*, p. 152; Hendin, *Suicide in America*, p. 17.

14. Halbwachs, *Causes of Suicide.*

15. Halbwachs, *Causes of Suicide*, chs. 8 and 9, and pp. 309–30. See also Douglas, *Social Meanings of Suicide*, p. 127; Vromen, "Sociology of Maurice Halbwachs," p. 97. Durkheim's only direct reference in *Suicide* to the city is at p. 137 n. 19, where he acknowledges that large cities generally had more suicides than small ones or rural districts, but he ascribes this to the overall level of social integration: "[L]arge cities are formed and develop under the influence of the same causes which themselves determine the development of suicide more than the cities

do themselves. Thus these cities are naturally numerous in regions rich in suicides, but without having any monopoly in them."

16. See Giddens, "Suicide Problem," p. 6.

17. Halbwachs, *Causes of Suicide*, p. 290.

18. Ibid., p. 10. Cf. Travis, "Halbwachs and Durkheim," p. 227. For Halbwachs's readiness "to enter the domain of motivation," see Bottomore and Nisbet, "Structuralism," pp. 573–74.

19. Halbwachs, *Causes of Suicide*, p. 11.

20. Ibid., p. 275. See also p. 330. The Epilogue to the present book presents, inter alia, an extended examination of Halbwachs's "unique cause of suicide . . . a feeling of a solitude."

21. Ibid., p. 317. See also Giddens's foreword to Halbwachs, *Causes of Suicide*, p. xviii; Douglas, *Social Meanings of Suicide*, pp. 129–30; Vromen, "Sociology of Maurice Halbwachs," pp. 63–64.

22. The following account of the Chicago School's "urban thesis" draws upon T. Morris, *Criminal Area*, p. 1; Snodgrass, "Clifford R. Shaw and Henry D. McKay," pp. 9–11; Davidson, *Crime and Environment*, p. 72; R. S. Cavan, "Chicago School of Sociology," p. 412; Bulmer, *Chicago School*, p. 61.

23. Park et al., *City*, p. 57. Cf. Lane, *Violent Death in the City*, p. 4.

24. Zorbaugh, "Dweller in Furnished Rooms," pp. 85–87.

25. R. Cavan, *Suicide*.

26. Ibid., p. 92.

27. Ibid., p. 93. A similar ecological argument appears in Schmid, *Suicide in Seattle*.

28. See Moksony, "Ecological Analysis of Suicide," p. 121.

29. R. Cavan, *Suicide*, pt. 2, "Suicide and Personal Disorganization."

30. Ibid., p. 326.

31. Ibid., p. 176. Here Cavan was following in the footsteps of the Chicago sociologist W. I. Thomas, joint author, with F. Znaniecki, of *Polish Peasant in Europe and America* (1918–20), who made a memorable remark about the importance of the subjective meaning that individuals attach to their action: "If men define situations as real, they are real in their consequences." Quoted in Bennett, *Oral History and Delinquency*, p. 131.

32. See Shaw, *Jack-Roller*, introduction by Howard Becker, pp. vi–vii; Elder, "Perspectives on the Life Course," p. 24.

33. R. Cavan, *Suicide*, p. 313. Cf. S. J. Smith, *Crime, Space and Society*, p. 15. For the view that Cavan ultimately failed "to connect her [statistical] data with personal motivations," see Kushner, *Self-Destruction*, pp. 66–67. Note, however, that Karl Meninger, *Man Against Himself*, p. 15, claimed that Cavan wrote "one of the earliest psychological studies of the modern era."

34. See Schmid, "Suicide in Minneapolis," pp. 30–31; Sainsbury, *Suicide in London*, passim; Walsh and McCarthy, "Suicide in Dublin's Elderly," p. 233; id.,

"Suicide in Dublin," p. 1395. Howard Kushner correctly points out that since the 1920's, "sociologists of suicide have refined their statistical skills in an attempt to determine *which* urban factors play the greatest role in causing suicide" (*Self-Destruction*, p. 65; emphasis in original). See also Baldwin, "British Areal Studies of Crime," p. 221.

35. The "urban thesis" also influenced the French historian Louis Chevalier, who embraced the "uprooting hypothesis" that large numbers of the poor, torn from their rural roots, migrated to nineteenth-century Paris, victims of "urban pathology" in the form of crime, madness, and suicide (*Labouring Classes and Dangerous Classes*, pp. 285–92). For commentary on Chevalier's "uprooting hypothesis," see Merriman, *Margins of City Life*, pp. 15–16; Ratcliffe, "Suicides in the City," pp. 1–70.

36. Douglas, *Social Meanings of Suicide*.

37. See Giddens, *Durkheim*, p. 115; Taylor, *Durkheim*, p. 44.

38. James Joyce, *Ulysses*, p. 98; Douglas, *Social Meanings of Suicide*, chs. 12–19, passim. Cf. Giddens, "Theory of Suicide," pp. 297–301; Atkinson, *Discovering Suicide*, pp. 50–51. Critics of the official suicide statistics also emphasize the gender bias in the data. Not only are female suicides more commonly concealed, it is argued, but *attempted* suicide, for which the rate is considerably higher for females than males (in part because women choose less lethal methods), eludes the statistical net entirely. See Ratcliffe, "Suicides in the City," p. 33.

39. See Douglas, *Social Meanings of Suicide*, p. 265; id., "Sociological Analysis of Social Meanings of Suicide," p. 261. Cf. Atkinson, *Discovering Suicide*, pp. 171–72; id., "Some Cultural Aspects of Suicide," pp. 157–58; Sainsbury, *Suicide in London*, p. 18; Taylor, *Durkheim*, pp. 60, 107. The same objection would apply to the city-country dichotomy that suicide data supposedly reveal (Ratcliffe, "Suicides in the City," p. 10). Douglas argues, in *Social Meanings of Suicide*, pp. 42–76, that Durkheim himself often fell back on "commonsense" knowledge or "shared social meanings" to interpret the associations between suicide and other "social facts." For example, to explain the different relationship between marriage and suicide for men and women, Durkheim appealed to the presumed difference between the sexes in their level of involvement in social life: "As she [woman] lives outside of community existence more than man, she is less penetrated by it; society is less necessary to her because she is less impregnated with sociability. . . . With a few devotional practices and some animals to care for, the old unmarried woman's life is full" (Durkheim, *Suicide*, p. 215; and cf. pp. 299, 385).

40. Douglas urged sociologists to work up from observable phenomena to abstractions about meanings, and to locate common "patterns of meaning" that actors construct for their suicidal actions. Douglas suggested the following meanings: revenge, escape, self-punishment, search for help, repentance, and expiation of guilt. See *Social Meanings*, ch. 17.

41. See Kushner, *Self-Destruction*, pp. 69, 72; Giddens, "Theory of Suicide,"

p. 304; Bauman, *Hermeneutics and Social Science*, p. 12. For a summary of the main characteristics of a sociology of social action, see Dawe, "Theories of Social Action," pp. 367–68, 373.

42. Baechler, *Suicides*, p. 65. Cf. p. 22: "[S]uicide is at every moment an objective possibility for every person. This objective abstract possibility will have a higher probability of being actualised if unsuccessful experiences accumulate or are particularly serious."

43. Ibid., p. 61.

44. For a general critique of the assumed link between urban industrialism and social pathology, see O. Anderson, "Did Suicide Increase with Industrialization," p. 166; Monkkonen, "Disorderly People?" p. 551. Michael Zell claims that historians, attracted to the Durkheimian model, "have treated suicide as a product of the rise of 'individualism,' of social disintegration and of the alleged rootlessness of modern societies" ("Suicide in Pre-Industrial England," p. 304). But Zell cites no specific historian to substantiate this claim. I would argue that historians have been more critical of the theory of social disorganization than Zell's comment implies.

45. Gatrell, "Decline of Theft and Violence," pp. 284–301. Cf. Lane, "Crime and the Industrial Revolution," p. 297; id., *Violent Death*, pp. 6–8.

46. See Lees, "Patterns of Lower-Class Life," pp. 364–83; id., *Exiles of Erin*, p. 247; R. Roberts, *Classic Slum*, passim.

47. See M. Anderson, *Family Structure*, ch. 10; Hareven, "History of the Family as an Interdisciplinary Field," p. 222; id., *Family Time and Industrial Time*, pp. 2–3; id., "History of the Family and the Complexity of Social Change," pp. 113–15; Alter, *Family and the Female Life Course*, pp. 3–5.

48. Lane, *Violent Death*, pp. 14–17, 120–39. Cf. id., *Roots of Violence*, pp. 13–16.

49. O. Anderson, "Did Suicide Increase with Industrialization," p. 149. See also pp. 153–60.

50. Ratcliffe, "Suicides in the City," p. 65.

51. O. Anderson, *Suicide*, chs. 3 and 4, passim.

52. MacDonald and Murphy, *Sleepless Souls*, pts. 1 and 2.

53. Ibid., p. 221.

54. Ibid., chs. 7–9, passim.

55. Ibid., p. 4.

56. For a defense of the official suicide figures, see Sainsbury, "Suicide: Opinions and Facts," pp. 579–82; Hindess, *Use of Official Statistics*, p. 12; Besnard, "Anti- ou ante-Durkheimisme?" pp. 313–41. Pescosolido and Mendelsohn argue that the social construction of suicide rates (particularly systematic misreporting) "has little discernible impact on the effects of variables commonly used to test sociological theories of suicide" ("Social Causation or Social Construction of Suicide?" p. 80).

57. Geertz, *Interpretation of Cultures*, p. 30; also quoted in Biersack, "Local Knowledge, Local History," p. 80.

58. Giddens, *Constitution of Society*, p. 2. For a discussion of the competing sociologies, one of social system, the other of social action, see Dawe, "Two Sociologies," pp. 207–18.

59. E. P. Thompson, *Poverty of Theory*, p. 345.

60. Ibid., p. 201, 298–99. For appreciations of Thompson's contribution to the agency-structure debate, see the essays by Sewell, Wood, Rosaldo, and Soper in Kaye and McClelland, eds., *E. P. Thompson*.

61. Bourdieu, *Outline of a Theory of Practice*, pp. 7–21, 80–81; id., "Marriage Strategies," p. 122. Cf. Henretta, "Social History as Lived and Written," pp. 1313–15; Medick and Sabean, eds., *Interest and Emotion*, pp. 2–3; Jenkins, *Pierre Bourdieu*, pp. 61, 97.

62. This paragraph is based on Giddens, *Profiles and Critiques*, pp. 8–14; id., *Constitution of Society*, pp. 1–26, 281–84; id., "Structuration Theory," pp. 204–15.

63. For Giddens's application of the theory of structuration to suicide, see "Typology of Suicide," pp. 287–95; id., "Theory of Suicide," pp. 306, 312–14. And cf. the "critical realist perspective" of Bhaskar, *Reclaiming Reality*, pp. 3–4.

64. Geertz, *Interpretation of Cultures*, p. 23.

65. Cobb, *Death in Paris*, p. 36.

66. See Lieberman, "Romanticism and the Culture of Suicide," p. 623.

67. N. Z. Davis, *Fiction in the Archives*; Ratcliffe, "Suicides in the City," p. 5. See also Corbin, "Cries and Whispers," p. 646.

68. Camus, *Myth of Sisyphus*, p. 4; Baechler, *Suicides*, p. 60. Cf. Alvarez, *Savage God*, p. 102; Styron, "Darkness Visible," p. 253.

69. Ginzburg, "Clues and Scientific Method," p. 27. Also quoted in Muir and Ruggiero, eds., *Microhistory*, p. xxvi n. 41.

70. Levinson, *Seasons of a Woman's Life*, pp. 5–14; *As You Like It* 2.7.139–66.

71. For the life-course approach, see Hareven and Vinovskis, eds., *Family and Population*, pp. 19–21; Hareven, *Transitions*, pp. 1–7; Hareven, *Family Time and Industrial Time*, pp. 6–8; Hareven and Adams, eds., *Aging and Life Course Transitions*, pp. xiii–xiv, 4–9. See also Levinson et al., *Seasons of a Man's Life*, pp. 40–46, for the concept of "the individual life structure," or "the basic pattern or design of a person's life at a given time," which "evolves through a standard sequence of periods."

72. My understanding of the urban life cycle or life course rests upon research done by historians of the family (see ch. 4), and upon evidence drawn from Kingston upon Hull (see ch. 5). The chapter on Hull uses an eclectic range of sources, including some material drawn from the decennial population censuses; it makes no pretense to be a study of the life cycle, based upon systematic use of the census, analogous to what family historians tend to construct.

73. See M. Anderson, "Emergence of the Modern Life Cycle," p. 85; Hareven, *Family Time and Industrial Time*, pp. 173–85. Cf. O. Anderson, *Suicide*, pp. 47, 54–55, 62–63, 65.

74. M. Anderson, "Emergence of the Modern Life Cycle," pp. 80, 87. Cf. Vincent, *Bread, Knowledge and Freedom*, p. 59. It could be argued, of course, that a suicide's position in the life course contributed only to the social construction of an unnatural death as suicide. Doubtless, there were contemporary cultural stereotypes of the trials and tribulations of each life stage, and these may well have informed the coroners' inquest. Again, however, I would argue that the interpretation of a suicidal death arose from the interaction between "folk" meanings and the "objective" circumstances associated with the suicide's life stage. I am aware, finally, that there could be a *generational* as distinct from a life-cycle effect. Each different life-cycle stage could accommodate a generation, sharing a structure of feeling (beliefs, customs, traditions), different from the structure of preceding and succeeding generations. I have not explored this issue, however. See Spitzer, "The Historical Problem of Generations," pp. 1353-85.

75. Alter, *Family and the Female Life Course*, p. 11; Maris, "Developmental Perspective of Suicide," p. 25. Cf. Levinson et al., *Seasons of a Man's Life*, pp. 46-49.

76. Abrams, *Historical Sociology*, p. 297.

77. Baechler, *Suicides*, p. xxi (emphasis in original).

Chapter 2

1. *Sir John Jervis on the Office and Duties of Coroners* (3d ed.), pp. 9-13; *Statutes of the Realm*, An Act to Consolidate the Law Relating to Coroners, 1887, 50 & 51 Vict., c. 71; O. Anderson, *Suicide*, pp. 15-16, 18, 347 n. 9. The Hull coroner's boundaries coincided, after 1836, with the boundaries of the municipal borough: see Public Record Office, H.O. 84/3, Atlas of Coroners' Districts, East Riding of Yorkshire.

2. See Havard, *Detection of Secret Homicide*, pp. 56 n. 3, 141-42; Jennings and Barraclough, "Legal and Administrative Influences," p. 410.

3. Coroners' Act, 1887 (cited n. 1 above).

4. O. Anderson, *Suicide*, p. 40.

5. See ch. 1; Douglas, *Social Meanings of Suicide*, passim; MacDonald and Murphy, *Sleepless Souls*, sect. 3.

6. For a similar conclusion concerning the reliability of suicide statistics, see Ratcliffe, "Suicides in the City," pp. 24-33.

7. *EMN*, Jan. 12, 1897, obituary.

8. Thorney had the assistance of the deputy coroners, J. A. Jackson, J. H. Gresham, and M. C. Lee.

9. *EMN*, Jan. 12, 1897.

10. These figures are drawn from "Return from the Clerks of the Peace and Town Clerks of the Number of Inquests held by each Coroner in the several counties, Cities, & boroughs in England & Wales, during the seven years ending 31 Dec. 1849 . . . ," PP, 1851 (148), 43: 416; *Hull News*, Jan. 3, 1857, p. 6; Jan. 5, 1867, p. 7; Jan. 8, 1870, p. 7; Annual Reports of the Medical Officer of Health, 1884-1900.

11. Quarter Sessions series, CQB/289–292 (1864). Examples of accidents at work were Richard Hagues, aged 41, a laborer in a paper mill, entangled in machinery, Feb. 25, 1864; Matthew Veal, aged 60, a timber merchant's laborer, crushed between a railway wagon and a timber truck. An example of an accident in the home was the case of Henry Smith, aged 2 years and six months, son of a cotton spinner, who drank boiling water, Nov. 21, 1864. The breakdown for the 105 inquests held in 1856 was: accident, 53.3%; illness and natural causes, 30.5%; found drowned, 10.5%; suicide, 5.7% (*Hull News*, Jan. 3, 1857, p. 6).

12. See n. 10 above. And cf. Forbes, "Coroners' Inquests," p. 392; Greenwald and Greenwald, "Coroners' Inquests," p. 58.

13. The monetary figures are drawn from "Coroners acting in England & Wales: Number of Inquests taken by each coroner, 1835–1839, charges made . . . ," PP, 1840 (209), 41: 324; "Return of Coroners' Inquests held in England & Wales, 1849–1859 . . . ," PP, 1860 (237), 57: 322; "Return of Number of Coroners for Counties, Boroughs, & other places in England & Wales, together with the salaries & emoluments paid to each," PP, 1883 (324), 55: 85; "Second Report of the Departmental Committee appointed to inquire into the Law relating to Coroners & Coroners' Inquests . . . ," PP, 1911, vol. 13, Minutes of Evidence, p. 667. See also William Brend, "Necessity for Amendment," p. 153; O. Anderson, *Suicide*, p. 23 n. 43.

14. For the stages in the process of defining a death as a suicide, I have been aided by Olive Anderson, *Suicide*, ch. 1, passim.

15. These statements are based upon scrutiny of all the suicide inquests in the Quarter Sessions series. The police took some of those who had poisoned themselves to the police station, where they subsequently died. It is possible that they were being arrested for the crime of attempted suicide. See CQB/379/15 (Thomas Dennison), May 1886; 401/8 (George Biffen), Nov. 1891. For a suicide who was taken to the hospital, see CQB/388/43 (Brown), Sept. 1888. Brown cut his throat; the house surgeon did a tracheotomy, but he died two days later. See also CQB/400/5 (Nelson), July 1891; 408/18 (Barnes), Aug. 1893.

16. The 73 suicides are in the dockets CQB/273 to CQB/312. Cf. Forbes, "Crowner's Quest," p. 37.

17. In large towns, medically uncertified deaths were never more than 2 percent of all deaths: O. Anderson, *Suicide*, p. 22 n. 39. For the role of the police, see, e.g., CQB/297 (Bulmer), Jan. 1866. Martha Ann Bulmer was found drowned in Lime Kiln Creek by a railway company policeman. He had seen her earlier and at first thought she was taking her services as a prostitute to the men who worked at the lime works. His deposition continued: "I thought she was going to destroy herself she was so quiet, that made me search for her, but it did not strike me until after she went away." The jury returned an open verdict. See also O. Anderson, *Suicide*, p. 377.

18. CQB/367/7 (Todd), Apr. 1883; 368/7 (Pitman), July 1883; CQB/298 (Woodhead), June 1866, and *EMN*, June 11, 1866, p .2.

19. CQB/394/9 (Clarke), Jan. 1890; 352/16 (Wilkinson), Aug. 1879.

20. CQB/281 (Goy), Mar. 1862; CQB/297 (Burton), Jan. 1866; 341/8 (Castle), Nov. 1876, and *EMN*, Nov. 22, 1876; 424/8 (Rosenston), July 1897, and *EMN*, July 28, 1897.

21. CQB/229/205 (Webb), Apr. 1849.

22. CQB/335/23 (Gilliard), June 1875; 412/11 (Bigby), Aug. 1894. See also 368/20 (Penny, a corn merchant's clerk), Aug. 1883; 427/46 (Kenning, a foreman fitter in a shipbuilding yard), May 1898.

23. CQB/224/132 (Graham), Dec. 1847. Dr. William Hendry had a chequered medical career. Two years later, he denied the possibility that Hull's drinking water had led to the cholera outbreak of 1849. In 1860, he was censured by the Board of Guardians for failing to visit a poor-law patient who was dying at home and for sending medicine unlabeled (Bickford and Bickford, *Medical Profession in Hull*, p. 57).

24. CQB/423/41 (Stokell), May 1897.

25. Havard, *Detection of Secret Homicide*, pp. 69–70; O. Anderson, *Suicide*, pp. 22–23.

26. CQB/325/16 (Atkinson), Feb. 1873; CQB/389/18 and *EMN*, Dec. 1, 1888.

27. CQB/430/5 and "Strange Conduct of the Family," *EMN*, Jan. 10, 1899.

28. See O. Anderson, *Suicide*, pp. 19–20.

29. See ch. 3.

30. CQB/330/19 (Cook) and *EMN*, June 12, 1874; 357/9 (Plant) and *EMN*, Nov. 18, 1880. See also CQB/301 (Stephenson) and *EMN*, Mar. 18, 1867; 399/24 (Bowen) and *EMN*, Apr. 13, 1891. "Among the working-classes it could not be concealed, of course, any more than a row could; everyone quickly knew about it," Richard Hoggart notes of suicide in the first half of the twentieth century (*Uses of Literacy*, p. 90). See also M. Anderson, "What Is New About the Modern Family?" pp. 83–84. And cf. Guillais, *Crimes of Passion*, pp. 28–29; Lis and Soly, "Neighbourhood Social Change," p. 15.

31. See Brend, *Inquiry into the Statistics of Deaths*, p. 71; Cawthon, "Thomas Wakley and the Medical Coronership," p. 194; O. Anderson, *Suicide*, pp. 23–25.

32. Cf. Forbes, "Crowner's Quest," p. 10; id., "Coroners' Inquests," p. 377; L. Rose, *Massacre of the Innocents*, p. 57. The use of pubs and taverns for inquests was abolished by the 1910 Licensing Act.

33. For example, CQB/230/374 (Ram), June 1849, inquest at police station; 222/106 (Wilson), June 1847, inquest at workhouse. Wilson, aged 70, a former bacon factor, was a workhouse resident. He cut his throat on Feb. 20, 1847, but did not die until June 15.

34. See CQB/198/87A (Erskin), May 1841; 203/158 (Jackson), June 1842; 219/108 (Whitty), Oct. 1846; 221/155 (Brandham), Sept. 1847; CQB/292 (Wood, landlord of the Whittington Inn), Nov. 1864. The inquest on an inmate of the

workhouse fever hospital was held in a tavern, too, perhaps to avoid infecting the coroner and his court: 221/173 (Walker), Sept. 1847.

35. See CQB/278/207 (Dossor), June 1861; CQB/191 (John), Aug. 1839; 205/136 (Noble), Mar. 1843.

36. See CQB/394/9 (Clarke), Jan. 1890; 431/33 (Jones), May 1899. Cf. O. Anderson, *Suicide*, p. 257. In 1889, Hull borough council sent a memorial to the Home Office criticizing the practice of holding inquests in public houses (on the grounds that it detracted from a proper evaluation of the cause of death, and increased the sufferings of bereaved relatives), and calling for an overhaul of the manner in which inquests were staged (Burney, "Decoding Death," pp. 162–63).

37. Cf. Sim and Ward, "Magistrate of the Poor?" pp. 246, 263; O. Anderson, *Suicide*, pp. 257–59.

38. Coroners' Act, 1887, 50 & 51 Vict., c. 71; Fenwick, "Accounting for Sudden Death," p. 197; Cawthon, "Medical Coronership," p. 195. In John Troutbeck's district, the summoning officer used the voters' list to select jurymen (Troutbeck, "Inquest Juries," p. 52).

39. CQB/185/17 (de Jonge), 1838; 382/5 (Good) and *EMN*, Jan. 26, 1887. City directories were used for the occupations of jurymen. For inquests with a similar jury composition, see 183/3 (Pinder), July 1837; 257/284 (Atkinson), Apr. 1856, and *Hull Advertiser*, Apr. 5, 1856. And cf. Greenwald and Greenwald, "Coroners' Inquests," p. 55.

40. Cawthon, "Medical Coronership," p. 195; O. Anderson, *Suicide*, p. 36 n. 76; CQB/223/194 (Shaw), Mar. 1847; 427/75 and *EMN*, July 1, 1898; 399/24 (Bowen) and *EMN*, May 26, 1891.

41. See E. A. Williams, *Open Verdict*, p. 45; Forbes, "Crowner's Quest," p. 12; Jennings and Barraclough, "Legal and Administrative Influences," p. 409.

42. See CQB/315 (Richardson), Sept. 1870, and *EMN*, Sept. 13, 1870, for Thorney's remarks at the start of an inquest.

43. CQB/300 (Colgan), Nov. 1866, and *Hull News*, Nov. 24, 1866; 339/30 (Brooke), Sept. 1876; 401/3 (Caley), Oct. 1891; 426/2 (Bodilly), Jan. 1898.

44. For the way the coroner questioned witnesses, see the case of Henry Hunter (CQB/416/27) in *EMN*, Aug. 20, 1895. See also CQB/273/038 (Leonard), Jan. 1860; 277/085 (Hindson), Feb. 1861; 418/18 (West), May 1896.

45. Some witnesses came from far afield. A silversmith and former employer of James Lewis (a watchmaker, aged 43, who poisoned himself) came from Grimsby, twenty miles away: CQB/349/13 (Lewis), Nov. 1878.

46. Cf. Jennings and Barraclough, "Legal and Administrative Influences," p. 409; Thurston, *Coroner's Practice*, pp. 121 ff.

47. CQB/411/4 (Steels). For inquests in which legal representatives were present, see 278/207 (Dossor), June 1861; 398/24 (Obee), Feb. 1891, and *EMN*, Feb. 17, 1891.

48. O. Anderson, *Suicide*, p. 219 n. 70.

49. CQB/400/24 (Wiles), Aug. 1891.

50. See, e.g., CQB/356/33 (Thornley), Sept. 1880; CQB/362/19 (Wood), Feb. 1882.

51. See CQB/243/39 (Dennison, aged 18), July 1852; CQB/385/18 (Lunn, aged 16), Dec. 1887; CQB/411/34 (Marsden, aged 18), May 1894; CQB/428/10 (Hinsbey, aged 23), July 1898. And cf. O. Anderson, *Suicide*, p. 59.

52. Ratcliffe, "Suicides in the City," p. 5. Cf. MacDonald and Murphy, *Sleepless Souls*, pp. 228–38. For the inquest on Jane Cooper, a 17-year-old servant, who jumped off the Monument in London, which "tried very hard to come up with a conventional narrative solution, concentrating especially on the plot of seduction and abandonment," see Pope, "A View from the Monument," p. 157.

53. It was not unknown, however, for lay witnesses to offer a diagnosis of the deceased's mental or physical condition that went beyond "melancholic" or "low-spirited." The widow of a rullyman said her husband suffered from "softening of the brain"; a daughter said her mother "laboured under religious monomania"; and a father said about his poorly daughter, "I have no doubt that she was a decided lunatic." See CQB/367/20 (Langrick), May 1883; 218/104 (Hunter), June 1846; 210/133 (Chapman), Apr. 1844.

54. Act for the Attendance and Remuneration of Medical Witnesses at Coroners' Inquests, 1836, 6 & 7 Will. 4, c. 89; Sim and Ward, "Magistrate of the Poor?" p. 249; O. Anderson, *Suicide*, p. 27 n. 54; Havard, *Detection of Secret Homicide*, pp. 9, 44; L. Rose, *Massacre of the Innocents*, p. 61; Forbes, *Surgeons at the Bailey*, p. 34; Crowther and White, *On Soul and Conscience*, p. 19. As Burney shows, many defended the practitioner-based autopsy on the grounds that the general practitioner was best placed to know the full story of any death ("Decoding Death," ch. 4).

55. Greenwald and Greenwald, "Medicolegal Progress in Inquests," pp. 208 (table 1), 228.

56. All the doctors are listed in Bickford and Bickford, *Medical Profession*. For the meaning of the different titles, see Waddington, "General Practitioners and Consultants," pp. 164–85. Surgeons performed operations, learning their skills by apprenticeship and practical training in wards of hospitals. By mid-century, surgeons were increasingly general practitioners. Physicians diagnosed illnesses and prescribed medicines, and were university-educated.

57. See ch. 6, table 6.5, for the methods of suicide.

58. For the reluctance to hold inquests for suicide by hanging and drowning on the part of Edwin Lankester, medical coroner of London, see O. Anderson, *Suicide*, p. 229 n. 104.

59. Burney discovered an increasing frequency of postmortem examinations at English inquests from the 1870's on ("Decoding Death," pp. 27–28).

60. CQB/186 (Dailey), May 1838; 207/133 (Smith), Oct. 1843.

61. CQB/214/161 (Binnington), Apr. 1845; 222/127 (Turpin), May 1847.

62. CQB/315 (Richardson), Sept. 1870, and *EMN*, Sept. 13, 1870; CQB/287 (Howson), Aug. 1863; 353/26 (Western), Dec. 1879.

63. CQB/431/60 (Dresser), May 1899; 405/24 (Gray), Nov. 1892.

64. For example, CQB/302 (Jennison), June 1867, and *Hull News*, June 22, 1867. Dr. Usher did a postmortem. At the inquest, he said that appearances were consistent only with poisoning by a narcotic that had been absorbed.

65. See Bickford and Bickford, *Medical Profession*, pp. 64, 102, 136.

66. CQB/411/34 (Marsden), May 1894; 344/43 (Smith), Oct. 1877, and *EMN*, Oct. 13, 1877. For Thompson, see also CQB/359/5 (Crawford), Apr. 1881.

67. CQB/334/8 (Birkett), Feb. 1875. At first, Dr. Quicke said he had observed no tendency to insanity in the deceased (a draper who had cut his throat). When further examined, he said that, having heard the evidence of the deceased's widow and friend, he thought the deceased was not in his right state of mind when he did the act.

68. See O. Anderson, *Suicide*, pp. 402, 405 n. 111; Tuke, *Dictionary of Psychological Medicine*, p. 1229; Scull, *Most Solitary of Afflictions*, pp. 305–6.

69. For Casson, see Bickford and Bickford, *Medical Profession*, p. 20. Cf. Small, *Love's Madness*, p. 22.

70. For the content of Victorian clinical manuals on mental disease, see O. Anderson, *Suicide*, pp. 382–83.

71. CQB/215/054 (Shaw), Oct. 1845; CQB/296 (Leach), Dec. 1865; 327/6 (Loveday), July 1873; 336/1 (Dick), July 1875. See also 283/142 (Whitton), Aug. 1842; 301 (Fenwick), Feb. 1867.

72. CQB/273/079 (Hall), Feb. 1860; 286 (Rose), Apr. 1863; 335/23 (Gilliard), June 1875.

73. CQB/268/058 (Haines), Dec. 1858; 399/26 (Teal), May 1891. The surgeon said of William Teal, aged 70, a color maker's laborer, who hanged himself: "I have heard that some members of his family have committed suicide. That is hereditary." The Coroner's Inquisition Book duly recorded: "probably hereditary." For a contemporary opinion on the inheritance of the suicidal propensity, see Strahan, *Suicide and Insanity*, pp. 188–90.

74. CQB/273/038 (Leonard), Jan. 1860; 368/20 (Penny), Aug. 1883; 405/24 (Gray), Nov. 1892; 369/12 (Bielfeldt), Nov. 1883. See also "Neglected Brain Disease—Suicide," *Journal of Psychological Medicine* 10 (July 1857): 414–22; Peterson, "Brain Fever in Nineteenth-Century Literature," pp. 447–50, 454; Scull, *Museums of Madness*, p. 160.

75. CQB/400/16 (Whitehead), Aug. 1891; 394/32 (Kirk), Mar. 1890; 417/37 (Panton), Dec. 1895. In the last case, Dr. Jackson said: "I believe she has had a sudden attack of influenza frenzy, following sleep." For another case of diseased bowels, see CQB/301 (Foster), Mar. 1867.

76. CQB/221/173 (Walker), Sept. 1847.

77. For delirium tremens resulting from excessive drinking, see CQB/303

(Batty), Aug. 1867; 353/3 (Kilgour), Oct. 1879. In the last case, Dr. Farbstein said: "When men suffer from that disease [delirium tremens] & are under delusions as to being followed or watched they have a tendency to commit suicide. A person suffering from delirium tremens is of unsound mind for the time." See also McCandless, "'Curses of Civilization': Insanity and Drunkenness," pp. 49–58. For hypochondriasis, see CQB/278/102 (Isaiah), May 1861; 376/28 (Pilfoot), Sept. 1885. For monomania, see CQB/195 (Massam), Oct. 1840; 212/104 (Gardner), Nov. 1844; 392/8 (Jefferson), July 1889. For the use of "puerperal mania," see Forbes, *Surgeons at the Bailey*, pp. 107–8.

78. See Oppenheim, *Shattered Nerves*, p. 107; Finnane, *Insanity and the Insane*, pp. 151–52; Digby, *Madness, Morality and Medicine*, p. 198; Scull, *Most Solitary of Afflictions*, p. 358; O. Anderson, *Suicide*, pp. 386–87. See also CQB/283/142 (Whitton), Aug. 1862. The keeper of the asylum for the insane had received Whitton under medical certificates of two surgeons; his insanity was described as a tendency to commit suicide.

79. See Scull, "A Convenient Place to Get Rid of Inconvenient People," p. 50. See also id., *Social Order/Mental Disorder*, pp. 215–21; Hodgkinson, "Provision for Pauper Lunatics," pp. 138–54.

80. CQB/233/277 (Frazer), Feb. 1850; 216/099 (Gray), Dec. 1845.

81. CQB/333/3 (Curry), Oct. 1874.

82. See CQB/235/488 (Smales), July 1850; 198/087A (Erskin), May 1841; 214/118 (Kay), May 1845; 215/044 (Dalton), Oct. 1845; 297 (Leggott), Feb. 1866; 265/145 (Canby), Jan. 1858; 372/33 (Lee), Sept. 1884; 399/16 (Blenkin), Apr. 1891.

83. CQB/355/9 (Simpson), May 1880.

84. CQB/346/28 (Woodhead), Mar. 1878; 259/81 (Wilkinson), Sept. 1856. See also 355/1 (Cooper), Apr. 1880.

85. CQB/412/41 (Skelton), Sept. 1894; 391/37 (Allen), June 1889. See also 367/20 (Langrick), May 1883. Langrick, a rullyman, suffered from "softening of the brain." A doctor had wanted the wife of the deceased to have him put into an asylum, as he thought the deceased was dangerous and suicidal. He had previously attempted suicide. But the son objected to committal.

86. CQB/308 (Thompson), Nov. 1868. See also 210/133 (Chapman), Apr. 1844.

87. CQB/310 (Martin), Apr. 1869; 368/2 (Anderson), July 1883. There were cases, finally, of suicidal patients moving in and out of asylums: 218/109 (Smithson), June 1846; 304 (Backhouse), Dec. 1867.

88. Cf. Finnane, *Insanity and the Insane*, p. 162; Scull, *Most Solitary of Afflictions*, pp. 351–52.

89. Walton, "Lunacy in the Industrial Revolution," pp. 2–18; id., "Casting Out and Bringing Back," pp. 132–41. Cf. M. Anderson, *Family Structure*, passim.

90. Six more suicide notes (3 female, 3 male) were found among open verdict cases.

91. CQB/423/3 (Appleyard), Apr. 1897, and *EMN*, Apr. 5, 1897; 302 (Jennison), June 1867; 415/18 (Smelt), May 1895.

92. CQB/378/28 (Gibson), Mar. 1886; 430/35 (Potts), Feb. 1899; 412/37 (Walker), Sept. 1894.

93. CQB/396/22 (Cullen), Aug. 1890.

94. CQB/277/085 (Hindson), Feb. 1861; 375/20 (Grice), June 1885; 368/28 (Bownes), Sept. 1883. See also 399/9 (Stephenson), Apr. 1891.

95. CQB/414/24 (Nixon), Jan. 1895; 419/35 (Hands), Aug. 1896.

96. Inquest depositions contain few references to the idea of suicide as sin. A rare example is that of William Page, a marine-stores dealer, aged 68, who hanged himself in May 1861. Page's son-in-law deposed: "Last Sunday week he spoke of committing suicide & said that any one doing so would go to hell." See CQB/278/173. And see CQB/340/6 (William Walker Hill), Apr. 1876. In a couple of other cases, the suicides spoke of Satan having tempted them to commit suicide: CQB/336/32 (Elizabeth Julian), Sept. 1875; CQB/419/22 (John Robert Hance), July 1896.

97. See Lieberman, "Romanticism and the Culture of Suicide," pp. 623–28; MacDonald and Murphy, *Sleepless Souls*, pp. 327–34.

98. CQB/433/7 (Martin), Dec. 1899. For a full discussion of felo de se verdicts, see ch. 3.

99. CQB/416/62 (Glew), Oct. 1895.

Chapter 3

1. O. Anderson, *Suicide*, p. 29.

2. CQB/230/387 (Dunn), May 1849; 411/40 (Dent), June 1894; 266/047 (Fish), Apr. 1858.

3. The number of ruminations on the classification and counting of suicides is legion. Sainsbury, "Suicide: Opinion and Facts," p. 579, and O'Carroll, "A Consideration of the Validity and Reliability of Suicide Mortality Data," p. 6, are two considerations of the subject that I have found useful.

4. CQB/312 (Thompson), Oct. 1869, and "Supposed Suicide," *Hull News*, Oct. 30, 1869; 236/404 (Purser), Dec. 1850, and *Hull Advertiser*, Dec. 27, 1850.

5. See Berridge and Edwards, *Opium and the People*, pp. 22–37, 80; Lomax, "Uses and Abuses of Opiates," p. 167; O. Anderson, *Suicide*, pp. 158, 185. The 1868 Pharmacy Act did little to diminish the habit of self-medication with opiates: see Berridge and Edwards, pp. 121–22.

6. CQB/231/172 (Crossland), July 1849; 378/16 (Oliver), Feb. 1886, and *EMN*, Feb. 13 and 25, 1886. See also CQB/205/153 (Cruikshanks), Jan. 1843: according to the *Hull Advertiser*, Feb. 3, 1843, the deceased got laudanum "under pretext that he was accustomed to take it, & wanted a sea stock"; CQB/253/078 (Parker), Feb. 1855: the druggist who sold her a pennyworth of opium said the deceased had the

appearance of an opium taker, and had she not done so, since she was a stranger, he would have declined.

7. CQB/279/161 (Holmes), Oct. 1861, and *Hull Advertiser* and *Hull News*, Oct. 5, 1861.

8. CQB/278/207 (Dossor), June 1861, and *Hull News*, June 8, 1861.

9. Juries were not entirely consistent, however. There were cases in which the jury returned a verdict of suicide by drowning while of unsound mind, but in which there was no depositional evidence to indicate that the deceased had been seen to jump into the water. It is hard to tell why such cases did not attract an open verdict. See CQB/311 (Anderson), Aug. 1869; 311 (Bennett), Sept. 1869.

10. CQB/303 (Mundy), June 1867.

11. CQB/368/28 (Bownes), Sept. 1883, and *EMN*, Sept. 8, 1883; 425/31 (Sherring), Nov. 1897, and *EMN*, Nov. 29, 1897. See also 410/49 (Renton), Mar. 1894.

12. CQB/398/38 (Kemp), Mar. 1891; 211/440 (Tomlinson), Aug. 1844, and *Hull Advertiser*, Aug. 16, 1844. See also 347/26 (Smith), June 1878; 284/113 (Whitworth), Nov. 1862.

13. The figure differs according to decade and gender. In the decade 1861–70, adding open verdicts to cases registered as suicide increases the annual average rate by 22 percent for males, and by 28 percent for females.

14. No previous historical study has included such cases. I have omitted open verdicts in which the circumstantial evidence was not compelling and/or in which the coroner advised the jury that there was no apparent motive that could lead them to arrive at the conclusion that the deceased had intentionally killed himself. See, e.g., CQB/380/21 (Bolton), Aug. 1886; 257/284 (Atkinson), Mar. 1856; 255/332 (Wilks), Sept. 1855.

15. MacDonald and Murphy, *Sleepless Souls*, p. 133; O. Anderson, *Suicide*, p. 221; Conley, *Unwritten Law*, p. 63. The final figure, from O. Anderson, *Suicide*, p. 265 n. 10, excluded those felo de se verdicts returned on murderers.

16. O. Anderson, *Suicide*, p. 224 n. 90.

17. CQB/214/131 (Hawley), May 1845, and *Hull Advertiser*, May 16, 1845. See also 233/305 (Lawler), Jan. 1850, and *Hull Advertiser*, Feb. 1, 1850.

18. O. Anderson, *Suicide*, pp. 220–21, 234, 266–70, 276, 278.

19. CQB/433/7 (Martin), Dec. 1899.

20. See O. Anderson, *Suicide*, pp. 216 n. 65, 220 n. 76, 222; MacDonald and Murphy, *Sleepless Souls*, pp. 129–37, 227; Conley, *Unwritten Law*, p. 63; Andrew and MacDonald, "Debate: The Secularization of Suicide," pp. 158–70.

21. CQB/190 (Hadley), 1839; 202/245 (Jackson), 1842.

22. In contrast, O. Anderson, *Suicide*, p. 239, states: "Where murder was followed by suicide . . . provincial juries seem to have been readier to judge the suicide *felo de se.*"

23. CQB/234/350 (Kelley), May 1850, and *Hull Advertiser*, May 24, 1850; 214/131 (Hawley), May 1845, and *Hull Advertiser*, May 16, 1845.

24. CQB/233/305 (Lawler), Jan. 1850, and *Hull Advertiser*, Feb. 1, 1850; 255/339

(Folly), Sept. 1855. For the other female felones de se, see CQB/202/194; 207/133; 226/135; 230/353; and CQB/194.

25. See "On Suicide—Verdicts of Felo-de-Se," pp. 27–30; Radcliffe, "Aesthetics of Suicide," p. 584; id., "English Suicide-Fields," pp. 708–9; *Sir John Jervis on the Office and Duties of Coroners*, p. 143.

26. CQB/392/22 (Willis), Aug. 1889.

27. CQB/368/32 (Hamwell), Sept. 1883.

28. CQB/257/223 (Ellerton), Jan. 1856; 223/143 (Messey), Jan. 1847.

29. CQB/200/143 (Hickson), Nov. 1841.

30. CQB/357/9 (Plant), Nov. 1880, and *EMN*, Nov. 18 and 19, 1880; 400/24 (Wiles), Aug. 1891, and *EMN*, Aug. 25 and 27, 1891.

31. O. Anderson, *Suicide*, pp. 223–24, 238. The first medium verdict in Hull was returned in 1854, and only in the final quarter of the nineteenth century was the verdict at all common. By contrast, almost one-fifth of suicide verdicts in the Rape of Hastings, East Sussex, between 1859 and 1866, were medium verdicts. Anderson, p. 158, argues that this was a function of the more forthright, unsentimental juries of rural regions.

32. CQB/359/18 (Carlson), May 1881; 427/61, June 1898.

33. CQB/409/38 (Benjamin), Dec. 1893; 431/6 (Isaksen), Apr. 1899. See also CQB/281 (Hardy), Jan. 1862.

34. CQB/353/2 (Zuccho), Sept. 1879; 395/7 (Broadley), Apr. 1890.

35. CQB/419/45 (van Kooten Duinkerk), Sept. 1896.

36. CQB/275/167 (Bullock), Oct. 1860, and *Hull News*, Oct. 13, 1860.

37. CQB/394/19 (Morris), Feb. 1890; 378/28 (Gibson), Mar. 1886.

38. CQB/430/5 (Shibko), Jan. 1899.

39. CQB/393/10 (Fussey), Nov. 1889; 406/43 (Thompson), Mar. 1893.

40. CQB/415/34 (Kemp), June 1895; 395/35 (Barnby), June 1890; 375/20 (Grice), June 1885; 424/31 (Waudby), Aug. 1897. See also CQB/294 (Ayton), May 1865; 404/5 (Shelbourne), July 1892.

41. The Hull findings are the reverse of those of Simon Cooke, who found a higher rate of medium verdicts among men aged 60 and above in Victoria, the Australian state he studied (Cooke, " 'Terminal Old Age' "). Finally, those given medium verdicts in Hull, male and female, used poison to kill themselves more frequently than suicides adjudged non compos mentis, but this is in keeping with their youthfulness.

42. CQB/400/20 (Leighton), Aug. 1891, and *EMN*, Aug. 20, 1891.

43. CQB/410/56 (Snell), Mar. 1894; CQB/311 (Bennett), Sept. 1869, and *Hull News*, Sept. 18, 1869; 339/3 (Bell), July 1876, and *EMN*, July 12, 1876.

44. CQB/200/143 (Hickson), Nov. 1841, and *Hull Advertiser*, Nov. 26, 1841.

45. CQB/211/440 (Tomlinson), Aug. 1844, and *Hull Advertiser*, Aug. 16, 1844; 400/24 (Wiles), Aug. 1891, and *EMN*, Aug. 25 and 27, 1891; CQB/315 (Richardson), Sept. 1870, and *Hull News*, Sept. 17, 1870.

46. See E. P. Thompson, *Customs in Common*, ch. 8; Hammerton, "Targets of

'Rough Music,'" pp. 23–44; id., *Cruelty and Companionship*, pp. 16–20. For additional examples of "rough music" in cases of suicide, see Conley, *Unwritten Law*, ch. 1; Chinn, *They Worked All Their Lives*, p. 43; O. Anderson, *Suicide*, p. 237; *Undertakers' & Funeral Directors' Journal & Monumental Masons' Review*, July 23, 1888 (Oates), Mar. 22, 1889 (Long). For older women "policing" the domestic habits of neighbors, see Tebbutt, *Women's Talk?*

47. CQB/188 (Buckton), Dec. 1838; 206/136 (Hutton), June 1843, and *Hull Advertiser*, June 30, 1843; 300 (Colgan), Nov. 1866, and *Hull News*, Nov. 24 1866; 257/284 (Atkinson), Mar. 1856, and *Hull Advertiser*, Apr. 5, 1856.

48. O. Anderson, *Suicide*, p. 32.

49. CQB/292 (Hardy), Nov. 1864, and *Hull News*, Nov. 26, 1864.

50. CQB/230/374 (Ram), June 1849, and *Hull Advertiser*, July 6, 1849; 214/161 (Binnington), Apr. 1845, and *Hull Advertiser*, Apr. 25, 1845; CQB/301 (Hilken), Feb. 1867, and *Hull News*, Feb. 23, 1867; CQB/186 (Dailey), May 1838, and *Hull Advertiser*, June 1, 1838.

51. CQB/400/5 (Nelson), July 1891, and *EMN*, July 24, 1891; CQB/315 (Smith), Aug. 1870, and *EMN*, Aug. 12, 1870; *EMN*, Sept. 14, 1883, Nov. 17, 1888, and Sept. 8 and 17, 1891.

52. *EMN*, June 15, 1881.

53. See Lane, *Violent Death in the City*, pp. 19–21.

54. MacDonald and Murphy, *Sleepless Souls*, pp. 134–35 and ch. 7, passim; O. Anderson, *Suicide*, pp. 224–32. Cf. Laqueur, "Bodies, Details, and the Humanitarian Narrative," p. 192.

Chapter 4

1. See M. Anderson, "Emergence of the Modern Life Cycle," pp. 69–87, passim; Hareven, "Family Time and Historical Time," p. 67; id., "Life-Course Transitions," p. 118. There are modern commentators, however, who argue that the traditional milestones of adult development (marriage, parenthood, retirement) are beginning to crumble, and that there is no longer a "standard life cycle." See Sheehy, *New Passages*.

2. See Elder, "Age Differentiation and the Life Course," p. 180; Mintz, "Life Stages," p. 2015. For cohort or generational dissimilarities in life-course patterns, see Hareven, "Last Stage," p. 171; Trovato, "Longitudinal Analysis of Divorce and Suicide," p. 200. It is possible, also, that perceptions of life-course transitions differed in the nineteenth century. Victorians may have viewed economic depression, strikes, or migration as transitions of more importance than normative life-course events.

3. The figures are from Hunt, *British Labour History*, p. 9.

4. See E. Roberts, "Working-Class Standards of Living," p. 311 n. 4; id., "Family," p. 20; Chinn, *They Worked All Their Lives*, p. 69. For the impact of work on

a 12-year-old boy, charged at Birmingham with attempting to commit suicide, see Patton, *Child and the Nation*, p. 89.

5. E. Roberts, *Woman's Place*, p. 34.

6. See Hunt, *British Labour History*, pp. 19–20, 22; McClelland, "Some Thoughts on Masculinity," p. 166; Ittman, *Work, Gender and Family*, p. 201.

7. Jordan, "Female Unemployment," pp. 177, 184–85.

8. Higgs, "Domestic Service and Household Production," pp. 130–32. See also Richards, "Women in the British Economy," p. 349.

9. M. Anderson, "Social Implications," p. 62; id., "What Is New About the Modern Family?" p. 83; Higgs, "Domestic Service and Household Production," p. 137.

10. Higgs, "Domestic Servants and Households," p. 207; id., "Domestic Service and Household Production," pp. 133–36; M. Anderson, "Social Implications," p. 63; Prochaska, "Female Philanthropy and Domestic Service," p. 83.

11. Higgs, "Domestic Service and Household Production," p. 134 (table 4.1).

12. See Davidoff, "Mastered for Life," p. 422; McBride, *Domestic Revolution*, pp. 102, 106, 108; Thane, "Late Victorian Women," p. 189; F. M. L. Thompson, *Rise of Respectable Society*, p. 179.

13. M. Anderson, "Social Implications," p. 32. In York, the mean age for first marriages of females (25.25 at mid-century) was a year higher than the national norm (24.4 in 1871); the mean age for first marriages of males (26.96) was over a year higher than the national norm (25.8): see Armstrong, *Stability and Change*, p. 163. In Preston in 1891, women married at an average of 25.9 years; in Barrow, it was 24.7 years: E. Roberts, *Woman's Place*, p. 81. For the impact on age of marriage of male occupational structure, see M. Anderson, "Marriage Patterns in Victorian Britain," pp. 62–63.

14. See Davidoff, "Family in Britain," p. 121; Wall, "Age at Leaving Home," pp. 190–200; Ittmann, "Family Limitation and Family Economy," p. 556; id., *Work, Gender and Family*, p. 201.

15. M. Anderson, *Family Structure*, p. 47. In Preston, 50% of all single male lodgers and 60% of single female lodgers were aged 15–24. Cf. Armstrong, *Stability and Change*, p. 182.

16. See Hareven, ed., *Family and Kin in Urban Communities*, p. 9; M. Anderson, *Family Structure*, pp. 53–54; id., "Social Implications," pp. 64, 69; id., "Modern Life Cycle," pp. 82–84.

17. See E. Roberts, *Woman's Place*, pp. 42–45; id., "Family," p. 27; Davidoff, "Family in Britain," p. 122; R. Roberts, *Classic Slum*, pp. 33–35; P. Thompson, *Edwardians*, p. 166. However, for the view that "the extent of dependence and the degree of subjugation to parental authority" of Preston boys aged 15–19 was "rather low," see M. Anderson, "Study of Family Structure," p. 51.

18. Armstrong, *Stability and Change*, p. 162 (table 6.8).

19. M. Anderson, "Modern Life Cycle," pp. 73–74 (fig. 3), 80. Cf. Hareven,

"Family Time and Historical Time," p. 63; id., "Last Stage," pp. 172–73; Chuda-coff, "Life Course of Women," pp. 285–86.

20. The description of the six life-cycle stages for married couples is as follows: (1) wife under 45, no children at home; (2) wife under 45, one child under 1 year at home; (3) children at home, but none in work; (4) children at home, and some, but under half, in work; (5) children at home, and half, or over half, in work; (6) wife 45 and over, no children, or one only aged 20, at home (M. Anderson, *Family Structure*, p. 202 n. 46). Cf. Koditschek, *Class Formation*, p. 372 (fig. 13.5). Cf. also Haines, "Industrial Work and the Family Life Cycle," p. 313.

21. Koditschek, *Class Formation*, pp. 371–72; M. Anderson, *Family Structure*, pp. 48, 53, 166; Armstrong, *Stability and Change*, p. 183.

22. Koditschek, *Class Formation*, pp. 371–72. Cf. Ittmann, "Family Limitation," p. 557 (fig. 1); Dupree, "Community Perspective in Family History," pp. 570–71 (fig. 16.1); Tilly and Scott, *Women, Work, and Family*, p. 127 (fig. 6.1); Lees, "Getting and Spending," p. 176 (fig. 1); Oppenheimer, "Life-Cycle Squeeze," pp. 229, 240.

23. Koditschek, *Class Formation*, pp. 372–74; Lees, "Getting and Spending," p. 173; P. Thompson, *Edwardians*, p. 180 (Will Thorn).

24. Koditschek, p. 448. Cf. Hareven, "Life-Course Transitions," p. 122. Among small shopkeepers and declining artisans, too, the exploitation of family labor was a familiar strategy for economic survival (Crossick and Haupt, "Shopkeepers, Master Artisans and the Historian," p. 9).

25. See Lockwood, *Blackcoated Worker*, pp. 23–25. The income of the lower class of clerk was often supplemented by a working wife, who would work at home in an attempt to safeguard "respectability" (ibid., p. 28).

26. Davidoff and Hall, *Family Fortunes*, p. 222. For the Victorian discussion of the "proper" time to marry, see Banks, *Prosperity and Parenthood*, ch. 3. For the drive for the education of children, see Crossick, "Petite Bourgeoisie," p. 79.

27. R. J. Morris, "Middle Class and the Property Cycle," pp. 91–92.

28. See Davidoff and Hall, *Family Fortunes*, chs. 7–9, esp. p. 226; Koditschek, *Class Formation*, pp. 209–10 and Appendix A; Crossick and Haupt, "Shopkeepers, Master Artisans and the Historian," p. 17.

29. In the woolen town of Bradford, 36% of all married women in the 1851 working-class census population were listed as holding outside employment (Koditschek, *Class Formation*, p. 378). See also E. Roberts, *Women's Work*, p. 22; Stearns, "Working-Class Women," p. 114. Cf. Modell et al., "Social Change and Transitions to Adulthood," p. 26.

30. See Alexander et al., "Labouring Women," pp. 177–79; August, "How Separate a Sphere?" pp. 286–304.

31. See Hunt, *British Labour History*, p. 18; Bourke, "Housewifery in Working-Class England," p. 168; E. Roberts, *Woman's Place*, p. 137; id., *Women's Work*, p. 16.

32. E. Roberts, *Women's Work*, p. 17. Cf. Guillais, *Crimes of Passion*, p. 117; Helly

and Reverby, eds., *Gendered Domains*, passim; Thane, "Late Victorian Women," pp. 175, 195.

33. Thane, "Late Victorian Women," p. 187; Tilly and Scott, *Women, Work, and Family*, pp. 126, 129, 228; Hunt, *British Labour History*, p. 17; E. Roberts, "Working-Class Standards of Living," p. 311; S. Rose, *Limited Livelihoods*, pp. 79–81; Hill, "Women, Work, and the Census," pp. 83–84. Cf. Alter, *Family and the Female Life Course*, p. 92. Underenumeration increased further when, in the 1881 census, women who worked at home (including those who helped run a family business) were returned as "unoccupied."

34. M. Anderson, "Social Position of Spinsters," p. 381; P. Joyce, "Work," p. 139.

35. Koditschek, *Class Formation*, p. 378. See also Bell, *At the Works*, p. 48; Armstrong, *Stability and Change*, pp. 180–81; Lees, "Getting and Spending," p. 174; Davidoff, "Separation of Home and Work?" pp. 83–84. While the working class took in boarders and lodgers, middle-class families were more likely to accommodate extended kin at particular points in the family cycle.

36. See Secombe, *Weathering the Storm*, p. 109; Ross, *Love and Toil*, p. 25; Bourke, "Housewifery in Working-Class England," p. 175.

37. See Chinn, *They Worked All Their Lives*, p. 35; Secombe, "Patriarchy Stabilized," p. 62; M. Anderson, *Family Structure*, p. 169.

38. See Thane, "Late Victorian Women," p. 179; M. Anderson, "Social Implications," p. 29; id., "Emergence of the Modern Life Cycle," p. 78; P. Thompson et al., *I Don't Feel Old*, p. 21.

39. See F. B. Smith, *People's Health*, p. 372; Vincent, *Bread, Knowledge and Freedom*, p. 52; R. Roberts, *Classic Slum*, p. 66; Bell, *At the Works*, pp. 50, 85; Armstrong, *Stability and Change*, p. 54; M. Anderson, *Family Structure*, pp. 138, 147. "Sickness," Gerry Kearns maintained, "was frequently implicated in downward social mobility in the nineteenth century." See "Biology, Class and the Urban Penalty," p. 13. According to P. Johnson, *Saving and Spending*, p. 69, "unskilled workers generally could not afford membership of sickness societies, which were the preserve of skilled workers." See also Lees, "Getting and Spending," p. 181.

40. M. Anderson, "Social Implications," p. 27 (table 1.2); id., "Emergence of the Modern Life Cycle," p. 78. The figures for the 1831 birth cohort were very similar.

41. Vincent, "Love and Death," p. 245; id., *Bread, Knowledge and Freedom*, pp. 58–59. Cf. Ross, *Love and Toil*, p. 159.

42. See Stearns, "Working-Class Women," p. 109; Ross, *Love and Toil*, pp. 191, 194; M. Anderson, *Family Structure*, pp. 69, 77.

43. See E. Roberts, *Woman's Place*, pp. 171–72; M. Anderson, *Family Structure*, p. 156. In Bradford, 40% of people in this life-cycle stage (single individuals with no coresident family) were below the poverty line, the next highest percentage after families in life-cycle stage 3.

44. Roebuck, "When Does 'Old Age' Begin?" pp. 416–18; id., "Grandma as Revolutionary," pp. 252–53; Jalland and Hooper, eds., *Women from Birth to Death*, pp. 281–84.

45. Johnson and Falkingham, *Ageing and Economic Welfare*, p. 23. Cf. Laslett, *Fresh Map of Life*, pp. 68–69; Jefferys and Thane, "Introduction: An Ageing Society and Ageing People," p. 5.

46. M. Anderson, "Emergence of the Modern Life Cycle," p. 70.

47. In the 1890's, in fact, old age as a distinct life stage was essentially "discovered." Cf. Hareven, "Last Stage," pp. 166, 168; Chudacoff, *How Old Are You?* p. 54.

48. Report of the Royal Commission on the Aged Poor, PP, 1895, vol. 15, Minutes of Evidence (7684-I), q. 17559, p. 925 (F. Compton). See also the evidence of Henry Allen, secretary of the Working Jewellers' Trade Society, q. 16576, p. 880. The Amalgamated Society of Engineers fixed its superannuation age at 55; the Amalgamated Carpenters & Joiners at 50: q. 17564, p. 925 (Crompton).

49. Sonya Rose treats those aged 55 and older as the elderly population of the communities she studied, on the grounds that such workers would have passed the time of their peak earnings and the older children would have begun to form their own households (S. Rose, "Varying Household Arrangements of the Elderly," p. 103).

50. The figures are from Mitchell and Deane, *Abstract of British Historical Statistics*, p. 12 (Population & Vital Statistics, 4); Johnson and Falkingham, *Ageing and Economic Welfare*, p. 23.

51. R. J. Morris, "Middle Class and the Property Cycle," pp. 109–10 (table 9); Crossick, "Petite Bourgeoisie," p. 83.

52. M. Anderson, "Emergence of the Modern Life Cycle," pp. 85–86; Stearns, *Be a Man!* p. 71. Cf. Bell, *At the Works*, p. 109; A. Williams, *Life in a Railway Factory*, p. 18. Older clerks, if let go, could also collapse into the ranks of the casual and unskilled (Crossick, "Emergence of the Lower Middle Class," p. 23). Finally, cf. Ransom and Sutch, "Impact of Aging on the Employment of Men," pp. 308–9.

53. Booth, *Life and Labour*, pp. 43–49; P. Johnson, "Employment and Retirement of Older Men," p. 118 (table 3). For penny-capitalist occupations (cowkeepers, coal dealers, shopkeepers) taken up by men who were no longer strong enough for manual labor, and helped by the Leeds Friendly Loan Society, see R. J. Morris, *Class, Sect and Party*, p. 257.

54. Crossick, "Petite Bourgeoisie," p. 78; F. B. Smith, *People's Health*, p. 321; Riley, *Sickness, Recovery and Death*, pp. 164–71, 192; Booth, *Aged Poor*, p. 321; Laslett, *Fresh Map of Life*, pp. 102–3; P. Thompson et al., *I Don't Feel Old*, p. 31.

55. P. Johnson, "Old Age and Ageing," pp. 5–8; P. Thompson, *I Don't Feel Old*, p. 31.

56. See Collins, "Introduction of Old Age Pensions," p. 254; Harrison, *Peaceable Kingdom*, p. 178; F. B. Smith, *People's Health*, p. 321; Hunt, *British Labour History*, p. 8.

57. See M. Anderson, "Impact on the Family Relationships of the Elderly," pp. 40–41; Thane, "History of Provision for the Elderly," p. 193; Meacham, *Life Apart*, pp. 134–35; G. L. Anderson, "Social Economy of Late-Victorian Clerks," pp. 113, 120; Crossick, "Petite Bourgeoisie," p. 65. See also Royal Commission on the Aged Poor, PP, 1895, vol. 15, Minutes of Evidence, q. 17559, p. 925 (F. Crompton): "[T]he tendency of modern industry is against the aged, and not merely the aged, but against even the elderly." And see evidence of Booth, qq. 10869–70, p. 880; and of A. R. Jephcott, a Birmingham engineer, qq. 14571–78, p. 797. Finally, cf. Fischer, *Growing Old in America*, p. 143.

58. See P. Joyce, "Work," p. 156; P. Johnson, "Employment and Retirement of Older Men," pp. 111–16, 126.

59. Bell, *At the Works*, p. 109.

60. PP, 1895, vol. 15, q. 14911, p. 815. James Callear was employed by the Patent Shaft and Axletree Company of Wednesbury; he represented ironworkers in the South Staffordshire Iron and Steel Wages Board. For later evidence that old men felt socially marginalized when their work lives came to an end, see Townsend, *Family Life of Old People*, pp. 144–47. And cf. Hareven, "Last Stage," p. 174.

61. Booth, *Life and Labour*, pp. 51–52; Tilly and Scott, *Women, Work, and Family*, p. 128; M. Anderson, "Social Implications," pp. 30–31; Rowntree, *Poverty*, pp. 32–33, 38, 45. Cf. Blom, "History of Widowhood," p. 193; Chudacoff and Hareven, "From the Empty Nest to Family Dissolution," p. 73.

62. See Stearns, "Old Women," pp. 44, 48, 51–53; Thane, "Women and the Poor Law," p. 33; id., "Late Victorian Women," pp. 177–78, 182; Booth, *Aged Poor*, p. 322. For the tensions of coresidence, see Bell, *At the Works*, pp. 110–12; M. Anderson, "Impact on the Family Relationships of the Elderly," p. 53.

63. P. Johnson, "Employment and Retirement of Older Men," p. 122 and n. 40; K. Williams, *From Pauperism to Poverty*, p. 208.

64. Thomson, "Welfare and the Historians," p. 370. See also id., "Welfare of the Elderly," p. 203.

65. See Thomson, " 'I Am Not My Father's Keeper,' " pp. 276–77; id., "Decline of Social Welfare," pp. 452–54; id., "Welfare and the Historians," pp. 372–74. See also Webb and Webb, *English Poor Law History*, p. 436; id., *English Poor Law Policy*, pp. 229–35; Quadagno, *Aging*, pp. 140–41, 154–55.

66. For the impact of the cutback in outdoor relief on women, see Quadagno, *Aging*, pp. 129–31; Roebuck and Slaughter, "Ladies and Pensioners," p. 107; Thane, "Women and the Poor Law," pp. 39–40; R. M. Smith, "Structured Dependence of the Elderly," p. 420. See also Thomson, "Workhouse to Nursing Home," pp. 49, 65; Booth, *Aged Poor*, p. 331; Crowther, *Workhouse System*, pp. 233–35; M. Anderson, "Social Position of Spinsters," pp. 382, 391.

67. In addition, 13% lived with their spouses; 5% with other kin; and 7% as lodgers: see M. Anderson, *Family Structure*, p. 139 (table 38). Cf. Armstrong, *Stability and Change*, p. 194.

68. Johnson and Falkingham, *Ageing*, p. 33 (table 2.5).

69. M. Anderson, *Family Structure*, p. 140 (table 39).

70. Thomson, "Welfare of the Elderly in the Past," pp. 209–10.

71. See Rowntree, *Poverty*, pp. 32–33, 38, 45; Armstrong, *Stability and Change*, p. 182; P. Thompson et al., *I Don't Feel Old*, pp. 32, 39–40. See also S. Rose, "Varying Household Arrangements of the Elderly," p. 101. And cf. Hareven, "Life-Course Transitions," p. 115; Dahlin, "Perspectives on the Family Life of the Elderly," p. 99.

Chapter 5

1. In 1872, the first year for which the Board of Trade Annual Abstracts gave separate figures of both imports and exports for particular ports, the total trade of Hull amounted to £39,568,823 (exports alone: £23,034,662); of London, £177,396,920; and of Liverpool, £205,561,708. For more on Hull's topography, see Lee, "Tramways," 1: 2.

2. Census data, 1841–1901; Forster, "Byelaw-Housing Morphology," pp. 42–43, 71–72.

3. See Bellamy, "Some Aspects," pp. 56–59; Cairncross, *Home and Foreign Investment*, p. 80. In 1882, the districts of Newington, Newland, Stoneferry, and Marfleet were incorporated into the borough. This boundary extension more than doubled the area of the borough, and took in 11,734 people (Victoria History, *County of York*, p. 7).

4. Lee, "Tramways," p. 11.

5. At the 1851 census, there were 111 females per 100 males in Hull, 104 females per 100 males in England and Wales.

6. At the 1851 census the ratio of women to men in the 15–24 age group was 117, while for England and Wales it was 105. By 1871, however, the Hull figure for this age group had fallen to 100, while the national average was 105.

7. Bellamy, "Some Aspects," p. 62; census data, 1841–1901. For a diagram of the age and sex distribution of the Hull population in 1851, see Tansey, "Residential Patterns," p. 150 (fig. 10).

8. Census data, 1861–1901.

9. Lee, "Tramways," ch. 1, passim; Victoria History, *County of York*, pp. 222, 245; Bellamy, *Trade and Shipping*, p. 15; Brown, *Waterfront Organisation*, ch. 1, passim.

10. Brown, *Waterfront Organisation*, p. 2; Lee, "Tramways," p. 9.

11. Victoria History, *County of York*, pp. 247–48; Gillett and MacMahon, *History of Hull*, p. 326; *Dr. Airy's Report*, p. 25.

12. Victoria History, *County of York*, p. 248; Bellamy, *Trade and Shipping*, p. 40 and table 4 at p. 64.

13. Bellamy, *Trade and Shipping*, p. 52. Imports became predominant in the trade pattern of the port from 1885. In Hull's total trade, imports increased from

46% in 1882 to 58% in 1900 (ibid., p. 48). In 1900, the most important imports (by value) were provisions (butter, bacon, and hams), grains (especially wheat), seeds, and wood; the most important exports were machinery, cotton goods and cotton yarn, coal, woolen and worsted goods, and metals (ibid., tables 4 and 5, pp. 64–65).

14. Lee, "Tramways," p. 8.

15. Bellamy, "Some Aspects," pp. 184, 221; id., *Trade and Shipping*, pp. 53–58.

16. See Victoria History, *County of York*, p. 188; Bellamy, *Trade and Shipping*, p. 59; Brooker, *Hull Strikes*, pp. 1–2.

17. Lee, "Tramways," p. 5.

18. Bellamy, *Trade and Shipping*, p. 33.

19. Only 16% of the 1,730 workers in cotton or flax manufacture in 1851 were born in Hull and district (Bellamy, "Cotton Manufacture," p. 91).

20. See Bellamy, "Cotton Manufacture," pp. 99–104; Hunt, *Regional Wage Variations*, pp. 202–3; Crawford, "Impact of the American Civil War," pp. 33–35. See also "Flax and Cotton Manufactures in Hull," *Hull Advertiser*, May 9, 1845; Rylands, *Distressed Cotton Operatives*, passim.

21. There were 2,000 voyages in 1860, over 4,000 in 1865 (Victoria History, *County of York*, p. 225).

22. Victoria History, *County of York*, pp. 225–26; Bellamy, *Trade and Shipping*, p. 38.

23. Bellamy, "Some Aspects," p. 256; Victoria History, *County of York*, pp. 222–24.

24. See Victoria History, *County of York*, pp. 253–57; Bellamy, *Trade and Shipping*, p. 45. And cf. F. M. L. Thompson, *Rise of Respectable Society*, p. 42.

25. See Victoria History, *County of York*, pp. 254–55; Lee, "Tramways," p. 11; Brown, *Waterfront Organisation*, pp. 24–25; Gillett and MacMahon, *History of Hull*, pp. 314–17; Bellamy, *Trade and Shipping*, p. 52; Victoria History, *County of York*, pp. 255–56. And cf. Benson, *Penny Capitalists*, p. 11.

26. Bellamy, "Some Aspects," pp. 56–59; Forster, "Byelaw-Housing Morphology," pp. 44, 49, 74. For shipbuilding and engineering, see Bellamy, "Hull Shipbuilding Firm," p. 35.

27. Bellamy, p. 264.

28. Bellamy, "Occupations," pp. 33–50 at p. 39 (table 3); Brown, *Waterfront Organisation*, pp. 8–9; Crossick, "Emergence of the Lower Middle Class," pp. 19–20.

29. Bellamy, "Occupations," p. 39 (table 4); id., "Some Aspects," p. 126; Hunt, *Regional Wage Variations*, p. 123.

30. The population included in the town part and Sculcoates was 86% of the total borough population.

31. "Handicrafts" included manual laborers and persons not belonging to any other class. A further 8.7% of occupied males were in the building trades.

32. Teachers were also in this category of women employed at home.

33. Statistical Society of Manchester, "Report on the Condition of the Working Classes," pp. 213, 217 (table 2). The society also noted that 21% of minors (under 21 years of age) were wage-earning in Hull, as against 35% in Manchester and Salford (ibid., p. 213).

34. For commentary on the occupation tables of the 1841 census, see Bellamy, "Occupations," pp. 35–37.

35. Ibid., pp. 39–40.

36. Ibid., pp. 37–40; Bellamy, "Some Aspects," p. 62. For women workers in cotton, see *Hull Advertiser*, Feb. 5, 1847, p. 7.

37. Bellamy, "Some Aspects," p. 124; id., *Trade and Shipping*, p. 52; Victoria History, *County of York*, pp. 258–59; Brown, *Waterfront Organisation*, ch. 5, passim; Abraham, "Hull Strike," pp. 358–62.

38. See Bellamy, "Occupations," pp. 40–42; id., "Some Aspects," p. 305; Brown, *Waterside Organisation*, p. 98. In 1892, Hull became a 100% union town in the building trades.

39. Victoria History, *County of York*, p. 258 (and n. 87 to p. 256); Bellamy, "Some Aspects," p. 305.

40. Bellamy, "Occupations," pp. 42–44; Victoria History, *County of York*, p. 258. Cf. Higgs, "Domestic Service and Household Production," p. 145.

41. Tansey, "Residential Patterns," p. 75. Cf. Ebey and Preston, *Domestic Service*, p. 30; McBride, *Domestic Revolution*, pp. 101, 114; Malcolmson, *English Laundresses*, pp. 9, 16.

42. "Census, 1901," PP, 1902 (1107), 121: 228–29 (County of York, County Borough of Kingston upon Hull, table 35). See also P. Johnson, "Employment and Retirement of Older Men," pp. 111–16.

43. A similar age profile existed for occupied males in all industrial districts, with the exception of the building trades. The latter trades were not particularly "youthful" at the national level: see "Supplement to the Registrar-General's 55th. Annual Report, 1881–90, Part II," PP, 1897 (8503), 21: clxvi–clxix (table 6).

44. Tansey, "Residential Patterns," p. 45. For W. A. Armstrong's scheme, see id., "Use of Information." In tables 5.1 and 5.2, class I includes professional occupations (solicitor, general practitioner); managerial occupations (employers with 25 or more employees); property owners; and those with a private income. Class II includes lower professionals (dentist, banker, schoolmaster); farmers; industrial employers (with up to 25 employees); shopkeepers employing assistants; police inspectors; masters of fishing smacks; agents and brokers. Class III, "skilled non-manual" (which appears in table 5.1 only), includes clerical occupations; small shopkeepers, chemists, and innkeepers; dealers; grocers; salesmen; and policemen. The category "skilled manual" includes skilled industrial craftsmen (boilermakers, ironfounders) and other skilled craftsmen (from bakers, blacksmiths, and boot and shoemakers to painters, plumbers, sailmakers, and shipwrights). The "semi-skilled" were essentially a class of assistants and servants. The category includes

agricultural workers and gardeners, seamen and fishermen, bargemen and watermen, color makers, cotton spinners, keelmen, oil millers, cellarmen, and general domestic servants. The category "unskilled" includes general laborers and dock laborers, and lower servants (chars, laundresses).

45. Brown, *Waterfront Organisation*, p. 21; Tansey, "Residential Patterns," pp. 181–82.

46. R. J. Morris estimated that 12 percent of males over 20 years of age in Hull in 1831 were middle class, reflecting the large number of shipowners ("Middle Class and British Towns," p. 288).

47. Cf. Crossick, "Urban Society and the Petty Bourgeoisie," pp. 314–25; id., "Petite Bourgeoisie," p. 82; R. Roberts, *Classic Slum*, pp. 4–6; Winstanley, *Shopkeeper's World*, chs. 9 and 10.

48. See Gosden, *Friendly Societies*, p. 242 (Appendix F); "Distressed State of Workmen," *Eastern Counties Herald*, June 28, 1849. For the cholera outbreak, see p. 121.

49. *Hull Advertiser*, Jan. 3, 1851, p. 8; Bellamy, *Trade and Shipping*, p. 33.

50. Sheahan, *History*, p. 238; "Distressed Sailors," *Hull Advertiser*, Mar. 15, 1862.

51. Gosden, *Friendly Societies*, p. 239; Lee, "Tramways," p. 7B (table A. 7).

52. Lee, "Tramways," p. 11.

53. Gillett and MacMahon, *History of Hull*, pp. 323–25. The summer of 1889 witnessed strikes of Hull engineers, shipwrights, and seamen, but wage gains were made in this outburst of "new unionism" (Victoria History, *County of York*, p. 259).

54. Brown, *Waterfront Organisation*, pp. 59, 65; Bellamy, "Some Aspects," p. 107; Lee, "Tramways," p. 11; Victoria History, *County of York*, p. 259.

55. Gill, *Hessle Road*, passim.

56. Tansey, "Residential Patterns," p. 74; Brooker, *Hull Strikes*, pp. 3–4; Victoria History, *County of York*, p. 227. Cf. Samuel, "Comers and Goers," pp. 147–48; E. Roberts, "Working-Class Standards of Living," p. 308.

57. Malcolmson, *English Laundresses*, p. 12; Brooker, *Hull Strikes*, p. 4.

58. See M. Anderson, "Social Implications," p. 22; Luckin, "Accidents, Disasters and Cities," pp. 180–83.

59. Gillett and MacMahon, *History of Hull*, p. 314. Cf. Riley, *Sickness, Recovery and Death*, p. 182; Schneer, "London's Docks," p. 21.

60. Victoria History, *County of York*, p. 238. Hull Union consisted of the two town parishes, St. Mary's and Holy Trinity. Sculcoates Union included the northern suburbs of Hull.

61. Ibid.

62. K. Williams, *From Pauperism to Poverty*, p. 102; F. B. Smith, *People's Health*, p. 383.

63. Victoria History, *County of York*, p. 238.

64. K. Williams, *From Pauperism to Poverty*, pp. 103–7; Thomson, "Welfare of

the Elderly," p. 217. For the view that out-relief was seen as an old-age pension, to which long payment of rates had established a claim, see Booth, *Aged Poor*, p. 148.

65. Victoria History, *County of York*, pp. 259–60; Gillett and MacMahon, *History of Hull*, p. 329.

66. Booth, *Aged Poor*, pp. 119, 121, 486 (Appendix A). In a memorandum to the Royal Commission on the Aged Poor, Charles Booth stated: "[P]auperism of some kind is the probable fate of 30 percent of our old people" (quoted in P. Johnson, *Saving and Spending*, p. 81). And cf. F. B. Smith, *People's Health*, p. 384.

67. Booth, pp. 88, 92, 118–21, 142–49.

68. Rowntree, *Poverty*, pp. 366, 375.

69. Forster, "Byelaw-Housing Morphology," p. 41; Forster, *Court Housing*, pp. 11–12; D. J. Smith, "Housing of the Poorer Classes," p. 11. See also J. Smith, *Report to the General Board of Health*, pp. 18–19, 26; *Homes of the People*, p. 5.

70. In all districts, it should be added, few Hull families were extended. To judge from Tansey's sample from the 1851 census, only 6.5% of the population were living as relatives in extended families. This limited development of the extended family is possibly explained by the large proportion of the population born outside Hull (47% in 1851), and by economic restraints on household size (Tansey, "Residential Patterns," p. 71).

71. Tansey, "Residential Patterns," pp. 202–10. The Statistical Society of Manchester in its "Report on the Condition of the Working Classes" in 1839 stated that houses in the town part of Hull were subdivided into separate chambers, and "consequently the separation of families is more distinct, and the system of taking in lodgers less generally practised" (p. 213).

72. Forster, *Court Housing*, p. 7; Victoria History, *County of York*, p. 450 (map); Sheahan, *History*, p. 389.

73. Lee, "Tramways," p. 7. According to the stipendiary magistrate T. H. Travis, there were 306 brothels known to the police in 1869 (*Eastern Counties Herald*, Oct. 21, 1869). For lists of lodging houses, see the Annual Reports of the Medical Officer of Health for 1882, 1884, 1888, and 1901. On the network of hotels, coffee and lodging houses around railway termini, see Kellett, *Impact of Railways*, p. 319. On "Little Ireland," see J. Smith, *Report to the General Board of Health*, p. 20.

74. Forster, *Court Housing*, p. 1.

75. Forster, "Byelaw-Housing Morphology," p. 53.

76. See "Social Evils: The Groves," *Hull Advertiser*, Feb. 5, 1847, p. 7.

77. Tansey, "Residential Patterns," pp. 86–97 (incl. fig. 6), pp. 201–2 (fig. 16); Dennis, *English Industrial Cities*, pp. 223, 229. Cf. Koditschek, *Class Formation*, pp. 450–51, on the residential segregation of the Bradford Irish.

78. Victoria History, *County of York*, pp. 239, 267–68, 316; Brown, *Waterfront Organisation*, p. 6; Tansey, "Residential Patterns," p. 58.

79. Tansey, "Residential Patterns," p. 70, found two concentrations of lodgers in Hull: among unskilled households and, surprisingly, skilled nonmanual (or white-collar) households.

80. Forster, "Byelaw-Housing Morphology," pp. 45–52; Gillett and Mac-Mahon, *History of Hull*, p. 309; Gill, *Hessle Road*, p. 20.

81. See Horobin, "Community and Occupation," pp. 347–50; Gill, *Hessle Road*, pp. 49, 53. Cf. P. Thompson et al., *Living the Fishing*, p. 206; P. Thompson, "Women in the Fishing," pp. 15, 22; Davidoff, "Family in Britain," p. 127.

82. Lee, "Tramways," p. 7; Gill, *Hessle Road*, p. 12.

83. See Dennis, *English Industrial Cities*, p. 214; Camm, "A Note on Residential Patterns," pp. 65–66.

84. Dennis, p. 84. Tansey, "Residential Patterns," p. 76, argued that the residential decision in the mid-nineteenth century was very dependent on economic factors. The development of a family would be more likely to promote a change of residence on economic grounds than considerations of the suitability of a neighborhood for family life. Cf. M. Anderson, "Social Implications," p. 13.

85. Dennis, p. 189.

86. Armstrong, *Stability and Change*, pp. 150–51.

87. Ibid., pp. 152–53; Victoria History, *County of York*, p. 234; "Cholera in Hull," *Hull Advertiser*, July 13, 1849, pp. 4–5; Aug. 3, 1849, p. 5; Aug. 24 1849, p. 4; Sibree, *Fifty Years' Recollections*, p. 63; Cooper, "On the Cholera Mortality," pp. 347–51. Cooper, a local physician, had campaigned to improve living conditions before the 1849 cholera outbreak. See also Forster, *Court Housing*, pp. 14–19.

88. Victoria History, *County of York*, p. 265; *Dr. Airy's Report*, passim. Bellamy, "Some Aspects," p. 57, refers to an earlier epidemic in 1875. See also F. B. Smith, *People's Health*, p. 323.

89. See the Annual Reports of the Medical Officer of Health for 1891 and 1903; Hull Fabian Society, *How the People of Hull Are Housed*, pp. 4–7.

Chapter 6

1. I have calculated crude suicide rates, not age-standardized ones. The latter would have been preferable, since they take account of changes in population structure, but my data would not allow it.

2. O. Anderson, *Suicide*, p. 43.

3. Ibid., pp. 90–92 (tables 3.1 and 3.2).

4. Ibid., pp. 80–81 (table 2).

5. Ibid., p. 43. On the signal contribution of women aged 25–44 to the sharp increase in the female suicide rate in the 1890's, see p. 131.

6. For the so-called suicidal mania and associated public anxiety of the 1890's, see Gates, "Suicide," pp. 598–99.

7. The national suicide rate for men slowly declined in the twentieth century, until the 1960's when the detoxification of gas sent the rate markedly down. However, the rate peaked in the 1930's during the Depression, and fell during the two world wars. For women, by contrast, the national suicide rate increased steadily and was less affected by depression and wars. The female rate was 33 percent higher

in 1974 than in 1901. In consequence, the rates for the sexes converged over the period 1900 to 1980. See Greenwood et al., "Deaths by Violence," p. 147 (table 1); Adelstein and Mardon, "Suicides 1961–74," pp. 13–14; Office of Health Economics, *Suicide*, pp. 8–9 (fig. 3); Clarke and Mayhew, "British Gas Suicide Story," pp. 83–84 (fig. 1); McClure, "Suicide," p. 309. Hull was particularly suicidal by 1950, with the highest crude suicide rate of the sixteen largest boroughs in England and Wales (those of 250,000 or more inhabitants): see "Suicide, 1901 to 1961," in *Registrar General's Statistical Review*, pp. 256–57 (table 130).

8. See Kushner, "Women and Suicide," p. 543; Hendin, *Suicide in America*, p. 49; W. N. East, "On Attempted Suicide," pp. 430–33, 442–43; O. Anderson, *Suicide*, pp. 239–40, 287–308, passim. And cf. Conley, *Unwritten Law*, pp. 64–65.

9. Strahan, *Suicide and Insanity*, p. 181.

10. Ogle, "On Suicides," pp. 102–3 (table 1), 104–5 (table 2). See also id., "On the Distribution of Suicides," p. 478; Greenwood et al., "Deaths by Violence," p. 155 (table 7).

11. Swinscow, "Some Suicide Statistics," pp. 1417–18 (figs. 1–4).

12. O. Anderson, *Suicide*, pp. 46, 51 (table 1.3), 54–55. The Victorian figures for young adult males are a far cry from those of today. The Samaritans estimate that male suicide among the under-25s went up by 50 percent between 1981 and 1991. See *New Society*, July 3, 1987, p. 40; A. Rankin, "The Ballad of the Sad Young Men," *Sunday Times*, Mar. 1, 1992.

13. I have drawn ages of suicides from the inquisitions, or, in default, from death certificates and press reports. There is some overrepresentation of whole figures (30, 40, 50), because when age had to be estimated by witnesses, the practice was to say, for example, "about 50 years of age."

14. The rate for the over-75s must be treated with circumspection, given the small number of suicides on which it is based in the case of both sexes.

15. See O. Anderson, *Suicide*, p. 48 (graph 1).

16. This confirms Anderson's judgment that "urban coroners rarely had to investigate a case of suicide by a really old woman" (ibid., p. 153). However, a small number of women over 64 years of age received open verdicts in which there was evidence of suicide: see CQB/329/13 (Feb. 1874); 378/16 (Feb. 1886); 414/50 (Mar. 1895).

17. O. Anderson, *Suicide*, p. 47.

18. Cf. R. Davies, " 'Do not go gentle into that good night'?" pp. 93–108: 47.2 percent of suicides in urban districts were aged 45–64.

19. Ogle, "On Suicides," p. 117. Cf. Radcliffe, "English Suicide-Fields," p. 704.

20. Durkheim, *Suicide*, p. 299.

21. MacDonald and Murphy, *Sleepless Souls*, p. 313; Merrick, "Patterns and Prosecution," p. 9. However, MacDonald and Murphy's figures include male and female suicides; and Merrick's figures include attempted as well as completed suicides.

22. Swinscow, "Some Suicide Statistics," p. 1421 (fig. 7). See also Sainsbury, *Suicide in London*, p. 81; McCulloch et al., "Ecology of Suicidal Behaviour," p. 316 (table 5); Meares et al., "Sex Difference in the Seasonal Variation of Suicide Rate," p. 322 (fig. 2); Adelstein and Mardon, "Suicides 1961–74," p. 17 (fig. 5).

23. "Suicide, 1901 to 1961," in *Registrar General's Statistical Review*, p. 252.

24. Greenwood et al., "Deaths by Violence," p. 159 (table 10).

25. Ibid.; O. Anderson, *Suicide*, pp. 172 n. 69, 361 n. 68, 373 n. 123.

26. No Hull suicide used domestic gas, which is not surprising since the rapid spread of the gas cooker was a post-1900 phenomenon.

27. Cf. O. Anderson, *Suicide*, pp. 367, 369 n. 107.

28. Cf. ibid., pp. 371–72.

29. Cf. Ogle, "On Suicides," pp. 120–21 (table 11).

30. These figures are higher than the national ones cited by O. Anderson, *Suicide*, p. 366 n. 89.

31. Ibid., p. 364 n. 83.

32. Both arsenic and strychnine were used for poisoning rodents. Arsenic was readily obtainable from grocers and chemists for one or two pence. Until 1851, there were no legal restrictions on its sale, and the Arsenic Act of 1851 did little to alter a system of free trade in arsenic. See Bartrip, " 'A Pennurth of Arsenic for Rat Poison,' " pp. 54, 65–67; Forbes, *Surgeons at the Bailey*, pp. 131, 144.

33. Cf. O. Anderson, *Suicide*, pp. 95, 364.

34. See CQB/379/8; 353/3; 412/21; 419/22; 335/5; 413/19.

35. Ogle, "On Suicides," pp. 108 (table 4), 109–10. According to Millar, "Statistics of Deaths by Suicide Among Her Majesty's British Troops," p. 189, over half the 663 deaths by suicide among British troops (exclusive of officers) during the ten years in question were "the result of gunshot wounds." On the proneness to suicide of doctors, see also Oppenheim, *Shattered Nerves*, p. 154.

36. Ogle, pp. 131, 135 (Dr. Robert Lawson). Another discussant suggested, however, that suicide deaths were recorded more accurately among soldiers than among civilians (p. 133).

37. Cf. Barnard, *To Prove I'm Not Forgot*, pp. 123, 130; Ratcliffe, "Suicides in the City," p. 54.

38. This explains the high suicide rates found in commercial, administrative, and residential centers, on which see O. Anderson, *Suicide*, pp. 92, 96.

39. Cf. Faris, *Social Disorganization*, pp. 307–8.

40. Ogle, "On Suicides," pp. 115–16. Lawyers, however, did not have a high general mortality rate. For the relatively high mortality levels of innkeepers, publicans, and shopkeepers, see Winter, *Great War*, pp. 111–14.

41. Giddens, ed., *Sociology of Suicide*, p. 423; and see also "Suicide, 1901 to 1961," in *Registrar General's Statistical Review*, pp. 252–54 (diagram 16).

42. See Miner, *Suicide*, pp. 50, 94.

43. See Dublin and Bunzel, *To Be or Not to Be*, p. 95.

44. It is necessary to examine the figures in two separate time periods, since a number of enumeration changes were made in the 1881 census. Before 1881, clerks were assigned to the particular branch of industry or commerce in which they worked; from 1881 on, they were grouped together under "commerce." Before 1881, retired persons and inmates of public institutions were assigned to their former occupations; from 1881 on, they were assigned to the unoccupied category. However, retired clergymen and medical practitioners were generally still included with the active members of their profession. Before 1881, a wife who assisted in her husband's business was included among the occupied population; from 1881 on, such women were not enumerated. These census amendments were closely followed in the allocation of suicides to the various occupational categories. It should be noted, finally, that unemployed suicides, in line with census rules, were assigned to the occupation they had followed when last in work. For all these census amendments, see Bellamy, "Occupation Statistics," pp. 168–69, 172; P. Johnson, "Employment and Retirement of Older Men," p. 109; Hunt, *Regional Wage Variations*, p. 185; E. Roberts, *Women's Work*, p. 42.

45. As stated in n. 44, clerks who did not work in commerce were listed under the relevant industry before 1881.

46. See Millar, "Statistics of Deaths by Suicide," pp. 189, 191. This led to an immediate reduction in the number of suicides in the national army.

Prisons also are conducive to suicide, to judge from the extant literature, which consistently reports high rates of suicide among prisoners: see Kushner, "Suicide, Gender, and the Fear of Modernity," p. 489 (n. 114). I am not able to compute a rate of suicide among Hull prisoners. In the entire Victorian period, nine male prisoners (or less than 2 percent of all male suicides) and one female prisoner killed themselves in the Borough Gaol. The occupations of the males were: three laborers, one draper's assistant, one merchant seaman, one painter, one tailor, and one shopkeeper.

47. In 1851 and 1861, "textiles" employed 12.7 and 11.2 percent, respectively, of all occupied women, suggesting that this occupation was not at all suicide prone.

48. Running the figures with open verdicts added did not alter the findings in tables 6.7 and 6.8 to any marked degree, with one exception. In the period 1881–99, when open verdicts are added, the number of female suicides rises from 9 to 20, and hence the occupational distribution of female suicide is affected. With suicide verdicts alone, only two occupations (food, drink, etc., and domestic service) are represented. When open verdicts are added, two other occupations (chemicals, oils, etc., and paper, books, etc.) are represented.

49. I have allocated suicides to the six classes that Tansey used in his study of Hull's social structure in 1851, viz.: class I (professionals, manufacturers employing more than 24 hands); class II (farmers, small manufacturers, and retailers employing more than one assistant); class III (other retailers, dealers, and clerks); class IV (skilled craft and industrial workers); class V (semi-skilled workers, including do-

mestic servants); and class VI (unskilled workers and laborers). The entire exercise rests, of course, on the assumption that occupation, typically that of the household head, correlates with social status. See Tansey, "Residential Patterns."

50. There were also a schoolmaster, a constable, and a lodging-house keeper.

51. Suicides were deemed to be unemployed if at time of death they were not in work owing to lack of employment, ill health, an accident, or old age. Those in irregular or casual employment were not counted as unemployed unless it was stated by inquest witnesses that they had been without work for an extended period. For the national late-century discussion of unemployment, see J. Harris, *Unemployment and Politics*, ch. 2. A number of modern studies have documented an association between unemployment and suicide, although the nature of the association is far from clear: see Sainsbury, *Suicide in London*, pp. 55, 74–75; Platt, "Unemployment and Suicidal Behavior," pp. 93–115; Pritchard, "Is There a Link Between Suicide in Young Men and Unemployment?" p. 755.

52. What little evidence there is of the relationship between strikes and suicide suggests, however, that strikes diminish the rate of male suicide owing to a rise in the strength of "collective sentiments": see Stack, "Effect of Strikes on Suicide," pp. 135–46; Haynes, "Strikes," p. 118. No such inverse relationship between strikes and suicide can be detected for the Hull dock strike of 1893.

53. It stands to reason that single or widowed women in the lowest social groups were most fully exposed to the problems surrounding unemployment.

54. Sainsbury, *Suicide in London*, p. 90.

55. Cf. O. Anderson, *Suicide*, pp. 32–33. Even so, it was not possible to surmount all such obstacles. Suicides in the workhouses, prisons, and insane asylums had to be allocated to the subdistricts in which the institution lay.

56. By the 1890's, the number of subdistricts was larger, owing to the 1882 and 1893 extensions of the municipal borough. The Hull Extension & Improvement Act, 1882 (44 & 45 Vict., c. 115), brought Marfleet, Stoneferry, Newland, and Newington within the borough boundaries; the Kingston-on-Hull Corporation Act, 1897 (60 & 61 Vict., c. 249), added part of the district of the Cottingham Urban District Council to the city municipal area. I did not calculate suicide rates for these new subdistricts, since the number of suicides was so small.

57. The rates for the 1840's are based on only 84 cases (46 male, 38 female). By contrast, the rates for the 1890's are based on 222 cases (152 male, 70 female), which is approximately 30 percent of all male and female suicides in Hull during the Victorian period.

58. See ch. 5, pp. 117–18.

59. In what follows, I have assumed that wives were subject to the same environments as their husbands, in view of the impact of the man's occupation upon standards of living and health.

60. This finding was doubtless affected by the closure of the Kingston cotton mill in 1894. However, only one male suicide came from the Groves cotton streets in the Sutton division, and he was a shipyard laborer.

61. A marine fireman, a marine steward, and a licensed porter, all from South Myton, also killed themselves, but the depositions do not suggest that these men were involved in the fishing industry.

62. Cf. O. Anderson, *Suicide*, p. 35.

63. See the epilogue to this book, however, for a sustained argument, based on coroners' case records, that many of the Hull suicides can be explained in terms of the degree of social isolation.

64. Since the religious denomination of suicides was nowhere systematically recorded, it has not been possible to examine the links between suicide and the different religions, of which Durkheim, for one, made so much.

Chapter 7

1. Ch. 4, pp. 86–89.

2. See Levinson et al., *Seasons of a Woman's Life*, p. 19; P. Thompson, *Edwardians*, pp. 70 ,75; M. Anderson, "What Is New About the Modern Family?" p. 85.

3. Durkheim, *Suicide*, p. 172. Durkheim goes on to say: "In France only one or two suicides per million inhabitants are found at this time of life."

4. See ch. 6, tables 6.2, 6.3, and 6.4. At the national level, according to Strahan, the suicide rate among females exceeded that of males in the 15–20 years age period. This he accounted for by the considerable constitutional change experienced by females (*Suicide and Insanity*, p. 181).

5. The categories have been adapted from Sainsbury, *Suicide in London*, pp. 62–64, table 11.

6. The inquest depositions did not always state definitively that the deceased was single; this often had to be arrived at by a process of elimination, i.e., no spouse gave evidence; no spouse was mentioned; the deceased lived with parents and siblings. In fact, it was because the information on civil status and living arrangements was that much "softer" than data on age or occupation that I decided to omit it from chapter 6 and use it in conjunction with material on the experience of suicide.

7. See ch. 5, p. 104.

8. See ch. 4, p. 88.

9. See ch. 4, p. 88.

10. See ch. 5, pp. 111–12.

11. See ch. 4, p. 87.

12. See ch. 5, p. 109.

13. CQB/333/3 (Josiah David Curry), open verdict; *EMN*, Oct. 30, 1874, p. 4.

14. CQB/368/20 (Henry Francis Penny). See also CQB/425/31 (George Sherring), Nov. 1897, open verdict.

15. CQB/230/371 (John Hawdon).

16. CQB/251/101 (James Rayner); *Hull Advertiser*, Aug. 26, 1854, p. 5.

17. CQB/400/43 (Frederick Thomas Robinson), open verdict. See also CQB/237/273 (Montagu Ayre), Mar. 1851.

18. CQB/338/32 (Thomas Holdstock), open verdict.

19. CQB/375/8 (John Holmes); *EMN*, May 9, 1885.

20. CQB/300 (Thomas Richardson Firth).

21. CQB/375/6 (Thomas Laister Tylee), open verdict.

22. CQB/421/19 (George Ellis), open verdict. See also *Hull News*, Mar. 29, 1862, p. 8 (William Goy); death certificate, 1862, Humber subdistrict, no. 412.

23. CQB/237/251 (William Miller); *Hull Advertiser*, Feb. 14, 1851, p. 6; *Eastern Counties Herald*, Feb. 13, 1851, p. 8. See also CQB/379/8 (David Henry Marshall); *EMN*, May 8, 1886.

24. O. Anderson, *Suicide*, p. 184; G. L. Anderson, *Victorian Clerks*, pp. 33–34.

25. CQB/239/70 (Alfred Pearson); *Hull Advertiser*, July 18, 1851, p. 5.

26. CQB/254/334 (Thomas Lovitt).

27. CQB/416/62 (Charles Henry Glew).

28. CQB/347/3 (George Johnson Butler).

29. CQB/431/56 (Albert Harold Garton Hill); *EMN*, June 6, 1899.

30. CQB/266/123 (Peter Dolby).

31. CQB/285/193 (Edwin William Whitaker); *Hull News*, Mar. 7, 1863, p. 4.

32. CQB/297 (John Cartwright); *EMN*, April 3, 1866, p. 2. See also CQB/428/41 (Arthur Conway), Aug. 1898.

33. CQB/282/108 (Henry Tindall). See *Hull News*, June 28, 1862, p. 6, for a report of the inquest on William Tindall, father of Henry Tindall, who died from natural causes two weeks after his son's suicide.

34. CQB/325/3 (Alfred Hawksley).

35. CQB/395/7 (George Broadley). See also CQB/416/11 (John Thomas Parkinson), July 1895.

36. CQB/399/35 (George Alfred Thorp), open verdict.

37. CQB/414/7 (John Ramsay), open verdict. Remarkably, according to one press report, the coroner stated at the end of the inquest that there did not seem to be any evidence that the lad had been ill-treated: *EMN*, Jan. 15, 1895. See also CQB/418/18 (George West), May 1896.

38. CQB/385/18 (Ada Lunn), open verdict.

39. CQB/411/34 (Annie Eliza Marsden). See also CQB/340/17 (Mary Ann Freeman), May 1876, open verdict.

40. CQB/257/223 (Mary Ellerton); *Hull Advertiser*, Jan. 19, 1856, p. 6.

41. CQB/326/30 (Louisa Hodsman).

42. CQB/394/38 (Martha Thompson). See also CQB/412/17 (Alice Graham White), Aug. 1894.

43. CQB/368/28 (Annie Elizabeth Bownes), open verdict.

44. CQB/375/27 (Kate Hird), open verdict.

45. CQB/284/169 (Jane Rowbottom); *Hull News*, Dec. 20, 1862, p. 7. See also CQB/297 (Martha Ann Bulmer), Jan. 1866, open verdict.

46. CQB/226/135 (Eliza Farrow), felo de se verdict; *Hull Advertiser*, June 23, 1848, p. 5.

47. CQB/207/133 (Lavinia Smith), felo de se verdict; *Hull Advertiser*, Oct. 13, 1843, p. 5.

48. CQB/194 (Eliza Brown), open verdict.

49. CQB/219/133 (Mary Ann Whyatt), open verdict; *Hull Advertiser*, July 31, 1846, p. 4.

50. CQB/396/31 (Lydia Stather), open verdict.

51. CQB/428/10 (Anne Elizabeth Maude Hinsbey). See also CQB/431/60 (Elizabeth Ann Dresser); *EMN*, May 31, 1899.

52. CQB/192 (Helen Lee); *Hull Advertiser*, Dec. 6, 1839.

53. CQB/311 (Elizabeth Anderson); *EMN*, Aug. 30, 1869, p. 2. See also CQB/223/143 (Harriet Messey); *Hull Advertiser*, Jan. 15, 1847, p. 5; CQB/243/39, July 15, 1852 (Ann Dennison); "Suicide by a Lover," *Hull Advertiser*, July 16, 1852, p. 5.

54. CQB/385/29 (Rebecca Ashton), open verdict.

55. CQB/427/39 (Ellen Hamilton); *EMN*, May 10, 1898. See also CQB/395/28 (Agnes Walsh), June 1890, open verdict.

56. CQB/255/339 (Sarah Folly), felo de se verdict; *Hull News*, Oct. 6, 1855, p. 6.

57. CQB/347/26 (Mary Elizabeth Smith), open verdict. See also CQB/400/24 (Mary Ann Emma Wiles); *EMN*, Aug. 25 and 27, 1891.

58. See ch. 2, p. 49.

59. CQB/359/5 (Harriet Crawford), open verdict.

60. CQB/392/7 (Grace Postill), open verdict.

61. CQB/398/38 (Mary Ann Kemp), open verdict.

62. CQB/419/74 (Annie Rogerson).

63. CQB/297 (Sarah Jane Raby), open verdict; *EMN*, Feb. 7, 1866, p. 2.

64. CQB/403/41 (Sarah Hope), open verdict.

65. O. Anderson, *Suicide*, pp. 60–61.

66. Cf. ibid., pp. 185–86.

67. Prints, paintings, and book illustrations all disseminated the image of the melancholic female suicide standing next to, and contemplating, a stream or river. Books and melodramas presented suicide as an appropriate response for a girl in trouble. See O. Anderson, *Suicide*, pp. 57, 146, 198; Gates, *Victorian Suicide*, p. 131; R. Davies, " 'Do not go gentle into that good night'?" p. 96; Barret-Ducrocq, *Love in the Time of Victoria*, p. 132; Small, *Love's Madness*, p. 5.

68. O. Anderson, *Suicide*, p. 146, discovered only one illegitimate pregnancy, and that in rural Sussex, not London. Three of the four Hull suicides who were pregnant were found drowned, and were assigned open verdicts. Between two of these suicides there was a direct emotional linkage, and an element of imitation. Isabella Kitching, aged 15, a domestic servant (actually a "nursegirl") at the Alexandra Hotel, was found drowned in September 1891. The two letters left in her hatbox were enigmatic. One stated: "I never spent a more miserable week in all my life; I have got low spirited & I cannot seem to cheer up;" the other said: "You little know what is hanging over my head." She was not pregnant, however. In Novem-

ber, Rebecca Brough, aged 20, a domestic servant, and the unmarried mother of a three-year-old child, was also found drowned in St. Andrew's Dock. Her employers would not keep the child any longer. Edith Kitching, who was a domestic in the same house, deposed: "My sister was a friend of hers & drowned herself in the St Andrews Dock about two months ago. Deceased has said she would drown herself since then." See CQB/400/37 (Isabella Kitching), open verdict; CQB/401/16 (Rebecca Brough), open verdict.

69. See O. Anderson, *Suicide*, p. 61; Behlmer, "Deadly Motherhood," pp. 419–20; Gillis, "Servants, Sexual Relations and the Risks of Illegitimacy," pp. 116, 128.

70. For the arduous conditions of domestic service, see Valenze, *First Industrial Woman*, pp. 171–79, which draws upon Liz Stanley, ed., *The Diaries of Hannah Cullwick, Victorian Maidservant* (London, 1984). And cf. Sainsbury, *Suicide in London*, p. 20; Baechler, *Suicides*, pp. 269–70; Ratcliffe, "Suicides in the City," p. 53.

Chapter 8

1. See ch. 5, p. 104.

2. See ch. 4, p. 94.

3. Cf. Stillion and McDowell, "Examining Suicide," p. 345; Levinson et al., *Seasons of a Woman's Life*, pp. 19–20.

4. See table 6.3. The rates for young adults (aged 15–24) were 5.6 (male) and 2.3 (female). These rates are based on suicide verdicts only. When open verdicts are added, the rates for those in the prime of life were 13.5 (male) and 7.7 (female); while for young adults they were 6.9 (male) and 4.3 (female). See table 6.4.

5. See tables 6.2 and 6.3.

6. The figure for single males could be larger, since in 11 percent of all male suicides in the prime of life, civil status could not be determined. No spouse gave evidence at these inquests, suggesting that the men were single. It is probably more accurate, however, to say that they were men, whether single or married, who did not reside in Hull. At the time of death, four were on board a vessel, two were seamen, one was at sea, three were emigrants, and three were in prison.

7. In the case of the women suicides, however, four of the singles, one of the widows, and three of the separated were cohabiting. If these cases are excluded, the figure for women outside of legal or common-law marriage drops from 43 to 35 percent.

8. The rate for married male suicides, moreover, includes a number of suicides who were married but separated. Without these cases, the rate for married suicides would fall to 12 suicides per 10,000. See Census 1901, PP, 1902 (1107), 121: 228–29 (table 35).

9. The figure for single female suicides, however, included two who were cohabiting. For modern confirmation of the finding that the incidence of suicide is lower among married persons than among either the single, the widowed, or the divorced, see Trovato, "Longitudinal Analysis," pp. 193–203.

10. Of the married men in lodgings, one was an emigrant, one was a visitor from York, and one was unable to support his wife.

11. The only accurate test of this factor, however, would be to know what proportion of married and widowed people in Hull were without children.

12. See ch. 6, p. 142.

13. See ch. 5, p. 111.

14. The proportions were as follows:

	Male suicides aged 25–44, 1837–99	All occupied males, 1851–71	All occupied males, 1881–99
Chemicals, oils	5.8%	3.3%	3.9%
Commerce	8.3	3.9	6.2
Government *	3.2	1.8	1.5
Professional	4.5	2.6	2.7
Domestic service	6.4	2.1	2.1

* National and local.

15. See O. Anderson, *Suicide*, p. 70.

16. The proportions were as follows:

Social Class	Percentage of household heads in each class, 1851 *	Suicides in prime of life, 1837–99
I. Professional, managerial	5%	4.5%
II. Lower professional, small employers	12	12.8
III. Skilled nonmanual	14	24.4
IV. Skilled manual	34	25.0
V. Semi-skilled manual	18	22.4
VI. Unskilled	18	10.3

* Based on 20% sample.

17. See ch. 5, p. 111.

18. Thus, of the 26 female suicides who were single, ten (or 38.5%) were occupied. One more single suicide was a prostitute.

19. See ch. 1, n. 19.

20. CQB/307 (Carl Magnus Hallonquest). See also CQB/321/93 (I. van Heyde) Jan. 1872; CQB/359/18 (Johan Ludwig Carlson), May 1881; *EMN*, May 17, 1887 (Hans Peter Hansen); CQB/431/10 (August Vilhelm Hallman), Apr. 1899.

21. CQB/321/85 (Timothy Cain). See also CQB/315 (Francis Pullen), Oct. 1870; CQB/323/10 (William Body), July 1872; CQB/336/38 (John Jones), Sept. 1875.

22. CQB/278/197 (Charles Brook); *Hull Advertiser*, June 8, 1861, p. 1.

23. CQB/339/30 (John Brooke); *EMN*, Sept. 28, 1876.

24. CQB/409/38 (Jacob Benjamin). See also CQB/287 (William Limb); *Hull Advertiser*, Oct. 10, 1863, p. 4. And for examples of suicides in which friendlessness or loneliness was specifically mentioned, see CQB/208/65 (Richard Wilson), Dec. 1843; CQB/404/34 (Bruno Carl Richard Behrendt), Aug. 1892.

25. CQB/302 (Charles Jennison); *EMN*, June 17, 1867, p. 2; June 19, 1867, p. 3.

26. CQB/423/54 (Albert Edward Hill). See also CQB/400/4 (George William Coltam), July 1891.

27. CQB/277/85 (Henry John Hindson); *Hull News*, Feb. 9, 1861, p. 5. See also CQB/399/9 (Tom Stephenson); *EMN*, Apr. 21, 1891; CQB/316 (Thomas Stork), Nov. 15, 1870, open verdict; CQB/345/20 (Marmaduke Walter Vavasour), Dec. 8, 1877; *EMN*, Dec. 8, 1877; CQB/391/28 (Robert Lowther), June 8, 1889.

28. CQB/200/143 (Robert Hickson); *Hull Advertiser*, Nov. 26, 1841, p. 6 For the inquest on Sarah Hickson, see CQB/200/137. The porter who was accused of being involved in the death of Hickson and his wife later preferred a charge against a policeman for taunting him as the murderer of Hickson. The Watch Committee reprimanded the policeman.

29. CQB/432/59 (José Perez); *EMN*, Sept. 15, 1899. See also CQB/353/2 (Marco Zuccho); *EMN*, Oct. 22, 1879; CQB/427/53 (Herbert Bellamy), May 30, 1898.

30. CQB/185/16 (George Heath); *Hull Advertiser*, Mar. 16, 1838.

31. CQB/376/28 (Frank Pilfoot). The deceased was a native of Lincolnshire.

32. CQB/407/30 (George Watson Kirkwood).

33. CQB/412/7 (Richard Bradford Richardson).

34. CQB/430/35 (Frank Potts); *EMN*, Feb. 8, 1899. The deceased was a native of Lincolnshire. For other examples of physical illness, see CQB/215/44 (Henry Dalton), Oct. 1845; CQB/330/17 (Robert Thomas Gant), June 1874, open verdict; CQB/339/25 (James Stathers), Sept. 1876, open verdict; CQB/351/25 (William H.C. Carter), June 1879; CQB/357/23 (William Rookledge), Dec. 1880; CQB/361/22 (John Henry Emes), Dec. 1881; CQB/414/24 (William Brighty Nixon), Feb. 1895; CQB/419/58 (Frederick Walter Woodall), Sept. 1896; CQB/426/39 (John William Cox), Feb. 1898; CQB/430/81 (George Henry Bearpark), Mar. 1899.

35. CQB/241/58 (Edward O'Brien).

36. CQB/283/142 (Edward Whitton).

37. CQB/300 (Thomas Colgan); *Hull News*, Nov. 24, 1866, p. 4. The deceased's wife said that he had attempted suicide eight weeks before.

38. CQB/397/33 (Henry Alfred Larkum). For other examples of mental illness, see CQB/198/87A (Thomas Erskin), May 1841; CQB/227/273 (John Cood), July 1848; CQB/241/83 (John Jackson), Feb. 1852, open verdict; CQB/270/178 (Alexander Gillies), July 1859; CQB/311 (George Martin Tune), July 1869; CQB/412/41 (George Skelton), Sept. 1894.

39. See P. Thompson, *Edwardians*, pp. 198–201. And cf. Perot, ed., *History of Private Life*, p. 637.

40. CQB/353/3 (Robert Sibbald Kilgour).

41. CQB/401/3 (Samuel Caley). See also CQB/221/155 (John Brandham); *Hull Advertiser*, Oct. 1, 1847.

42. CQB/412/1 (Joseph Lucas). See also CQB/415/7 (Henry Welborn); *EMN*, Apr. 15, 1895. For other examples of drink-induced suicide, see CQB/259/81 (Joseph Wilkinson), Oct. 1856; CQB/292 (James Hardy), Nov. 1864; *EMN*, Nov. 26, 1864,

p. 2; CQB/312 (Joseph Hair), Nov. 1869; CQB/326/23 (Thomas Proctor Tonge), June 1873, open verdict; CQB/393/13 (John Dolphin), Dec. 1889; CQB/404/5 (Ernest Collins Sherbourne), July 1892; CQB/411/46 (Richard Freeman), June 1894; CQB/416/8 (William Clayton), July 1895; CQB/418/4 (Thomas Hannen), Apr. 1896; *EMN*, Apr. 27, 1896; CQB/428/9 (Joseph Gallon), July 1898.

43. CQB/395/35 (George Henry Barnby).

44. CQB/407/35 (Anton Henricks).

45. CQB/426/11 (Robert Wiles Pattison). See also CQB/219/108 (William Whitty), Oct. 1846; CQB/267/89 (William Lewsley), July 1858; CQB/338/3 (James Mason Palmer), Jan. 1876; CQB/345/17 (Abraham Taylor), Nov. 1877; CQB/359/7 (Edward Carey), Apr. 1881; CQB/364/44 (John Stapleton), Oct. 1882.

46. CQB/389/18 (John William Oliver); *EMN*, Dec. 1, 1888.

47. CQB/411/45 (Joseph Brown). See also CQB/423/81 (Matthew Pape), June 1897.

48. CQB/291 (William Barratt); *EMN*, Sept. 8, 1864, p. 2.

49. CQB/396/18 (Andrew Moir Benoit). See also CQB/372/16 (Gerard Louis Petre), July 1884.

50. CQB/411/4 (John Steels). See also CQB/315 (William Drant), Sept. 1870.

51. This is exclusive of the cases in which drink and work were interconnected. For those cases, see the CQB references in nn. 46–50.

52. CQB/303 (George Sanderson Mundy), open verdict.

53. CQB/361/28 (Amos Paulson), open verdict; *EMN*, Dec. 20, 1881.

54. CQB/431/2 (John Anderson Soutter).

55. CQB/356/15 (John Thomas Spink); *EMN*, Aug. 17, 1880.

56. CQB/427/28 (Robert Leonard Caley). See also *EMN*, June 16, 1887 (William J. N. Usher); Coroners' Inquisition Book.

57. See ch. 5, p. 115.

58. CQB/415/37 (Herbert Mawe Belton).

59. CQB/330/11 (George Fosby Stones), open verdict. See also CQB/377/22 (Stephen Spence), Jan. 1886; CQB/431/74 (Charles William O'Neill), June 1899.

60. CQB/190 (William Garton); *Hull Advertiser*, May 17, 1839.

61. CQB/214/131 (John Hawley); *Hull Advertiser*, May 16, 1845, p. 5.

62. CQB/344/43 (Joseph Smith); *EMN*, Oct. 13, 1877. See also CQB/331/8 (William Laking), Aug. 1874; *EMN*, Aug. 4, 1874, p. 4.

63. CQB/288 (Thomas Iveson); *Hull News*, Jan. 2, 1864, p. 4.

64. CQB/416/60 (Thomas Clark). See also CQB/278/207 (William James Dossor), open verdict; *Hull Advertiser*, June 8, 1861, p. 5; CQB/340/6 (William Walker Hill); *EMN*, Apr. 21, 1876; CQB/393/10 (William Fussey); CQB/412/21 (Frank Tinson Martindale), Aug. 1894.

65. CQB/216/99 (John Gray).

66. CQB/352/26 (William Bradshaw Pool); *EMN*, Sept. 10, 1879.

67. CQB/412/37 (William Walker).

68. CQB/430/34 (Henry Grint). See also CQB/244/109 (William Collins), Nov. 1852; CQB/284/89 (John Unwin), Nov. 1862; CQB/320/96 (James McCrakan), Dec. 1871; CQB/329/22 (John Jackson), Mar. 1874; CQB/361/4 (Benjamin Thornton), Oct. 1881; CQB/377/3 (Thomas Haigh), Oct. 1885, open verdict; CQB/414/45 (Septimus Ringrose), Mar. 1895.

69. CQB/335/5 (John Wilkinson).

70. CQB/413/19 (Thomas Joseph Redhead).

71. CQB/365/13 (Francis Johnson). See also CQB/363/1 (Niels Rasmussen), Apr. 1882.

72. CQB/323/18 (Selina Wardle).

73. CQB/336/32 (Elizabeth Julian); *EMN*, Sept. 4, 1875.

74. CQB/417/37 (Eliza Ellen Panton). See also CQB/287 (Sarah Auckland); *Hull News*, Oct. 3, 1863, p. 4; CQB/362/23 (Eliza Belcher), Mar. 1882, open verdict; Coroners' Inquisition Book. For an example of a suicide whose baby had been ill for a week, and who consequently was worn out, see CQB/389/2 (Emily Kennedy), Oct. 1888, open verdict.

75. CQB/356/32 (Emily Heron); *EMN*, Sept. 24, 1880. See also CQB/210/133 (Helen Chapman), May 1844; CQB/268/58 (Elizabeth Haines), Dec. 1858; CQB/319/132 (Elizabeth Stephenson), Aug. 1871; CQB/385/28 (Emily Foster), Jan. 1888, open verdict.

76. CQB/315 (Eliza Smith); *EMN*, Aug. 12, 1870. See also CQB/402/27 (Harriet W. G. Alexander), Feb. 1892. For other examples of suicides induced by physical illness and/or depression, see CQB/184 (Alice Wright), Nov. 1837; *Hull Advertiser*, Nov. 10, 1837; CQB/301 (Betsey Foster), Mar. 1867; CQB/323/6 (Alice Glen), July 1872; CQB/390/29 (Elizabeth Parker), Mar. 1889, open verdict; CQB/394/29 (Ann Gall), Mar. 1890; CQB/394/32 (Alice Mary Kirk), Mar. 1890.

77. CQB/368/2 (Matilda Annie Anderson). See also CQB/373/16 (Sarah Morris), Dec. 1884, open verdict; CQB/424/75 (Charlotte Elizabeth Johnson), Oct. 1897.

78. CQB/221/142 (Jane Curtis).

79. CQB/217/117 (Elizabeth Hudson). See also CQB/412/51 (Christiana O'Donoghue), Oct. 1894; CQB/392/8 (Matilda Jefferson), July 1889; Coroners' Inquisition Book.

80. CQB/262/81 (Jane Gordon); *Hull News*, June 20, 1857, p. 7.

81. CQB/339/3 (Eliza Bell). Several jurymen rebuked the druggist for allowing the deceased, of known intemperate habits, to have access to laudanum (*EMN*, July 12, 1876). For other examples of drink-induced suicides, see CQB/268/53 (Charlotte Levett); *Hull News*, Nov. 27, 1858, p. 7; CQB/339/32 (Mary Ann Heron), Oct. 1876, open verdict; CQB/365/15 (Jane Dyas), Nov. 1882; CQB/373/4 (Sarah Blakeley), Oct. 1884; *EMN*, May 27, 1887 (Mary Ann Heaton); Coroners' Inquisition book; CQB/422/3 (Alice Dawson), Jan. 1897; CQB/428/5 (Emma Palmer), July 1898; CQB/431/33 (Elizabeth Jones), May 1899.

82. CQB/400/20 (Mary Ann Leighton); *EMN*, Aug. 20, 1891.

83. CQB/427/59 (Annie Snowden). For other examples of drink-induced suicides involving marital strife, see CQB/184 (Jane Sharp), Dec. 1837; CQB/356/3 (Mary Ann Rymer), July 1880, open verdict; Coroners' Inquisition book; CQB/362/9 (Elizabeth Smith), Feb. 1882; CQB/364/4 (Maria Johnson), July 1882; CQB/426/26 (Lucy Alice Shakesby), Feb. 1898; CQB/428/35 (Rose Amy Wilson), Aug. 1898.

84. CQB/276 (Charlotte Gower); *Hull News*, Oct. 27, 1861, p. 6.

85. CQB/311 (Margaret Sirvoizza).

86. CQB/390/23 (Elizabeth Ann Richardson), open verdict. See also CQB/432/64 (Elizabeth Hair Wilkinson), Sept. 1899; *EMN*, Sept. 19, 1899.

87. CQB/315 (Mary Ann Richardson); *Hull News*, Sept. 17, 1870, p. 6; *EMN*, Sept. 13, 1870, p. 4.

88. CQB/396/22 (Amy Alice Cullen).

89. CQB/374/25 (Lucy Willman), Mar. 1885, open verdict.

90. CQB/398/43 (Sarah Ellen Stamp), Mar. 1891, open verdict. See also CQB/307 (Martha Stringer), Sept. 1868; *Hull News*, Sept. 5, 1868, p. 4. For a 30-year-old housemaid who left her situation, declaring she was pregnant, when in fact she was not, see *EMN*, Dec. 21, 1899 (Elizabeth Jones).

91. CQB/245/112 (Hannah Pattinson).

92. CQB/313 (Ann Carroll), open verdict. See also CQB/202/194 (Mary Thirsk), June 1842; *Hull Advertiser*, June 24, 1842, p. 3; CQB/311 (Sarah Ann Bennett), Sept. 1869; *Hull News*, Sept. 18, 1869, p. 7; CQB/353/26 (Ellen Western or Gollicker), Dec. 1879; *EMN*, Dec. 30, 1879; CQB/425/52 (Frances Maria Petersen), Dec. 1897.

93. CQB/410/49 (Mary Elizabeth Renton), open verdict.

94. CQB/275/40 (Ann Baker); *Hull News*, July 21, 1860, p. 6.

95. CQB/211/471 (unknown woman).

96. CQB/286 (Sarah Rose). See also CQB/370/26 (Betsy Bell), Mar. 1884; *EMN*, Mar. 15, 1884; CQB/425/9 (Kate Booth), Nov. 1897.

97. CQB/198/81 (Jane Bell).

98. CQB/211/440 (Mary Tomlinson), open verdict; *Hull Advertiser*, Aug. 16, 1844, p. 6. For the inquest on the child, see CQB/211/441 (Charles Tomlinson). A rumor having got afloat that Tomlinson had destroyed herself because of her husband's ill-treatment—a rumor that the coroner scotched—crowds of women collected in the vicinity, ready it seems to make their feelings on the matter known.

99. CQB/405/21 (Mary Barnes), open verdict. See also CQB/231/172 (Sarah Crossland), July 1849.

100. CQB/423/5 (Mary Ann Wray), open verdict. See also CQB/386/2 (Gertrude Hind); *EMN*, Jan. 24, 1888.

101. CQB/275/167 (Jane Bullock); *Hull News*, Oct. 13, 1860, p. 6.

102. CQB/424/46 (Patrina Watthem). See also CQB/333/26 (Isabella Reoch); *EMN*, Jan. 5, 1875; CQB/370/16 (Mary Ann Skeggs), Feb. 1884; Coroners' Inquisition Book.

103. Cf. Sainsbury, *Suicide in London*, p. 82.

104. See ch. 5, p. 115.

105. Cf. Ayers and Lambertz, "Marriage Relations, Money, and Domestic Violence," p. 199.

106. Cf. Tomes, " 'Torrent of Abuse,' " pp. 331–32.

107. See Sainsbury, *Suicide in London*, p. 80; Canetto, "She Died for Love and He for Glory," pp. 4–7; Kushner, "Women and Suicidal Behavior," pp. 13–19.

108. For the argument that female suicide often occurs in the context of abuse, hostility, and neglect by male partners (as distinct from the standard view that female suicide is the outcome of individual pathology), see Canetto and Lester, "Epidemiology of Women's Suicidal Behavior," pp. 51–52. And cf. Ayers and Lambertz, "Marriage Relations, Money, and Domestic Violence," p. 210.

109. See ch. 5, p. 108.

Chapter 9

1. See ch. 4, p. 94.

2. Stillion et al., *Suicide Across the Life Span*, p. 172.

3. Ibid.

4. Stillion and McDowell, "Examining Suicide," p. 346.

5. Ibid., pp. 348–49; Kirsling, "Review of Suicide," pp. 363–64.

6. Radcliffe, "On the Prevalence of Suicide," p. 464.

7. See table 6.2.

8. See table 6.3. When open verdicts were added, the rates were 41.4 and 12.3, respectively. See table 6.4.

9. Census, 1901, PP, 1902 (1107) 121: 228–29 (County of York, County Borough of Kingston upon Hull, table 35).

10. The civic status of 10 percent of male suicides and 2.6 percent of female suicides could not be discovered from the inquest documents.

11. The male figure would doubtless exceed 35 percent if those of unknown civic status who were, in fact, single or widowed could be included.

12. The rate for married male suicides includes a number of suicides who were married but separated. Without these cases, the rate for married suicides would fall to 30 per 10,000 living. See Census 1901, PP, 1902, 121: 228–29 (table 35).

13. Durkheim, *Suicide*, p. 192.

14. Of the 22 males whose civic status was unknown, two were in the asylum and one was in the workhouse.

15. Durkheim, *Suicide*, p. 188.

16. The proportions were as follows:

	Male suicides aged 45–64, 1890–99	Occupied men aged 45 and above, 1890–99
Agriculture	2.3%	1.1%
Metals, engineering	12.3	11.4
Textiles	3.2	1.1
Dress	6.4	3.0
Food and drink	10.9	7.7
Commerce	7.8	4.4
Domestic service	5.0	0.9

17. See ch. 4, p. 95.
18. Ibid.
19. The proportions were as follows:

Social Class	Percentage of household heads in each class, 1851 *	Suicides in early old age, 1837–99
I. Professional, managerial	5%	2.4%
II. Lower professional, small employers	12	10.0
III. Skilled nonmanual	14	24.3
IV. Skilled manual	34	38.0
V. Semi-skilled manual	18	15.7
VI. Unskilled	18	9.5

* Based on 20% sample.

20. CQB/202/245 (John Jackson); *Hull Advertiser*, May 6, 1842, p. 3. The verdict in this case was felo de se.

21. CQB/384/47 (Robert Collison), open verdict; *EMN*, Oct. 11, 1887. See also *Hull News*, Feb. 1, 1862, p. 4 (John Hardy); *Hull Advertiser*, Feb. 1, 1862, p. 5; CQB/406/25 (William Hall), Feb. 1893; CQB/411/36 (William Henry Wheelwright), June 1894.

22. CQB/258/478 (Robert Quinn).

23. CQB/412/31 (William Grainger). Two emigrants who committed suicide also claimed they were leaving home to evade the law: CQB/351/26 (Carl Wilborg); *EMN*, June 30, 1887; CQB/323/5 (Christian Schreiber), July 1872.

24. CQB/292 (Anthony Wood); *EMN*, Nov. 22, 1864, p. 2.

25. CQB/404/48 (George Adamson). See also CQB/412/11 (Thomas Bigby), Aug. 1894; CQB/415/15 (Henry Michael Lord), Apr. 1895; CQB/417/32 (Stephen Pedder), Dec. 1895; CQB/418/20 (Matthew Ord), May 1896.

26. CQB/284/113 (Philip Henry Whitworth), open verdict. See also CQB/382/1 (William Henry Lazenby), Jan. 1887; *EMN*, Jan. 12, 1887.

27. CQB/314 (John Hewson). And for the effect of a sister's death, see CQB/323/7 (Adam Large), July 1872, open verdict; *Hull & Eastern Counties Herald*, July 18, 1872, p. 5. For suicides prompted by the death of a close friend, see CQB/334/8 (Samuel Birkett), Feb. 1875; CQB/343/38 (Joseph Schack), July 1877; *EMN*, July 4, 1877; CQB/423/79 (John Arthur Harris), June 1897.

28. CQB/331/24 (William Mudd); *EMN*, Sept. 16, 1874, p. 4. See also CQB/389/9 (James Featherstone), Oct. 1888.

29. CQB/357/9 (Charles Plant); *EMN*, Nov. 18 and 19, 1880. For the inquest on Ann Plant's body, see CQB/357/8. The jury returned a verdict of "wilful murder" against Charles Plant.

30. CQB/419/45 (John Henry van Kooten Duinkerk). For the inquest on Hester Ann Duinkerk's body, see CQB/419/44. See also CQB/404/38 (Thomas Clayton). For the impact on a father of his son's remand to prison on a theft charge, see CQB/293 (Joseph Woodhead); *EMN*, Jan. 16, 17, and 18, 1865. For other examples of suicides in which there was a disturbance in a personal relationship, see CQB/356/40 (William Kitching), Oct. 1880; CQB/379/26 (Alfred Gilbert Gauntlett), June 1886.

31. CQB/204/99 (John Shaw).

32. CQB/252/124 (Edward Skerrow). See also CQB/252/161 (William Hartley), Oct. 1854; CQB/260/446 (John Taylor), 1856.

33. CQB/323/26 (William Clark). CQB/407/41 (Thirtle Cork). For some of the other examples of drink-induced suicides, see CQB/218/136 (John Taylor), Apr. 1846; *Hull Advertiser*, May 1, 1846, p. 5; CQB/301 (Collings Stephenson), Mar. 1867; *EMN*, Mar. 18, 1867, p. 3; CQB/331/28 (John Bennington), Sept. 1874; CQB/381/11 (Charles Simpson Hare), Nov. 1886; CQB/388/43 (John Brown), Oct. 1888; CQB/394/11 (Richard Rand), Jan. 1890; CQB/415/34 (Thomas Kemp), June 1895; CQB/428/42 (John Williams), Aug. 1898.

34. CQB/416/45 (Philip Gilsenan). For other examples of drink and marital violence, see CQB/303 (George Batty); CQB/310 (William Francis Brown), Apr. 1869; CQB/362/19 (Anthony Wood), Feb. 1882; CQB/407/15 (Robert Johnson Wildbore), Apr. 1893.

35. CQB/326/24 (Samuel Hodgson), open verdict.

36. CQB/394/19 (Joseph Morris).

37. CQB/423/30 (George Waddingham).

38. CQB/298 (Henry Woodhead); *EMN*, June 11, 1866, p. 2. For other examples of suicides in which intemperance was associated with financial or work troubles, see CQB/266/119 (William Slingsby), June 1858, open verdict; CQB/274/140 (John Smith), June 1860; CQB/279/126 (Thomas Everatt), Sept. 1861; *Hull Advertiser*, Sept. 14, 1861, p. 4; CQB/300 (Joseph Mann); *EMN*, Nov. 19, 1866, p. 3; CQB/356/36 (Frederick Johannsen), Sept. 1880, open verdict; CQB/366/25 (William Porter), Mar. 1883; *EMN*, Mar. 15, 1883; CQB/371/10 (William Challis), Apr. 1884.

39. CQB/191 (George John); *Hull Advertiser*, Aug. 16, 1839.

40. CQB/221/173 (John Walker); *Hull Advertiser*, Sept. 17, 1847.

41. CQB/369/28 (Joseph Lyon Jacobs), open verdict; *EMN*, Dec. 15, 1883.

42. CQB/416/53 (Henry Capes). For some of the other suicides caused by physical illness, see CQB/230/364 (William Rea), June 1849; *Eastern Counties Herald*, June 28, 1849; CQB/242/26 (William Sherwood), May 1852; CQB/274/43

(Tom Lee), Apr. 1860; CQB/287 (John Atkinson); *Hull News*, Sept. 19, 1863, p. 4; CQB/304 (Frederick Backhouse), Dec. 1867, open verdict; CQB/368/7 (Martin Pitman), July 1883; CQB/417/17 (Job Lee), Nov. 1895; CQB/427/49 (John Dixon), May 1898; CQB/430/5 (Louis Shibko), Jan. 1899.

43. CQB/215/54 (George Shaw). It was unclear from the inquisition whether Shaw was a sailor or a tailor. See also CQB/296 (James Leach), Dec. 1865; CQB/336/1 (Robert Dick), July 1875. For suicides who had previously been in an asylum, see CQB/374/13 (Richard McDonald), Jan. 1885; CQB/431/67 (George Waller), June 1899.

44. CQB/239/103 (John James); *Hull Advertiser*, Sept. 5, 1851, p. 6.

45. *EMN*, Oct. 13, 1899 (Edward Roberts).

46. CQB/392/50 (Elias Fox Peachey), open verdict. For a sample of the large number of suicides who were said to be in a desponding and melancholic state, see CQB/196/128 (John Martin Seaton), Nov. 1840; CQB/197 (John Johnson), Feb. 1841; CQB/219/103 (Henry Tomlinson), Oct. 1846; CQB/369/32 (George Topham), Dec. 1883; CQB/391/39 (Joseph Windle), July 1889.

47. CQB/251/125 (William Lilinston Scott). See also CQB/311 (Ephraim Phillips), Oct. 1869, open verdict; CQB/357/13 (Charles Frederick Holdorf), Dec. 1880; CQB/429/46 (Henry Selby), Dec. 1898, open verdict.

48. CQB/385/21 (William Lonsdale). For other examples of suicides in which illness led to unemployment, see CQB/238/156 (George Robinson); *Eastern Counties Herald*, June 12, 1851, p. 5; CQB/374/3 (Robert Belt), Jan. 1885, open verdict; CQB/391/37 (George Martin Allen), June 1889; CQB/408/18 (Elias Barnes), Aug. 1893; CQB/413/25 (William Hillam), Dec. 1894; CQB/422/27 (John Basil Ferrar), Feb. 1897, open verdict; CQB/425/6 (William Henry Pettit); *EMN*, Oct. 29, 1897; CQB/427/46 (Charles Henry Kenning), May 1898.

49. CQB/426/21 (Henry Spencer). For the impact of old age on painters and decorators in the Edwardian years, see Robert Tressell's legendary novel *The Ragged Trousered Philanthropists*, first published in 1914.

50. Thirty-seven of the 41 unemployed suicides in this age group were either directly affected by economic troubles or were affected by the economic impact of intemperance or illness. Of all the male suicides in all age groups who were unemployed at the time of death, 46 percent were in early old age.

51. CQB/206/136 (Thomas Hutton). The jury subscribed 16 shillings for Hutton's widow, who was destitute (*Hull Advertiser*, June 30, 1843, p. 5).

52. CQB/367/7 (Thomas Todd).

53. CQB/400/5 (John Nelson); *EMN*, July 20, 1891. For some of the other suicides directly affected by unemployment, with their occupation, see CQB/235/476 (Thomas Cumpston, mast and block maker), Aug. 1850, open verdict; CQB/242/8 (William Whitehead, sloopmaster), Apr. 1852, open verdict; *Hull Advertiser*, Apr. 23, 1852, p. 4; CQB/289 (Edward Carter, sloopman), Jan. 1864, open verdict; *Hull News*, Jan. 16, 1864, p. 7; CQB/325/16 (Thomas Atkinson, oil miller), Feb. 1873;

CQB/351/21 (George Crosskill, bricklayer), June 1879; CQB/392/23 (William Glenton, mariner), Aug. 1889, open verdict; CQB/398/24 (Thomas Obee, managing clerk to a wine merchant); *EMN*, Feb. 17, 1891; CQB/404/18 (Thomas Hill, dock laborer), July 1892; CQB/412/6 (Henry Grant, marine fitter), July 1894, open verdict; CQB/424/29 (Robert Wardell, plumber), Aug. 1897; CQB/424/42 (Thomas Richard Johnson, ship's steward), Sept. 1897; CQB/430/30 (William McKay, boilermaker), Jan. 1899; CQB/430/68 (William Lawsley, driller), Mar. 1899.

54. CQB/225/150 (John Davey); *Hull Advertiser*, Mar. 10, 1848, p. 5.

55. CQB/352/19 (Henry Greenwood), open verdict. See also CQB/348/34 (John Bainton), Oct. 1878, open verdict; *EMN*, Oct. 10, 1878; CQB/360/35 (Charles Story), Oct. 1881.

56. CQB/423/51 (George Ward). For additional examples of suicides whose business was in trouble, with details of their trade, see CQB/306 (William Young, twine spinner), May 1868; CQB/331/34 (Benson Harper, cartman and night soil collector), Oct. 1874; CQB/402/53 (John Franksen, money changer, lender, and waggonette proprietor), Mar. 1892; CQB/423/78 (Hugh Barrett, woolen merchant), June 1897.

57. CQB/241/104 (Patrick Duffy); *Hull Advertiser*, Jan. 16, 1852, p. 4; *Hull News*, Jan. 10, 1852, p. 2.

58. CQB/351/22 (William Johnson); *EMN*, June 11, 1879.

59. CQB/429/61 (John William Hudson), open verdict. For additional examples of suicides affected by accidents, the most common accident being falling into a dock or a ship's hold, see CQB/270/119 (Richard Paul, coal cartman), May 1859; CQB/297 (James Leggott, sawyer and joiner), Feb. 1866; CQB/347/11 (John Gibson, timber merchant's laborer), May 1878; CQB/350/19 (James Smith, dock laborer), Feb. 1879; CQB/381/12 (William Fowler, boilermaker's laborer), Nov. 1886; CQB/389/14 (William Smith, tailor), Nov. 1888; CQB/398/47 (George Winter, boilermaker), Mar. 1891; CQB/412/40 (Thomas John Bartlett, master mariner), Sept. 1894; CQB/430/12 (James Starkey, railway gangsman), Jan. 1899, open verdict.

60. CQB/239/79 (Robert Stephens); *Hull Advertiser*, Aug. 1, 1851, p. 6.

61. CQB/353/20 (Robert Clark); *EMN*, Dec. 12, 1879. For additional examples of suicides affected by debt and poverty, see CQB/208/81 (Edmund Halley), Nov. 1843; CQB/241/50 (William Blenkin), Mar. 1852; *Hull News*, Apr. 3, 1852, p. 6; CQB/249/250 (George Thornton), Feb. 1854; CQB/297 (William Burton), Jan. 1866; *EMN*, Jan. 11, 1866, p. 2; CQB/307/88 (William Maltby); *EMN*, July 29, 1868, p. 2; CQB/347/23 (Charles Hawkins), June 1878, open verdict; CQB/388/36 (Jesse Sainsbury), Sept. 1888, open verdict.

62. CQB/408/20 (John Sykes). See also CQB/423/3 (Alfred Appleyard); *EMN*, Apr. 5, 1897.

63. CQB/203/158 (Jane Jackson); *Hull Advertiser*, July 1, 1842, p. 3.

64. CQB/402/18 (Mary Ann Hill).

65. CQB/233/277 (Rebecca Frazer).

66. CQB/421/37 (Clarissa Mary Kennard). See also CQB/271/109 (Catherine Jones), Sept. 1859; *Hull News*, Oct. 1, 1859, p. 7.

67. CQB/279/161 (Jane Holmes), open verdict; *Hull Advertiser*, Oct. 5, 1861, p. 4. For additional examples of female suicides affected by economic or work troubles, see CQB/218/101 (Amelia English, unemployed housekeeper), June 1846; CQB/323/16 (Frances McKirdy, unemployed housekeeper), July 1872; CQB/405/26 (Fanny Holmes, dock laborer's wife), Nov. 1892.

68. CQB/358/18 (Sarah Ann Major), open verdict.

69. CQB/253/78 (Mary Parker).

70. CQB/423/41 (Mary Stokell). For other examples of drink-induced suicides, see CQB/223/194 (Jane Shaw), Mar. 1847; *Hull Advertiser*, Mar. 26, 1847, p. 5; CQB/341/8 (Isabel Castle), Nov. 1876; CQB/344/6 (Emma Griffiths), July 1877; CQB/355/11 (Jemma Wallis), June 1880; CQB/374/28 (Ann Wiles), Mar. 1885; CQB/424/31 (Emily Waudby), Aug. 1897.

71. CQB/256/84 (Elizabeth Appleyard); *Hull Advertiser*, Oct. 27, 1855, p. 5.

72. CQB/309 (Martha Arnett).

73. CQB/360/6 (Mary Dent); *EMN* July 13, 1881. See also CQB/192 (Martha Halley), Nov. 1839; *Hull Advertiser*, Dec. 6, 1839. Halley's husband, a coachmaker, had committed suicide two years earlier.

74. CQB/360/27 (Harriet Reynolds).

75. CQB/415/18 (Ellen Smelt).

76. CQB/220/142 (Elizabeth Hanson). For additional examples of bereavement for a child, see CQB/303 (Sarah Bell), Aug. 1867; CQB/346/30 (Ann Bennington), Apr. 1878; CQB/412/54 (Sarah Ann Howard), Oct. 1894.

77. CQB/379/24 (Ann Sweeting). For examples of suicides who were unhappily married, see CQB/407/32 (Jane Brocklebank), May 1893; CQB/262/36 (Charlotte Pocklington), Apr. 1857.

78. CQB/267/211 (Mary Crossland).

79. CQB/399/16 (Sarah Blenkin).

80. CQB/415/25 (Martha Naylor). For a sample of the other cases in which physical illness motivated suicide, see CQB/189 (Susannah Agars), Mar. 1839, open verdict; CQB/323/8 (unknown woman), July 1872; CQB/355/9 (Sarah Simpson), May 1880; CQB/360/19 (Mary Martinson), Aug. 1881, open verdict; CQB/399/24 (Louisa Bowen), Apr. 1891; *EMN*, Apr. 13 and 15, 1891; CQB/405/2 (Christiana Bateson), Oct. 1892, open verdict; CQB/424/2 (Phoebe Gower), July 1897; CQB/426/41 (Matilda Ward), Feb. 1898.

81. CQB/298 (Sarah Gilliard), open verdict.

82. CQB/308 (Mary Simpson). For other examples of religious despondency, see CQB/207/113 (Ann Denton), Aug. 1843; CQB/218/109 (Mary Smithson), June 1846; CQB/371/28 (Elizabeth Pearson), June 1884.

83. CQB/308 (Harriet Thompson).

84. CQB/327/6 (Sarah Ann Loveday). For a sample of the other suicides who were afflicted with depression and nervous complaints, see CQB/183/11 (Ann Balk), Aug. 1837; *Hull Advertiser*, Aug. 25, 1837; CQB/197/193 (Elizabeth Peart), Mar. 1841; CQB/214/118 (Elizabeth Kay), May 1845, open verdict; *Hull Advertiser*, May 23, 1845, p. 5; CQB/246/89 (Esther Rayner), June 1853; CQB/258/386 (Elizabeth Hart), May 1856, open verdict; CQB/263/76 (Elizabeth Rushforth), Aug. 1857; CQB/388/13 (Ann Rhodes), July 1888, open verdict; CQB/433/1 (Harriet Spring), Oct. 1899.

85. The Workmen's Compensation Act made employers wholly liable for accidents at work, and required them to make payments to injured workmen over and above their common-law obligations. See Bartrip, "Rise and Decline of Workmen's Compensation," p. 157. See also Luckin, "Accidents, Disasters and Cities," p. 183 n. 23.

86. See ch. 5, pp. 114-15.

87. See Kushner, "Women and Suicidal Behavior," pp. 13-19.

88. See CQB/357/13 (Charles Frederick Holdorf), Dec. 1880; CQB/392/50 (Elias Fox Peachey), Oct. 1889, open verdict; CQB/408/18 (Elias Barnes), Aug. 1893.

89. See CQB/303 (George Batty), Aug. 1867; CQB/310 (William Francis Brown), Apr. 1869; CQB/362/19 (Anthony Wood), Feb. 1882; CQB/407/15 (Robert Johnson Wildbore), Apr. 1893; CQB/416/45 (Philip Gilsenan), Sept. 1895. See also CQB/252/124 (Edward Skerrow), Oct. 1854; CQB/287 (John Lodge), Oct. 1863.

90. See CQB/208/81 (Edmund Halley), Nov. 1843; CQB/307/88 (William Maltby), July 1868; CQB/400/5 (John Nelson), July 1891; CQB/274/140 (John Smith), June 1860; CQB/353/20 (Robert Clark), Dec. 1879; CQB/408/20 (John Sykes), Aug. 1893; CQB/388/36 (Jesse Sainsbury), Sept. 1888, open verdict; CQB/289 (Edward Carter), Jan. 1864, open verdict; CQB/241/104 (Patrick Duffy), Jan. 1852. See also CQB/279/126 (Thomas Everatt), Sept. 1861; CQB/430/68 (William Lawsley), Mar. 1899.

91. See CQB/298 (Henry Woodhead), June 1866; CQB/371/10 (William Challis), Apr. 1884; CQB/239/79 (Robert Stephens), July 1851; CQB/266/119 (William Slingsby), June 1858.

92. See CQB/355/11 (Jemma Wallis), June 1880; CQB/358/18 (Sarah Ann Major), Feb. 1881, open verdict; CQB/424/31 (Emily Waudby), Aug. 1897.

93. See CQB/183/11 (Ann Balk), Aug. 1837; CQB/263/76 (Elizabeth Rushforth), Aug. 1857; CQB/267/211 (Mary Crossland), Oct. 1858; CQB/323/8 (unknown woman), July 1872; CQB/399/24 (Louisa Bowen), Apr. 1891.

94. Cf. Tebbutt, *Women's Talk?* p. 117.

95. This paragraph and the next one has been informed by Canetto, "Gender and Suicide in the Elderly," pp. 89, 92-94; Girard, "Age, Gender, and Suicide," pp. 555-57; Canetto and Lester, "Epidemiology of Women's Suicidal Behavior," pp. 48-51. See also ch. 4, p. 97.

Chapter 10

1. See ch. 4, p. 97; P. Johnson, "Employment and Retirement of Older Men," pp. 111–16, 126.

2. This was particularly true of the later Victorian period. Between 1850 and 1900, according to James C. Riley, there was "a transition from an age of death to an age of sickness." As mortality decreased, morbidity increased; those surviving longer were prey to sickness (Riley, *Sickness, Recovery and Death*, p. 192).

3. See P. Thompson et al., *I Don't Feel Old*, p. 64.

4. See ch. 5, p. 111.   5. Ibid., 104.

6. See ch. 4, p. 98.   7. See ch. 5, p. 117.

8. See ch. 4, p. 98.

9. See table 6.2. The number of female suicides aged 75 and over was small and extremely variable from decade to decade. There was, for example, no recorded suicide by a woman aged 75 and over in the 1850's, 1870's, 1880's, and 1890's. Thus the suicide rate for this age group is unreliable. For the comparison with all industrial towns and London in the decade 1861–70, see O. Anderson, *Suicide*, p. 49 (table I.I).

10. See table 6.3. When open verdicts were added, the rates were 37.7 and 16.7, respectively. See table 6.4.

11. Census 1901, PP, 1902, 121 (1107): 228–29 (County of York, County Borough of Kingston upon Hull, table 35). For a comparison with the elderly in early modern England, see MacDonald and Murphy, *Sleepless Souls*, p. 256.

12. The civic status of 6 percent of male suicides could not be discovered from the inquest documents.

13. The figure for male suicides includes 6 percent of cases in which it was unclear from the inquest documents whether the suicide was single or a widower.

14. The rate for married male suicides includes a number of suicides who were married but separated. Without these cases, the rate for married suicides would fall to 9.4 per 10,000 living. See Census 1901, PP, 1902, 121: 228–29 (table 35).

15. The suicide rates for females in the 1890's are based on very small numbers. A rate for single females could not be given, since no single woman committed suicide in this decade.

16. For the main characteristics of old-age living arrangements in the nineteenth century, based upon evidence from other regions, see ch. 4, p. 99.

17. The proportions were as follows:

	Male suicides aged 45–64	Occupied men aged 45 and above, 1890–99
Dress	9.7%	3.0%
Food and drink	17.0	7.7
Commerce	7.3	4.4

18. See ch. 4, p. 95. And cf. Booth, *Life and Labour*, pp. 48–49.

19. The proportions were as follows:

Social Class	Percentage of household heads in each class, 1851 *	Suicides in early old age, 1837–99
I. Professional, managerial	5%	2.4%
II. Lower professional, small employers	12	11.9
III. Skilled nonmanual	14	19.0
IV. Skilled manual	34	26.2
V. Semi-skilled manual	18	26.2
VI. Unskilled	18	14.3

* Based on 20% sample.

20. CQB/317/197 (Christopher Fairbotham), open verdict.

21. CQB/423/39 (Jacob Charles Hewitt).

22. CQB/395/22 (John Douse).

23. CQB/273/98 (Jacob Crowther), open verdict.

24. CQB/356/33 (Joseph Thornley); *EMN*, Sept. 28, 1880. For other suicides in which heavy drinking figured, see CQB/213/125 (William Oliver); *Hull Advertiser*, Jan. 17, 1845, p. 5; CQB/267/156 (William Luck), Sept. 1858, open verdict; CQB/346/23 (Abraham Leonard), Mar. 1878; CQB/356/20 (Thomas Maddra), Aug. 1880; CQB/379/15 (Thomas Dennison), May 1886, open verdict; *EMN*, May 13, 1886; CQB/409/4 (James Story), Oct. 1893.

25. CQB/331/9 (Richard Jackson).

26. CQB/374/2 (William Carlisle); *EMN*, Jan. 10, 1885.

27. CQB/382/14 (George Willingham).

28. CQB/403/2 (James Holliday Bowen). For other cases of somatic illness, see CQB/381/26 (Thomas Colbridge), Dec. 1886; CQB/387/2 (Robert Fox Thacker), Apr. 1888; CQB/419/37 (James Leake), Aug. 1896; CQB/427/10 (David Johnson), Apr. 1898.

29. CQB/273/38 (Thomas Leonard). For other cases of head pain, see CQB/222/106 (William Wilson), June 1847; CQB/333/5 (John James Best), Nov. 1874.

30. CQB/397/39 (John Hibbs). For other cases of old age, see CQB/248/284 (John Beautyman), Nov. 1853, open verdict; *Hull News*, Dec. 3, 1853, p. 6; CQB/312 (Samuel Thompson), open verdict; *Hull News*, Oct. 30, 1869, p. 4.

31. CQB/301 (Thomas Fenwick); *EMN*, Feb. 16, 1867, p. 2.

32. CQB/310 (Thomas Martin). For other cases of insanity and melancholia, see CQB/211/468 (Richard Wray), Oct. 1844, open verdict; *Hull Advertiser*, Oct. 4, 1844, p. 5; CQB/334/34 (Henry Garthorne), Apr. 1875; CQB/335/23 (John Gilliard), June 1875; CQB/397/11 (William Henry Thompson), Oct. 1890, open verdict.

33. CQB/258/485 (Robert Hardy).

34. CQB/322/30 (Thomas Inman). It was unclear from the depositions whether Inman was single or widowed.

35. CQB/375/10 (James Garrod); *EMN*, May 12, 1885. For other examples of business or money troubles, with details of their business, see CQB/344/37 (John Hockless, coal dealer), Sept. 1877; CQB/352/16 (Joah Swaine Wilkinson, retired

keelman and house owner), Aug. 1879; CQB/360/37 (Harris Grodditer, jewelery dealer), Oct. 1881; CQB/367/39 (John Hill, cowkeeper), June 1883.

36. CQB/399/26 (William Teal). For other examples of illness and work troubles, see CQB/400/21 (William Harford), Aug. 1891; CQB/412/13 (Joseph Shields), Aug. 1894; CQB/412/50 (John Cumpston), Oct. 1894, open verdict.

37. CQB/371/11 (Thomas Benson Lacey).

38. CQB/374/31 (John Wray). See also CQB/405/9 (John Arnold), Oct. 1892, open verdict.

39. CQB/331/32 (Frederick Sutton).

40. CQB/372/29 (James Francis Porter). See also CQB/378/28 (John Gibson), Mar. 1886.

41. CQB/278/173 (William Page); *Hull Advertiser*, May 25, 1861, p.1.

42. CQB/418A/48 (Eliza Fowler).

43. CQB/255/303 (Hannah Simpson).

44. CQB/294 (Ann Ayton); *EMN*, May 17, 1865, p. 2. For other suicides in which intemperance figured, see CQB/186 (Mary Dailey); *Hull Advertiser*, June 1, 1838; CQB/378/16 (Elizabeth Oliver), Feb. 1886, open verdict; *EMN*, Feb. 13 and 25, 1886; CQB/430/60 (Annie Mylett), Mar. 1899.

45. CQB/271/95 (Mary Cain).

46. CQB/217/128 (Mary Chamberlain).

47. CQB/299 (Dinah King). For other examples of ill and desponding suicides, see CQB/230/421 (Rachel Fenton), Apr. 1849; CQB/312 (Amelia Rowlett), Nov. 1869; CQB/428/32 (Esther Gosschalk), Aug. 1898.

48. CQB/313 (Martha Carrick). For another example of "religious monomania," see CQB/218/104 (Mary Hunter), June 1846. For other examples of delusional, hysterical, and eccentric suicides, see CQB/223/201 (Elizabeth Savage), Mar. 1847; CQB/228/150 (Elizabeth Thompson), Dec. 1848; CQB/311 (Ann Jameson), Sept. 1869; CQB/313 (Sarah Wilkinson), Jan. 1870; CQB/416/41 (Eliza Gibson), Aug. 1895; CQB/423/32 (Hannah Foster), Apr. 1897.

49. CQB/251/116 (Pleasant Robinson); *Hull Advertiser*, Sept. 16, 1854. See also CQB/258/445 (Mary Martin), June 1856, open verdict.

50. CQB/258/419 (Phoebe Gansby).

51. CQB/329/13 (Elizabeth Joys), open verdict.

52. CQB/414/50 (Mary Squires), open verdict. See also CQB/423/29 (Isabella Allcock), Apr. 1897.

53. Ogle, "On Suicides," p. 102.

54. Strahan, *Suicide and Insanity*, p. 181.

55. See table 6.2.

56. CQB/218/104 (Mary Hunter), June 1846; CQB/311 (Ann Jameson), Sept. 1869; CQB/423/32 (Hannah Foster), Apr. 1897.

57. CQB/222/106 (William Wilson), June 1847; CQB/273/38 (Thomas Leonard), Jan. 1860; CQB/397/39 (John Hibbs), Dec. 1890; CQB/311 (William Sissons), July 1869.

58. CQB/186 (Mary Dailey), May 1838; CQB/294 (Ann Ayton), May 1865; CQB/299 (Dinah King), Oct. 1866; CQB/414/50 (Mary Squires), Mar. 1895.

59. CQB/403/2 (James Holliday Bowen), Mar. 1892; CQB/397/39 (John Hibbs), Dec. 1890; CQB/301 (Thomas Fenwick), Feb. 1867; CQB/381/26 (Thomas Colbridge), Dec. 1886; CQB/427/10 (David Johnson), Apr. 1898; CQB/335/23 (John Gilliard), June 1875; CQB/352/16 (Joah Swaine Wilkinson), Aug. 1879; CQB/375/10 (James Garrod), May 1885; CQB/344/37 (John Hockless), Sept. 1877.

60. CQB/273/38 (Thomas Leonard), Jan. 1860; CQB/427/10 (David Johnson), Apr. 1898; CQB/381/26 (Thomas Colbridge), Dec. 1886; CQB/397/11 (William Henry Thompson), Oct. 1890; CQB/334/34 (Henry Garthorne), Apr. 1875.

61. CQB/331/32 (Frederick Sutton), Oct. 1874; CQB/371/11 (Thomas Benson Lacey), Apr. 1884; CQB/372/29 (James Francis Porter), Aug. 1884; CQB/378/28 (John Gibson), Mar. 1886.

62. CQB/213/125 (William Oliver), Jan. 1845; CQB/273/98 (Jacob Crowther), Mar. 1860; CQB/346/23 (Abraham Leonard), Mar. 1878; CQB/356/33 (Joseph Thornley), Sept. 1880; CQB/409/4 (James Story), Oct. 1893; CQB/403/2 (James Holliday Bowen), Mar. 1892; CQB/400/21 (William Harford), Aug. 1891; CQB/374/31 (John Wray), Mar. 1885; CQB/405/9 (John Arnold), Oct. 1892; CQB/278/173 (William Page), May 1861.

63. See the case cited in n. 36 above.

64. CQB/186 (Mary Dailey), May 1838; CQB/255/303 (Hannah Simpson), Aug. 1855; CQB/299 (Dinah King), Oct. 1866; CQB/329/13 (Elizabeth Joys), Feb. 1874; CQB/423/29 (Isabella Allcock), Apr. 1897.

65. There is a useful discussion of the same issue in O. Anderson, *Suicide*, pp. 62–65.

Epilogue

1. Halbwachs, *Causes of Suicide*, p. 317. My understanding of Halbwachs has been greatly assisted by Vromen, "Sociology of Maurice Halbwachs," ch. 1. For Halbwachs's wider contribution to the sociology of suicide, see pp. 18–20.

2. Ibid., p. 330.   3. Ibid., pp. 270–73.

4. Ibid., p. 278.   5. Ibid., p. 283.

6. Ibid., p. 285.   7. O. Anderson, *Suicide*, p. 180.

8. Ratcliffe, "Suicides in the City," pp. 69–70. See also Cooke, " 'Terminal Old Age,' " pp. 81–88.

9. See, e.g., CQB/199/123 (James Clegg), Sept. 1841; CQB/351/21 (George Crosskill), June 1879.

10. CQB/307/88 (William Maltby).

11. Sainsbury, *Suicide in London*, p. 76.

12. CQB/351/21 (George Crosskill).

13. CQB/430/68 (William Lawsley).

14. CQB/405/21 (Mary Barnes), open verdict.

15. CQB/398/24 (Thomas Obee); *EMN*, Feb. 17, 1891.

16. CQB/288 (Thomas Iveson), Dec. 1863.

17. CQB/425/6 (William Henry Pettit); *EMN*, Oct. 29, 1897.

18. CQB/289 (Edward Carter), open verdict. See also CQB/412/37 (William Walker), Sept. 1894.

19. CQB/378/28 (John Gibson).

20. CQB/423/5 (Mary Ann Wray), open verdict.

21. CQB/400/21 (William Harford).

22. CQB/408/20 (John Sykes). See also CQB/298 (Henry Woodhead), June 1866; CQB/423/3 (Alfred Appleyard), Apr. 1897.

23. CQB/399/26 (William Teal).

24. CQB/311 (William Sissons). See also CQB/222/106 (William Wilson), June 1847.

25. CQB/384/47 (Robert Collison), open verdict. See also CQB/339/30 (John Brooke), Sept. 1876; CQB/347/3 (George Johnson Butler), Apr. 1878.

26. CQB/202/245 (John Jackson); *Hull Advertiser*, May 6, 1842. For suicide in prison, see CQB/206/136 (Thomas Hutton), June 1843; CQB/416/27 (Henry Hodgson Hunter), Aug. 1895.

27. CQB/412/31 (William Grainger).

28. CQB/403/41 (Sarah Hope), open verdict.

29. CQB/410/49 (Mary Elizabeth Renton), open verdict.

30. CQB/398/38 (Mary Ann Kemp), open verdict. See also CQB/392/7 (Grace Postill), July 1889, open verdict; CQB/398/43 (Sarah Ellen Stamp), Mar. 1891, open verdict.

31. CQB/307 (Martha Stringer).

32. CQB/313 (William Sharp), open verdict.

33. CQB/396/22 (Amy Alice Cullen), Aug. 1890. See also CQB/311 (Elizabeth Anderson), Aug. 1869.

34. CQB/399/9 (Tom Stephenson); *EMN*, Apr. 21, 1891. See also CQB/419/45 (John Henry van Kooten Duinkerk), Sept. 1896.

35. CQB/323/35 (Elizabeth Swift), Sept. 1872.

36. CQB/400/4 (George Coltam).

37. CQB/302 (Charles Jennison). See also CQB/360/6 (Mary Dent), July 1881; CQB/428/10 (Anne Elizabeth Maude Hinsbey), July 1898.

38. CQB/311 (Sarah Ann Bennett); *Hull News*, Sept. 18, 1869, p. 7. See also CQB/424/75 (Charlotte Elizabeth Johnson), Oct. 1897.

39. CQB/419/37 (James Leake). See also CQB/430/35 (Frank Potts), Feb. 1899.

40. CQB/427/49 (John Dixon).

41. CQB/287 (Sarah Auckland).

42. CQB/217/117 (Elizabeth Hudson).

43. CQB/239/103 (John James).

44. Halbwachs, *Causes of Suicide*, p. 285.

45. CQB/362/9 (Elizabeth Smith).   46. CQB/404/38 (Thomas Clayton).

47. CQB/409/4 (James Story).   48. CQB/381/26 (Thomas Colbridge).

49. CQB/312 (Samuel Thompson), open verdict.

50. CQB/428/32 (Esther Gosschalk). Cf. Achte, "Suicidal Tendencies in the Elderly," p. 59.

51. CQB/208/81 (Edmund Halley); CQB/208/65 (Richard Wilson).

52. CQB/415/7 (Henry Welborn). See also CQB/412/1 (Joseph Lucas), July 1894.

53. CQB/431/6 (Anna M. Isaksen). See also CQB/237/251 (William Miller), Feb. 1851; CQB/379/8 (David H. Marshall), May 1886.

54. CQB/353/20 (Robert Clark). See also CQB/289 (Edward Carter), Jan. 1864, open verdict; CQB/400/4 (George W. Coltam), July 1891.

55. CQB/271/109 (Catherine Jones).

56. Halbwachs, *Causes of Suicide*, p. 154.

57. See pp. 154–60.

58. See pp. 234–35.

59. O. Anderson, "Did Suicide Increase with Industrialization," p. 153.

BIBLIOGRAPHY

Primary Sources

I. Unpublished Sources

Kingston upon Hull City Records Office: Coroners' registers and case papers for the borough of Kingston upon Hull, Quarter Sessions series, CQB, 1838–99.

Kingston upon Hull Local History Library: City directories.

Kingston upon Hull Office of Registrar of Births, Deaths & Marriages: Death certificates.

Kingston upon Hull Coroners' Office: Coroners' Inquisition Book.

Public Record Office: Home Office papers, H.O. 84/3, Atlas of Coroners' Districts, East Riding of Yorkshire.

II. Newspapers and Other Periodical Publications

Eastern Morning News (absorbed the *Hull Advertiser* in 1868).
Hull Advertiser
Hull & Eastern Counties Herald
Hull Daily News
Hull News
Undertakers' & Funeral Directors' Journal & Monumental Masons' Review

III. Parliamentary Papers

Censuses of England and Wales, 1841–1901.

Judicial Statistics, England and Wales: Part I. Criminal Statistics, 1838–1900.

Registrar-General of Births, Deaths and Marriages, Annual Reports and Decennial Supplements.

[For the appropriate volume of the parliamentary papers for the above, see the *General Index to House of Commons Papers*.]

1840 (209), vol. 41, Coroners Acting in England and Wales: Number of Inquests Taken by Each Coroner, 1835–39.

1851 (148), vol. 43, Return from the Clerks of the Peace and Town Clerks of the Number of Inquests Held by Each Coroner in the Several Counties, Cities, & Boroughs in England and Wales, During the Seven Years Ending 31 Dec. 1849.

1860 (237), vol. 57, Return of Coroners' Inquests Held in England & Wales, 1849–59.

1883 (324), vol. 55, Return of Number of Coroners for Counties, Boroughs, &
Other Places in England and Wales, Together with the Salaries & Emoluments
Paid to Each.

1895 (7684-I), vol. 15, Minutes of Evidence Taken Before the Royal Commission
on the Aged Poor.

1897 (8503), vol. 21, Supplement to the Registrar-General's 55th Annual Report,
1881–90, Part II.

1911 (5492), vol. 13, Minutes of Evidence Taken Before the Departmental Committee Appointed to Inquire into the Law Relating to Coroners & Coroners'
Inquests.

IV. Other Official Publications

Annual Reports of the Medical Officer of Health, Kingston upon Hull, 1882–1903.
Office of Health Economics, *Suicide and Deliberate Self-Harm* (1981).
Statutes of the Realm.

Secondary Sources

Place of publication is London unless otherwise indicated.

Abraham, W. H. "The Hull Strike." *Economic Review* 3 (1893): 357–63.
———. *The Studies of a Socialist Parson.* Hull, 1892.
Abrams, P. *Historical Sociology.* Ithaca, N.Y., 1982.
Achte, K. "Suicidal Tendencies in the Elderly." *Suicide & Life-Threatening Behavior*
18 (1988): 55–65.
Adelstein, A., and C. Mardon. "Suicides 1961–74." *Population Trends* 2 (1975):
13–18.
Alexander, S., A. Davin, and E. Hostettler. "Labouring Women: A Reply to Eric
Hobsbawm." *History Workshop* 8 (1979): 174–82.
Alter, G. *Family and the Female Life Course: The Women of Verviers, Belgium,
1849–1880.* Madison, 1988.
Alvarez, A. *The Savage God: A Study of Suicide.* New York, 1972.
Anderson, G. L. "The Social Economy of Late-Victorian Clerks." In G. Crossick,
ed., *The Lower Middle Class in Britain, 1870–1914,* 113–33. 1977.
———. *Victorian Clerks.* Manchester, 1976.
Anderson, M. "The Emergence of the Modern Life Cycle in Britain." *Social History*
10 (1985): 69–87.
———. *Family Structure in Nineteenth-Century Lancashire.* Cambridge, 1971.
———. "The Impact on the Family Relationships of the Elderly of Changes Since
Victorian Times in Governmental Income-Maintenance Provision." In E. Shanas
and M. B. Sussman, eds., *Family, Bureaucracy, and the Elderly,* 36–59. Durham,
N.C., 1977.
———. "Marriage Patterns in Victorian Britain: An Analysis Based on Registra-

tion District Data for England and Wales, 1861." *Journal of Family History* 1 (1976): 55–78.

———. "The Social Implications of Demographic Change." In F. M. L. Thompson, ed., *The Cambridge Social History of Britain, 1750–1950*, 2: 1–70. Cambridge, 1990.

———. "The Social Position of Spinsters in Mid-Victorian Britain." *Journal of Family History* 9 (1984): 377–93.

———. "The Study of Family Structure." In E. A. Wrigley, ed., *Nineteenth-Century Society*, 47–81. Cambridge, 1972.

———. "What Is New About the Modern Family?" In M. Drake, ed., *Time, Family and Community*, 67–89. Oxford, 1994.

Anderson, O. "Did Suicide Increase with Industrialization in Victorian England?" *Past & Present* 86 (1980): 149–73.

———. *Suicide in Victorian and Edwardian England*. Oxford, 1987.

Andrew, D. T., and M. MacDonald. "Debate: The Secularization of Suicide in England 1660–1800." *Past & Present* 119 (1988): 158–70.

Armstrong, W. A. *Stability and Change in an English County Town: A Social Study of York, 1801–51*. Cambridge, 1974.

———. "The Use of Information About Occupation." In E. A. Wrigley, ed., *Nineteenth-Century Society: Essays in the Use of Quantitative Methods for the Study of Social Data*. Cambridge, 1972.

Aron, R. *Main Currents in Sociological Thought*. 2 vols. New York, 1970.

Atkinson, J. M. *Discovering Suicide: Studies in the Social Organization of Sudden Death*. 1978.

———. "Some Cultural Aspects of Suicide in Britain." In N. L. Farberow, ed., *Suicide in Different Cultures*, 135–58. Baltimore, 1975.

August, A. "How Separate a Sphere? Poor Women and Paid Work in Late-Victorian London." *Journal of Family History* 19 (1994): 285–309.

Ayers, P., and J. Lambertz, "Marriage Relations, Money, and Domestic Violence in Working-Class Liverpool, 1919–39." In J. Lewis, ed., *Labour and Love: Women's Experience of Home and Family, 1850–1940*, 195–219. Oxford, 1986.

Baechler, J. *Suicides*. New York, 1979. Translated by Barry Cooper. Originally published as *Les Suicides*. Paris, 1975.

Baldwin, J. "British Areal Studies of Crime: An Assessment." *British Journal of Criminology* 15 (1975): 211–27.

Banks, J. A. *Prosperity and Parenthood: A Study of Family Planning Among the Victorian Middle Classes*. 2d ed. 1965.

Barnard, S. M. *To Prove I'm Not Forgot: Living and Dying in a Victorian City*. Manchester, 1990.

Barret-Ducrocq, F. *Love in the Time of Victoria*. New York, 1992.

Bartrip, P. "A 'Pennurth of Arsenic for Rat Poison': The Arsenic Act, 1851 and the Prevention of Secret Poisoning." *Medical History* 36 (1992): 53–69.

————. "The Rise and Decline of Workmen's Compensation." In P. Weindling, ed., *The Social History of Occupational Health*, 157–79. 1985.

Bauman, Z. *Hermeneutics and Social Science*. New York, 1978.

Behlmer, G. K. "Deadly Motherhood: Infanticide and Medical Opinion in Mid-Victorian England." *Journal of the History of Medicine and Allied Sciences* 34 (1979): 403–27.

Bell, Lady Florence. *At the Works: A Study of a Manufacturing Town* [Middlesbrough]. 1907. Reprint with a new introduction by Frederick Alderson. Newton Abbot, 1969. Reprint, 1985.

Bellamy, J. M. "Cotton Manufacture in Kingston upon Hull." *Business History* 4 (1962): 91–108.

————. "A Hull Shipbuilding Firm: The History of C. & W. Earle and Earle's Shipbuilding and Engineering Company Ltd." *Business History* 6 (1963): 27–47.

————. "Occupation Statistics in the Nineteenth-Century Censuses." In R. Lawton, ed., *The Census and Social Structure*, 165–78. 1978.

————. "Occupations in Kingston upon Hull, 1841–1948." *Yorkshire Bulletin of Economic and Social Research* 4 (1952): 33–50.

————. "Some Aspects of the Economy of Hull in the Nineteenth Century with Special Reference to Business History." Ph.D. diss., University of Hull, 1965.

————. *The Trade and Shipping of Nineteenth-Century Hull*. Hull: East Yorkshire Local History Society, 1979.

Bennett, J. *Oral History and Delinquency*. Chicago, 1981.

Benson, J. *The Penny Capitalists: A Study of Nineteenth-Century Working-Class Entrepreneurs*. New Brunswick, N.J., 1983.

————, ed. *The Working Class in England, 1875–1914*. 1985.

Berridge, V., and G. Edwards. *Opium and the People*. 1981.

Besnard, P. "Anti- ou ante-Durkheimisme? Contribution au débat sur les statistiques officielles du suicide." *Revue Française de Sociologie* 17 (1976): 313–41.

Bhaskar, R. *Reclaiming Reality: A Critical Introduction to Contemporary Philosophy*. 1989.

Bickford, J. A. R. *The Old Hull Borough Asylum (1849–1883)*. Hull, 1981.

Bickford, J. A. R., and M. E. Bickford, *The Medical Profession in Hull, 1400–1900*. Hull, 1983.

Biersack, A. "Local Knowledge, Local History: Geertz and Beyond." In L. Hunt, ed., *The New Cultural History*, 72–96. Berkeley, Calif., 1989.

Blom, I. "The History of Widowhood: A Bibliographic Overview." *Journal of Family History* 16 (1991): 191–210.

Bohannan, P., ed. *African Homicide and Suicide*. Princeton, N.J., 1960.

Booth, C. *The Aged Poor in England and Wales*. 1894.

————. *Life and Labour of the People in London*. 1889–1903. 2d ser. *Industry*. 1903.

Boris, E. "The Home as a Workplace: Deconstructing Dichotomies." *International Review of Social History* 39 (1994): 415–28.

Bottomore, T., and R. Nisbet, "Structuralism." In Bottomore and Nisbet, eds., *A History of Sociological Analysis*, 557–98. New York, 1978.

Bourdieu, P. "Marriage Strategies as Strategies of Social Reproduction." In R. Forster and O. Ranum, eds., *Family and Society: Selections from the Annales: Economies, sociétés, civilisations*, 117–44. Translated by Elborg Forster and Patricia M. Ranum. Baltimore, 1976.

———. *Outline of a Theory of Practice*. Cambridge, 1977.

Bourke, J. "Housewifery in Working-Class England 1860–1914." *Past & Present* 143 (1994): 167–97.

Brend, W. A. *An Inquiry into the Statistics of Deaths from Violence and Unnatural Causes in the United Kingdom*. 1915.

———. "The Necessity for Amendment of the Law Relating to Coroners and Inquests." *Transactions of the Medico-Legal Society for 1912–1913* 10 (1913): 143–97.

Brooker, K. *The Hull Strikes of 1911*. Hull: East Yorkshire Local History Society, 1979.

Brown, R. *Waterfront Organisation in Hull, 1870–1900*. Hull, 1972.

Bruner, E. M. *Text, Play, and Story: The Construction and Reconstruction of Self and Society*. Washington, D.C., 1984.

Bryant, C. G. A., and D. Jary, eds. *Giddens' Theory of Structuration: A Critical Appreciation*. 1991.

Buckle, H. T. *History of Civilization in England*. 3 vols. 1857. Reprint, 1871.

Bulmer, M. *The Chicago School of Sociology*. Chicago, 1984.

Bulusu, L., and M. Alderson, "Suicides 1950–82." *Population Trends* 35 (1984): 11–17.

Burney, I. A. "Decoding Death: Medicine, Public Inquiry, and the Reform of the English Inquest, 1836–1926." Ph.D. diss., University of California, Berkeley, 1993.

Cairncross, A. *Home and Foreign Investment, 1870–1913*. 1953. Reprint, Aldershot, 1992.

Camm, E. "A Note on Residential Patterns and Social Formations." *Journal of Regional & Local Studies* 6 (1986): 64–74.

Camus, Albert. *The Myth of Sisyphus and Other Essays*. Translated by Justin O'Brien. New York, 1955. Originally published as *Le Mythe de Sisyphe: Essai sur l'absurde*. Paris, 1942.

Canetto, S. S. "Gender and Suicide in the Elderly." *Suicide & Life-Threatening Behavior* 22 (1992): 80–97.

———. "She Died for Love and He for Glory: Gender Myths of Suicidal Behavior." *Omega* 26 (1992–93): 1–17.

Canetto, S. S., and D. Lester. "The Epidemiology of Women's Suicidal Behavior." In S. S. Canetto and D. Lester, eds., *Women and Suicidal Behavior*, 35–57. New York, 1995.

Cavan, R. S. "The Chicago School of Sociology, 1918–1933." *Urban Life* 11 (1983): 407–20.

———. *Suicide*. Chicago, 1928.

Cawthon, E. "Thomas Wakley and the Medical Coronership: Occupational Death and the Judicial Process." *Medical History* 30 (1986): 191–202.

Chevalier, L. *Labouring Classes and Dangerous Classes in Paris During the First Half of the Nineteenth Century*. Translated by Frank Jellinek. 1973. Originally published as *Classes laborieuses et classes dangereuses à Paris pendant la première moitié du XIXe siècle*. Paris, 1958.

Chinn, C. *Poverty Amidst Prosperity. The Urban Poor in England, 1834–1914*. Manchester, 1995.

———. *They Worked All Their Lives: Women of the Urban Poor in England, 1880–1939*. Manchester, 1988.

Chudacoff, H. P. *How Old Are You? Age Consciousness in American Culture*. Princeton, N.J., 1989.

———. "The Life Course of Women: Age and Age Consciousness, 1865–1915." *Journal of Family History* 5 (1980): 274–92.

Chudacoff, H. P., and T. K. Hareven. "From the Empty Nest to Family Dissolution: Life Course Transitions into Old Age." *Journal of Family History* 4 (1979): 69–83.

Clarke, R. V., and P. Mayhew. "The British Gas Suicide Story and Its Criminological Implications." In M. Tonry and N. Morris, eds., *Crime and Justice*, 10: 79–113. Chicago, 1988.

Clegg, J., ed. *Autobiography of a Lancashire Lawyer, Being the Life and Recollections of John Taylor, Attorney-at-Law, and First Coroner of the Borough of Bolton*. Bolton, 1883.

Cobb, R. *Death in Paris: The Records of the Basse-Geôle de la Seine, October 1795–September 1801, Vendémiaire Year IV–Fructidor Year IX*. Oxford, 1978.

———. *A Sense of Place*. 1975.

Collins, D. "The Introduction of Old Age Pensions in Great Britain." *Historical Journal* 8 (1965): 246–59.

Colt, G. H. *The Enigma of Suicide*. New York, 1991.

Conley, C. A. *The Unwritten Law: Criminal Justice in Victorian Kent*. Oxford, 1991.

Cooke, S. "'Terminal Old Age': Ageing and Suicide in Victoria, 1841–1921." *Australian Cultural History* 14 (1995): 76–89.

Cooper, H. "On the Cholera Mortality in Hull During the Epidemic of 1849." *Journal of the Statistical Society of London* 16 (1853): 347–51.

———. "On the Relative Prevalence of Diseases in Hull, and the Effects of Season upon Disease." *Journal of the Statistical Society of London* 16 (1853): 352–55.

Corbin, A. "Cries and Whispers." In M. Perrot, ed., *A History of Private Life*, 4: 615–67. Cambridge, 1990.

Crawford, P. G. "The Impact of the American Civil War on Hull, 1861–1865." *Journal of Regional & Local Studies* 4 (1984): 31–40.

Creighton, C. "The Rise of the Male Breadwinner Family: A Reappraisal." *Comparative Studies in Society and History* 38 (1996): 310–37.

Crossick, G. "The Emergence of the Lower Middle Class in Britain: A Discussion." In G. Crossick, ed., *The Lower Middle Class in Britain, 1870–1914*, 11–60. 1977.

———. "The Petite Bourgeoisie in Nineteenth-Century Britain: The Urban and Liberal Case." In G. Crossick and H.-G. Haupt, eds., *Shopkeepers and Master Artisans in Nineteenth-Century Europe*, 62–94. 1984.

———. "Urban Society and the Petty Bourgeoisie in Nineteenth-Century Britain." In D. Fraser and A. Sutcliffe, eds., *The Pursuit of Urban History*, 307–26. 1983.

Crossick, G., and H.-G. Haupt, "Shopkeepers, Master Artisans and the Historian: The Petite Bourgeoisie in Comparative Focus." In Crossick and Haupt, eds., *Shopkeepers and Master Artisans in Nineteenth-Century Europe*, 3–31. 1984.

Crowther, M. A. *The Workhouse System.* 1983.

Crowther, M. A., and B. White. *On Soul and Conscience: The Medical Expert and Crime.* Aberdeen, 1988.

Dahlin, M. "Perspectives on the Family Life of the Elderly in 1900." *Gerontologist* 20 (1980): 99–107.

Davidoff, L. "The Family in Britain." In F. M. L. Thompson, ed., *The Cambridge Social History of Britain, 1750–1950*, 2: 71–129. Cambridge, 1990.

———. "Mastered for Life: Servant and Wife in Victorian and Edwardian England." *Journal of Social History* 7 (1974): 406–28.

———. "The Separation of Home and Work? Landladies and Lodgers in Nineteenth- and Twentieth-Century England." In S. Burman, ed., *Fit Work for Women*, 64–97. 1979.

Davidoff, L., and C. Hall. *Family Fortunes. Men and Women of the English Middle Class, 1780–1850.* Chicago, 1987.

Davidson, R. N. *Crime and Environment.* 1981.

Davies, R. " 'Do not go gentle into that good night'? Women and Suicide in Carmarthenshire, c. 1860–1920." In A. V. John, ed., *Our Mothers' Land: Chapters in Welsh Women's History, 1830–1939*, 93–108. Cardiff, 1991.

Davis, N. Z. *Fiction in the Archives.* Stanford, 1987.

Dawe, A. "Theories of Social Action." In T. Bottomore and R. Nisbet, eds., *A History of Sociological Analysis*, 362–417. New York, 1978.

———. "The Two Sociologies." *British Journal of Sociology* 21 (1970): 207–18.

D'Cruze, S., and J. Turnbull. "Fellowship and Family: Oddfellows' Lodges in Preston and Lancaster, c. 1830–c. 1890." *Urban History* 22 (1995): 25–47.

Dennis, R. *English Industrial Cities of the Nineteenth Century: A Social Geography.* Cambridge, 1984.

Digby, A. *Madness, Morality and Medicine: A Study of the York Retreat, 1796–1914.* Cambridge, 1985.

Douglas, J. D. *The Social Meanings of Suicide.* Princeton, N.J., 1967.

———. "The Sociological Analysis of Social Meanings of Suicide." *Archives Européennes de Sociologie* 7 (1966): 249–75.

Dr. Airy's Report to the Local Government Board on the Sanitary State of Hull. Hull, 1882.

Dublin, L. I., and B. Bunzel. *To Be or Not to Be: A Study of Suicide.* New York, 1933.

Dupree, M. "The Community Perspective in Family History: The Potteries During the Nineteenth Century." In A. L. Beier, D. Cannadine, and J. M. Rosenheim, eds., *The First Modern Society,* 549–73. Cambridge, 1989.

Durkheim, E. *Suicide: A Study in Sociology.* Translated by J. A. Spaulding and G. Simpson. 1951. Reprint, New York, 1966. Originally published as *Le Suicide: Etude de sociologie.* Paris, 1897.

East, W. G. "The Port of Kingston-upon-Hull During the Industrial Revolution." *Economica* 11 (1931): 190–212.

East, W. N. "On Attempted Suicide, with an Analysis of 1,000 Consecutive Cases." *Journal of Mental Science* 59 (1913): 428–78.

Ebey, M., and B. Preston. *Domestic Service in Late Victorian and Edwardian England, 1871–1914.* Reading, 1976.

Elder, G. H. "Age Differentiation and the Life Course." *Annual Review of Sociology* 1 (1975): 165–90.

———. "Perspectives on the Life Course." In G. H. Elder, ed., *Life Course Dynamics. Trajectories and Transitions, 1968-1980,* 23–49. Ithaca, N.Y., 1985.

Emmison, F. G. *Archives and Local History.* Chichester, 1974.

Erikson, E. H. *Identity and the Life Cycle.* 1959. Reprint, New York, 1980.

Faris, R. E. L. *Social Disorganization.* New York, 1955.

Fedden, H. R. *Suicide: A Social and Historical Study.* 1938.

Fenwick, J. "Accounting for Sudden Death: A Sociological Study of the Coroner System." Ph.D. diss., University of Hull, 1984.

Finnane, M. *Insanity and the Insane in Post-Famine Ireland.* 1981.

Fischer, D. H. *Growing Old in America.* New York, 1977.

Fleury, Maurice de. *L'Angoisse humaine, avec une introduction touchant le renouveau de la psychologie.* Paris, 1924.

Forbes, T. R. "Coroners' Inquests in the County of Middlesex, England, 1819–42." *Journal of the History of Medicine* 32 (1977): 375–94.

———. "Crowner's Quest." *Transactions of the American Philosophical Society* 68 (1978): 5–50.

———. *Surgeons at the Bailey: English Forensic Medicine to 1878.* New Haven, Conn., 1985.

Forster, C. A. *Court Housing in Kingston upon Hull.* Hull, 1972.

———. "The Historical Development and Present-Day Significance of Byelaw-Housing Morphology, with Particular Reference to Hull, York and Middlesborough." Ph.D. diss., University of Hull, 1969.

Gates, B. T. "Suicide." In G. A. Cevasco, ed., *The 1890s,* 598–99. New York, 1993.

———. *Victorian Suicide: Mad Crimes and Sad Histories.* Princeton, N.J., 1988.

Gatrell, V. A. C. "The Decline of Theft and Violence in Victorian and Edwardian

England." In V. A. C. Gatrell, Bruce Lenman, and Geoffrey Parker., eds., *Crime and the Law: The Social History of Crime in Western Europe Since 1500*, 238-370. 1980.

Gay, P. *The Bourgeois Experience: Victoria to Freud*. New York, 1984.

Geertz, C. *The Interpretation of Cultures*. New York, 1973.

Gibson, J., and C. Rogers. *Coroners' Records in England and Wales*. Birmingham, 1988.

Giddens, A. *The Constitution of Society*. Berkeley, Calif., 1984.

———. *Durkheim*. 1978.

———. *Profiles and Critiques in Social Theory*. Berkeley, Calif., 1982.

———. "The Suicide Problem in French Sociology." *British Journal of Sociology* 16 (1965): 3-18.

———. "A Theory of Suicide." In A. Giddens, *Studies in Social and Political Theory*, 297-321. 1977.

———. "A Typology of Suicide." *Archives Européennes de Sociologie* 7 (1966): 276-95.

———, ed. *The Sociology of Suicide: A Selection of Readings*. 1971.

Gill, A. *Hessle Road*. Beverley, 1987.

Gillett, E., and K. A. MacMahon. *A History of Hull*. Oxford, 1980.

Gillis, J. R. "Servants, Sexual Relations and the Risks of Illegitimacy in London, 1801-1900." In J. Newton, M. P. Ryan, and J. R. Walkowitz, eds., *Sex and Class in Women's History*, 114-45. 1983.

Ginzburg, C. "Morelli, Freud and Sherlock Holmes: Clues and Scientific Method." *History Workshop* 9 (1980): 5-36.

Girard, C. "Age, Gender, and Suicide: A Cross-National Analysis." *American Sociological Review* 58 (1993): 553-74.

Gosden, P. H. J. H. *The Friendly Societies in England, 1815-1875*. Manchester, 1961.

Greenwald, G. I., and M. W. Greenwald. "Medicolegal Progress in Inquests of Felonious Deaths: Westminster, 1761-1866." *Journal of Legal Medicine* 2 (1981): 193-264.

Greenwald, M. W., and G. I. Greenwald. "Coroners' Inquests: A Source of Vital Statistics: Westminster, 1761-1866." *Journal of Legal Medicine* 4 (1983): 51-86.

Greenwood, M., et al. "Deaths by Violence, 1837-1937." *Journal of the Royal Statistical Society* 104 (1941): 146-63.

Guillais, J. *Crimes of Passion: Dramas of Private Life in Nineteenth-Century France*. Cambridge, 1990.

Haines, M. R. "Industrial Work and the Family Life Cycle, 1889-1890." *Research in Economic History* 4 (1979): 289-356.

Halbwachs, M. *The Causes of Suicide*. Translated by Harold Goldblatt. New York, 1978. Originally published as *Les Causes du suicide*. Paris, 1930.

Hammerton, J. *Cruelty and Companionship: Conflict in Nineteenth-Century Married Life*. 1992.

————. "The Targets of 'Rough Music': Respectability and Domestic Violence in Victorian England." *Gender & History* 3 (1991): 23–44.

Hanawalt, B. "Seeking the Flesh and Blood of Manorial Families." *Journal of Medieval History* 14 (1988): 33–45.

————. *The Ties That Bound*. Oxford, 1986.

Hareven, T. K. "Family Time and Historical Time." *Daedalus* 106 (1977): 57–70.

————. *Family Time and Industrial Time: The Relationship Between the Family and Work in a New England Industrial Community*. New York, 1982.

————. "The History of the Family and the Complexity of Social Change." *American Historical Review* 96 (1991): 95–124.

————. "The History of the Family as an Interdisciplinary Field." In T. K. Rabb and R. I. Rotberg, eds., *The Family in History*, 211–26. New York, 1976.

————. "The Last Stage: Historical Adulthood and Old Age." In D. Van Tassel, ed., *Aging, Death, and the Completion of Being*, 165–89. Philadelphia, 1979.

————. "Life-Course Transitions and Kin Assistance in Old Age: A Cohort Comparison." In D. Van Tassel and P. N. Stearns, eds., *Old Age in a Bureaucratic Society*, 110–25. Westport, Conn., 1986.

————. *Transitions: The Family and the Life Course in Historical Perspective*. New York, 1978.

————, ed. *Family and Kin in Urban Communities, 1700-1930*. New York, 1977.

Hareven, T. K., and K. J. Adams, eds. *Aging and Life Course Transitions: An Interdisciplinary Perspective*. New York, 1982.

Hareven, T. K., and M. Vinovskis, eds. *Family and Population in Nineteenth-Century America*. Princeton, N.J., 1978.

Harris, A. "Studies in the Historical Geography of the East Riding of Yorkshire." Ph.D. diss., University of Hull, 1962.

Harris, J. *Unemployment and Politics*. Oxford, 1972.

Harrison, B. *Peaceable Kingdom: Stability and Change in Modern Britain*. Oxford, 1982.

Havard, J. D. J. *The Detection of Secret Homicide: A Study of the Medico-Legal System of Investigation of Sudden and Unexplained Deaths*. 1960.

Haynes, M. J. "Strikes." In J. Benson, ed., *The Working Class in England*, 89–132. 1985.

Helly, D. O., and S. M. Reverby, eds. *Gendered Domains. Rethinking Public and Private in Women's History*. Ithaca, 1992.

Hendin, H. *Suicide in America*. New York, 1982.

Henretta, J. A. "Social History as Lived and Written." *American Historical Review* 84 (1979): 1293–1322.

Higgs, E. "Domestic Servants and Households in Victorian England." *Social History* 8 (1983): 201–10.

————. "Domestic Service and Household Production." In A. V. John, ed., *Unequal Opportunities: Women's Employment in England, 1800-1918*, 125–50. Oxford, 1986.

Higonnet, M. "Speaking Silences: Women's Suicide." In S. R. Suleiman, ed., *The Female Body in Western Culture*, 68–83. Cambridge, 1986.

———. "Suicide: Representations of the Feminine in the Nineteenth Century." *Poetics Today* 78 (1973): 1353–85.

Hill, Bridget. "Women, Work and the Census: A Problem for Historians of Women." *History Workshop* 35 (1993): 78–94.

Hindess, B. *The Use of Official Statistics in Sociology.* 1973.

Hodgkinson, R. G. "Provision for Pauper Lunatics, 1834–1871." *Medical History* 10 (1966): 138–54.

Hoggart, Richard. *A Measured Life: The Times and Places of an Orphaned Intellectual.* New Brunswick, N.J., 1994.

———. *The Uses of Literacy.* 1957. Reprint, Harmondsworth, 1973.

Homes of the People: Report of the Conference Held in the Town Hall, Hull, 1 Feb. 1884. Hull, 1884.

Horobin, G. W. "Community and Occupation in the Hull Fishing Industry." *British Journal of Sociology* 8 (1957): 343–56.

Hosgood, C. P. "The 'Pigmies of Commerce' and the Working-Class Community: Small Shopkeepers in England, 1870–1914." *Journal of Social History* 22 (1989): 439–60.

Hull Fabian Society. *How the People of Hull Are Housed.* Hull, 1910.

Hunt, E. H. *British Labour History, 1815–1914.* 1981.

———. *Regional Wage Variations in Britain, 1850–1914.* Oxford, 1973.

Ittmann, K. "Family Limitation and Family Economy in Bradford, West Yorkshire, 1851–1881." *Journal of Social History* 25 (1992): 547–73.

———. *Work, Gender and Family in Victorian England.* New York, 1995.

Jalland, P., and J. Hooper, eds. *Women from Birth to Death: The Female Life Cycle in Britain, 1830–1914.* Brighton, 1986.

Jefferys, M., ed. *Growing Old in the Twentieth Century.* 1989.

Jefferys, M., and P. Thane. "Introduction: An Ageing Society and Ageing People." In M. Jefferys, ed., *Growing Old in the Twentieth Century,* 1–18. 1989.

Jenkins, R. *Pierre Bourdieu.* 1992.

Jennings, C., and B. Barraclough. "Legal and Administrative Influences on the English Suicide Rate Since 1900." *Psychological Medicine* 10 (1980): 407–18.

Jervis, Sir J. *Sir John Jervis on the Office and Duties of Coroners.* 1829. 3d ed., 1866. Edited by C. W. Lovesy.

Johnson, K. K. "Durkheim Revisited: 'Why Do Women Kill Themselves?' " *Suicide & Life-Threatening Behavior* 9 (1979): 145–53.

Johnson, P. "The Employment and Retirement of Older Men in England and Wales, 1881–1981." *Economic History Review* 47 (1994): 106–28.

———. "Old Age and Ageing in Britain." *Refresh* 17 (1993): 5–8.

———. *Saving and Spending: The Working-Class Economy in Britain, 1870–1939.* Oxford, 1985.

Johnson, P., and J. Falkingham, *Ageing and Economic Welfare.* 1992.

Jones, D. J. V. *Crime, Protest, Community and Police in Nineteenth-Century Britain.* 1982.

Jordan, E. "Female Unemployment in England and Wales, 1851–1911: An Examination of the Census Figures for 15–19 Year Olds." *Social History* 13 (1988): 175–90.

Joyce, James. *Ulysses.* 1934. Reprint, Harmondsworth, 1969.

Joyce, P. "Work." In F. M. L. Thompson, ed., *The Cambridge Social History of Britain, 1750–1950,* 2: 131–94. Cambridge, 1990.

Kaye, H. J., and K. McClelland, eds. *E. P. Thompson: Critical Perspectives.* 1990.

Kearns, G. "Biology, Class and the Urban Penalty." In G. Kearns and C. W. J. Withers, eds., *Urbanising Britain. Essays on Class and Community in the Nineteenth Century,* 12–30. Cambridge, 1991.

Kellett, J. R. *The Impact of Railways on Victorian Cities.* 1969.

King, P. "Female Offenders, Work and Life-Cycle Change in Late-Eighteenth-Century London." *Continuity and Change* 11 (1996): 61–90.

Kirsling, R. A. "Review of Suicide Among Elderly Persons." *Psychological Reports* 59 (1986): 359–66.

Knox, W. "Apprenticeship and De-Skilling in Britain, 1850–1914." *International Review of Social History* 31 (1986): 166–84.

Koditschek, T. *Class Formation and Urban-Industrial Society: Bradford, 1750–1850.* Cambridge, 1990.

Kohli, M. "The World We Forgot: A Historical Review of the Life Course." In V. W. Marshall, ed., *Later Life: The Social Psychology of Aging,* 271–303. Beverly Hills, Calif., 1986.

Kushner, H. I. *Self-Destruction in the Promised Land: A Psychocultural Biology of American Suicide.* New Brunswick, N.J., 1989. Republished as *American Suicide.* New Brunswick, N.J., 1991.

———. "Suicide, Gender, and the Fear of Modernity in Nineteenth-Century Medical and Social Thought." *Journal of Social History* 26 (1993): 461–90.

———. "Women and Suicidal Behavior: Epidemiology, Gender and Lethality in Historical Perspective." In S. S. Canetto and D. Lester, eds., *Women and Suicidal Behavior,* 11–34. New York, 1995.

———. "Women and Suicide in Historical Perspective." *Signs* 10 (1985): 537–52.

LaCapra, D. *Emile Durkheim: Sociologist and Philosopher.* Ithaca, N.Y., 1972.

Lane, R. "Crime and the Industrial Revolution: British and American Views." *Journal of Social History* 7 (1974): 287–303.

———. *Roots of Violence in Black Philadelphia, 1860–1900.* Cambridge, 1986.

———. *Violent Death in the City.* Cambridge, 1979.

Laqueur, T. W. "Bodies, Details, and the Humanitarian Narrative." In L. Hunt, ed., *The New Cultural History,* 176–204. Berkeley, Calif., 1989.

Laslett, P. *A Fresh Map of Life: The Emergence of the Third Age.* 1989.

Lee, G. A. "The Tramways of Kingston upon Hull: A Study in Municipal Enterprise." Ph.D. diss., University of Sheffield, 1967–68.

Lees, L. H. *Exiles of Erin: Irish Migrants in Victorian London.* Ithaca, N.Y., 1979.

———. "Getting and Spending: The Family Budgets of English Industrial Workers in 1890." In J. M. Merriman, ed., *Consciousness and Class Experience in Nineteenth-Century Europe*, 169–86. New York, 1979.

———. "Patterns of Lower-Class Life: Irish Slum Communities in Nineteenth-Century London." In S. Thernstrom and R. Sennett, eds., *Nineteenth-Century Cities*, 359–85. New Haven, Conn., 1969.

Levinson, D. J., et al. *The Seasons of a Man's Life.* New York, 1978.

———. *The Seasons of a Woman's Life.* New York, 1996.

Lieberman, L. "Romanticism and the Culture of Suicide in Nineteenth-Century France." *Comparative Studies in Society and History* 33 (1991): 611–29.

Lis, C., and H. Soly. "Neighbourhood Social Change in West European Cities." *International Review of Social History* 38 (1993): 1–30.

Lockwood, D. *The Blackcoated Worker.* 1958. Reprint, Oxford, 1989.

Lomax, E. "The Uses and Abuses of Opiates in Nineteenth-Century England." *Bulletin of the History of Medicine* 47 (1973): 167–76.

London, Jack. *The People of the Abyss.* 1903. Reprint, 1992.

Luckin, B. "Accidents, Disasters and Cities." *Urban History* 20 (1993): 177–90.

Lukes, S. *Emile Durkheim: His Life and Work.* Stanford, 1985.

McBride, T. M. *The Domestic Revolution: The Modernisation of Household Service in England and France, 1820–1920.* New York, 1976.

McCandless, P. " 'Curses of Civilization': Insanity and Drunkenness in Victorian Britain." *British Journal of Addiction* 79 (1984): 49–58.

McClelland, K. "Some Thoughts on Masculinity and the 'Representative Artisan' in Britain, 1850–1880." *Gender & History* 1 (1989): 164–77.

McClure, G. M. G. "Suicide in England and Wales, 1975–1984." *British Journal of Psychiatry* 150 (1987): 309–14.

McCulloch, J. W., A. E. Philip, and G. M. Carstairs. "The Ecology of Suicidal Behaviour." *British Journal of Psychiatry* 113 (1967): 313–19.

MacDonald, M. "The Secularization of Suicide in England, 1660–1800." *Past & Present* 111 (1986): 50–100.

MacDonald, M., and T. R. Murphy. *Sleepless Souls: Suicide in Early Modern England.* Oxford, 1990.

McHugh, M. P. "The Influence of the Coroner's Inquisition on the Common Law and the Medico Legal System." Ph.D. diss., University College, London, 1976.

Malcolmson, P. E. *English Laundresses: A Social History, 1850–1930.* Urbana, Ill., 1986.

Maris, R. W. "The Developmental Perspective of Suicide." In A. A. Leenars, ed., *Life Span Perspectives of Suicide. Time-lines in the Suicide Process*, 25–38. New York, 1991.

Martineau, H. "Self-Murder." *Once a Week*, Dec. 17, 1859, 510–14.

Meacham, S. *A Life Apart: The English Working Class, 1890–1914.* Cambridge, Mass., 1977.

Meares, R., et al. "A Sex Difference in the Seasonal Variation of Suicide Rate: A Single Cycle for Men, Two Cycles for Women." *British Journal of Psychiatry* 138 (1981): 321-25.

Medick, H., and D. W. Sabean, eds. *Interest and Emotion: Essays on the Study of Family and Kinship.* Cambridge, 1984.

Meninger, K. *Man Against Himself.* New York, 1938.

Merrick, J. "Patterns and Prosecution of Suicide in Eighteenth-Century Paris." *Historical Reflections* 16 (1989): 1-43.

Merriman, J. M. *The Margins of City Life: Explorations on the French Urban Frontier, 1815-1851.* New York, 1991.

Millar, W. H. "Statistics of Deaths by Suicide Among Her Majesty's British Troops Serving at Home and Abroad During the Ten Years 1862-71." *Journal of the Royal Statistical Society* 37 (1874): 187-92.

Miller, J., ed. *On Suicide.* San Francisco, 1992.

Miner, J. R. *Suicide and Its Relation to Climatic and Other Factors.* Baltimore, 1922.

Mintz, S. "Life Stages." *Encyclopedia of American Social History*, 2011-22. New York, 1993.

Mitchell, B. R., and P. Deane. *Abstract of British Historical Statistics.* Cambridge, 1962.

Modell, J., F. F. Furstenberg, and T. Hershberg. "Social Change and Transitions to Adulthood in Historical Perspective." *Journal of Family History* 1 (1976): 7-32.

Moksony, F. "Ecological Analysis of Suicide: Problems and Prospects." In D. Lester, ed., *Current Concepts of Suicide*, 121-38. Philadelphia, 1990.

Monkkonen, E. H. "A Disorderly People? Urban Order in the Nineteenth and Twentieth Centuries." *Journal of American History* 68 (1981): 539-59.

Morris, R. J. *Class, Sect and Party: The Making of the British Middle Class, Leeds 1820-1850.* Manchester, 1990.

———. "The Middle Class and British Towns and Cities of the Industrial Revolution, 1780-1870." In D. Fraser and A. Sutcliffe, eds., *The Pursuit of Urban History*, 286-306. 1983.

———. "The Middle Class and the Property Cycle During the Industrial Revolution." In T. C. Smout, ed., *The Search for Wealth and Stability*, 91-113. 1979.

Morris, T. *The Criminal Area: A Study in Social Ecology.* 1957.

Morselli, E. *Suicide: An Essay on Comparative Moral Statistics.* New York, 1882.

Muir, E., and G. Ruggiero, eds. *Microhistory and the Lost Peoples of Europe.* Baltimore, 1991.

Neave, D. R. J. "Friendly Societies in the Rural East Riding, 1830-1912." Ph.D. diss., University of Hull, 1985.

"Neglected Brain Disease—Suicide." *Journal of Psychological Medicine* 10 (1857): 414-22.

O'Carroll, P. W. "A Consideration of the Validity and Reliability of Suicide Mortality Data." *Suicide & Life-Threatening Behavior* 19 (1989): 1-16.

Office of Health Economics. *Suicide and Deliberate Self-Harm.* 1981.

Ogle, W. "On Suicides in England and Wales in Relation to Age, Sex, Season and Occupation." *Journal of the Royal Statistical Society* 49 (1886): 101–35.

———. "On the Distribution of Suicides in England and Wales." *Journal of Psychological Medicine* 12 (1859): 469–83.

"On Suicide—Verdicts of Felo-de-Se." *Journal of Psychological Medicine & Mental Pathology* 3 (1850): 27–30.

Oppenheim, J. *Shattered Nerves: Doctors, Patients, and Depression in Victorian England.* New York, 1991.

Oppenheimer, V. K. "The Life-Cycle Squeeze: The Interaction of Men's Occupational and Family Life Cycles." *Demography* 11 (1974): 227–45.

Park, R. E., E. W. Burgess, and R. E. McKenzie. *The City.* Chicago, 1925.

Parkes, C. M. *Bereavement: Studies of Grief in Adult Life.* 1972.

Parkin, F. *Durkheim.* Oxford, 1992.

Patton, G. M. *The Child and the Nation.* 1915.

Perot, M., ed. *A History of Private Life,* vol. 4. Cambridge, Mass., 1990.

Pescosolido, B. A., and R. Mendelsohn. "Social Causation or Social Construction of Suicide? An Investigation into the Social Organization of Official Rates." *American Sociological Review* 51 (1986): 80–100.

Peterson, A. C. "Brain Fever in Nineteenth-Century Literature: Fact and Fiction." *Victorian Studies* 19 (1976): 445–64.

Platt, S. "Unemployment and Suicidal Behavior: A Review of the Literature." *Social Science and Medicine* 19 (1984): 93–115.

Pope, Norris. "A View from the Monument: A Note on *Martin Chuzzlewit.*" *Dickens Quarterly* 4 (1987): 153–60.

Porter, T. M. *The Rise of Statistical Thinking, 1820–1900.* Princeton, N.J., 1986.

Prior, L. *The Social Organization of Death: Medical Discourse and Social Practices in Belfast.* New York, 1989.

Pritchard, C. "Is There a Link Between Suicide in Young Men and Unemployment? A Comparison of the UK with Other European Community Countries." *British Journal of Psychiatry* 160 (1992): 750–56.

Prochaska, F. K. "Female Philanthropy and Domestic Service in Victorian England." *Bulletin of the Institute of Historical Research* 54 (1981): 79–85.

Quadagno, J. *Aging in Early Industrial Society.* New York, 1982.

Radcliffe, J. N. "The Aesthetics of Suicide." *Journal of Psychological Medicine* 12 (1859): 582–602.

———. "English Suicide-Fields, and the Restraint of Suicide." *Medical Critic & Psychological Journal* 8 (1862): 701–10.

———. "On the Prevalence of Suicide in England." *Transactions of the National Association for the Promotion of Social Science* 1862: 461–73.

Ransom, R. L., and R. Sutch. "The Impact of Aging on the Employment of Men in American Working-Class Communities at the End of the Nineteenth Century."

In D. I. Kertzer and P. Laslett, eds., *Aging in the Past: Demography, Society, and Old Age*, 303-27. Berkeley, Calif., 1995.

Ratcliffe, B. M. "Suicides in the City: Perceptions and Realities of Self-Destruction in Paris in the First Half of the Nineteenth Century." *Historical Reflections* 18 (1992): 1-70.

Richards, E. "Women in the British Economy Since About 1700: An Interpretation." *History* 59 (1974): 337-57.

Richardson, R. *Death, Dissection and the Destitute*. 1987.

Riley, J. C. *Sickness, Recovery and Death: A History and Forecast of Ill Health*. Iowa City, 1989.

Roberts, E. "The Family." In J. Benson, ed., *The Working Class in England, 1875-1914*, 1-35. 1985.

———. *A Woman's Place: An Oral History of Working Class Women 1890-1940*. Oxford, 1984.

———. *Women's Work, 1840-1940*. Basingstoke, 1988.

———. "Working-Class Standards of Living in Barrow and Lancaster, 1890-1914." *Economic History Review* 30 (1977): 306-21.

Roberts, R. *The Classic Slum: Salford Life in the First Quarter of the Century*. Manchester, 1971.

Roebuck, J. "Grandma as Revolutionary: Elderly Women and Some Modern Patterns of Social Change." *International Journal of Aging and Human Development* 17 (1983): 249-66.

———. "When Does 'Old Age' Begin? The Evolution of the English Definition." *Journal of Social History* 12 (1979): 416-28.

Roebuck, J., and J. Slaughter, "Ladies and Pensioners: Stereotypes and Public Policy Affecting Old Women in England, 1880-1940." *Journal of Social History* 13 (1979): 105-14.

Rose, L. *The Massacre of the Innocents: Infanticide in Britain, 1800-1939*. 1986.

Rose, S. *Limited Livelihoods: Gender and Class in Nineteenth-Century England*. Berkeley, Calif., 1991.

———. "The Varying Household Arrangements of the Elderly in Three English Villages: Nottinghamshire, 1851-1881." *Continuity and Change* 3 (1988): 101-22.

Rosen, G. "History in the Study of Suicide," *Psychological Medicine* 1 (1971): 267-85.

Ross, E. *Love and Toil: Motherhood in Outcast London, 1870-1918*. New York, 1993.

Rowntree, B. S. *Poverty: A Study of Town Life*. 1901.

Rylands, J. *The Distressed Cotton Operatives*. Hull, 1864.

Sainsbury, P. *Suicide in London: An Ecological Study*. 1955.

———. "Suicide: Opinions and Facts." *Proceedings of the Royal Society of Medicine* 66 (1973): 579-87.

Samuel, R. "Comers and Goers." In H. J. Dyos and M. Wolff, eds., *The Victorian City*, 1: 123-60. 1976.

Schmid, C. F. "Suicide in Minneapolis, Minnesota: 1928-32." *American Journal of Sociology* 39 (1933): 30-48.

———. *Suicide in Seattle, 1914 to 1925*. Seattle, 1928.

Schneer, J. "London's Docks in 1900: Nexus of Empire." *Labour History Review* 59 (1994): 20-33.

Scull, A. "A Convenient Place to Get Rid of Inconvenient People: The Victorian Lunatic Asylum." In A. D. King, ed., *Buildings and Society*, 37-60. 1980.

———. *The Most Solitary of Afflictions: Madness and Society in Britain 1700-1900*. New Haven, Conn., 1993.

———. *Museums of Madness*. 1979.

———. *Social Order/Mental Disorder*. Berkeley, Calif., 1989.

Secombe, W. "Patriarchy Stabilized: The Construction of the Male Breadwinner Wage Norm in Nineteenth-Century Britain." *Social History* 11 (1986): 53-76.

———. *Weathering the Storm: Working-Class Families from the Industrial Revolution to the Fertility Decline*. 1993.

Sharpe, J. "History from Below." In P. Burke, ed., *New Perspectives on Historical Writing*, 24-41. Philadelphia, 1992.

Shaw, C. R. *The Jack-Roller: A Delinquent Boys Own Story*. 1930. Reprint, Chicago, 1966.

Sheahan, J. J. *History of the Town and Port of Kingston-upon-Hull*. Beverley, 1866.

Sheehy, G. *New Passages: Mapping Your Life Across Time*. New York, 1995.

Sibree, J. *Fifty Years' Recollections of Hull*. Hull, 1884.

Sim, J., and T. Ward, "The Magistrate of the Poor? Coroners and Deaths in Custody in Nineteenth-Century England." In M. Clark and C. Crawford, eds., *Legal Medicine in History*, 245-67. Cambridge, 1994.

Small, Helen. *Love's Madness. Medicine, the Novel, and Female Insanity, 1800-1865*. Oxford, 1996.

Smith, D. J. "The Housing of the Poorer Classes in Kingston-upon-Hull." Thesis, Royal Institute of British Architects, 1937.

Smith, F. B. *The People's Health 1830-1910*. 1979.

Smith, J. *Report to the General Board of Health on a Preliminary Inquiry into the Sewerage, Drainage, and Supply of Water, and the Sanitary Condition of the Inhabitants of the Town and Borough of Kingston-upon-Hull*. 1850.

Smith, R. M. "The Structured Dependence of the Elderly as a Recent Development: Some Sceptical Historical Thoughts." *Ageing and Society* 4 (1984): 409-28.

Smith, S. J. *Crime, Space and Society*. Cambridge, 1986.

Snodgrass, J. "Clifford R. Shaw and Henry D. McKay: Chicago Criminologists." *British Journal of Criminology* 16 (1976): 1-19.

Spitzer, A. B. "The Historical Problem of Generations." *American Historical Review* 78 (1973): 1353-85.

Sprott, S. E. *The English Debate on Suicide from Donne to Hume*. La Salle, Ill., 1961.

Stack, S. "The Effect of Strikes on Suicide: A Cross-National Analysis." *Sociological Focus* 15 (1982): 135-46.

Statistical Society of Manchester. "Report on the Condition of the Working Classes in the Town of Kingston-upon-Hull." *Journal of the Statistical Society of London* 5 (1842): 213–17.

Stearns, P. N. *Be a Man! Males in Modern Society.* New York, 1979.

———. "Old Women: Some Historical Observations." *Journal of Family History* 5 (1980): 44–57.

———. "Working-Class Women in Britain, 1890–1914." In M. Vicinus, ed., *Suffer and Be Still,* 100–120. Bloomington, Ind., 1972.

Stengel, E., and N. G. Cook. "Contrasting Suicide Rates in Three Industrial Communities." *Journal of Mental Science* 107 (1961): 1011–19.

Stewart, I. "Suicide: The Influence of Organic Disease." *Lancet,* Oct. 22, 1960, 919–20.

Stillion, J., and E. E. McDowell. "Examining Suicide from a Life Span Perspective." *Death Studies* 15 (1991): 327–54.

Stillion, J., E. E. McDowell, and J. H. May. *Suicide Across the Life Span.* 1989.

Stokes, J. *In the Nineties.* Chicago, 1989.

Strahan, S. A. K. *Suicide and Insanity.* 1893.

Styron, William. "Darkness Visible." In J. Miller, ed., *On Suicide,* 247–69. San Francisco, 1992.

"Suicide, 1901 to 1961." In *The Registrar General's Statistical Review of England and Wales for 1961.* 1964.

Sullivan, W. C. "Alcoholism and Suicidal Impulses." *Journal of Mental Science* 45 (1898): 259–71.

———. "The Relation of Alcoholism to Suicide in England, with Special Reference to Recent Statistics." *Journal of Mental Science* 46 (1900): 260–81.

Swinscow, D. "Some Suicide Statistics." *British Medical Journal,* June 23, 1951, 1417–23.

Tansey, P. A. "Residential Patterns in the Nineteenth-Century City: Kingston upon Hull, 1851." Ph.D. diss., University of Hull, 1973.

Taylor, S. *Durkheim and the Study of Suicide.* 1982.

Tebbutt, M. *Women's Talk? A Social History of 'Gossip' in Working-Class Neighbourhoods, 1880–1960.* Aldershot, 1995.

Thane, P. "The History of Provision for the Elderly to 1929." In D. Jerrome, ed., *Ageing in Modern Society,* 191–99. 1983.

———. "Late Victorian Women." In T. R. Gourvish and A. O'Day, eds., *Later Victorian Britain, 1867–1900,* 175–208. New York, 1988.

———. "Women and the Poor Law in Victorian and Edwardian England." *History Workshop* 6 (1978): 29–51.

Thompson, E. P. *Customs in Common.* New York, 1993.

———. *The Poverty of Theory and Other Essays.* 1978.

Thompson, F. M. L. *The Rise of Respectable Society.* Cambridge, 1988.

Thompson, P. *The Edwardians.* 1979.

Thompson, P., C. Itzin, and M. Abdendstern. *I Don't Feel Old: The Experience of Later Life*. Oxford, 1990.

Thompson, P., T. Wailey, and T. Lummis. *Living the Fishing*. 1983.

―――. "Women in the Fishing: The Roots of Power Between the Sexes." *Comparative Studies in Society and History* 27 (1985): 3–32.

Thomson, D. "The Decline of Social Welfare: Falling State Support for the Elderly Since Early Victorian Times." *Ageing and Society* 4 (1984): 451–82.

―――. " 'I am not my father's keeper': Families and the Elderly in Nineteenth-Century England." *Law and History Review* 2 (1984): 265–86.

―――. "Welfare and the Historians." In L. Bonfield, R. M. Smith, and K. Wrightson, eds., *The World We Have Gained*, 355–78. Oxford, 1986.

―――. "The Welfare of the Elderly in the Past: A Family or Community Responsibility?" In M. Pelling and R. M. Smith, eds., *Life, Death, and the Elderly: Historical Perspectives*, 194–221. 1991.

―――. "Workhouse to Nursing Home: Residential Care of Elderly People in England Since 1840." *Ageing and Society* 3 (1983): 43–69.

Thurston, G. *Coroner's Practice*. 1958.

Tilly, L., and J. W. Scott. *Women, Work, and Family*. New York, 1978.

Tiryakian, E. A. "Emile Durkheim." In T. Bottomore and R. Nisbet, eds., *A History of Sociological Analysis*, 187–236. New York, 1978.

Tomes, N. "A 'Torrent of Abuse': Crimes of Violence Between Working-Class Men and Women in London, 1840–1875." *Journal of Social History* 11 (1978): 328–45.

Townsend, P. *The Family Life of Old People*. Glencoe, Ill., 1957. New abridged ed., Harmondsworth, 1963.

Travis, R. "Halbwachs and Durkheim: A Test of Two Theories of Suicide." *British Journal of Sociology* 41 (1990): 225–43.

Tressell, R. *The Ragged Trousered Philanthropists*. 1914. Reprint, 1968.

Troutbeck, J. "Inquest Juries." *Transactions of the Medico-Legal Society* 1 (1902–4): 49–58.

Trovato, F. "A Longitudinal Analysis of Divorce and Suicide in Canada." *Journal of Marriage & the Family* 49 (1987): 193–203.

Tuke, D. H. *A Dictionary of Psychological Medicine*. 2 vols. Philadelphia, 1892.

Valenze, D. *The First Industrial Woman*. New York, 1995.

Victoria History of the Counties of England. *A History of the County of York, East Riding*, vol. 1: *The City of Kingston upon Hull*. Oxford, 1969.

Vincent, D. *Bread, Knowledge and Freedom: A Study of Nineteenth-Century Working-Class Autobiography*. 1981.

―――. "Love and Death and the Nineteenth-Century Working Class." *Social History* 5 (1980): 223–47.

Vromen, S. "The Sociology of Maurice Halbwachs." Ph.D. diss., New York University, 1975.

Waddington, I. "General Practitioners and Consultants in Early Nineteenth-

Century England." In J. Woodward and D. Richards, eds., *Health Care and Popular Medicine in Nineteenth-Century England*, 164–88. 1977.

Wall, R. "The Age at Leaving Home." *Journal of Family History* 3 (1978): 181–202.

Walsh, D., and P. D. McCarthy. "Suicide in Dublin." *British Medical Journal* 1 (1966): 1393–96.

——. "Suicide in Dublin's Elderly." *Acta Psychiatrica Scandinavica* 41 (1965): 227–35.

Walton J. K. "Casting Out and Bringing Back in Victorian England: Pauper Lunatics, 1840–70." In W. F. Bynum, R. Porter, and M. Shepherd, eds., *The Anatomy of Madness*, 2: 132–46. 1985.

——. "Lunacy in the Industrial Revolution: A Study of Asylum Admissions in Lancashire, 1848–50." *Journal of Social History* 13 (1979): 1–22.

Ward, D. "Victorian Cities: How Modern?" *Journal of Historical Geography* 1 (1975): 135–51.

Watt, J. R. "The Family, Love, and Suicide in Early Modern Geneva." *Journal of Family History* 21 (1996): 63–86.

Webb, Sidney, and Beatrice Webb. *English Poor Law History*. 1929.

——. *English Poor Law Policy*. 1910. Reprint, 1963.

Williams, A. *Life in a Railway Factory*. 1915.

Williams, E. A. *Open Verdict: An Ex-Coroner Looks Back*. 1967.

Williams, K. *From Pauperism to Poverty*. 1981.

Winstanley, M. *The Shopkeeper's World, 1830–1914*. Manchester, 1983.

Winter, J. *The Great War and the British People*. 1986.

Zell, M. "Suicide in Pre-Industrial England." *Social History* 11 (1986): 303–17.

Zorbaugh, H. W. "The Dweller in Furnished Rooms: An Urban Type." *American Journal of Sociology* 32, pt. 2 (1926).

INDEX

In this index an "f" after a number indicates a separate reference on the next page, and an "ff" indicates separate references on the next two pages. A continuous discussion over two or more pages is indicated by a span of page numbers, e.g., "57–59." *Passim* is used for a cluster of references in close but not consecutive sequence.

Library of Congress Cataloging-in-Publication Data

Bailey, Victor

This rash act : suicide across the life cycle in the

Victorian city / Victor Bailey.

p.   cm.

Includes bibliographical references and index.

ISBN 0-8047-3123-3 (alk. paper). —

ISBN 0-8047-3124-1 (pkb. : alk. paper)

1. Suicide—Sociological aspects—England—Hull.

2. Suicide—England—Hull—History—19th century.   I. Title.

HV6548.G7B35   1998

362.28′09428′3709034—dc21   97-32785

Original printing 1998

Last figure below indicates year of this printing:

06 05 04 03 02 01 00   99 98